ENCYCLOPEDIA
—— OF ——
TRACK & FIELD

D1127632

ENCYCLOPEDIA
OF
TRACK & FIELD

PRENTICE-HALL PRESS
New York

Contributors and technical consultants
Enrico Arcelli, Erminio Azzaro,
Pasquale Bellotti, Renato Canova,
Renato Carnevali, Alessandro Donati,
Pino Dordoni, S. Filippini, Luigi
Gianoli, Luciano Gigliotti, Giampaolo
Lenzi, Elio Locatelli, Dante Merlo, E. di
Monteventano, Ennio Preatoni,
R. Quercetani, Ugo Ranzetti, Giorgio
Rondelli, E. Trifari

Picture acknowledgements
Archivio Rizzoli, A.R.T. Foto, A.S.L.,
D. Basanisi, H. Hommel, Image Bank,
Mark Shearman and Olympia

This material was first published by
RIZZOLI EDITORE
in the partwork ''Conoscere l'Atletica''

© Proprietà letteraria riservata
Copyright 1983 by Rizzoli Editore,
Milano

Published 1986 by Prentice-Hall Press
A Division of Simon & Schuster, Inc.
Simon & Schuster Building
1230 Avenue of the Americas
New York, New York 10020

Copyright © English text Hamlyn
Publishing 1985

**Library of Congress Cataloging in
Publication Data**
Main entry under title:

Encyclopedia of track & field.

1. Track-athletics.   I. Arco
Publishing.
II. Title: Encyclopedia of track and field.
GV1060.5.E52   1985   796.4'2
85-13503
ISBN 0-671-61916-0

Printed in Italy

Contents

Preface

This book should be of great interest to the sports enthusiast and aspiring athlete alike. All aspects of the background to training are given, and the complex techniques and the stresses they create on the body are carefully explained. Schedules are given for each event for accomplished athletes, and for some events a section is devoted to specific training for the young. The book will be of considerable value as a training and instruction manual for use by coaches and serious athletes.

Introduction

From the earliest times running has been a natural part of man's existence, whether he was catching animals for food or escaping from predators. However, he also began to run for pleasure and then competitively, leading to a desire to improve on his speed or ability to run farther.

In time, running came to be used as a means of communication and the fastest runners became messengers between villages or countries, carrying news of important events or of war. Later there were long-distance messengers who ran for a whole day bearing tidings affecting the lives of their compatriots, such as the legendary Pheidippides (or Phillipides) who is supposed to have run from Athens to Sparta to request help against an invading Persian force.

One of the earliest examples of competitive running can be found in the works of Homer, who tells of races run in the 12th century BC. Thus man has been racing on foot for over three thousand years.

It was the Greeks who elevated running and sports to the level of their gods at Olympia, and the spectacle of athletes running and engaged in other contests of exertion suggested to sculptors fertile images of human beauty. The Greek word for race was 'agone', from the word 'agonia' meaning to live to the very last breath; for the athlete this meant running to the very last breath in order to win victory.

At Olympia, there was only one contest at the early Olympiads, the 'stadium', and this was a race over about 200 m. Later the diaulos (400 m) and the dolichos (2400 m) were added, the prize being a simple crown of olive leaves. When the powerful Spartans began to compete, they exerted a great influence, and the 18th Olympiad included jumping and throwing events in addition to running.

The Olympic Games continued to expand, but their growth fostered professionalism among the competitors, and winners even had statues of themselves erected. Eventually the Games were banned by the Roman emperor Theodosius in AD394, as he felt that they had pagan connotations.

Running as a sport then disappeared for several centuries, but interest in running as an art was rekindled after the Middle Ages first by the Italians, and then by the Germans and Swedes. However, it was England in the Industrial Revolution that revived the passion for racing, and sport in general. Today we see people from all walks of life pounding city streets and competing in fun-runs over all sorts of distances – just to take part is an honour, whether you win or come 14105th in the London Marathon. The ancient Olympian spirit has been rediscovered.

In order to help the judges when the finish of a race is very close, photo-finish equipment has been devised which freezes the athletes on film as soon as the beam at the finish line is broken; the athlete whose torso first crosses the line is the winner (the head and the arms do not count).

Timing and measurement of athletics events

In the early days of athletics, there were few rules and regulations to be observed by the competitors, and races were very informal (the start of a race was pretty well by mutual consent of the participants rather than by the direction of an official).

In fact it was only about 100 years ago that amateur athletics organizations began to be formed, the first of these being in England. In 1913 the International Amateur Athletics Federation (IAAF) was formed, and has since been responsible for the administration of the sport and ratification of world records. Now when important athletics meetings are held, a large staff of officials and judges is present to ensure that the events are as fair as possible for the competitors involved.

Up until the late 1950s, manual timing was used exclusively for all timed athletics events, but then auto-

Below. With the ever-increasing standard of competition, the wind has become an important factor in the sprint and long-jump events; equipment has been designed which records the wind speed at the moment the event takes place, and if the value obtained is greater than 2 m/sec. any record obtained cannot be ratified.

The picture shows a close-up of the high-jump uprights and bar. For the high-jump the uprights must be between 4.00 m and 4.04 m apart and the bar

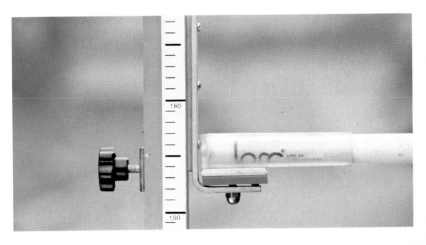

must be between 3.98 m and 4.02 m long. In the pole-vault, the vertical supports must be 4.30–4.37 m apart and the bar must be 4.48–4.52 m long.

matic electronic timing was introduced as a back-up. Subsequently, automatic timing completely superseded hand timing, which is now used only as an emergency back-up. With manual timing, the timekeeper started his watch when he saw the flame or smoke from the starting pistol. Automatic timing systems are linked electronically to the pistol so that the clock is started at the instant the trigger is pressed. The difference between the two methods is roughly 20/100 sec. for the 200 m, manual timing giving a slightly lower figure.

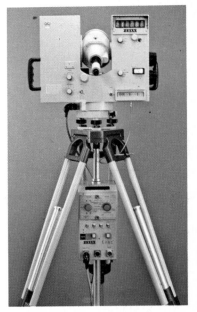

Up until a few years ago the throwing events were measured with a metric expanding ruler, but now a more sophisticated system is used, called the 'magic eye'. This apparatus makes use of an infra-red light source and a prism to calculate the distance between the edge of the throwing circle and the point where the object (discus, javelin, etc.) landed.

100 m
How it is run

'Are sprinters born or are they made?' This question is often asked, but the answer is not a simple one. Although it is true that you need to have a natural gift for sprinting in order to do well in the sprint events, it is equally true that this alone is not enough. In order to become a successful sprinter, you need to perfect such talent through training.

In the past, natural ability was considered to be sufficient and coaches of the early decades of the 20th century used to recruit sprinters from among those who proved to have 'swift legs'. Indeed, one fundamental quality for a sprinter is being able to act and react quickly. Thus at the time it was thought that the ideal type of sprinter had to be very muscular, but not tall. It was not until later that it was discovered that no precise type exists, and athletes of all shapes and sizes have become world-class sprinters.

At the beginning of the century, and for a while after, there was a marked difference between the Anglo-Saxon (and therefore American and German) training schools and those that might be classified as belonging to Latin Europe. The principles of preparing and creating sprinters were considerably more advanced among the British, Americans and Germans, because they started from a base of athletic activities already well-tried at school, whereas elsewhere sporting activity in schools was practically non-existent.

There was therefore a gulf between the two groups. The Americans then entered in races black athletes who had exceptional talent. Moreover, their ability at that time was further enhanced by training methods that were exceptionally advanced for their time. In fact, American athletes of the 1930s and 1940s underwent training schedules not very different from those used now. It was Europe that made enormous progress regard-ing the building up and preparation of sprinters. By applying scientific principles, it was possible first to make up for the late starting point, and then even to achieve superiority.

These days, therefore, talent is no longer sufficient for success — constant and careful application is needed. A record cannot be improvised; years of preparation are also required. Pietro Mennea is a good example. As a boy, he quickly demonstrated that he had remarkable qualities, but he worked hard for ten years to achieve success. There has been nothing fortuitous in his athletics career. Each goal has been worked for conscientiously and he never attempted to speed up the process.

Having explained the basic concepts, we can now examine the guidelines to be followed when creating a sprinter.

THE QUICK YOUNGSTER
A child who is on the way to becoming an athlete, and who thinks he has the necessary talent to get to the top,

must first realize that in order to develop speed an individual must make the most of his whole body.

The feet are certainly the most important part, because they are the base, but there are also the legs which take the load, the gluteus muscles, which are the basic hinge of the sprinter, the trunk and the arms. If we study the structure of a sprinter, we find the figure of a complete athlete, strong and very muscular in all parts of the body.

Thus, the first thing to do with a beginner is to concentrate on building up the body, which must have developed muscles geared towards rapid movements. His sporting activities must therefore not be limited to those which utilize only the lower limbs. In this way, the young athlete should strive for that muscle harmony which is essential for a balanced action.

There is a wide range of free-standing exercises followed by exercises carrying weights (for older participants; younger beginners should use circuit training) that help to build up strength in a controlled manner which, together with running training, enable the young athlete to improve and progress and therefore to move more rapidly.

THE FIRST 100 METRES

First of all when tackling the 100 m, the shortest distance in the Olympic programme, one should not think of running it all in one breath without any thought. A period of 10–11 sec. is a comparatively short space of time, but to the man running 100 m it can seem an eternity. He must consider only what he is capable of doing and what he has learned, since, if he makes a mistake, only in this way is he

The starting technique of Pietro Mennea, 1980 Olympic champion and world record holder in the 200 m with 19.72 sec.
In picture 1, Mennea prepares to take his position on the starting blocks. He supports himself on his hands so that he can find the most suitable point of contact between his feet and the blocks, and ensure that the blocks are properly fixed (in former times, athletes dug small holes in the cinder track, in which they placed their feet). In picture 2 he is in the 'on your marks' position. In picture 3, when the starter gives the command 'set', Mennea raises his pelvis. Note that the pelvis is higher than the shoulders, which are almost perpendicular to the hands. In picture 4, the start, Mennea shoots forward, pushing off with his left foot and advancing his right knee; the left arm is brought forward, while the right is flung backwards. In picture 5, the initial supporting leg is drawn back after the start. In picture 6, Mennea advances with co-ordinated, powerful movements.

in a position to correct himself. To run fast does not mean to move feverishly or to strain every part of the body to the full; speed is also self-control. To move in an exaggerated state of tension means to proceed jerkily.

THE 100 METRES: FROM START TO FINISH

In a 100 m race there are four distinct phases: the start, pick-up, acceleration and the development of maximum speed.

The start, i.e. the sudden change from a stationary to a running position, is the most precarious phase. It is fundamental, for anyone who wishes to perform well in a sprint, to spring away from the start as quickly as possible. In particular, the beginner must sharpen up his ability to react to the starter's signal.

In order to train for the start, initially some standing starts can be attempted, without kneeling down in front of the starting blocks, first with the feet in a line, then later with the feet apart (one in front of the other). Without his hands resting on the ground, the sprinter would pitch forward and the start would be turned into an instinctive reaction against the fear of falling. This progressive approach is advisable because starting correctly from blocks requires a certain strength and ability.

Let us now examine the techniques employed by top athletes in the 100 m.

On your marks. An athlete preparing to take part in a sprint race moves into his lane behind his starting blocks. When the starter gives the command 'on your marks', he moves forward, kneels in front before touching the blocks, then backs into them and rests his feet on the blocks, so that they are secure (see sequence on pages 10–11). The crouching position that he adopts depends mainly on the arrangement of the blocks in relation to one another, and their distance from the starting line. There are no standard measurements to follow when securing the blocks on the metal rod to which they are fixed, but they should be positioned according to the physique of the particular athlete and thus the length of his

limbs. The distance between the two blocks must enable the knee of the rear leg, once the crouching position has been adopted, to project about 10–15 cm beyond the front foot. Usually, the average distance between the blocks is about the length of the athlete's foot (between 28 and 32 cm). The distance between the front block and the starting line must be such that the front knee just meets the plane passing through the arms; this distance is usually equal to twice the length of the athlete's foot (50–60 cm).

With his feet on the blocks, the competitor bends his legs and places his hands, thumbs inwards, just behind the starting line. His fingers too must always be behind this line. His shoulders should be perpendicular to his hands with his arms extended, and his eyes firmly on the ground.

Set. At the command 'set', the athlete extends his legs, and lifts his pelvis. His pelvis is slightly higher than his shoulders, which are slightly farther forward than his hands. His gaze should be directed towards his thumbs. At this point, the athlete should feel the weight of his body supported equally by his hands and feet. If there is insufficient weight on his hands, he should lean slightly further forward with his shoulders, while excessive weight on his arms means that he should lean further back.

Go. At the command 'go', or when the pistol is fired, the athlete removes his hands from the ground and swings his arms, one in front and the other behind in a co-ordinated movement with the lower limbs. The front leg drives hard against the block and the rear leg comes forward with the knee bent towards the chest. In this swinging movement, the arm opposite the leg which is bent forward from behind is brought forward, while the arm opposite the leg which is extended is pulled back and propels the body forwards. In the act of straightening to maximum extension, the head, perfectly relaxed on the neck, must not be raised to look at the finish line, but must remain in a straight line extending from the trunk, with the eyes looking down at the track.

The position adopted on the starting blocks must as far as possible be comfortable and not cause high muscular tension, which would be detrimental to the runner's speed, agility and ability to accelerate. A basic prerequisite for efficient acceleration is relaxation, i.e. the controlled eagerness that the athlete shows in moving from a state of immobility and to achieve high speed. The start and acceleration phases, which are extremely tricky, are the basis of the whole race.

Pick-up. The young sprinter must not think that to start and run quickly means maximum and total commitment, and nothing else. The acceleration phase, i.e. an increase in speed, usually lasts for about 45–50 m in the case of highly trained athletes, whereas with youngsters this phase is progressively shorter the younger and less accomplished they are. Generally, an initial part of the complete acceleration phase can be distinguished. This comprises the first 7–8 steps and is called 'pick-up', since the positions adopted by the athlete in this phase are visibly different from those immediately following the start of the race. The force that the athlete exerts by thrusting his legs on the ground is more pronounced than the force exhibited in the start phase.

As the speed increases, the force exerted by the athlete in the initial phase decreases progressively and gives way to more agile movements, which are the result of a more emphatic and lively reaction from the feet. The first strides are called 'pick-up', since it is in these strides that there is the greatest variation in speed, given that in the short space of about 10 m the athlete passes from zero speed to a speed of about 9 m/sec., or the equivalent of 32.4 km/h (20.25 mph).

Acceleration. Between the first 10 m and 40–45 m (and thus within a distance of 35 m) the athlete's acceleration is reduced in that his maximum speed reaches 11.6–11.8 m/sec., i.e. between 41.76 and 42.48 km/h (26.1 and 26.55 mph). This represents an increase of about 3 m/sec. in relation to the speed reached at the end of the 'pick-up' phase.

Maximum speed. Having reached maximum speed, the athlete must proceed in complete relaxation so as to maintain the speed he has attained almost constantly until the finish.

Maximum speed is the speed at which the athlete is still in control, i.e. where he does not feel at its mercy and does not end up overrunning himself. This means that the sprinter must think of the 100 m race not as a crack of the whip, an extremely intense and brief effort, but as an easy and fluent action.

With his final stride, an accomplished sprinter thrusts out his chest, with his arms parallel behind him. This enables him to push further forward the point on his body which will interrupt the beam of the photofinish light.

Note: The training for the 100 m is almost the same as for the 200 m, and the two are combined in the next chapter.

The starter's rules and disqualification

The starter must position himself at the side of the runners so that he can spot any breaks. He should be aided by one or two assistants, who check that no competitor has his fingers over or in front of the starting line.

The starter should start the race by firing a pistol or similar device. If he is not convinced that everything is ready for the start, once the competitors are at their marks and on their blocks, he must order them to stand up again.

At the command 'set', the competitors must adopt the full and final 'set' position. Failure to execute this movement after a reasonable time constitutes a false start and the offending competitor is cautioned. If this is repeated, he is disqualified.

Should an athlete shift his position with his hands or feet after the word 'set' and before the gun goes off, this is considered a false start, and he receives a warning. If the same competitor is responsible for a second infringement of the same kind, he is disqualified.

A competitor can also be disqualified if he leaves the lane assigned to him. Track judges and marksmen can threaten disqualification, but they can leave the competitor in the race if they consider that the result is not affected.

Usually in races at international level, after the first false start, a warning is displayed by means of a flag or red light at the foot of the blocks or on the board indicating the runner's lane.

The stars

BERNARD WEFERS (USA)
Among the many runners in the 19th century who were given the title of the 'world's fastest human', the most worthy champion was probably Bernard Wefers. Between 1895 and 1897 he dominated the American sprint scene, at that time the strongest in the world. He did not take part in the first Olympic Games (Athens, 1896), but demonstrated that he was the best sprinter of the time in the historic encounter between the athletics clubs of New York and London on 21 Sept. 1895 at Manhattan Field, New York, easily winning the 100 yards in 9.8 sec. and the 220 yards (run in a straight line) in 21.6 sec. He won the American championships over the same distances three years in a row. Some of the times that he recorded, including a 9.4 sec. in the 100 yards, were disbelieved by the judges and officials of the time, who dared not ratify them. Two times recorded by him in 1896 – 21.2 sec. in the 220 yards in a straight line and 30.6 sec. in

the 300 yards – came to be entered on the official IAAF register of world records, and remained unbeaten for a quarter of a century.

RALPH METCALFE (USA)
In the impressive array of great American sprinters, Metcalfe achieved the largest number of victories in the national championships: three in the 100 m and five in the 200 m between 1932 and 1936. However, he had no success in the Olympic Games. In Los Angeles in 1932 he lost the 100 m by a few centimetres to his compatriot, Eddie Tolan, sharing with him a world record of 10.3 sec. The two of them were the first black Americans to win Olympic medals in the sprints. In Berlin in 1936, he was up against the great Jesse Owens in the 100 m and again finished second after a difficult start and a superb but late recovery. He finally struck gold in the 4 × 100 m relay when, for the first time ever, his team broke the 40 sec. barrier (39.8 sec.). Because of

his difficulties in starting, he was considered by many to be mediocre in this respect; but Owens's trainer, Larry Snyder, having seen the film of the Berlin 100 m in slow motion, declared that Metcalfe had the quickest start, but lost ground immediately afterwards through his bad habit of running with small strides in the initial phase. Having got into gear, with his large strides, Metcalfe was invincible, one of the greatest of his time. His personal records were: 100 yards in 9.4 sec., 100 m in 10.2 sec., 200 m with partial curve 20.6 sec., 220 yards in a straight line 20.4 sec. and with a following wind 19.8 sec. When his career was over, he entered political life and was elected to Congress in Washington.

JESSE OWENS (USA)
Today, the name Jesse Owens still holds a special fascination. To understand his unique abilities, it is sufficient to hear what he managed on his 'Day of days', 25 May 1935, in Ann

Jesse Owens

Arbor (Michigan); in an hour and a quarter he broke three world records (220 yards, 220 yards hurdles and long jump), and equalled a fourth (100 yards). In his 'Week of Weeks', from 2 to 9 Aug. 1936 in Berlin, he won four Olympic gold medals (100 m and 200 m, long jump, 4 × 100 m relay). Without specializing in any of these events, he was the greatest sprinter of his time with 9.4 sec. in the 100 yards and 20.3 sec. in the 220 yards (straight); 10.2 sec. in the 100 m and 20.7 sec. in the 200 m (with full curve). He was also the best long jumper, breaking the 8 m barrier at Ann Arbor with a leap of 8.13 m (26ft 5in). This record remained unbeaten for 25 years. At the climax of two exceptional years, 1935 and 1936, he retired from the athletics scene without discovering his full potential.

ARMIN HARY (GERMANY)

The key to his success lay in an extraordinary speed of reflex, and he then learned how to increase this advantage by 'premature' acceleration. His most important victory was achieved in the 100 m in the 1960 Olympic Games in Rome. After a false start, for which he was cautioned, he regained his composure and set off perfectly. He won in 10.2 sec. (electronic time, 10.32 sec.), spoiling the comeback of the American, Dave Sime. Hary became the second European to win the 100 m in the Olympics, after the Englishman, Harold Abrahams, who won in 1924.

In 1958, in Stockholm, he won the 100 m European title in 10.3 sec. after an unbelievably good start. He achieved the first '10 dead' in 1959 in Friedrichshafen, but on a slightly sloping track. He repeated this time twice on 21 June 1960 in Zurich: the first race was rendered null and void 'after the event' due to a false start. In the re-run race he recorded the same time under normal conditions, even though the electronic timing device, used as a back-up, showed no better than 10.25 sec. His attempts at the 200 m were not frequent, but he nonetheless achieved a convincing 20.5 sec. on a track with a partial curve. From 1961 onwards, he had various ups and downs which led him to give up athletics prematurely.

BOB HAYES (USA)

If you were to ask a group of experts who was the fastest man ever seen in the 100 m, the majority would probably mention the name of Bob Hayes. In the 1964 Olympics in Tokyo, Hayes won the 100 m in 10.06 sec., 0.19 sec. faster than the second-placed competitor, an extraordinary margin for an Olympic final over this distance. Later, on the last leg of the 4 × 100 m relay, he took the baton in fourth position, almost three metres behind the leader, but he overhauled everyone else to win the race by three metres. These two exhibitions of sheer speed, on a cinder track, startled experts from all over the world. In that relay, Hayes must have reached an average speed very close to 41 km/h (25.6 mph) once he had got into his stride. Tall and powerful he was superbly muscular. Although not much better than mediocre at starting, his acceleration was incredible. Over the first 20–30 m, he almost gave the impression of staggering, so disjointed was his action, but after this point he adopted a very efficient running style and was uncatchable.

He managed to break the 6 sec. barrier for the first time in the 60 yards, the classic distance of US indoor meetings, with 5.9 sec. in 1964 in New York. He was the co-holder of world records in the 100 yards (9.1 sec. and 100 m (10.0 sec.) and equalled that of the 220 yards with curve (20.5 sec.), although it was not ratified. Three years running (1962–64) he won the American title for the 100 yards and 100 m. During his years at high school, he distinguished himself at American football rather than in athletics, and after his successes at the Tokyo Olympics, he returned to football as a professional with the Dallas Cowboys, achieving great success in this sport too.

JIM HINES (USA)

The name of Jim Hines has passed into history as the first person to run the 100 m in less than 10 sec., which he accomplished on 20 June 1968 in Sacramento, in a semi-final of the American championships; his time according to hand-operated instruments was 9.9 sec. Previously, he had won his heat in a wind-assisted time of 9.8 sec. In the final he was beaten by his great rival Charles Greene, who won the title in a wind-assisted 10.0 sec. Four months later, Hines repeated his feat in the Olympic final in Mexico, this time timed on the much more reliable automatic timing device. His world record of 9.95 sec.

Jim Hines in the 1968 Olympics.

was assisted by the rarefied air of the Mexican capital, which is situated more than 2000 m above sea level. In the same Olympic Games, Hines ran a sparkling last leg to win the 4 × 100 m relay for America in a world record time of 38.23 sec. Jim Hines did not have the power of Bob Hayes, nor the technical efficiency of Valeri Borzov, first in Munich in 1972, but he had no weak points and he stood out above everyone in 1968. Besides equalling the world records for the 60 yards indoor (5.9 sec.) and the 100 yards (9.1 sec.), he was also a very strong 200 m runner. He also showed his ability over a longer distance when he ran 440 yards in the relay in 45.5 sec. Like Bob Hayes he subsequently entered the world of American football, but did not

Valeri Borzov

achieve the success of his predecessor.

VALERI BORZOV (USSR)

To date, he is the only European to have won the 100 m/200 m double in the Olympic Games, which he achieved at Munich in 1972. In the 100 m he won in 10.14 sec., almost a metre ahead of the American Robert Taylor, having broken the European record with a time of 10.07 sec. in the heats. In the 200 m, his time was 20.00 sec., another European record, beating the American Larry Black by two metres.

It has often been said that Borzov's talent was 'constructed' rather than natural. Indeed, he and his trainer, Valentin Petrovski, studied at length every technical detail of sprinting and there is no doubt that his preparation was guided by rigorous scientific principles. However, his talent had shown itself very early – he won the 100 m in the European Championships in Athens in 1969, one month before his 20th birthday; also, the USSR has still not managed to produce another sprinter of a class even remotely comparable to Borzov's in the years since Munich. Borzov often gave the impression of running like a machine, and his competitive strength is reflected in an extraordinary series of international successes: four outdoor European titles (100 m in 1969, 1971 and 1974, 200 m in 1971) and seven indoor (50 m and 60 m). In the Olympic Games, apart from his double gold in Munich, he won a silver medal in the 4 × 100 m in 1972, and two bronze medals in 1976 in the 100 m and 4 × 100 m. He is the only 100 m Olympic champion who has managed to return to the rostrum at this event at the next Games. He always showed a marked preference for the 100 m over the 200 m, but, if he had wished, he could probably have made a name for himself in the 400 m, which he ran in 47.6 sec. at the age of 20. Two operations to his Achilles tendons prevented him competing in the 1980 Games in Moscow.

FANNY BLANKERS (HOLLAND)

The first great figure in women's athletics, she came to the fore in the most remarkable way in 1935, when only 17.

By running the 800 m in 2 min. 29.0 sec., she collected the first of an amazing series of national records.

In 1936 she made her first appearance in the Olympics, finishing sixth in the high jump and helping Holland to gain fifth place in the 4 × 100 m relay. In 1938 her name appeared for the first time in the register of world records: 11.0 sec. in the 100 yards. Having married in 1940, by the end of the war she held the world records for the 80 m hurdles, the high jump and the long jump.

In 1946, in the European Championships in Oslo, she won gold in the 80 m hurdles and in the 4 × 100 m relay. Her fame is mainly connected with the success she had in the 1948 Olympics in London, where she emulated Jesse Owens's feat in winning four gold medals: 100 m and 200 m, 80 m hurdles and 4 × 100 m relay, and by then she was 30 years old.

Between 1938 and 1951, she achieved world records in seven events: 100 yards (10.8 sec.), 100 m (11.5 sec.), 220 yards (24.2 sec.), 80 m hurdles (11.0 sec.), high jump (1.71 m), long jump (6.25 m) and pentathlon (4692 points).

WILMA RUDOLPH (USA)

For many years, black athletes have monopolized sprints in the USA. In the women's sprint events, this tradition was begun by Wilma Rudolph, who in the 1960 Rome Olympics won the 100 m and 200 m, as well as the 4 × 100 m relay – a triple gold that no female sprinter has managed to equal. In childhood, she was afflicted by polio, and it was only at the age of eleven that she was able to do without an iron support on her right leg. Yet at sixteen she managed to qualify for the American Olympic team and in Melbourne, in 1956, she won a bronze medal in the 4 × 100 m relay. Four years later, in Rome, she showed overwhelming superiority, winning both sprints by a clear three metres. Her time in the 100 m, 11.0 sec., would have constituted a new world record, had she not had wind assistance of 2.8 m/sec. According to the automatic timing device, her time was 11.18 sec., which is still impressive, particularly since it was achieved on a

Wilma Rudolph

WYOMIA TYUS (USA)

In the long history of the Olympic Games, the feat of twice winning the 100 m has up to now eluded the efforts of all the greatest male sprinters. However, it has been achieved by women, including Wyomia Tyus. Before she was 18, she went 'on tour' in Europe and immediately demonstrated her talent. Before her 19th birthday, she gained an indoor world record, running the 60 yards in 7.5 sec. In the same year, 1964, she qualified for the Tokyo Olympic Games. She did not go there as the favourite to win, but she proved to be the strongest. In the quarter-finals, she equalled Wilma Rudolph's world record of 11.2 sec., improving upon her pre-Games personal best by three-tenths of a second. In the final, she won in 11.4 sec., running against the wind, beating her compatriot Edith McGuire and the Pole Ewa Klobukowska. Tyus also won a silver in the 4 × 100 m relay. Four years later, at the Mexico Games, Tyus again won the 100 m, this time in a world record time of 11.0 sec., corrected to 11.08 on the electronic timer.

Tyus won the third and final gold medal of her career in the 4 × 100 m relay, with her team finishing in a world record time of 42.87 sec. In between the Olympics, she also held the world record for the 100 yards (10.3 sec.). Although generally ignoring the 200 m, she managed to run the distance in 23.0 sec.

EVELYN ASHFORD (USA)

She is the only female sprinter who in recent years has been able to break the monopoly of Eastern Europe, in particular East Germany, in this event. In two World Cups she managed to achieve a double win in the 100 m and 200 m, with 11.06 sec. and 21.83 sec. in 1979 in Montreal, and with 11.02 sec. and 22.18 sec. in 1981 in Rome. On these occasions, she had to defeat the East Germans Marlies Göhr, Marita Koch and Bärbel Wöckel, twice Olympic champion in the 200 m.

At the 1976 Olympics in Montreal, just 19 years old, she had to content herself with fifth place in the 100 m. The American boycott of the Moscow Olympics in 1980 prevented her from

Evelyn Ashford

having a second attempt, but at the Los Angeles Olympics in 1984 she proved she is still a champion by taking the gold medal in the women's 100 m in a new Olympic record of 10.97 sec.

Regarding times, she finally managed to dent the supremacy of the East Germans in the 100 m, replacing Göhr as the world record holder with a time of 10.79 sec. achieved on 3 July 1983 in Colorado Springs, situated 2194 m above sea level.

MARLIES GÖHR (GDR)

For seven seasons, between 1977 and 1983, she was one of the best women's 100 m runners in the world, if not the best of all time, but she never won a race in the Olympics, except in the relay races. She has held world records for the 100 m with 10.81 sec., achieved on 8 June 1983 in East Berlin, and 10.88 sec., gained in 1977 in Dresden. She has beaten 11 sec. nine times, rivalled in this achievement only by the American Evelyn Ashford. In her first Olympic Games in 1976, when she was 18, the East German girl finished eighth in the 100 m and then won the gold in the 4 × 100 m relay. Four years later in Moscow, she started as clear favourite in the absence of Ashford. However,

cinder track. In her brief career, she held the world records for the 100 m (11.2 sec.) and 200 m (22.9 sec.), as well as the 4 × 100 m (44.3 sec.). She gave up athletics even earlier than Jesse Owens, at the age of 22, and might have become the greatest female athlete of all time had she continued with the sport, above even Koch and Göhr.

Wyomia Tyus

Marlies Göhr

she was beaten by a hundredth of a second (11.07 sec. as against 11.06 sec.) by the Russian Lyudmila Kondratyeva. She obtained at least partial consolation with another success in the 4 × 100 m relay, with the East German team winning in a world record time of 41.60 sec.

Still in the 100 m, Göhr triumphed in the European Championships in 1978 and 1982, and also in the first World Cup (1977), beating Ashford, among others, who nevertheless twice took her revenge in subsequent World Cups (1979 and 1981).

In the 200 m, Göhr has competed infrequently, although finishing second in the European Championships in 1978. Her personal best is 22.36 sec.

Charles Paddock (USA) – *See the 200 m.*
Carl Lewis (USA) – *See the 200 m.*
Pietro Mennea (ITALY) – *See the 200 m.*
Tommie Smith (USA) – *See the 200 m.*

Men

sec.
10.6 Donald Lippincott (USA) 1912
10.6 Jackson Scholz (USA) 1920
10.4 Charles Paddock (USA) 1921
10.4 Eddie Tolan (USA) 1929
10.3 Percy Williams (Canada) 1930
10.3 Eddie Tolan (USA) 1932
10.3 Ralph Metcalfe (USA) 1933
10.3 Eulace Peacock (USA) 1934
10.3 Christiaan Berger (Holland) 1934
10.3 Ralph Metcalfe (USA) 1934
10.3 Takayoshi Yoshioka (Japan) 1935
10.2 Jesse Owens (USA) 1936
10.2 Harold Davis (USA) 1941
10.2 Lloyd La Beach (Panama) 1948
10.2 Barney Ewell (USA) 1948
10.2 McDonald Bailey (GB) 1951
10.2 Heins Fütterer (Germany) 1954
10.2 Bobby Morrow (USA) 1956
10.2 Ira Murchison (USA) 1956
10.1 Willie Williams (USA) 1956
10.1 Ira Murchison (USA) 1956
10.1 Leamon King (USA) 1956
10.1 Ray Norton (USA) 1959
10.0 Armin Hary (Germany) 1960
10.0 Harry Jerome (Canada) 1960
10.0 Horacio Esteves (Venezuela) 1964
10.0 Bob Hayes (USA) 1964
10.0 Jim Hines (USA) 1967
10.0 Enrique Figuerola (Cuba) 1967
10.0 Paul Nash (S. Africa) 1968
10.0 Oliver Ford (USA) 1968
10.0 Charlie Greene (USA) 1968
10.0 Roger Bambuck (France) 1968
9.9 Jim Hines (USA) 1968
9.9 Charlie Greene (USA) 1968
9.9 Ronnie Ray Smith (USA) 1968
9.9 Eddie Hart (USA) 1972
9.9 Reynaud Robinson (USA) 1972
9.9 Steve Williams (USA) 1974
9.9 Silvio Leonard (Cuba) 1975
9.9 Steve Williams (USA) 1975
9.9 Steve Williams (USA) 1976
9.9 Harvey Glance (USA) 1976
9.9 Donald Quarrie (Jamaica) 1976

Automatic times
9.95 Jim Hines (USA) 1968
9.93 Calvin Smith (USA) 1983

Women

sec.
11.7 Stanislawa Walasiewicz (Poland) 1934
11.6 Stanislawa Walasiewicz (Poland) 1937
11.5 Fanny Blankers-Koen (Holland) 1948
11.5 Marjorie Jackson (Australia) 1952
11.4 Marjorie Jackson (Australia) 1952
11.3 Shirley de la Hunty (Australia) 1955
11.3 Vera Krepkina (USSR) 1958
11.3 Wilma Rudolph (USA) 1960
11.2 Wilma Rudolph (USA) 1961
11.2 Wyomia Tyus (USA) 1964
11.1 Irena Kirszenstein (Poland) 1965
11.1 Wyomia Tyus (USA) 1965
11.1 Barbara Ferrell (USA) 1967
11.1 Ludmilla Samotyosova (USSR) 1968
11.1 Irena Szewinska (Poland) 1968
11.0 Wyomia Tyus (USA) 1968
11.0 Chi Cheng (Taiwan) 1970
11.0 Renate Meissner (GDR) 1970
11.0 Eva Gleskova (Czechoslovakia) 1972
11.0 R. Meissner-Stecher (GDR) 1971
11.0 R. Meissner-Stecher (GDR) 1972
11.0 Ellen Strophal (GDR) 1972
10.9 R. Meissner-Stecher (GDR) 1973
10.8 R. Meissner-Stecher (GDR) 1973
10.8 Annegret Richter (W. Germany) 1976

Automatic times
11.07 Wyomia Tyus (USA) 1968
11.07 R. Meissner-Stecher (GDR) 1972
11.04 Inge Helten (W. Germany) 1976
11.01 Annegret Richter (W. Germany) 1976
10.88 Marlies Göhr (GDR) 1977
10.81 Marlies Göhr (GDR) 1983
10.79 Evelyn Ashford (USA) 1983

Note: Up until the 1964 Olympics, the two Germanies (Federal Republic of Germany and German Democratic Republic) competed under the same flag. Subsequently, they competed as West Germany and East Germany, respectively.

200 m

How it is run

As in the case of the 100 m, there are no standard physical attributes that enable some runners to excel at 200 m; also, different methods of preparation have been employed by the various schools of sprinting.

The old American and Anglo-Saxon schools did not differentiate between training methods for the 100 m and 200 m. Thus, a sprinter trained to run the 100 m also tried his hand at the 200 m, and obtained good results. The two schools of thought were highly advanced in terms of performances, particularly as a result of instruction and the generalized spread of fitness and sporting activity. By implementing training programmes, the athletes of the countries concerned were therefore in a position to outdistance competitors from other countries by several metres. Furthermore, black sprinters left everyone behind, and because they were more gifted than whites, they were therefore more likely to perform better in this event. However, from the 1960s onwards, 'old' Europe, because of its better appreciation of the training methods to be used in the case of the 200 m, recovered and wiped out those metres that represented the difference between its athletes and the black Americans. Champions such as Borzov, Mennea

and Wells have illustrated with their achievements Europe's technical change of direction. Their results are the fruits of the new training theories which have been perfected little by little.

To date, there are two examples of systematic training coming from the USA: that of Evelyn Ashford, who undergoes intensive work sessions, which enabled her to beat clearly the East Germans, those running machines; and Edwin Moses, master of the 400 m hurdles. Others have mostly followed their instinct and training programmes owing more to tradition than to current thinking.

Differences. We will now explain the differences that might be defined as 'technical' between the 100 m and 200 m events.

While it is essential for the 200 m runner to be able to develop high peaks of speed, as for the 100 m, the most obvious difference between the two distances lies in 'speed endurance', which can be defined as the capacity to maintain high speeds over longer distances.

A distinction therefore needs to be made in the training for the 100 m and 200 m. Indeed, the 200 m runner must include in his training schedule a slightly heavier work load over long-

er distances. Thus, he should generally carry out repeated trials over 300 m and 400 m, as well as repeating shorter distances, between 60 m and 150 m, more often and in greater quantities. Another significant difference between the 100 m and 200 m lies in acquiring the technique to run the curve (turn) correctly.

Finally, we should consider the different rhythmical approach to the race, which leads to a different development of speed. In the 200 m, the acceleration phase is slightly less dynamic and furious than in the 100 m, and a slightly lower speed is reached than that developed for the shorter race. In the first part of the race, the 200 m runner must take a slightly longer time (about 20–30 hundredths of a second more) than his personal record for the 100 m and attempt to keep this speed almost steady until the finish.

The correct differential between the first and second sections of the 200 m must be in the region of half a second, for example, the first 100 m in 10.20 sec. and the second in 9.80 sec. This occurs when the race is tackled correctly according to the principles outlined.

How to tackle it. We have already explained that the 200 m is tackled in

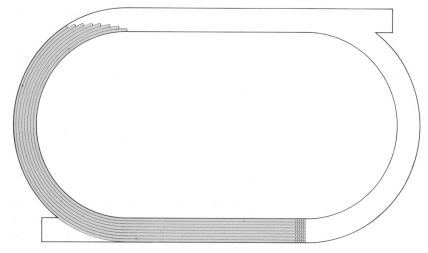

Left: *The diagram shows a complete running track, the shaded area representing the section run in the 200 m race; the finishing straight is always in front of the main stand in a stadium. Note that the staggered start is to allow for the extra distance run by competitors in the outside lanes.* **Opposite:** *This sequence shows Borzov's perfect technique in running the curve . Note how the athletes lean into the bend in order to counteract the centrifugal force encountered.*

a slightly calmer manner than the 100 m. The runner's emotional state must be more controlled, because the speed to be developed both at the start and in the acceleration phase must be definitely more restrained, and because it is vital to consider that the first 100 m is run on a curve.

The start. Bearing in mind that the start takes place on a curve, the starting blocks are positioned near the outer line that delimits the lane, so as to follow a starting trajectory which is tangential to the curve itself, 5–6 m beyond the starting line. The inner lanes force the athlete to run a more pronounced curve than the outer lanes. When positioning the start-

ing blocks, this fact must be taken into account.

Running on a curve. When building up high speeds on a curve, centrifugal force tends to make the athlete skid outwards. In order to overcome this force, the sprinter has to lean into the bend. It is vitally important, therefore, for the athlete to be relaxed and supple, particularly in the upper part of the body, because any rigidity in his trunk would cause his entire body to advance as a single unit and thus be more likely to be affected by the centrifugal force pushing him outwards. The swinging of the arms must not be too extensive. In order to facilitate his action on the curve, the

runner must try, apart from leaning into the bend, to twist his trunk slightly so as to advance his left shoulder; this will help the whole body of the athlete to run in a more co-ordinated manner. The 200 m is an all-out sprint event, but it is controlled. Too fast a start causes a high consumption of energy, which is needed to overcome the powerful centrifugal force.

The straight. The most tricky part of the 200 m is the 'junction' between the curve and the straight. In this section of the track, which is between 80 m and 120 m from the start, the runners reach their peak speed, i.e. they are travelling at around

CONFIGURATION OF THE CURVE

The track on which the races are run consists of two straights (stretches) joined by two full curves.

For various reasons, tracks are designed with curves with a single centre, rounded, with a radius varying between 36.6 m and 40 m measured at the kerb, the centre being at the median of the tangents drawn from the end of the straights. However, it is considered best to make the radius 39.7 m, because it offers a number of advantages, including (a) a football pitch of a suitable size for international matches (105 × 68 m) can be put inside the running track; (b) with a broader curve, the athlete has less of a problem with centrifugal force, which pushes him outwards, and thus it helps his running action.

In order for a complete track to conform to regulations and for the results obtained on it to be ratifiable, it has to be monocentric and measure 389.12 m at the kerb and consequently 400 m in the inside lane (this measurement is taken 30 cm from the kerb), regardless of the radius chosen, bearing in mind that the straights become longer as the radius of curvature decreases and vice versa.

Whereas the inside lane is measured 30 cm from the kerb, the other lanes are measured 20 cm from the line painted on the track and which delimits it. In the inside lane the measurement is taken at a distance of 30 cm, since this lane is delimited by the kerb which protrudes 5 cm above the track, for which reason the athlete is obliged to run a little further inside the lane

Line of tangential points

radius

30 cm

20 cm

so as not to trip over the kerb. The width of tracks varies between 7.57 m (six-lane tracks) and 10.11 m (eight-lane tracks). The width of each lane is 1.27 m (however, the outside lane is 1.22 m, the difference being the width of the line which separates one lane from another).

On the subject of curves of running tracks, the International Technical Regulations for athletics races stipulate: 'The record must be achieved on a track where the radius of the curve of the outside lane does not exceed 60 m'.

Valeri Borzov (lane 2, arms raised) wins the final of the 100 m at the Munich Olympics. Robert Taylor of the USA (middle of the picture) was second, and the Jamaican Lennox Miller was third (on Taylor's right).

11 m/sec. (25 mph). It is important at this point not to skid. The sprinter who maintains a correct running position on the bend with the left shoulder slightly ahead of the other one naturally feels propelled towards the straight, on which he must try to maintain the speed that he has previously achieved. As on the bend, the runner must make sure that his upper body is supple and relaxed.

The athlete must think only about how his lower limbs are acting; the contact of his feet with the track must be explosive.

Pietro Mennea, in his fastest 200 m, covered the final 100 m in a time of around 9.5 sec., a time which can be broken down as follows: from 100 m to 150 m in 4.65 sec., from 150 m to 200 m, i.e. the final 50 m, in 4.85 sec.

The catching-up that athletes sometimes appear to be achieving in the final section of a race is more often as a result of the competitor in front slowing down, than the competitor in pursuit accelerating.

The sequence of photographs opposite shows the finish of the 200 m final at the Moscow Olympics. Pietro Mennea (nearest the camera) overhauls the Scotsman Allan Wells to win by 0.02 sec. in 20.19 sec., with the 1976 gold medallist (Jamaican Don Quarrie) just taking third place at the line.

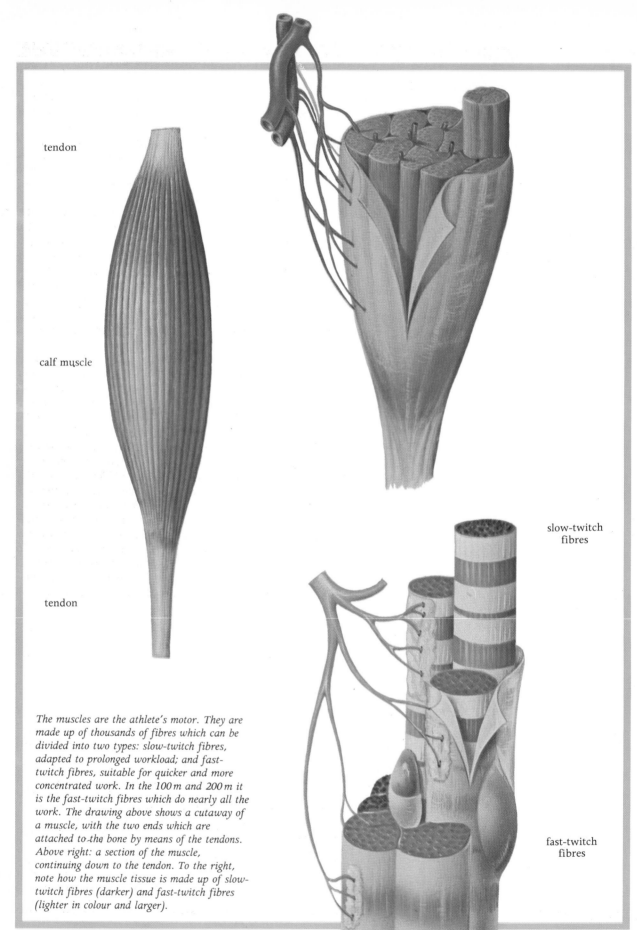

tendon

calf muscle

tendon

slow-twitch
fibres

fast-twitch
fibres

The muscles are the athlete's motor. They are
made up of thousands of fibres which can be
divided into two types: slow-twitch fibres,
adapted to prolonged workload; and fast-
twitch fibres, suitable for quicker and more
concentrated work. In the 100 m and 200 m it
is the fast-twitch fibres which do nearly all the
work. The drawing above shows a cutaway of
a muscle, with the two ends which are
attached to the bone by means of the tendons.
Above right: a section of the muscle,
continuing down to the tendon. To the right,
note how the muscle tissue is made up of slow-
twitch fibres (darker) and fast-twitch fibres
(lighter in colour and larger).

The sprinter's engine

For humans a distance of 40–50 m is sufficient to reach top speed. Not even the car, proportionately, is capable of that.

Once in their stride, the best sprinters in the world run faster than 40 km/h (25 mph). Youngsters who run the 100 m in around 12.0 sec. or the 80 m in around 10.0 sec. achieve about 35 km/h (22 mph). In the 200 m the best athletes (but often a number of youngsters too) manage to maintain an average speed which is very similar to a 100 m speed.

The muscles that determine the forward movement of the body are more or less the same whether the athlete is running at top speed, or is running very slowly. However, there are a few differences.

Certain muscles work slightly differently depending on the speed at which the athlete runs; one is the calf muscle, the sural triceps: the faster one runs, the greater the power this muscle has to exert.

The muscle can be contracted or relaxed (shortened or lengthened) because it consists of thousands of fibres which are capable of becoming shorter or longer. In a given athlete, when many fibres come into operation at once, the muscle exerts high levels of force. If few fibres come into operation, the force exerted is much less.

However, these fibres are not all the same: some are suited to prolonged work, known as slow-twitch fibres. Other fibres have a greater aptitude for rapid, explosive and concentrated work over a short time: these are called fast-twitch fibres. When an athlete runs very fast, not all his muscle fibres are in operation: it is his fast-twitch fibres that are at work. Whereas in a normal person, about half his fibres are of this type and the other half are slow-twitch fibres, there are champions of some events who have a predominance of one type of fibre: the best marathon runners, for example, have 85% (or more) slow-twitch fibres, while those who excel in the 100 m have more than 65% fast-twitch fibres. These differences are partly hereditary, but they are also partly due to specific training for a given event. We shall now examine the characteristics of the fast-twitch fibres, which are the most important in the short races, and the only ones that come into action when the athlete runs as fast as possible.

These fibres are of larger diameter and are capable of shortening in a very rapid time: in 40–90 thousandths of a second they reach the highest degree of contraction. They are also geared to using, every fraction of a second, a large quantity of the muscle's 'fuel' – ATP (adenosine triphosphate). In order to exert great power – as they are capable of doing – these fibres must burn up large amounts of energy each second. And because the 'fuel' tanks, which are in the muscles, can only contain a limited quantity, it is essential that the fibres themselves produce ATP, so as not to run out of fuel.

The mechanisms for producing this fuel are of three different types. In the shorter races (the 100 m and 200 m) the far greater amount required is produced by the 'alactacid anaerobic' mechanism, which has two fundamental characteristics for the purposes of exertions which are concentrated in short periods of time: it can be activated more speedily than the other two mechanisms, and it can provide a large quantity of energy every second which is used to produce ATP.

The alactacid anaerobic mechanism is like a flow of energy from one tank to another: what happens is that the energy in the creatine phosphate (CP) molecule is transferred to the ATP, the molecule which is used as the only possible fuel by the muscle fibres.

In the 100 m, but much more significantly in the 200 m, the fuel also comes from another energy mechanism, called 'lactacid anaerobic', as soon as it starts to produce a substance called lactic acid. This mechanism becomes much more important in the 400 m and the two most typical distances of fast middle-distance running, the 800 m and 1500 m.

AT HIGH ALTITUDE YOU BECOME FASTER

The higher up you go, the faster you become: this was asserted by scientists and confirmed by the Olympics held in Mexico City in 1968, which devastated the register of world records for the sprinting and jumping events.

It was already thought that running in a rarefied atmosphere offers many advantages, but this had never been quantified. Now, however, using Mexico City (2250 m above sea level) as a basis, calculations have been made regarding the improvements that can be obtained over events held at sea level: in the 100 m you gain about 11/100 sec. (for example, a time of 10.11 sec. in Rome is the equivalent of 10.00 sec. in Mexico City); in the 200 m about 20/100; in the 400 m about 36/100. The maximum gain occurs in a full circuit of the track, whereas the situation is reversed with the longer distances, where the consumption of oxygen by the athlete increases.

Training for the young

FIRST TRAINING PHASE

We shall now describe the characteristics of the first period, which is the phase for establishing the qualities of specific endurance of the youngster. This ought to be carried out between mid-October and mid-December, followed by a period of recuperation between 16 Dec. and 3 Jan.

In compiling the training programme, we have borne in mind that the youngster, in his first contact with sporting activity, must find aspects to stimulate his interest. Only after this first phase of work will he be made to understand the need to make good the failings encountered and to develop the various qualities by taking measures (not specific to the sprinter), which could have been 'tedious' in the introductory part. Gradually the athlete can be made to understand the importance and necessity of building himself up bodily and psychologically.

Therefore, the purpose of this first period is to get the young athlete to acquire experience. Thus, sprinting technique, the acceleration phase and starting from blocks, as well as hurdling techniques, will be explained and corrected simply by the use of exercises. At the end of each unit, periods lasting about 15 days will be inserted, ending with races and possibly followed by a period (the length of which may vary) of recuperation.

These competitions can be carried out in or between schools, and are extremely important for checking progress and for the interest that they arouse in the youngsters, who are especially attracted at this age by any form of competitive activity. It is worth remembering that the play element is of fundamental importance to children. Also, such a schedule of preparation should make allowance for rest. When dealing with youngsters, the main problem to overcome is that of the boredom that arises from a continuous, overwhelming work load.

Session 1

Warm-up: walking exercises for the feet, that is, exercises which mainly concern the reactivity of the feet and which can also be carried out with weights. For example, the athlete can move forward with a springy step, wearing a belt weighing 6–7 kg.

Technical exercises possibly with low hurdles, different distances apart; three spurts, each of 60–80 m, at a progressive speed.

Jumps: jumps with feet together between hurdles 50–76 cm high; there can be 5–8 hurdles, in a sequence of 6–10 repetitions; single jumps (standing long jump); triple, quintuple, decuple jumps, using alternate legs or both legs together (frog jumps).

Exercises with steps about 40–50 cm high; the athlete jumps up, using alternate feet or both feet together (frog jumps) with 6–10 steps, repeating the exercise 3–5 times.

Specific endurance: this is one of the fundamental prerequisites of endurance training for young sprinters. It consists of repeated runs of between 60 m and 500 m, broken up by rests of sufficient length to assist speed.

Recommended runs for the first day: 3 × 60 m, then 2 × 80 m, 15 min. recovery; 100 m, 8 min. recovery; 200 m, 12–15 min. recovery; 300 m.

Session 2

Warm-up: exercises with ropes over 15–20 m.

Suppleness and stretching exercises; three spurts of 80–100 m at progressive speed.

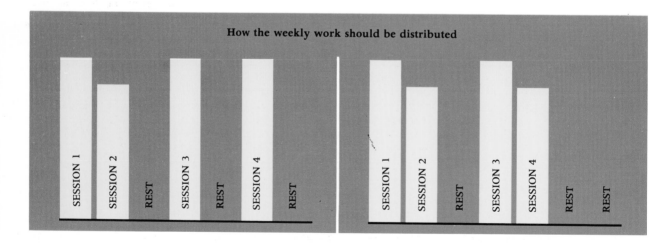

How the weekly work should be distributed

SESSION 1 | SESSION 2 | REST | SESSION 3 | REST | SESSION 4 | REST

SESSION 1 | SESSION 2 | REST | SESSION 3 | SESSION 4 | REST | REST

First example – The four training sessions are distributed as follows: two consecutive days of work at the beginning, one rest day, one day's training, one rest day, another day's training. When the work days are consecutive, the schedule of the second training session must be less demanding than the first.

Second example – The four training sessions are distributed as follows: two consecutive work days at the beginning, one rest day, two further consecutive work days, followed by two rest days. This distribution allows greater recovery than the other one.

Running uphill: this is an exercise to promote muscle development and specific endurance. It is carried out in stretches of 30 m and 50 m at a sustained, almost maximum, speed: 3–4 min. pauses after 30 m; 5–6 min. after 50 m.

Sprinting from blocks: studying the starting phase with starts from blocks progressing over about 30 m. These can be alternated with acceleration exercises from a standing start, again over stretches of 30 m, with 3 min. pauses between exercises. The number of starts can vary between 8 and 12 repetitions.

Game: Choose games which from the muscular point of view have more to do with the performance of the sprinter, i.e. basketball, football, volley-ball and hand-ball.

Session 3

Warm-up: walking exercises for the feet; technical exercises with possibly low hurdles, different distances apart; three spurts, each of 60–80 m, at a progressive speed.

Jumps: jumps with feet together between hurdles 50–76 cm high; there can be 5–8 hurdles, in a sequence of 6–10 repetitions; single jumps (standing long jump); triple, quintuple,

decuple jumps, with alternate legs or both legs together (frog jumps). Exercises with steps about 40–50 cm high; the athlete jumps up, using alternate feet or both feet together (frog jumps) with 6–10 steps, repeating the exercise 3–5 times.

Specific endurance: 3–4 × 60 m with 4 min. pauses; 2–3 × 80 m with 6 min. pauses; 300 m after 15 min.; 500 m after 12–15 min.

Session 4

Warm-up: exercises with ropes over 15–20 m; suppleness and stretching exercises; three spurts of 80–100 m at progressive speed.

Resistance work: runs are carried out over distances of 20 m and 30 m with a load of about 10 kg. In these runs it is advisable to have the athletes start by supporting themselves on their hands and knees, in order to perfect even further the technique of springing away from the blocks and the acceleration phase; 8–12 repetitions can be done with pauses of 3–4 min.

Sprints from blocks: starts from blocks progressing over about 30 m. These can also be alternated with acceleration exercises from a standing start, again over stretches of 30 m, with 3 min. pauses between exercises,

Pietro Mennea demonstrates a stretching exercise. He has adopted the hurdling position with his right hand towards his left leg. This position is then reversed.

which can vary between 8 and 10 repetitions.

Game: choose one of the following ballgames: basketball, football, volley-ball and hand-ball.

SECOND TRAINING PHASE

The second phase, general and specific building, ought to be carried out in January and February and should end before the period of recuperation which runs from 1 to 14 March.

After the previous phase, in which the characteristics of the individual are studied, and having assessed his potential, we shall be concerned mainly with the work of muscle building and with introducing exercises which will develop so-called aerobic power.

The exercises suggested will be directed towards all the muscle areas, from the trunk and the lower and upper limbs, to the feet muscles.

All the proposals should follow naturally from the previous phase of learning and dialogue with the young beginner.

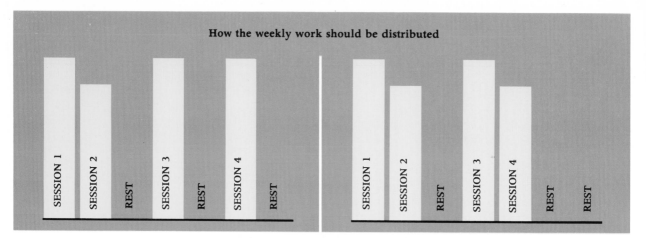

How the weekly work should be distributed

SESSION 1 | SESSION 2 | REST | SESSION 3 | REST | SESSION 4 | REST

SESSION 1 | SESSION 2 | REST | SESSION 3 | SESSION 4 | REST | REST

First example – The four training sessions are distributed as follows: two consecutive work days at the beginning, one rest day, one day's training, one rest day, another day's training. When the work days are consecutive, the schedule of the second training session must be less demanding than the first.

Second example – The four training sessions are distributed as follows: two consecutive work days at the beginning, one rest day, two further consecutive work days, followed by two rest days. This distribution allows greater recovery than the other one.

Pierfrancesco Pavoni performs a series of jumps over hurdles, which serve to increase the response and elasticity of the athlete. The hurdles can be 50–76 cm high and the exercises are carried out 5–8 times with 6–10 repetitions, with the feet together.

Session 1

Warm-up: exercises with ropes over 15–20 m. Suppleness or stretching exercises; three sprints of 80–100 m at progressive speed.

Strength building: exercises which involve the muscle areas between the glutei and the feet. For example: from the prone position, kick alternate legs upwards. From the prone position, keeping the ankles on the ground, bend upwards with the chest. Running while kicking backwards over distances of 100 m, 200 m, 300 m and 400 m with 1 kg weights on the ankles.

Adjustment sprints: the purpose of these is to regulate and improve the acceleration phase. Stretches of at least 30 m are covered, both after walking a few steps and from a stationary start, and with very close to maximum effort.

Sprints for running technique: distances of 60–80 m are covered at a sustained speed with lengthy pauses; the latter will enable the athlete to recover properly and to be in a position to perfect his technique and to put the suggestions into practice.

Aerobic power: this is gained by means of continuous and progressive running, allowing pulse rates to exceed 150 beats per minute, over distances between 2000 m and 5000 m.

Session 2

Warm-up: walking exercises for the feet; technical exercises with possibly low hurdles, different distances apart; three sprints of 60–80 m, at a progressive speed.

Strength building: exercises that involve the muscular areas between the abdomen and the neck. For example: swinging the arms, wearing armlets weighing about 2 kg, bending the arms, abdominal exercises on the wall bars and on the ground.

Jumps: jumps with feet together between hurdles 50–76 cm high; there can be 5–8 hurdles, in a sequence of 6–10 repetitions; single jumps (standing long jump); triple, quintuple, decuple jumps, with alternate legs or both legs together (frog jumps). Exercises with steps about 40–50 cm high; the athlete jumps up, using alternate feet or both feet together (frog jumps) with 6–10 steps, 3–5 repetitions.

Adjustment sprints: distances of at least 30 m are run, both from a moving as well as a stationary start, with near maximum effort.

Game: Choose one from basketball, football, volley-ball and hand-ball.

Session 3

Warm-up: exercises with ropes over 15–20 m. Suppleness or stretching exercises; three spurts of 80–100 m at progressive speed.

Strength building: exercises which involve the muscle areas between the glutei and the feet. For example: from the prone position, kick alternate legs upwards. From the prone position, keeping the ankles on the ground, bend upwards with the chest. Running while kicking backwards over distances of 100 m, 200 m, 300 m and 400 m with weights of about 1 kg on the ankles.

Adjustment sprints: the purpose of these is to regulate and improve the acceleration phase. Stretches of at least 30 m are covered, both after walking a few steps and from a stationary start, and with very close to maximum effort.

Sprints for running technique: distances of 60–80 m are covered at a sustained speed with lengthy pauses; the latter will enable the athlete to recover properly and to be in a position to perfect his technique and to put the suggestions of his trainer into practice.

Aerobic power: as before (Session 1).

Session 4

Warm-up: walking exercises for the feet; technical exercises with possibly low hurdles, different distances apart; three sprints of 60–80 m at a progressive speed.

Strength building: exercises that involve the muscular areas between the abdomen and the neck, as before.

Jumps: as before.

Adjustment sprints: as before.

Aerobic power: as before.

THIRD TRAINING PHASE

The third period, again involving general and specific building, but more thorough, ought to be carried out between 15 and 30 April, therefore finishing at the beginning of the actual competitive season itself.

In this final phase, we shall continue the work for a period of four weeks, making use of some elements already used in the previous units.

In the final two weeks, the work will be perfected and other special methods will be introduced, which are designed to prepare the athlete properly for the now imminent competitions.

We shall thus resume the hurdling technique (both for short races and for the 300 m) and starting from blocks. The work should take place on alternate days.

FIRST PART

Session 1

Warm-up: traditional type, which may consist of 10–12 min. of light jogging, springing forward on the balls of the feet; series of highly reactive jumps, between hurdles 30–40 cm high, with 6–8 repetitions over 6–8 hurdles; suppleness and stretching exercises, three stretches of 80–100 m, at progressive speed.

Strength building: exercises as before.

Hurdling technique: exercises for lateral clearance with first and second leg, and for central clearance and rhythm tests over the race distances.

Aerobic power: as before.

Session 2

Warm-up: as per previous training session.

Jumps: as before.

Sprints from blocks: sprints of 30 m are carried out starting at the shot from a pistol or other audible signal.

Specific endurance: this involves runs of 200–250–300 m or 200–200–300 m or 300–300 m with 15–20 min. recovery periods. This work can be combined with rhythm tests over hurdles.

Session 3

Warm-up: as per previous training session.

Strength building: as in Session 1 of the second phase.

Resistance work: runs can be made over distances of 30–50 m and even 100 m, dragging loads of various weights. It is advisable to use pneumatic tyres weighed down with loads of about 10 kg in the case of 30 m runs, and 6–8 kg in the case of 50 m and 100 m runs. If the work is carried out

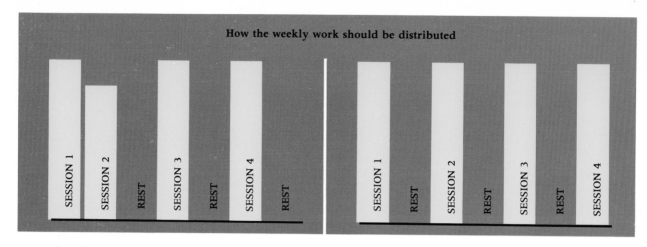

How the weekly work should be distributed

SESSION 1	SESSION 2	REST	SESSION 3	REST	SESSION 4	REST

Opening period – In the initial part of the third the third phase, the work should be: two consecutive work days at the beginning, a rest day, a work day, a rest day, a work day. As in the previous units, the content of the consecutive work days is different.

SESSION 1	REST	SESSION 2	REST	SESSION 3	REST	SESSION 4

Competitive period – In the competitive period of the third unit, the distribution of the weekly training is different from the previous examples. A day of training is always followed by a rest day, and the amounts of work are uniform.

in a single session, it can be structured as follows: 4 × 30 m, plus 2 × 50 m, plus 1 × 100 m, with pauses of 3, 5, 6 and 8 min., respectively.

Adjustment sprints: these are carried out over distances of at least 30 m, starting both from a moving as well as a stationary position, with very close to maximum effort, with a view to regulating the acceleration phase.

Sprints for running technique: distances of 60–80 m are covered at a sustained speed with lengthy pauses. The latter will enable the athlete to recover properly and to be in a position to perfect his technique and to put the suggestions into practice.

Session 4

Warm-up: as in previous training session.

Jumps: as before.

Sprints from blocks: sprints of 30 m are made, starting at the shot from a pistol or other audible signal.

Specific endurance: trials of 400–500 m or 500–300 m or 500–500 m. Over the longer distances, great attention should be paid to the distribution of the runner's effort. This work may also be combined with rhythm tests over hurdles.

SECOND PART

Session 1

Warm-up: as before.

Exercises for hurdling technique: ex-

ercises are performed for lateral clearance with first and second leg, and for central clearance and rhythm tests are carried out over the race distances.

Synthesis trials: Sprints are made over distances of 100–150 m (with or without the use of starting blocks), the times after every 50 m being recorded. For the 150 m, a full or half curve can be used. The recovery times for the 100 m must be 10–12 min. and 15–20 min. for the 150 m.

Session 2

Warm-up: as per the previous training session.

Sprints from blocks: sprints of 30 m are made, starting at the shot from a pistol or other audible signal.

Specific endurance: as in the first part.

Session 3

Warm-up: as per previous training session.

Jumps: as before.

Speed runs: sprints are made over distances of 60 m from a standing start (timing the first and second 30 m sections) and the trainer assesses the runner's acceleration capabilities as well as those once under way. Comparing the times obtained over the first 30 m with those recorded in the sprints with starting blocks, he can evaluate the athlete's starting ability in the crouching position, that is, on all fours (losses of 25 hundredths of a

second are considered excellent). Trials are also carried out over 1, 3 and 5 hurdles, positioned at the race distances.

Session 4

Warm-up: as per the previous training session.

Sprints from blocks: sprints of 30 m, starting at the shot from a pistol.

Specific endurance: trials of 400–500 m or 500–300 m or 500–500 m. These can also be combined with rhythm tests over hurdles.

SOME BASIC EXERCISES

Weights A

Exercise 1: 5–8 sets of five repetitions of half squats (that is, lifting a bar-bell while half bending the legs). The exercise must be executed rapidly and be timed.

Because the bending angle is always equal to about 90°, it is necessary to use a stool or a chair of sufficient height to correspond to the required knee angle. When the athlete quickly bends his legs, he must only touch the stool lightly before stretching up again equally quickly.

Use a weight of approximately the same as the athlete's body weight, increasing this gradually as the preparation progresses, to about 150% of his body weight.

Exercise 2: Four sets of 4–5 repetitions of squat-jumps (that is, lifting a bar-bell while fully bending the legs and jumping up with the legs a little way apart). The jumps with the bar-bell on the shoulders must be carried out with maximum effort in order to reach maximum height. The starting weight can be something like 20 kg and eventually reach about 50% of the athlete's body weight

Exercise 3: bouncing up and down on the balls of the feet.

3–4 sets of 20–30 repetitions carrying a bar-bell on the shoulders. This exercise must be executed very rapidly; the heels must rise very high and fall until they almost touch the ground. In order to keep his balance during this exercise (which does not involve jumping), the athlete must move his feet together slightly. The initial weight should be 30–40 kg, rising as high as 60 kg or even 70 kg.

Weights B

Exercise 1: walking, bending the knees, legs apart.

8–10 steps forward, bending the knees and stretching up rapidly, without coming off the ground, carrying a bar-bell on the shoulders.

The exercise is repeated in 6–8 sets. The weight used is initially 50% of the athlete's body weight, rising, by the end, to very near the athlete's full body weight.

Exercise 2: squat-jumps.

4–5 half squat-jumps with bar-bell. This exercise is almost identical to the second exercise under 'Weights A', with the difference that in this one the legs are kept together. The weights, sets and repetitions are identical to the above-mentioned exercise.

Exercise 3: this is the same as exercise 3 under 'Weights A'.

Useful advice

The weight-lifting system adopted uses sets of repetitions with varying weights. This means that within the sets the weight varies. Two or three weights can be chosen, for example, 60–65 kg or 60–65–70 kg. In the first case, the sets shall be organized as follows: 60–65–60, etc. In the second case, the sets should be 60–65–70–65–60–65–70, etc.

When using weights, put on a rigid weight-lifter's belt to protect the lumbar region of the spine.

When doing the half-squat, it is advisable to put a block 5–6 cm thick under the heels, to make the trunk more vertical and thus to reduce the bending stresses in the spine.

In pauses between sets, it is advisable always to do some compensatory exercises: (i) rapid skipping with knees high, lasting for 10–12 skips; (ii) a fast sprint of 4–5 paces; (iii) 3–4 half squat-jumps in quick succession.

Exercises on the move

These exercises, which involve the feet and legs, are performed by moving forward using small weights or normal body weight. The former are used in the basic and general cycles, the latter (without weights) are used in the special cycles.

Exercise 1: walking on the heels–balls of the feet, wearing a 6–7 kg belt (or bicycle tyre inner tube filled with sand). To start with, the athlete's heel is in contact with the ground, then, with a powerful spring, he gets on tiptoe. He walks forward in this way, with a light, lithe step, interspersing 60–80–100 m walks with the same amount of light running.

Exercise 2: walking on the balls of the feet–heels–balls of the feet. This takes the form of a powerful, rapid and full springy foot action, with the tip of the toes, and not the metatarsus, coming into contact with the ground; thus, the athlete pushes off from the tip of his toes, following his rapid springy movement. The knees remain almost locked. Sets will be carried out as in the previous example, totalling, for the two exercises together, distances

of 800 m and over. The two exercises are carried out very carefully, and a belt is worn.

Exercise 3: hopping. Again wearing the belt, the athlete bounces up and down rapidly and powerfully in such a way that it makes him feel higher than when running. Instead of bringing his knees forward, he raises his feet behind him towards the gluteus. Carry out in sets.

Exercise 4: short skips. This is a running action, keeping the knees high (at least horizontal), either wearing ankle weights of 1.5–2 kg or a belt, but not both. The exercise is co-ordinated with a swinging movement of the arms.

Rapid sets of 50–60 skips.

Exercise 5: long skips. The difference from the previous example lies in the more pronounced forward movement that is made with each step. The difference may seem hardly noticeable, but it is considerable.

In fact, it is simply a more powerful and decisive thrust from the foot which determines the dynamism and forward movement of the sprinter. The rhythm must of course be slower, the trunk (which can very easily fall backwards) must remain vertical, and the arms must swing more fully.

Sets should be carried out over initial distances of 60–80 m up to 100–150 m, in the case of sprinters, and up to 200 m for 400 m runners.

The belt should also be worn for this exercise, in which case, the maximum distance should be reduced by 30–40% (that is, about 120–150 m).

Training for mature athletes

Having explained the work recommended for training youngsters who are on the way to becoming sprinters, we now deal with mature sprinters.

Once again we give the schedules prepared by the sprint section of the Federazione Italiana di Atletica Leggera. While in the case of work programmes for youngsters there were rest days during the week, in the case of mature athletes, more sophisticated modulation of training is provided, particularly regarding the sequence of work loads.

We set out below some examples of weekly training schedules in order to prepare the athlete for the indoor season, which usually ends by mid-March, and then for the outdoor season, which begins in April and finishes in September. These schedules take account of this, so a training programme has been drawn up which allows for participation in high-level races at the end of each period. We shall therefore refer to two major work cycles, indicating the recommended period for each.

WEEKLY TRAINING SCHEDULES

Standard week of the introductory cycle. Preparation for indoor races (from 16 Oct. to 12 Nov.)

Session 1

- Weights A (see pp. 28–29)
- Jumps: 8 triple, 6 quintuple.
- Sprints: 8–10 × 30 m from moving or standing start.

Session 2

- Strength building: exercises which involve the flexor and extensor muscles (flexors of the thighs, ischiofemorals, glutei).
- Uphill runs (gradient 15%): two sets of 4–5 repetitions × 30 m; one set of 3–4 repetitions × 50 m; pauses of 3, 4, and 8 min. between sets.

Session 3

- Weights B (see p. 29).
- Compensatory exercises and prolonged running with raised knees, with or without ankle bands of 1–2 kg.

Session 4

- Jumps: 6 triple, 4 quintuple, 3 decuple.
- Sprints: 6–8 × 30 m.
- Strides, that is, progressive runs: 5–6 × 100 m.

Session 5

- Weights A.
- Strength building: exercises which involve the flexor and extensor muscles (flexors of the thighs, ischiofemorals, glutei).
- Adjustment sprints: distances of at least 30 m are covered, with stationary or moving starts; effort very close to maximum and spurts.

Session 6

- Uphill runs (gradient 15%): one set of 4 × 30 m; two sets of 4 × 50 m.
- Jumps: triple, 3 decuple.
- 3–4 runs of 100 m.

Standard week of the basic cycle. Preparation for indoor races (from 13 Nov. to 10 Dec.)

Session 1

- Jumps: 5 triple, 3 quintuple, 2 decuple.
- Speed strength: two sets of 3 × 60 m; 2 × 80 m; 1 × 100 m; pauses of 2, 3 and 10 min.

Session 2

- Strength building: exercises which involve the flexor and extensor muscles (flexors of the thighs, ischiofemorals, glutei).
- Resistance work: sprints dragging a load of 12–15 kg; two sets of 4 × 30 m; pauses of 2, 3 and 8 min.
- Adjustment sprints with standing starts and starts from blocks.

Session 3

- Weights A: half squats; half squat-jumps; bouncing up and down on balls of feet.
- Compensatory exercises and spurts.

Session 4

- Jumps: 5 triple, 3 decuple.
- Speed endurance: one set of 4–5 × 60 m; one set of 3–4 × 80 m; pauses of 2, 3, 10 min.

Session 5

- Weights B: walking with legs apart; half squat-jumps; bouncing up and down on balls of feet.
- Resistance work: sprints, dragging 12–15 kg; one set of 4 × 20 m; one set of 4 × 30 m; pauses of 3 and 8 min.
- Strength building: exercises which involve the flexor and extensor muscles.
- Jumps: 6 triple, 4 quintuple.
- Adjustment sprints with standing starts and starts from blocks.
- Spurts: 3–4 × 100 m.

Standard week of the special completion cycle. Preparation for indoor races (from 2 Jan. to 22 Jan.)

Session 1

• Jumps: springy jumps between hurdles.

• Sprints from blocks.

• Alactacid power (runs on the flat): sprints of 60–80–80 m; or 60–60–80 m.

Session 2

• Weights: half squat-jumps (normal body weight).

• Jumps: 3 frog, 2 triple, 2 quintuple.

• Running, acceleration and speed exercises.

Session 3

• Jumps: springy jumps between hurdles.

• Sprints from blocks: 5–6 × 30 m.

• Speed endurance; 3 × 60 m; 2 × 80 m, 1 × 100 m.

Session 4

• Weights: half squat-jumps (normal body weight).

• Jumps: 3 triple, 2 decuple.

• Running, acceleration and speed exercises.

Session 5

• Jumps: springy jumps between hurdles.

• Sprints from blocks: 30 and 60 m.

• Spurts: 3 × 100 m.

Session 6

• Weights: half squat-jumps (normal body weight).

• Running, acceleration and speed exercises.

• Spurts at will.

Standard week of the basic cycle. Preparation for outdoor races (from 1 Mar. to 20 Mar.)

Session 1

• Uphill runs: 5 × 30 m plus 4–5 × 50 m; maximum speed, pauses of 3, 4 and 10 min. between the trials; 15–20 min. between the sets.

• Lactacid capacity (or specific endurance in relation to race distances): sets of sprints of this kind can be carried out: 200 m – 8 min. pause; 200 m – 8 min. pause; 300 m or 200 m – 8 min. pause; 300 m – 10 min. pause; 300 m or 200 m – 8 min. pause; 300 m. Run the distances at 85% the speed of personal best.

Session 2

• Weights A: reducing the programme of half-squats to six repetitions and six sets.

• Sprints from the blocks: 6–10 of about 30 m.

• Alactacid capacity (or speed endurance): 4–5 × 60 m, 2 min. pauses between the trials and 8 min. between the sets; 4–5 × 60 m; 4–5 × 60 m; 4–5 × 60 m; 3–4 × 80 m, 3 min. pause between the runs (paying attention to the rhythm, frequency and fullness of the stride and the ease of running).

Session 3

• Jumps: 5–6 standing long jumps; 5–10 triples, half on each leg; 3–5 alternate decuple jumps.

• Lactacid capacity: in sets of 150–250 m with 6 min. recovery between the runs and 10 min. between the sets; 150–250 m with 6 min. recovery between the runs and 10 min. between the sets; 150–250 m with 6 min. recovery between the runs. The distances are run at 85% of maximum speed.

Session 4

• Weights B: reducing to six steps and six sets the movements with knee bends, legs apart.

• Alactacid capacity: 4–5 × 60 m; 4–5 × 60 m; 3–4 × 80 m; 3–4 × 80 m; looking to the best compromise between fullness and frequency of stride, relaxation and ease of running.

Session 5

• Uphill runs: 5 × 30 m at maximum speed; 4 × 50 m at maximum speed; 3 × 100 m at controlled speed, 3 min. pause for 30 m; 4 min. for 50 m, 5 min. for 100 m; 8–10 min. between sets.

Session 6

• Jumps: 5–6 standing long jumps, six successive triples (three per leg), 3–5 alternate quintuples, three alternate decuples.

• Mixed capacity: 60–80–100 m, with recovery between the runs of 2, 3 and 4 min. then 10–12 min. between the sets; then 60–80–100–300 m.

Standard week of the intensive basic cycle. Preparation for outdoor races (from 29 Mar. to 25 Apr.)

Session 1

• Uphill runs: 5 × 30 m; plus 4–5 × 50 m, same pauses and gradient, greater intensity after 15–20 min.

• Lactacid capacity: the speed should be 90% of maximum. The sets can be structured as follows: 200 m – 10 min. recovery; 200 m – 10 min. recovery; 300 m – 12 min. recovery; 300 m or 200 m – 10 min. recovery; 300 m – 12 min. recovery; 300 m or 200 m – 10 min. recovery; 200 m – 10 min. recovery; 300 m.

Session 2

• Sprints from blocks: 8–10 × 30 m.

• Alactacid capacity: 5 × 50 m, 2 min. recovery between runs and 8 min. between sets; 5 × 60 m; 4 × 80 m, 3 min. pause between runs (always paying attention to a relaxed running style and the fullness/ frequency of stride).

Session 3

• Jumps: 4–5 standing long jumps, eight alternate triples, four alternate decuples.

• Lactacid capacity: in sets of 150–250 m, 6 min. recovery between runs, 10 min. between sets; 150–250 m, 6 min. recovery between runs, 10 min. between sets; 150–250 m, 6 min. recovery between runs. The speed of execution must be equal to 90% of the maximum.

Session 4

• Weights A: reducing the half-squats to three repetitions and six sets; sets of exercises for agility.

• Alactacid capacity: 4 × 60 m; 4 × 60 m; 3 × 80 m; 2 min. recovery between the 60 m runs, 8 min. between the sets, 3 min. recovery between the 80 m runs.

Session 5

• Sprinting while dragging a weight: two sets of 4 × 30 m with 3 min. recovery between the runs and 8 min. between the sets; 8–10 tenths longer than record over 30 m without dragging a weight. The weight dragged should be between 12 and 15 kg, and can consist of a rubber tube containing sand pulled along a synthetic track.

Session 6

• Jumps: six standing long jumps, six successive triples (three with the left, three with the right), three alternate quintuples, two alternate decuples.

• Mixed capacity: runs of 60–80–100–200 m, 12 min. recovery; 60–80–100–200 or 300 m, faster than the previous cycle.

Standard week of the special cycle. Preparation for outdoor races (from 26 Apr. to 15 May)

Session 1

• Sprints from blocks: 6–8 × 30 m.

• Lactacid power (synthesis tests): 4–5 × 150 m with 12–15 min. pause. The speed must be 95% of the maximum; time after every 50 m covered.

Session 2

• Warm-up with stretching exercises.

• Jumps over hurdles: five sets with ten hurdles 76 cm high; five sets with ten hurdles from 50 to 30 cm high.

• Alactacid capacity: 200 m – 10–12 min. recovery; 250 m – 10–12 min. recovery; 300 m. Speed must be equal to 95% of maximum.

Session 3

• Rest.

• Winding down, i.e. reduce the commitment, with sprints and dragging a weight.

• 5 × 30 m adjustment sprints.

Session 4

• Jumps over hurdles: five sets with ten hurdles 76 cm high; five sets with ten hurdles 50 and 30 cm high.

• Alactacid power and lactacid power: 60 m at maximum speed; 60 m at maximum speed; 100 m at almost maximum speed; 150 m at almost maximum speed; time the 30 m sections of the 60 m, the final 30 m sections of the 80 m and the 50 m sections in the 100 m and 150 m.

Session 5

• Alternate jumps: four standing long jumps, four triples, three quintuples, two decuples.

• Spurts: 80–100 m of controlled intensity.

Session 6

• Jumps over hurdles: eight sets of 10 hurdles 50 and 30 cm high, the bouncing action must be as rapid as possible.

• Sprints from blocks: 3 × 30 m + 2 × 60 m (with training partners).

• Lactacid power: 2 × 100 m with 6 min. pause, speed 95–98%, 15–20 min. recovery; 1 × 300 m, speed 95%.

■ The stars ■

CHARLES PADDOCK (USA)

In the 1920s he was one of the first globe trotters of athletics and he toured the world described as 'The World's Fastest Human'. He had earned this title with a fine series of records and victories, and he knew how to exploit it to the full thanks to his feeling for publicity.

He made his first appearance in Europe at the Inter-Allied Games of 1919 in Paris. A year later, in the Olympic Games at Antwerp, he won the 100 m and the 4 × 100 m relay and was second in the 200 m. In Paris in 1924, he was second in the 200 m and fifth in the 100 m. In 1928 in Amsterdam, he failed by a whisker to reach his third consecutive final of the 200 m — a feat achieved by Pietro Mennea half a century later.

His golden year was 1921, when he equalled the world record for the 100 yards (9.6 sec.) and improved on those for the 100 m (10.4 sec.) and 220 yards in a straight line (20.8 sec.). In the same season he was credited with an incredible 10.2 sec. in the 110 yards (100.58 m), recognized by the American Federation only as a noteworthy performance. In 1926 he ran the 100 yards in just over 9.5 sec.: this would have been a new world record, but according to the rules of the time, it had to be rounded up to the nearest tenth of a second, and so it became 9.6 sec.

Paddock was in the habit of hurling himself at the tape with a 'long jump' of about 5 m — a style that was much debated by the experts. Certainly of great significance for the time were two times obtained by him in 1921, which remained unequalled for many years: 30.2 sec. in the 300 yards and 33.2 sec. in the 300 m.

He fought in the Second World War as a captain in the Marines and died in action in 1943.

HAROLD DAVIS (USA)

The Second World War prevented many champions from enjoying Olympic success. Among such athletes was Harold Davis. It is generally agreed that if the Games of 1940 and 1944 had not been cancelled because of the Second World War, he could

have won several gold medals, perhaps rivalling the great Jesse Owens.

From 1940 to 1943, Davis was almost invincible, and there was only one way in which he could lose a race: at the start.

However, he was able to equal the world records for the 100 yards (9.4 sec.) and the 100 m (10.2 sec.) and he ran the 220 yards in a straight line in 20.4 sec., and in 20.2 sec. with the wind over the limit. In the American Championships he obtained four victories in the 200 m and three in the 100 m. In these important championships he was beaten only once, by Barney Ewell in the 100 m in 1941. But even on that occasion he provided the clearest evidence of his worth: a more dreadful start than usual meant that he had to make up a deficit of three metres. He nearly succeeded and finished a few centimetres behind Ewell, timed at 10.3 sec. (the world record being 10.2 sec.). On that occasion Davis probably achieved one of the fastest speeds ever recorded on an athletics track.

In the summer of 1943, Davis enlisted in the Marines. When the war was over he tried to compete again, but muscular problems forced him to give up.

BOBBY MORROW (USA)

Between 1956 and 1958, Bobby Morrow dominated the USA and the world at the 100 m and 200 m. At just 21 years of age, he proved to be the fastest man in the world at the 1956 Olympic Games in Melbourne, where he won the men's 100 m and 200 m and helped the USA to win the 4 × 100 m relay. He was the last white American sprinter to dominate the world scene.

In the three-year period of his supremacy, he was rarely beaten. He was the joint-holder of world records for the 100 yards (9.3 sec.), 100 m (10.2 sec.) and 200 m with curve (20.6 sec.).

HENRY CARR (USA)

A great 200 m runner, he could probably have excelled at 400 m had he wished. In the Tokyo Olympics in 1964, he won the 200 m in 20.36 sec., a time which stands up well today, especially as it was obtained on a cinder track against a wind of almost

Bobby Morrow

1 m/sec. In the same Games, he helped the American 4 × 400 m relay team to success, running the last leg in 44.5 sec.

A mediocre starter, he never had a great love for the 100 m, and yet stood out among the best in the USA, running the 100 yards in 9.3 sec. and the 100 m in 10.2 sec. At the 200 m he dominated for two seasons (1963–64), often winning by a wide margin.

As a youngster, his natural power helped him to come to the fore very quickly: before the age of 17 he ran the 100 yards in 9.7 sec. and the 220 yards in 21.0 sec. He tried his hand at the 400 m (or 440 yards) only eight times in his career, and was never beaten.

After his Olympic success in Tokyo, he was attracted by American professional football, but never distinguished himself at this sport.

TOMMIE SMITH (USA)

In terms of sustained speed, he was probably the greatest of all. In the Mexico Olympics in 1968, he won the 200 m in 19.83 sec., finishing the race with arms raised.

He had emerged as a top sprinter in 1966, taking the world records for the 220 yards with a curve (20.0 sec.) and in a straight line (19.5 sec.). While bearing in mind that these were timed manually, the second of them represents the highest speed ever recorded in a race from a stationary start: an average speed of 37.139 km/h (23.21 mph). In the same season, he contributed to the USA achieving its first 'under 3 minutes' in the 4 × 400 m relay, running his leg in 43.8 sec. He also jumped 7.90 m in the long jump, giving away many centimetres in his take-off.

In 1967 he took on Lee Evans at 400 m and beat him, at the same time improving on the world records for the 400 m (44.5 sec.) and the 440 yards (44.8 sec.).

He was involved in the boycott staged in the Mexico Games by a number of blacks in the US team. At the end of his relatively short career, he had to his credit 9.3 sec. in the 100 yards and 10.1 sec. in the 100 m.

DONALD QUARRIE (JAMAICA)

He was already a first-rate athlete at the age of 17, when he ran the 100 m in 10.3 sec. and was selected for the Olympic Games in Mexico. However, he had the misfortune to injure himself in training and was unable to compete. He did not take long to recover, and by the age of 20 he had bagged six international gold medals having won the 100 m, 200 m and 4 × 100 m in the 1970 Commonwealth Games and the 1971 Pan-American Games. On the latter occasion, in Cali (Colombia), he achieved a world record of 19.86 sec. in the 200 m.

In his second Olympic engagement, in Munich in 1972, he was again unlucky when pain from a previously pulled muscle stopped him in the semi-final of the 200 m. Four years later in 1976 in Montreal, he shot ahead of everyone in the 200 m (20.22 sec.), after losing the 100 m by a whisker to the Trinidadian Hasley Crawford (10.07 sec. to 10.06 sec.).

In 1980, his thirteenth year of international competition, he again won an Olympic medal, finishing third in the 200 m in Moscow in 20.29 sec., behind Pietro Mennea and the Scotsman Allan Wells. In 1982,

Don Quarrie

now 31 years old, he ran this distance in 20.39 sec.

In his long career he won an unparalleled number of titles. Apart from his Olympic medals, he collected six, all gold, in the Commonwealth Games. He was US champion three times in the 200 m and twice in the 100 m.

Three of his manually timed world records have been: for the 100 m (9.9 sec.), 200 m (19.8 sec.) and 220 yards (19.9 sec.).

Small in stature compared with the average for world-class sprinters, his leg action was one of the quickest ever known.

PIETRO MENNEA (ITALY)

Mennea proved himself to be a sprinter of international class at the age of 19, in 1971, when he finished sixth in the 200 m in the European Championships in Helsinki, with a new personal record of 20.88 sec. In 1972, he duelled with Borzov in Milan, losing by a narrow margin in the 100 m, but equalling, together with the Russian, the European record (10.0 sec.). In the absence of Borzov, he won the 200 m in 20.2 sec., again equalling the European record. In the Munich Olympics, he finished third in the 200 m in 20.30 sec., three

metres behind Borzov. After this experience, he constantly had Borzov in his sights, aiming to equal him and, if possible, to beat him. In the European Championships in 1974, he again finished second in the 100 m behind Borzov, and won the 200 m. He finally achieved his goal in the final of the 1975 European Cup in Nice, when he finished ahead of his Russian rival in the 200 m. However, in his second Olympics, in 1976 in Montreal, he could finish no better than fourth in the 200 m. At the World University Games in Mexico in 1979, he first took the European record for the 100 m (10.01 sec.) and then the world record for the 200 m (19.72 sec.), succeeding Borzov and Tommie Smith, respectively.

Next came his third Olympics at Moscow in 1980. After being eliminated in the 100 m, Mennea took revenge in the 200 m, beating the Scotsman Allan Wells in the final in 20.19 sec. He thus became the first sprinter to figure among the finalists for the 200 m in three Olympics. The autumn of 1980 saw him at the peak of his career: in eight consecutive races over 200 m he obtained a tremendous average of 20.07 sec. In 1983, now 31, he came third in the World Championships in Helsinki.

The 1984 Olympics saw Mennea competing in his fourth consecutive Olympic final at 200 m, but he could do no better than 20.55 sec. to take seventh place.

CARL LEWIS (USA)

Carlton 'Carl' Frederick Lewis is the true heir of Jesse Owens. The great athlete from the past was also a friend of the Lewis family.

Forty-eight years after the exceptional exploits of Owens, Lewis wrote a new page in the history of the sprint and the long jump.

On 18 June 1983, on the fast track at Indianapolis, Carl Lewis won the 100 m in the United States Championships in 10.27 sec. against a strong wind. The next day, he appeared on the long jump runway and executed a leap of 8.79 m, the longest distance ever achieved at sea level. This was not enough for him and so he attempted a second jump: 8.71 m. At this point he decided to leave it there because he wanted to run in the semi-finals of the 200 m, which proved a formality for him. He had a great ambition: to win three American titles, achieving a triple win never before accomplished.

Later that evening, in the 200 m final, he devastated the opposition with a time of 19.75 sec. Nobody had ever been so fast at sea level. Mennea's record, achieved in Mexico City with the help of rarefied air, was 19.72 sec.

At Modesto, California, in May 1983, he had run the 100 m in 9.97 sec., the first athlete to beat 10 sec. at sea level.

In the 1984 Los Angeles Olympics, Carl Lewis managed to emulate the achievements of the great Jesse Owens by taking four gold medals – in the 100 m, 200 m, 4 × 100 m relay and long jump. In the 100 m, he pulled back a couple of metres deficit to win by the largest margin in Olympic history, nearly 2.5 m, in a time of 9.99 sec. His time of 19.83 sec. in the 200 m took three hundredths off Tommie 'Jet' Smith's 1968 Olympic record, while in the 4 × 100 m relay his final leg of 8.94 sec. helped the US team to a new world record of 37.83 sec. His long jump of 8.54 m was 30 cm longer than the second competitor and it was his only valid jump of the final, the other five being a foul and four passes.

RENATE STECHER (GDR)
In the 1972 Olympics in Munich, she earned the nickname of 'Borzov in a skirt'. Like the Russian champion, she won two gold medals (100 m and 200 m) and a silver (4 × 100 m relay).

Renate Stecher

Carl Lewis (left)

Over the twin distances 100 m/200 m, she is the female sprinter who has up to now had the most success. In the 1976 Olympics in Montreal she won another three medals: gold in the 4 × 100 m relay, silver in the 100 m and bronze in the 200 m.

She has also made a terrific impact on the register of records. On 7 June 1973, in Ostrava, she became the first woman to beat the 11 second barrier in the 100 m, running it in 10.9 sec. Later on in the season, she took the record to 10.8 sec. (the automatic timing version being 11.07 sec.). In the 200 m she acquired the world record in 1972 in Munich with 22.4 sec. and within the space of one year she took it to 22.1 sec. (22.38 sec. electronic).

Her talent emerged early as, at the age of 16, she helped East Germany to success in the 4 × 100 m relay in the European Junior Games. When these were next held, in 1968, she won three silver medals (100 m, 200 m and 4 × 100 m relay). In occasional breaks from sprinting, she recorded 5.65 m in the long jump and totalled 4297 points in the pentathlon.

Jesse Owens (USA) – *See the 100 m.*
Valeri Borzov (USSR) – *See the 100 m.*
Valerie Brisco-Hooks (USA) – *See the 400 m.*

WORLD RECORDS

Men
sec.
20.6 Andy Stanfield (USA) 1951
20.6 Andy Stanfield (USA) 1952
20.6 Thane Baker (USA) 1956
20.6 Bobby Morrow (USA) 1956
20.6 Manfred Germar (Germany) 1958
20.6 Ray Norton (USA) 1960
20.5 Peter Radford (GB) 1960
20.5 Stone Jackson (USA) 1960
20.5 Ray Norton (USA) 1960
20.5 Livio Berruti (Italy) 1960
20.5 Paul Drayton (USA) 1962
20.3 Henry Carr (USA) 1963
20.2 Henry Carr (USA) 1964
20.0 Tommie Smith (USA) 1966
19.8 Tommie Smith (USA) 1968
19.8 Donald Quarrie (Jamaica) 1971
19.8 Donald Quarrie (Jamaica) 1975

Automatic times
19.83 Tommie Smith (USA) 1968
19.72 Pietro Mennea (Italy) 1979

Women
sec.
23.6 Stanislawa Walasiewicz (Poland) 1935
23.6 Marjorie Jackson (Australia) 1952
23.4 Marjorie Jackson (Australia) 1952
23.2 Betty Cuthbert (Australia) 1956
23.2 Betty Cuthbert (Australia) 1960

22.9 Wilma Rudolph (USA) 1960
22.9 Margaret Burvill (Australia) 1964
22.7 Irena Kirszenstein (Poland) 1965
22.5 Irena Kirszenstein (Poland) 1968
22.4 Chi Cheng (Taiwan) 1970
22.4 R. Meissner-Stecher (GDR) 1972
22.1 R. Meissner-Stecher (GDR) 1973

Automatic times
22.21 Irena Szewinska (Poland) 1974
22.06 Marita Koch (GDR) 1978
22.02 Marita Koch (GDR) 1979
21.71 Marita Koch (GDR) 1979

Note: up until 1966, the IAAF also recorded world records obtained over 200 metres in a straight line.

21.2 Bernie Wefers (USA) 1896
21.2 Ralph Craig (USA) 1910
21.2 Donald Lippincott (USA) 1913
21.2 Howard Drew (USA) 1914
21.2 Willie Applegarth (Germany) 1914
21.2 George Parker (USA) 1914
20.8 Charles Paddock (USA) 1921
20.8 Charles Paddock (USA) 1924
20.6 Roland Locke (USA) 1926
20.6 Ralph Metcalfe (USA) 1933
20.3 Jesse Owens (USA) 1935
20.2 Mel Patton (USA) 1949
20.1 Dave Sime (USA) 1956
20.0 Frank Budd (USA) 1962
20.0 Tommie Smith (USA) 1965
19.5 Tommie Smith (USA) 1966

400m

How it is run

The 400 m, one complete lap of the track, is known as 'the killer event' — because the athlete's effort is intense and sustained over a comparatively long distance.

Anyone trying to compete over 400 m for the first time following instinct rather than a specific plan will be on his knees before the end of the race. Even the top competitors at this distance can experience a severe headache, nausea, and some disorientation.

Of course, this is short-lived, but it could still have a deleterious effect on the runner's future performance since it is not encouraging to settle on the

starting blocks in a subsequent race with the memory of the suffering experienced in the previous one.

Because of this, the one-lap race should be approached by studying the most economical distribution of energy, since it is only by interpreting this race correctly and rationally that a young runner will subsequently be able to face it with confidence.

The finish of the 400 m final in the 1968 Olympics. Lee Evans (on the left of the picture) took the gold medal in a world record time of 43.86 sec., which still stands today.

TEST OF SPEED

The 400 m is classified as a sprint, because it still requires an ability to achieve peak speed. Top athletes in the 400 m can run the 200 m in 20.50–20.60 sec. or faster. This speed quality is combined with the ability to withstand intense effort, defined as the lactic acid capacity.

To start with, let us look at the following theory. The time in which the runner is able to run 400 m should be the same as the athlete's performance over 100 m multiplied by four, or his best performance over 200 m multiplied by two, plus 3.5–4 sec. in each case. Where an athlete with

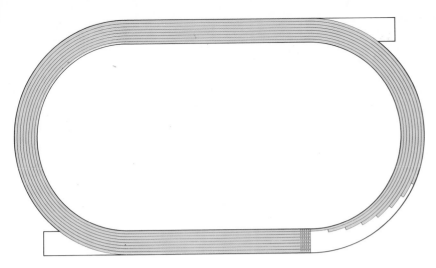

In the 400 m, the athletes run one complete lap of the track; the stagger for runners in the outside lanes is to compensate for the larger circuit which would otherwise be run.

personal bests of 10.5 sec. in the 100 m and 21.0 sec. in the 200 m fails to achieve a time of around 45.8 or 46.0 sec., this may be due to either (a) poorly judged distribution of effort, or (b) lack of the necessary lactic acid resistance.

The second shortcoming can be corrected straight away by training, concentrating primarily on lactic acid resistance, but not to the detriment of work designed to increase both muscular strength and speed, as there is always a risk that concentrating on one type of training in preference to another will not prove beneficial. The first fault can be corrected by advice from the athlete's coach, because the 400 m runner's racing technique differs from those adopted by sprinters over shorter distances. Above all, the stride must be long and relaxed.

HOW TO RUN THE RACE

Firstly, it should be remembered that the race begins on a bend (turn), and that in the first 100 m it is not necessary to develop a particularly high speed, or the speed achieved in the second 100 m. Effort should therefore be progressively increased so that the maximum speed is achieved in the second half of the first straight (stretch), i.e. between 150 m and 200 m, the runner entering the second bend at a sustained pace.

The 200 m mark is the critical point in the event, as the athlete entering the second bend begins to experience fatigue, and at this point the stagger begins to be evened out. If the speed achieved in the first half of the race has been extremely high, its reduction in the second half will be quite pronounced, and the athlete eventually pays heavily for too fast a start.

If fatigue is beginning to be felt on entering the bend, the discomfort is accentuated at the end. The athlete also begins to experience some difficulty in moving his lower limbs. It is at this point that the 400 m runner has to concentrate on not losing speed, endeavouring to keep it constant even if this is extremely difficult. He must certainly not stiffen up in his efforts to react, but must maintain some flexibility. An athlete who becomes rigid will waste energy in jerky pointless movements, energy that may be required in the final stages.

HINTS FOR YOUNG ATHLETES

A young athlete intending to concentrate on this event must approach it with a clear mind and should not initially specialize in this event to the exclusion of all others; his efforts should be divided between the various sprint events. In addition – and here trainers should be able to help a great deal – they should run 400 m races using different racing tactics so that they do not stagnate. However, it is wrong to force a young runner to take part in the 400 m if he is not fully prepared, both physically and mentally.

Physiology:
What happens in the 400 m

Anyone who has tried to run the 400 m will know that at a certain point – nowhere near the finish line – the runner begins to experience great fatigue: the legs become extremely heavy, the muscles do not seem to respond, and the brain no longer functions properly. It is always hard to get to the finish line and, even after reaching it, exhaustion persists for some time and recovery is slow.

What makes the 400 m so demanding, both physically and mentally?

What happens to the muscles and in the body as a whole over the 45 seconds taken to run one lap of the track?

Almost everything is governed by what happens in the muscles. The muscular system (i.e. the calf, thigh and gluteal muscles), which is put under considerable stress in the race, represents a substantial proportion of the body's entire mass. A large amount of lactic acid is produced in these muscles; this is waste material and creates problems for the body.

To understand how lactic acid is formed, the point should be made that this is not something that affects all running events, only those in which effort is sustained for at least several seconds and is quite intense: the events that result in the maximum production of this substance are the 400 m to 1500 m inclusive.

To be able to work at the necessary levels of intensity and duration of these particular events, the muscles need a plentiful supply of adenosine triphosphate (ATP), their fuel. Part of this has to be manufactured via the 'anaerobic lactic acid mechanism', which leads to the production of lactic acid.

The muscles contain quantities of glycogen, a form of amide comprising many molecules of glucose. During periods of high-intensity effort the molecule of this sugar (which has a chain of six carbon atoms) is broken into two parts through a series of biochemical reactions; each of these parts has three carbon atoms. If oxygen is available, the reactions continue until the chains are completely broken, so that each carbon atom is separate from the others. If, however, the oxygen arriving at and usable by the muscles is insufficient, the reactions are interrupted and first pyruvic acid then lactic acid are formed.

The object of producing the 'fuel' to enable the muscles to function is also achieved, but, at the same time, the negative effect represented by the production of the waste material, the lactic acid, is experienced; its acid part in particular (the hydrogen ion) greatly disturbs the body's efficiency and is responsible for fatigue.

The muscle at rest has a minimum degree of acidity; if the fibres are examined, the pH value (the acidity index) is found to be 6.9, compared with a neutral pH of 7, the fluid being more acidic the lower the value. In an athlete having run 400 m pushing himself to the limit, on the other hand, the pH value falls to 6.4 or even lower.

Under these conditions, the ability of the muscle fibres to function at their best is impaired; when contracted they are only able to provide much less power. This is why, at the end of a 400 m race, one's muscles feel weak and the thighs extremely heavy, requiring much more force than usual to lift them.

The hydrogen ions pass from the muscles into the blood. These are extremely small molecules and, in a relatively short period of time, a significant number pass through the muscular fibres: in a person at rest, the blood pH is about 7.4, which is slightly alkaline. The movement of so many hydrogen ions from the large muscle masses into the blood causes the blood to become slightly acidic and reach low pH values that do not occur in human beings at any other time.

This blood also reaches the brain, an extremely sensitive organ. Its functioning becomes slightly disturbed, and it is probably this acidity in the blood that causes the muddled sensation and the reduced co-ordination typical in people who have exerted themselves leading to substantial production of lactic acid. The reduced efficiency of the muscles (due to the lactic acid present) and the diminished co-ordination (following the acidification of the blood) explain why frequently in the final stretch of a 400 m race, the athletes' running style deteriorates markedly.

Training, when carried out properly and with strict adherence to the working schedules put forward by an expert, can improve the ability to supply the muscles with a greater quantity of ATP produced in the anaerobic lactic acid mechanism.

■ Training ■

In the chapter on the 200 m, we examined the commitment required from a young runner considering the speed events, i.e. 100 m, 200 m and 400 m. For training of the young, therefore, see the previous chapter.

However, for experienced athletes, we reproduce here the training schedules prepared by the sprint section of the Federazione Italiana di Atletica Leggera. The schedule covers two periods: one relating to winter activities (therefore involving indoor racing), and the other devoted to outdoor activities.

The first period consists of four sections: an introductory phase, two basic phases, each of three weeks, and a special 21-day phase. This period ends with participation in races, after which the athlete has a ten-day recuperation period.

The second period consists of a basic phase of 20 days, and a special phase of 21 days. This is followed by a completion phase of 20 days which closely follows the schedules of the previous phase, and provides for participation in the first outdoor races.

GENERAL STRENGTHENING

This relates to a series of exercises designed to strengthen virtually all of the athlete's muscular regions.

Small weights and particular items of equipment are used (e.g. bows and expanders). The object is to work on specific areas: on the feet and the extensor muscles which lift the heels (from the erect position) when the knees are extended; on the ischiocrural muscles (at the back of the thighs), on the gluteal muscles, the lumbar muscles, the abdominal muscles (both by bringing the lower limbs on to the chest, held stationary, and by bringing the chest down to the legs, held stationary); on the muscles of the scapulo humeral girdle, the pectoral and dorsal muscles and the extensor muscles of the arm (the triceps bracchii), the flexural muscles of the arm (the biceps, the anterior bracchial muscles, etc.).

For the feet, in addition to the example already described in the weights session, with a 5−6−7 kg belt around the waist, fast wide springs can be carried out with the body leaning forward, the arms extended and the hands resting on the wall.

Rapid movements are carried out on both legs or on one leg at a time until exhausted, repeating the same series two or three times, and timing.

For the ischiocrural muscles, a bow or expander may be used. Starting from a sitting position on a stool with the legs extended, the bow or expander is applied to the ankles, and backward knee bends are performed.

Alternatively, although not replacing the above exercise, backward kick running may be carried out, with 1.5 and 2 kg ankle bands.

For the gluteal muscles, the same ankle bands or any weight attached to the feet may be used.

Starting from a prone position on the floor, the athlete performs a series of successive alternating jerks (one leg at a time) (with both legs in the scissors position).

Still with the ankle bands or other weight applied to the feet, the athlete, starting from the upright position, quickly raises one leg to the chest repeatedly until exhausted, then repeats the exercise with the other leg. This strengthens the flexor muscles of the thighs.

It is not necessary to go into detail on strengthening the abdominal muscles. For the muscles of the scapular girdle, the thorax and the arms, either bar-bells or the weight of the body may be used.

From the prone position, with the feet resting on a stool, height 30–40 cm, and the arms bent with the hands on the floor next to the shoulders, simultaneous extensions of the arms are carried out followed by successive rapid bends, in a continuous series.

To make this exercise more demanding, a bar-bell of a suitable weight may be placed on the athlete's shoulders. For the arm flexor muscles, a bar at a height of approximately 2 m may be used, on which the athlete hangs with back and outwards thumb grip. He then carries out bends and stretches until his chin touches the bar and returns to the extended arm position.

If desired, when the athlete is sufficiently strong, any weight suited to the athlete's new condition may be fixed to the feet or to the ankle bands.

The bar-bell may be lowered to the chest with the bar under the chin and the elbows raised, or starting with the bar-bell at the chest, upward thrusts may be carried out, co-ordinating with a rapid thrusting movement of the legs.

The classic movement of stretching the arms from the bench may also be carried out, i.e. starting from a sitting position on the bench with the arms folded, with the bar-bell lightly touching the chest. Other exercises can, however, be performed: those described here are intended as a guideline only.

Useful advice
Strengthening is carried out by increasing speed and dynamism in sets of repetitions taking the athlete to increasing states of discomfort.

The two classic weightlifter's exercises are carried out with the bar-bell: the snatch and the thrust, with a simultaneous bending movement of the lower legs instead of the legs being wide apart. These exercises, in addition to acting on the whole of the body's muscular system, are designed to stimulate the nervous system to respond by means of fast and explosive action, and to improve its nutritional uptake.

WEEKLY TRAINING SCHEDULES

Typical week in the introductory phase of Period 1 (typical dates 10 Oct. to 2 Nov.)

Session 1
- Weights B (see training for the 200 m, page 29).
- Sprint: 10 × approx. 30 m, with standing and flying starts.
- Steady runs: 4–5 × 80 m.
- Aerobic strength: fast 4 km cross-country run with maximum heart rate 180 beats per minute.

Session 2
- General strengthening.
- Steady runs: 10–12 × 100 m, at sustained speed.

Session 3
- Hill runs: 8–10 × 100 m with 12% gradient and approx. 90% exertion, 5 min. between.
- Steady runs: 2–3 × 100 m at moderate speed.
- Aerobic strength: phased runs: 600 m, with 4 min. recovery; 600 m, with 12 min. recovery; 600 m, with 4 min. recovery; 600 m.

Session 4
- General strengthening (see explanation below).
- Sprint: 10–12 × approx. 30 m with standing and flying starts.
- Steady runs: 10 × 100 m at sustained speed.

Session 5
- Hopping: 8–10 alternating sets of five; five alternating sets of ten; 3 × alternating 50 m.
- Aerobic strength with phased runs: 600 m with 5 min. recovery; 500 m with 4 min. recovery; 400 m with 4 min. recovery; 300 m with 3 min. recovery; 200 m.

Session 6
- Hill runs: two sets of 4–5 × 100 m, with 3 min. recovery between and with 10 min. recovery between sets (same gradient and exertion as Session 3). Aerobic strength: 3 km progressive cross-country (heart rate 150–160 beats per minute).

Day 7, Rest

In the next phase, the first basic phase, a general strengthening session is replaced by a session of hopping, a phased run session (for aerobic strength) is eliminated, and so is the fast continuous cross-country. Two alactic acid capacity sessions and two lactic acid capacity sessions are added.

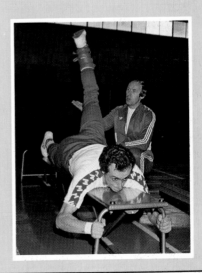

Typical week in the first basic phase of period 1 (typically from 7 Nov. to 4 Dec.)

Session 1
- Hopping: alternating from standing, 6 trebles, 5 tens, 4 × 50 m.
- Lactic acid capacity in sets of runs: 300/400/300 m; 300/400/300 m; 300/400 or 200 m; 300/200 m; 200/300 m; 300 m; 300 m; with intervals of 4 min. between runs and 10 min. between sets: times equal to 80% of previous year's record over the distance.

Session 2
- Hill runs: 8–10 × 100 m, with 5 min. between and 90% exertion, improved times in comparison with the earlier phase.
- Aerobic strength: progressive 3 km cross-country run (heart rate 150–160 beats per minute).

Session 3
- General strengthening.
- Sprint: 8 × 30 m with flying start.
- Alactic acid capacity: 4–5 × 60 m, with an interval of 1½ min. between runs, and 8 min. interval between sets: 4–5 × 60 m with intervals of 1½ min. and 8 min.; 3–4 × 80 m with intervals of 2 min.; virtually current maximum speed, paying attention to running technique.

Session 4
- Alternating hops from standing; 6 fives; 3–4 × 100 m.
- Lactic acid capacity in repeated runs: 300 m with interval of 8–10 min.; 500 m with interval of 8–10 min.; 500 m; times equivalent to 85% of previous year's record over the distance.

Session 5
- Weights B.
- Sprints: 8–10 × 30 m with flying start.
- Alactic acid capacity: series of 3–4 (60–80–100 m) with intervals of 1½ min., 2 min. and 8 min. between sets. Attention to be paid to technique and rhythm to be controlled, compromising between length and frequency of stride.

Session 6
- Hill runs: two sets of 4 × 100 m with interval of 3 min. between runs and 10 min. between sets.
- Aerobic strength in phased runs: 600 m, with interval of 6 min.; 500 m with interval of 5 min.; 400 m with interval of 4 min., 200 m; run slightly faster than previous phase.

Day 7, Rest

The next phase eliminates the last weights session and one hill run session. The aerobic strength session in interval runs becomes lactic acid capacity training in repeat runs. An alactic acid capacity unit is added. The general strengthening session becomes shorter, limiting the work of the flexor muscles of the thighs, the ischiocrural and gluteal muscles.

Typical week in the second basic phase (e.g. 5 Dec. to 1 Jan.)

Session 1
- Steady runs: several at progressive speeds.
- Lactic acid capacity in sets: 300/400/300 m, with interval of 4 min. between runs and 10 min. between sets; 300/400 m, with intervals of 4 min. and 10 min.; 200/300 m, with interval of 4 min. and 1 min.; intensity: some runs 80%, others 85%.

Session 2
- Alternating hops: 5 triples, 4 sets of 10, 3 × 50 m.
- Alactic acid capacity: 5 × 60 m, with intervals of 1½ min. between runs: 10 min. recovery; 4 × 100 m, with 3 min. interval. Speed almost current maximum, paying attention to running technique.

Session 3
- Strengthening: limited to lower leg muscles (thigh flexors, ischiocrural and gluteal muscles and sural triceps).
- Lactic acid capacity, repetition runs: 300 m, with interval of 12 min.; 300 m, with interval of 12 min.; 500 m or as alternative training 5–6 × 300 m with interval of 12 min.

Session 4
- Alternate hopping: 5 fives; 3 × 100 m.
- Alactic acid capacity: 3–4 (80/100/80 m) with intervals of 2 min. 20 sec.–3 min. between runs and intervals of 10–12 min. between series, paying attention to the use of the feet, finding a compromise between length and frequency of stride.

Session 5
- Hill running: 6–8 × 100 m with 5 min. interval at faster speed than previous phase.
- Several 30 m sprints.
- Aerobic strength: progressive cross-country over 3 km, or continuous cross-country over 4 km.

Session 6
- Alactic acid capacity: two sets of 3–4 × 100 m, with intervals of 3 min. between runs and 10 min. between sets, paying attention to the length and frequency of stride; then 15–20 min. active interval.
- Lactic acid capacity in repetition runs: 600 m with 12 min. interval; 500 m at 600 m pace, with 12 min. interval; 400 m with 12 min. interval, 90% speed.

Typical week in the special phase of period 1 (e.g. 2 to 23 Jan.)

Session 1
- Hopping between hurdles: five sets with 10 hurdles, 76 cm; five sets with 10 hurdles, 40 cm.
- Lactic acid strength: 6–8 × 150 m with intervals of 12–15 min. Speed virtually current maximum. Times should improve in successive weeks to regain maximum and above in second phase.

Session 2
- Lactic acid capacity in repetition runs: 200 m, with interval of 10–12 min.; 200 m with interval of 12–15 min.; 300 m. Speed to be approx. 95% with tendency to increase in successive phases, with increased intervals.

Session 3
- Alternating hops: 3 fives, 3 tens, 1 × 100 m, or:
- Hill runs: 5 × 100 m, speed near maximum, with 6 min. intervals.
- Sprint and compensatory steady runs.

Session 4
- Hopping between hurdles: five sets with 10 hurdles of 76 cm; five sets with 10 hurdles, 50 cm.
- Lactic acid strength: 3 × 100 m, with 6 min. interval.
- Lactic acid capacity: 500 m with 12–15 min. interval, 95%; 400 m with 12–15 min. interval, 90%; 300 m at 95%. Times to improve in successive phases but always with this differentiated modulation.

Session 5
- Running and acceleration exercises on the spot and in forward movement.
- Aerobic strength: progressive cross-country over 3 km or alternatively continuous cross-country over 4 km.

Session 6
- Hopping between hurdles, eight sets with 10 hurdles, 50 cm.
- Lactic acid strength: 2 × 100 m, with 8 min. interval; 2 × 150 m with 10 min. interval.
- Lactic acid capacity: 1 × 150 m. Speed 95% or above, increasing gradually until record exceeded.

Typical week in the basic phase of the second preparatory period (e.g. 10 Mar. to 6 Apr.)

Session 1
- A number of steady runs at progressive speeds.
- Lactic acid capacity in sets of 300/400/300 m with intervals of 4 min. between, then 10 min. interval; 300/400 m with 4 min. between.
- Intensity: some runs at 80%, some at 85%.

Session 2
- Alternating hops, 5 threes, 4 tens, 3 × 50 m.
- Lactic acid capacity: 5 × 60 m with interval of 1½ min. between sets, then 10 min. recovery; 5 × 80 m with interval of 2 min. between, then 10 min. recovery; 4 × 100 m with 3 min. interval. Speed almost current maximum, paying attention to technique.

Session 3
- Strengthening limited to lower leg muscles (thigh flexors, ischiocrurals, gluteal muscles and sural triceps).
- Lactic capacity in repetition runs: 300 m, with interval of 12 min.; 300 m, with interval of 12 min.; 300 m, with interval of 12 min.; 500 m. The longer interval should improve intensity, at 90%.

Session 4
- Alternating hops: 5 fives; 3 × 100 m.
- Alactic capacity: 3–4 sets of 80/100/80 m with intervals of 2½–3 min. between runs and with intervals of 10–12 min. between sets, paying attention to use of the feet, respecting the compromise between the length and frequency of stride.

Session 5
- Hill running: 6–8 × 100 m, with interval of 5 min. at speed higher than runs in previous phase.
- A number of 30 m sprints.
- Aerobic strength: progressive cross-country over 3 km, or alternatively continuous cross-country over 4 km.

Session 6
- Alactic acid capacity: two sets of 3–4 × 100 m, with interval of 3 min. between runs and 10 min. interval between sets, paying attention to length and frequency of stride. Then 15–20 min. active interval.
- Lactic acid capacity in repeat runs: 600 m, with 12 min. interval; 500 m with 12 min. interval; 400 m with 12 min. interval; speed 85% over 600 m.

Day 7, Rest

In the next cycle, work is somewhat reduced to increase intensity. The number of demanding sessions is reduced to four, with more gentle sessions and one day's rest. Lactic acid strength runs of 100 m and 150 m are added, with hopping between hurdles of 76–50 cm.

Session 1
- Hopping between hurdles: five sets with 10 hurdles of 76 cm; five sets with 10 hurdles of 50 cm.
- Lactic acid strength: 6–8 × 150 m, with interval of 12–15 min., speed almost current maximum. Times to improve over successive weeks, to reach the maximum and above in phase 2.

Session 2
- Lactic acid capacity in repetition runs: 200 m, with interval of 10–12 min.; 300 m with interval of 12–15 min.; 300 m. Speed to be approximately 95% with tendency to increase in successive phases, together with intervals. Times to improve on record in the second special phase.

Session 3
- Alternating hops: 3 fives, 3 tens; 2 × 100 m, or:

- Hill running: 5 × 100 m, speed near maximum, with 6 min. intervals between.
- Sprint and compensatory steady runs.

Session 4
- Hops between hurdles: five sets with 10 hurdles of 76 cm; five sets with 10 hurdles of 50 cm.
- Lactic acid strength: 3 × 100 m, with 6 min. intervals between.
- Lactic acid capacity: 500 m, 95% with interval of 12–15 min.; 400 m 90% with interval of 12–15 min.; 300 m at 95%. Times to improve in successive phases, but always with this differentiated modulation.

Session 5
- Running and acceleration exercises on the spot and in forward motion.
- Aerobic strength: progressive cross-country over 3 km or alternatively continuous cross-country over 4 km.

Session 6
- Hops between hurdles: eight sets with 10 hurdles, 50 cm.
- Lactic acid strength: 2 × 100 m, with interval of 8 min.; 2 × 150 m with interval of 10 min.
- Lactic acid capacity: 1 × 500 m, speed 95% and upwards, gradually increasing as schedule proceeds, until record is exceeded.

Day 7, Rest

The tendency in the next phase is to increase the speed at which runs are carried out. Session 5 may be eliminated completely and replaced by a unit without a specific work scheme, or total rest.

◼ The stars ◼

LON MYERS (USA)
One of the greatest athletes, if not the greatest, in the 19th century, between 1879 and 1884, he won 15 championship races in the USA, and at one time held all the national records for distances between 50 yards and the mile.

In the 440 yards, he was the first man to achieve times of less than 50 sec. regularly, and on four occasions he clocked under 49 sec. In the 880 yards, he twice achieved 1 min. 55.4 sec. when times of less than 2 min. were relatively rare. In order to leave some excitement in races, he often had to give away a handicap to his opponents. At the time, such 'handicap' races were extremely popular, and livened up betting.

The only opponent competitive with Myers was the Englishman Walter George. The two attracted large crowds when they met in a 'test match' over three distances in 1882 in New York. Myers won the 880 yards, but George, who was a better distance runner, won the mile and the $\frac{3}{4}$ mile, thus winning the challenge.

BILL CARR (USA)
In the 1932 Los Angeles Olympic 400 m final, Carr won in 46.2 sec., a new world record, and his great rival Ben Eastman finished 2/10 sec. behind him. Carr ended that summer by contributing towards the victory of the USA in the 4 × 400 m relay (3 min. 08.2 sec., a world record that was to remain unbeaten for 20 years). A few months later, he was involved in a road accident, suffering serious fractures that brought an end to his brief career.

HERB MCKENLEY (JAMAICA)
He is the only athlete in recent times to have succeeded in winning Olympic medals in both the 100 m and the 400 m. It happened in 1952 in Helsinki, when he finished second in the 100 m, a few inches behind the American Lindy Remigino, and sec-ond in the 400 m. McKenley had already won a silver medal at the 1948 Olympics in London, finishing behind his compatriot, Arthur Wint, in the 400 m. He moved up from the silver in the last race of the Helsinki Games, the 4 × 400 m relay, when together with Wint, Laing and Rhoden he brought Jamaica to victory following a memorable battle with the US team. His amazing third leg run (44.6 sec.) was instrumental in their gaining the world record (3 min. 03.9 sec.).

He revolutionized the approach to the 400 m. He would run the first 200 m as a sprinter (sometimes he had mid-race times of nearly 21 sec.), then try to survive. He established some major world records (45.9 sec. in the 400 m, 46.0 sec. in the 440 yards, both in 1948), but he also suffered defeats because of his speed fall-off towards the finish.

OTIS DAVIS (USA)
Few athletes have begun their careers as sprinters at the age of 26. It would

Otis Davis just holds off Karl Kaufmann in the 1960 Olympic final.

Alberto Juantorena, double gold medallist at the Montreal Olympics in 1976 in the 400 m/800 m.

be unusual anywhere, but particularly so in a country such as the USA, where it is more common for many careers already to have ended at that age. Otis Davis was an exception, however. He changed from basketball to athletics in 1958 and quickly showed great talent, running the 100 yards in 9.7 sec. and the 220 yards in 21.5 sec. In 1959 he proved his ability at the 440 yards, after half a dozen official races clocking 46.2 sec., the third best time in the world that year.

In the 400 m final at the 1960 Olympics, he was involved in a memorable race with the German, Karl Kaufmann. After accelerating suicidally in the third quarter, which he covered in 10.8 sec., he entered the back straight with a lead of around six metres on Kaufmann. The latter, who had distributed his effort more sensibly, put in a strong finish, but at the line, Davis just managed to hold his lead. For both, manual timing showed a new world record of 44.9 sec.; the electronic timing used as a standby gave Davis 45.07 sec. and Kaufmann 45.08 sec. The American then contributed to the success of the US team in the 4 × 400 m relay with a leg of 44.4 sec. and a new world record (3 min. 02.2 sec.). Davis ended his brief career in 1961. Among his best times, he clocked 9.5 sec. over 100 yards and 20.9 sec. over 220 yards.

LEE EVANS (USA)

For consistency of performance Lee Evans has been unequalled among one-lap runners. He won the US championship title five times (1966–69 and 1972), narrowly missing the record of six wins established in the last century by Lon Myers. Competition nowadays is also of course much more intense than in the days of the nonetheless excellent Myers. Stylistically he was not a text-book runner, but his strength and temperament helped him to force his way through in the most critical phase of each race, the finish.

Evans' greatest run was in the Olympic finals in Mexico in 1968, which he won with a world record of 43.86 sec. ahead of Larry James. Since then, no-one has ever clocked less than 44 sec., but it has been calculated that the rarefied air in Mexico (at an altitude of 2250 m) probably gave 400 m runners an advantage of about 0.4 sec. His intermediate splits were clocked unofficially as 10.7, 10.4 (21.1), 11.1 (32.2) and 11.6 (43.8) sec. Evans was also a member of the US team which set the world record for the 4 × 400 m relay of 2 min. 56.16 sec. at the same Games, another record which still stands. Over his career, he ran the 200 m in 20.4 sec. and the 440 yard hurdles in 50.2 sec.

ALBERTO JUANTORENA (CUBA)

Central America has for several decades been a great source of sprinters and 400 m runners. In Cuba, the first 'great' over this distance was Alberto Juantorena. His name is associated with an unprecedented achievement in the history of the Olympic Games: the double gold medal in the 400 m/800 m, which he pulled off in 1976 in Montreal. These distances are not regarded these days as being in the same category; to triumph in both in a competition such as the Olympic Games is a fantastic feat. In Montreal, the 400 m came after the 800 m, and for Juantorena the final was his seventh race in seven days. Yet he recorded a time of 44.26 sec., which to date is the best 'automatic' time recorded at or near sea level. The only comparable figure is the 'manual' 44.1 sec. which American Wayne Collet achieved in 1972 at Eugene. In Montreal, the Cuban ran only the heat and final of the 4 × 400 m relay. Juantorena moved into athletics from basketball in 1971. He first proved himself in the 400 m and in 1972 in Munich he almost made the Olympic finals. He virtually began in the 800 m in 1976, and immediately achieved some exceptional times, culminating in a world record of 1 min. 43.50 sec. in the Montreal final. In 1977 he did even better with 1 min. 43.44 sec. and managed to repeat the 400 m/800 m double in the World Cup in Düsseldorf.

Following a number of relatively serious injuries, he re-emerged in 1980, finishing fourth in the 400 m at the Moscow Olympics, and he officially ended his career in 1984.

MARIA ITKINA (USSR)

The 400 m was unavailable to women for some considerable time, and only appeared in the Olympic programme for the first time in 1964 in Tokyo. This was too late for Maria Itkina, the world's number one at the distance for several seasons previously. Now 32, she could manage only fifth place.

She was the first real 400 m specialist, and among the first to combine successfully the 200 m and the 400 m. At the European Championships, she won three titles: the 200 m in 1954 and the 400 m in 1958 and 1962. At the Olympic Games in 1960, in the absence of her preferred race, she had to be content with fourth place in the 200 m. With the USSR's 4 × 100 m relay team she was fourth on two occasions, in 1956 and 1960.

Her career as a one-lap runner began in 1952 (58.4 sec.) and culminated in 1962, when for the sixth time she improved on the world record at 53.4 sec. She succeeded in doing better still (53.2 sec. in 1963) having lost the record to the North Korean, Shin Geum Dan.

In the other sprint races, she had personal bests of 11.4 sec. (100 m) and 23.4 sec. (200 m).

IRENA SZEWINSKA (POLAND)

Irena Szewinska has left her mark on women's athletics records. She took part in five Olympic Games, from Tokyo in 1964 to Moscow in 1980, collecting seven medals, a record equalled only by the Australian Shirley Strickland de la Hunty. The Polish athlete appeared for the first time in the Olympic arena as an 18 year old,

Maria Itkina (1)

and was second in the 200 m with 23.1 sec. (European record), second in the long jump at 6.60 m (national record), and first in the Polish 4 × 100 m relay team in 43.6 sec. (world record).

At the 1968 Games in Mexico she won the 200 m with a world record of 22.58 sec., after winning a bronze medal in the 100 m. In 1972, at the Munich Olympics, came another bronze medal in the 200 m. Having moved up to the 400 m, at the 1976 Olympics in Montreal, she won in a world record time of 49.28 sec., leaving her nearest opponent more than ten metres behind. She ended her Olympic career in a rather sad way: at the Moscow Olympics an Achilles tendon injury pulled her up in the 400 m semi-finals.

Irena Szewinska

At the European championships her record is unequalled: ten medals, half of them gold, between 1966 and 1978. She also has the distinction of having beaten Marita Koch in the 400 m World Cup Final in 1977, at the age of 31, and was the first woman to clock less than 50 sec. for the 400 m (49.9 sec. in 1974). At the 1974 European Games in Rome, she clocked 48.5 sec. in a relay leg.

Her amazing range of records is as follows: 10.9 sec. (manual) and 11.13 sec. in the 100 m, 22.0 sec. (manual) and 22.21 sec. in the 200 m, 49.28 sec. in the 400 m, 14.0 sec. (manual) in the 100 m hurdles, 56.62 sec. in the 400 m hurdles, 1.68 m in the high jump, 6.67 m in the long jump and 4705 points in the pentathlon.

MARITA KOCH (GDR)

Marita Koch has the distinction of having held the world records for both 200 m and 400 m at 21.71 sec. and 48.16 sec. respectively. Between 1978 and 1982, she improved on the world record for the 400 m on six occasions, taking it at 49.19 sec., and bringing it down to 48.16 sec. at the 1982 European games in Athens, beating her Czech rival Jarmila Kratochvilova.

Koch appeared on the scene while very young, winning a silver medal at the European Junior Championships in 51.60 sec. in 1975 when only 18. At the Montreal Olympics, she had the misfortune to be eliminated by a

Marita Koch

muscle injury after the first heat of the 400 m. Her first great rival over this distance was to be Irena Szewinska, eleven years her senior. For three seasons, from 1978 to 1980, the East German was virtually unbeatable, dominating the world field in the 400 m; she crowned this period by contributing to the GDR's second place in the 4 × 400 m relay at the Moscow Olympics, running her leg in 48.3 sec. She competed in the 200 m too on a number of occasions, but was beaten in the 1979 World Cup by the American Evelyn Ashford. Koch nevertheless holds the two best times ever: 21.71 sec. in 1979 and 21.76 sec. in 1982. In the 100 m, she has a personal best of 10.83, which is the third fastest time ever.

Men

sec.
47.8 Maxie Long (USA) 1900
47.4 Ted Meredith (USA) 1916
47.0 Emerson Spencer (USA) 1928
46.4 Ben Eastman (USA) 1932
46.2 Bill Carr (USA) 1932
46.1 Archie Williams (USA) 1936
46.0 Rudolf Harbig (Germany) 1939
46.0 Grover Klemmer (USA) 1941
46.0 Herb McKenley (Jamaica) 1948
45.9 Herb McKenley (Jamaica) 1948
45.8 George Rhoden (Jamaica) 1950
45.4 Lou Jones (USA) 1955
45.2 Lou Jones (USA) 1956
44.9 Otis Davis (USA) 1960
44.9 Karl Kaufmann (Germany) 1960
44.9 Adolph Plummer (USA) 1963
44.9 Mike Larrabe (USA) 1964
44.5 Tommie Smith (USA) 1967
44.1 Larry James (USA) 1968
43.8 Lee Evans (USA) 1968

Automatic times
43.86 Lee Evans (USA) 1968

Women

57.0 Marlene Mathews (Australia) 1957
57.0 Marise Chamberlain (New Zealand) 1957
56.3 Nancy Boyle (Australia) 1957
55.2 Polina Lazareva (USSR) 1957
54.0 Maria Itkina (USSR) 1957
53.6 Maria Itkina (USSR) 1957
53.4 Maria Itkina (USSR) 1959
53.4 Maria Itkina (USSR) 1962
51.9 Shin Geum Dan (N. Korea) 1962
51.7 Nicole Duclos (France) 1969
51.7 Colette Besson (France) 1969
51.0 Marilyn Neufville (Jamaica) 1970
51.0 Monika Zehrt (GDR) 1972
49.9 Irena Szewinska (Poland) 1974
49.8 Christine Brehmer (GDR) 1976
49.8 Irena Szewinska (Poland) 1976
49.3 Irena Szewinska (Poland) 1976

Automatic times

50.14 Ritta Salin (Finland) 1974
49.77 Christine Brehmer (GDR) 1976
49.75 Irena Szewinska (Poland) 1976
49.29 Irena Szewinska (Poland) 1976
49.19 Marita Koch (GDR) 1978
49.03 Marita Koch (GDR) 1978
48.94 Marita Koch (GDR) 1978
48.89 Marita Koch (GDR) 1979
48.60 Marita Koch (GDR) 1979
48.16 Marita Koch (GDR) 1982
47.99 Jarmila Kratochvilova (Czechoslovakia) 1983

Valerie Brisco-Hooks, who in 1984 completed a unique Olympic double by taking the gold medal in the 200 m and 400 m, in both races breaking the Olympic record.

Jarmila Kratochvilova (411), the first woman to break 48 sec. in the 400 m.

Relay

Relay races as we know them today first appeared towards the end of the 19th century in the USA, being 'invented' by two enthusiasts from the University of Pennsylvania, Frank B. Ellis and H. Laussat Geyelin. They conceived a one-mile race in which each team was represented by four athletes; each ran with a cylindrical wooden baton in his hand and, after covering a quarter of a mile (402.34 m), passed it to a partner, who then repeated the procedure, and so it continued until the fourth and final stage. Two teams took part in the first

competition held in 1893: the University of Pennsylvania won in a time of 3 min. 25.2 sec. The new race was so successful that it was decided to hold a meeting based on relay races of varying lengths at the end of April each year. Thus the 'Pennsylvania Relay Carnival' was born, known as the 'Penn Relays'. Since 1895 this meeting has been held each spring, with the exception of the war years, at Franklin Field, Philadelphia.

The success of the 'Penn Relays' subsequently brought about the birth of similar festivals in other parts of the

USA, and relay races are exceptionally popular there.

The sprint relay, the 4 × 110 yards, began much later, and the 4 × 100 m first appeared in Czechoslovakia in 1897. The first significant time in the 4 × 110 yards was in 1913, when an English team completed the race in 43.2 sec. The metric version, the 4 × 100 m, has now been perfected by the Americans, who hold the world record for this event with 37.83 sec. This was achieved at the 1984 Oympic Games, with Carl Lewis recording 8.94 sec. on the final leg.

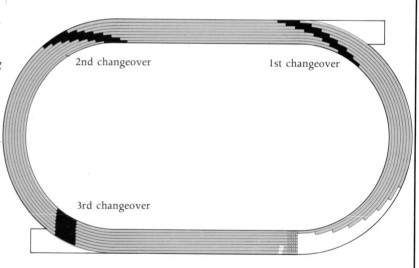

THE 4 × 100 M RELAY

The 4 × 100 m relay is divided into four 100 m legs to be covered by the same number of athletes who are required to take over a baton before starting their leg of the track.

The baton must be passed within a 20 m long designated 'changeover' zone (shown darkened on the diagram), on penalty of disqualification. As the diagram shows, the lead-off runner starts from the finish line, runs the bend and passes the baton to the second runner at the transition between the bend and the straight opposite the finish line. The second changeover takes place in the transition zone between the straight and the second bend. The third takes place on the transition between the bend and the finish straight.

2nd changeover

1st changeover

3rd changeover

The 4 × 100 m relay

The 4 × 100 m relay uses four sprinters together running a complete lap of the track, passing on a baton which has to arrive at the finish line with the runner of the last leg. The athletes on each leg run 106 m, 126 m, 126 m and 120 m respectively, assuming the three baton changeovers take place

26 m from the start of the pre-changeover zone. The sum of the legs run by each athlete is greater than 400 m, due to the fact that in the changeover zone, both athletes – the holder of the baton and the receiver – are running together. The trickiest phase is of course the moment when

the baton passes from the current carrier to the recipient, preferably without excessive loss of speed. To do this, the recipient has to start off before the carrier is too close; therefore he marks a reference point on the track. When his partner crosses the mark, he will start moving. This

Pietro Mennea demonstrates the starting position on the first leg of the 4 × 100 m relay. The position is exactly the same as in the 100 m sprint, except that the lead-off runner has to hold the baton in his right hand and then pass it to his partner. The baton is held with the fourth and little fingers and in the space between the thumb and index finger, these latter two being used with the middle finger as the support for starting. The baton has to be a smooth hollow tube of circular section made of a single piece of wood, metal or other rigid material to a length of 28–30 cm. The circumference must be between 12 and 13 cm and the baton must not weigh less than 50 g.

distance, from the reference point to the waiting athlete, is 6–8 m, depending on the athlete's ability.

Alternated technique. In the currently favoured 'alternated changeover', the baton alternates successively between the right and left hands of the four runners – the first and third, who run the bends, use the inside of the lane, while the second and fourth, moving on the straight, run on the outside. The first and third runners will therefore carry the baton in their right hand, and the other two in their left.

The acceleration zone. It is important for the three recipients to start in the pre-changeover zone with a high impetus, enabling them to achieve as fast a speed as possible after 25–26 m (the point by which they are required to have taken over the baton).

Before the start of the race, the three receiving athletes must mark on the track using adhesive tape the distance from which each of them is required to start running, based on their training runs.

This is the trickiest phase of the relay, as the athlete is required to be fast and precise, when highly tense, and has to transfer the baton within the changeover zone, generally demarcated by continuous yellow lines.

The takeover athletes are allowed to use an acceleration zone of 30 m, while the changeover, the baton passing, must take place within the last 20 m, otherwise the team is disqualified. The changeover must not take place in the pre-changeover zone.

Start. The athletes on the second, third and fourth legs can start from either a crouching or a standing position. In recent years the former method has been virtually abandoned because the athlete does not reach as high a speed as with the other method by the time the baton is handed over.

Changeover. Baton passing can be carried out in two ways, downsweep or upsweep, although there is not a lot of difference between them. The choice is left to the individual's preference, as both methods have similar points for and against.

Choice of runners for the individual stages. The choice of men and their distribution over the track is extremely important. Generally, coaches select sprinters with high acceleration and speed resistance, i.e. runners who can maintain high speeds for stretches of more than 100 m since, as already stated, they run between 106 m and 126 m. The lead-off runner must be a good starter and, like the third leg runner, must be good on the curve, in order not to lose too much ground compared with the straight run.

All members of the team must therefore be psychologically strong, being able to keep cool when the baton is being passed over. Naturally the team's cohesion is achieved with time and training, but only in proper races will athletes become accustomed to tension and the competitive environment.

The result. For high-quality teams, it is possible to calculate a table which will predict their theoretical performance. If the team consists of four athletes with personal bests of

Pietro Mennea and Pierfrancesco Pavoni demonstrate changeover training (photos right to left). They are running on a straight and pass the baton backwards and forwards between one another to familiarize themselves with the race requirement. This exercise is designed to make the movements involved become automatic. Mennea is following Pavoni in photographs 2 and 3, and passing the baton to him. Then, in photographs 4, 5 and 6, Pavoni, continuing the running action and arm movement, returns the baton to him. Running continues, and Mennea repeats the previous action, returning the baton to Pavoni. This exercise is repeated several times to accustom the athletes to reacting to the stimulus required by the arrival of the baton-carrying partner. Only repeated trial runs will make relay runners able to tackle a race properly, carrying out the baton transfer automatically.

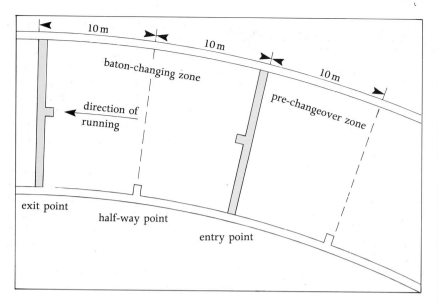

baton-changing zone

←— direction of running

pre-changeover zone

10 m   10 m   10 m

exit point

half-way point

entry point

❶

❷

There are two techniques in the changeover – the downsweep and upsweep. Photos 1 and 2 show the first technique, and the upsweep is shown in photos (a)–(c).

ⓐ

ⓑ

ⓒ

The 'hot zone' is the changeover zone where the baton is passed between two runners; there are three such zones for the three changes in a 4 × 100 m relay. There is a pre-changeover zone of 10 m which the recipient of the baton uses to accelerate. The baton must then be passed within the next 20 m otherwise the team will be disqualified.

Here Pierfrancesco Pavoni demonstrates the standing-start position used by runners on the second to fourth legs of a relay.

10.30 sec., the calculations should be as follows.

For the lead-off runner, assume a time equivalent to his best, 10.30 sec., for the second and subsequent runners, their personal bests less approximately 0.2 sec. This gives leg times of 10.30, 10.10, 10.10 and 10.10 sec. The times of the first and third runners, running on a bend, need to be weighted by approximately 0.25 sec., giving 10.55, 10.10, 10.35 and 10.10 sec., resulting in a total of 41.10 sec.

From this total deduct between 2.5 sec. and 2.8 sec., as the athletes receive the baton when they have already started, giving $41.10 - 2.8 = 38.30$ sec. These are approximate calculations, but they do equate with reality when the changeover techniques have been sufficiently well practised and their execution has become almost automatic.

Changeover calculations. In the 4 × 100 m relay, the last changeover between the third and fourth leg runners is crucial. The placement of the individual members of the team over the various legs should take into account the particular strengths of each runner. This is especially important for the last two runners who, to a certain extent, can make good earlier errors, provided the third leg runner is a good bend runner, and provided the baton is passed without hesitation. If the changeover has been a good one, the fourth-leg runner can develop this acceleration.

The 4 × 400 m relay

The 4 × 400 m relay, as we saw in the introduction, was the first relay event. The mile, the classic distance for the British, was divided into four parts, but metric distances were subsequently standardized, resulting in the current version. This race is a great spectacle when the opposing teams are closely matched. Each competitor in the 4 × 400 m runs a complete lap of the track and, unlike the 4 × 100 m, the second and third changes take place on the finish line, within a 20 m zone. There is no acceleration zone as in the 4 × 100 m. Only the first stage is run entirely in lanes, the changeover taking place in lane. The zone straddles the starting line for the 800 m, starting 10 m before and ending 10 m after this line. The second leg runner, having taken over the baton, runs the entire bend in lane and cuts into line, i.e. in the first lane, at the end of the bend. On the track, corresponding with the re-entry line, there is a band marking the end of the 'guided' run. From this point onwards, the athletes have the same distance to run. Two flags placed on either side of the track provide a clear marker of the re-entry points.

The baton. The baton is carried in the right hand, the recipients taking it with the left. The changeover technique provides for the recipient to set off turned slightly to the left. Once the baton has been taken, the athlete immediately transfers it to the other hand. This transfer is important. If he forgets, the athlete can arrive at the changeover zone with the baton in the wrong hand and baton passing will then be crosswise. This involves a loss of speed and the risk of falling due to collision between incoming runners arriving simultaneously at the changeover.

In this relay, too, the success of the changeover can allow valuable metres to be gained. The changeover must be practised over and over again in training, if possible also simulating the combative situations which frequently occur at the second and third changeovers. In these two baton passes, the recipients are required to

take up their position on the starting line of the changeover zone, based on the order in which the carrying runners arrive. This means that if a carrier is in third position on the incoming straight, the relevant recipient must take up his position third, starting from the line internally demarcating the track. Logically, this is possible when positions are clear and well defined. What often happens is that changes in position occur over the very last few metres, and then there is a tremendous battle. It should be remembered that once the finish line has been crossed – and this applies to all relay racing – the baton must not be used to express any emotion, such as throwing it into the air or on to the ground. It must be handed to one of the officials on arrival, otherwise the team will be disqualified.

Strategy. The strategy to be adopted in the placement of athletes is important. Usually the least strong athlete is put in first, as he has to run a shorter distance, of approximately 390 m. The strongest, on the other hand, usually runs last, his task being to

make up any disadvantage or to maintain any advantage gained. Contingencies may sometimes cause this order to be varied. The object is always to make up the team as a function of the opponent to be beaten. Often the 4 × 400 m is run by 800 m specialists, who have great stamina and a natural propensity for shoulder to shoulder struggle.

It should be noted that many athletes in relay racing can obtain stage times of less than their own personal bests over the same distance individually. This is due mainly to the fact that the athlete is moving outside his usual field, and the struggle with the other competitors results in an even greater effort.

4 × 400 m calculations. Unlike the 4 × 100 m sprint relay, it is not possible in this event to theorize on the finishing time by adding the times for the individual runners, with a downward correction to take into account successful baton changeovers.

At the end of each relay stage in the 4 × 400 m the baton holders arrive in a state of exhaustion, and the successful transfer of the baton is no longer attributable to a co-ordinated process, instead depending more on determination.

Marita Koch

If the stage runner is a strong 400 m runner, the task of transferring the baton will be carried out more easily. Any delay will be difficult to make up by successive recipients.

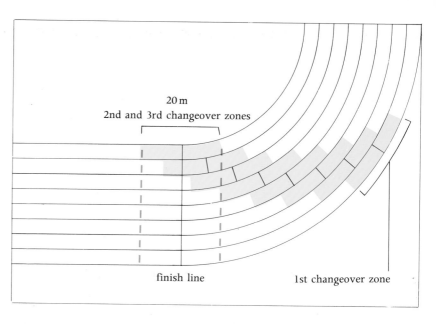

20 m
2nd and 3rd changeover zones

finish line

1st changeover zone

The first changeover in the 4 × 400 m The diagram shows where the changeover should take place on each leg of the 4 × 400 m relay. In the first changeover, the baton must be passed in lane. On the second changeover, the athletes hand the baton to each other within a 20 m zone straddling the start. The photo on the left shows Stefano Malinverni (Italy) in the final of the 4 × 400 m relay at the Moscow Olympics in 1980. In the other photo, Zuliani has turned partly to his left in order to receive the baton from Malinverni in the same race. If the baton is dropped, it can be picked up only by the athlete who was carrying it at the time.

4 × 100 Men
sec.
42.3 Germany (Röhr, Kern, Hermann, Rau) 1912
42.2 USA (Scholz, Murchison, Kirksey, Paddock) 1920
42.0 Great Britain (Abrahams, Rangeley, Royle, Nichol) 1924
42.0 Netherlands (Boot, Broos, De Vries, Van den Berghe) 1924
41.1 USA (Clarke, Hussey, Leconey, Murchison) 1924
41.0 Newark A.C. (USA) (Bowman, Curie, Pappas, Cumming) 1927
41.0 Sport Club Eintracht (Germany) (Geerling, Wichmann, Metzner, Salz) 1928
40.8 Germany (Jonath, Corts, Houben, Körnig) 1928
40.8 S.C. Charlottenburg (Germany) (Körnig, Grosser, Natan, Schloske) 1929
40.8 Univ. S. California (USA) (Delby, Maurer, Guyer, Wykoff) 1931
40.0 USA (Kiesel, Toppino, Dyer, Wykoff) 1932
39.8 USA (Owens, Metcalfe, Draper, Wykoff) 1936
39.5 USA (Murchison, King, Baker, Morrow) 1956
39.5 Germany (Steinbach, Lauer, Fütterer, Germar) 1958
39.5 Germany (Cullman, Hary, Mahlendorf, Lauer) 1960
39.5 Germany (Cullman, Hary, Mahlendorf, Lauer) 1960
39.1 USA (Jones, Budd, Frazier, Drayton) 1961
39.0 USA (Drayton, Ashworth, Stebbins, Hayes) 1964
38.6 Univ. S. California (USA) (McCullouch, Kuller, Simpson, Miller) 1967
38.6 Jamaica (Stewart, Fray, Forbes, Miller) 1968
38.3 Jamaica (Stewart, Fray, Forbes, Miller) 1968
38.2 USA (Greene, Pender, Smith, Hines) 1968

Automatic times
38.19 USA (Black, Taylor, Tinker, Hart) 1972
38.03 USA (Collins, Riddick, Wiley, Williams) 1977
37.86 USA (King, Gault, Smith, Lewis) 1983
37.83 USA (Graddy, Brown, Smith, Lewis) 1984

4 × 100 Women
sec.
46.4 Germany (Albus, Krauss, Dollinger, Dorffeldt) 1936
45.9 Germany (Knabe, Sander, Klein, Petersen) 1952
45.6 Soviet Union (Kalashnilova, Safronova, Hnikina, Turova) 1953
45.6 Soviet Union (Vinogradova, Itkina, Safronova, Polinichenko) 1955
45.2 Soviet Union (Krepinkina, Kosmoleva, Itkina, Botchkareva) 1956
45.1 Germany (Fisch, Kohler, Stubnick, Mayer) 1956
44.9 Germany (Kohler, Mayer, Sander, Stubnick) 1956
44.7 Great Britain (Pashley, Scrivens, Paul, Armitage) 1956
44.5 Soviet Union (Krepkina, Maslovskaja, Itkina, Schelkanova) 1961
44.5 Poland (Ciepla, Piatkowska, Sobota, Szyroba) 1962
43.4 Netherlands (Van den Berg, Stierke, Hennipman, Bakker) 1968
43.4 Soviet Union (Sarcova, Bukharina, Popkova, Samotesova) 1968
43.3 West Germany (Schittenheim, Helten, Irrgang, Mickler-Becker) 1971
42.9 GDR (Kauffer, Heinich, Struppel, Stecher) 1972
42.8 West Germany (Krause, Mickler, Richter, Rosendhal) 1972
42.6 GDR (Kandarr, Stecher, Heinrich, Selmigkeit) 1973
42.6 GDR (Maletzki, Stecher, Heinich, Eckert) 1974
42.5 GDR (Maletzki, Stecher, Heinich, Eckert) 1974

Automatic times
42.51 GDR (Maletzki, Stecher, Heinich, Eckert) 1974
42.50 GDR (Oelsner, Stecher, Bodendorf, Blos) 1976
42.27 GDR (Klier, Hamman, Bodendorf, Göhr) 1978
42.10 GDR (Koch, Schneider, Auerswald, Göhr) 1979
42.09 GDR (Brehmer, Schneider, Auerswald, Göhr) 1979
42.09 GDR (Muller, Wockel, Auerswald, Göhr) 1980
41.85 GDR (Muller, Wockel, Auerswald, Göhr) 1980
41.60 GDR (Muller, Wockel, Auerswald, Göhr) 1980
41.53 GDR (Gladisch, Koch, Auerswald, Göhr) 1983

4 × 400 Men
min.sec.
3:18.2 USA (Schaff, Sheppard, Gissing, Rosenberger) 1911
3:16.6 USA (Sheppard, Reidpath, Meredith, Lindberg) 1912
3:16.0 USA (Cochrane, Stevenson, McDonald, Helffrich) 1924
3:14.2 USA (Baird, Spencer, Alderman, Barbuti) 1928
3:13.4 USA (Baird, Taylor, Barbuti, Spencer) 1928
3:12.6 Stanford Univ. (USA) (Shore, A.A. Hables, L.T. Hables, Eastman) 1931
3:08.2 USA (Fuqua, Ablowich, Warner, Carr) 1932
3:03.9 Jamaica (Wint, Laing, McKenley, Rhoden) 1952
3:02.2 USA (Yerman, Young, G. Davis, O. Davis) 1960
3:00.7 USA (Cassell, Larrabee, Williams, Carr) 1964
2:59.6 USA (Frey, Evans, Smith, Lewis) 1966
2:56.16 USA (Matthews, Freeman, James, Evans) 1968

4 × 400 Women
3:47.4 Moscow Club (USSR) Finogenova, Medvedeva, Voitenko, Klein) 1969
3:43.2 Estonia (USSR) (Zagere, Verbele, Shtula, Dundare) 1969
3:37.6 Great Britain (Pawsey, Attwood, Simpson, Board) 1969
3:34.2 France (Mombet, Jacq, Duclos, Besson) 1969
3:33.9 West Germany (Czekay, Gleichfeld, Eckhoff, Frese) 1969
3:30.8 Great Britain (Stirling, Lowe, Simpson, Board) 1969
3:30.8 France (Martin, Duclos, Jacq, Besson) 1969
3:29.3 GDR (Kuehne, Lohse, Seidler, Zehrt) 1971
3:28.8 GDR (Kaesling, Seidler, Zehrt, Rohde) 1972
3:28.5 GDR (Kaesling, Kuehne, Siedler, Zehrt) 1972
3:23.0 GDR (Kaesling, Kuehne, Siedler, Zehrt) 1972
3:19.23 GDR (Maletzki, Rohde, Streidt, Brehmer) 1976
3:19.04 GDR (Siemon, Busch, Rubsam, Koch) 1982
3:15.92 GDR (Walther, Busch, Rubsam, Koch) 1984

800 m
How it is run

The 800 m was inaugurated for the first time as an official event at the 1896 Olympics in Athens; at that time the 880 yards (British half-mile) was the standard distance.

For a long while the 800 m was considered as an event to which the athlete should trade up from the 400 m; but in recent years Britain's Sebastian Coe and Steve Ovett in particular appear to have confirmed that the 800 m is an event to which the 1500 m runner should trade down, i.e. athletes who can demonstrate stamina at speed are most likely to do well at the 800 m distance.

TACTICS
The 800 m is an extremely tactical event in that it is run according to the athlete's specific objective – to qualify for the next round, to win a championship, or to set a record. However, tactics are worthless without speed and stamina.

It is essential to know how to take the best advantage of speed and stamina, and what their relationship is to one another. There are two ways of tackling the 800 m: setting a fast pace to start with, and trying to maintain this to the finish; or a fairly even distribution of effort with perhaps a kick off the final bend.

YOUNG RUNNERS
Before worrying about the race tactics described above, the young runner should first of all learn to run properly, using the correct technique, and the instructions suggested by the experts responsible for the middle-distance running sector of the Federazione Italiana di Atletica Leggera are clear on this. We set out here their suggestions for the 14–15 year old age range.

At the end of the first stages of training, the young runner should be taught the running technique best suited to his skeletal and muscular characteristics. The development of

physical qualities (strength, speed and flexibility) make it continuously necessary for the running technique to be brought into line with his own development. In addition, running technique is also related to the youngster's joint movement, which will develop with suitable exercises designed to improve the functioning of the ankle, the hip joint and the shoulders, and the spine.

RUNNING TECHNIQUE
The coach of a young athlete should draw attention to the essential aspects of running, rather than concentrating on less important details, as follows.

(a) the youngster should learn to run springing on his feet

(b) immediately after the leading part of the foot has left the ground, the leg should tend to bend naturally towards the thigh, and the limb, thus bent, should advance, allowing the knee to project adequately forward and up

(c) the trunk should be kept upright to assist forward movement and lifting of the knee and correct support of the foot

(d) the upper limbs should swing sufficiently widely, co-ordinated with the lower limbs

(e) the upper part of the body should be as relaxed as possible.

The same instructions suggest exercises to improve the use of the feet, and running exercises. The exercises in the first group, which should be carried out with a natural load and then with an additional load (a small bar-bell of 20–30 kg on the shoulders, or a 5–6 kg belt) are designed to strengthen the muscles of the feet, in the gemellus, the soleus, the posterior tibial and the flexor muscles of the

toes, and they consist of rising on the balls of the feet, or on the ball of one foot only. In the first instance, the 'up and down' movement may be repeated 30–60 times in accordance with the individual's muscle efficiency. With the extra load, given the greater effort required, the repetitions should be halved.

The running exercises cover swinging the arms, designed to improve the functioning of the shoulder joints, in addition to skipping, alternate hops forward, to fast bounding, short sprints and extended running. These exercises, in addition to training youngsters, help the coach to identify and correct any faults in technique.

To make the exercises more useful, it is essential for the young runner to be told to 'spring', applying little force for long endurance times and a great deal of force for short endurance times, to achieve maximum ability to perform rapid changes in speed, a decisive factor in the 800 m race.

Training

Training of the middle-distance runner, whether for true middle distance (800 m and 1500 m) or long distance (5000 m and 10 000 m), is complex and requires general psychological/physical training to be carried out over long periods.

Because of its complexity and the long periods of time involved, it is important to understand the fundamental points.

For juniors (boys aged 14 and 15, girls aged 13 and 14), training should be designed to provide a basis for the future, not expecting to collect major competitive results for the moment. Only with increased age will training bear fruit.

Alberto Juantorena leads in the 800 m final at the Montreal Olympics. In the chasing group are Wohlhuter, Van Damme, Wülbeck and Susanj. Juantorena went on to win the race, in the first part of a unique double which gave him the gold medal in the 400 m and 800 m.

The young runner is trained to develop general stamina, muscle efficiency and running technique.

General stamina training is provided involving continuous running for periods of 20–50 min., carried out on natural terrain, possibly undulating to be covered at constant, increasing or varied speed.

These exercises effect a gradual increase in running speed in relation to the youngster's progress. When running of this kind in a natural environment is carried out in groups,

avoid assigning individuals who have difficulty in maintaining the pace of the others, or who maintain it with excessive ease, to the same groups.

Muscle efficiency is the main condition required of a middle-distance runner, as the mechanical work in the race is carried out by the muscles, which use their own chemical energy and that received via the cardio-circulatory system.

With respect to running technique, see the introduction to the section on the 800 m. As for the need to give preference to basic training for the young, we would add two extremely valid reasons:
1. This avoids making the mistake of overestimating the young runner's talents, anticipating the achievement of good results having prematurely insisted on the development of specific stamina;

2. It avoids the danger involved in premature heavy training of specific stamina, causing stagnation of the youngster's future performance potential; this can lead to the youngster rejecting the event and eventually giving up running altogether.

So one should never be in a hurry with a budding middle-distance runner.

For youngsters of up to 14–15, there are no specific tables provided for the middle-distance athlete.

For the older age ranges, still retaining the characteristics of a more generalized training, the training 'guidelines' for the young runner are directed towards the future 800 m and 1500 m specialist. The typical weeks suggested relate specifically to youngsters of 17–18 who have the talent and experience to do well in middle-distance running.

Typical week in the first introductory general phase, lasting 6−8 weeks between October and November

Session 1
• Running exercises: 6−8 sets in the first week of the phase, 12−15 in the last week.
• Trunk muscle strengthening: 3−4 series of exercises in the first week, to 6−8 in the final week.
• Aerobic or general stamina 8−10 km at steady speed in the first week to 12−15 km in the final week.

Session 2
• Strengthening of the lower limbs: 5−6 sets of exercises in the first week to 10−12 in the final week.
• Aerobic or general stamina: initially running 7−8 km in gentle speed progression in the first week to achieve 10−12 km, still in gentle progression, in the final week.

Session 3
• Strengthening of the trunk: From 4−6 series of exercises in the first week, progressively developing to up to 6−8 in the final week.
• Running exercises: 8−10 series in the first week to 15−20 in the final week.

Session 4
• Strengthening of the lower limbs: 5−6 series of exercises from the first week to the last.
• Aerobic or general stamina: from 2.5 to 3 km running in gentle progression from the first week to 4−5 km in the last week.

Session 5
• Running exercises: from 6−8 sets in the first week to 12−15 in the final week.
• Aerobic or general stamina: from 8−10 km running at constant speed in the first week to 12−15 in the final week.

Session 6
• Running exercises: from 4−5 sets in the first week to 6−8 in the final week.
• Trunk strengthening: from 3−4 series of exercises in the first week to 5−6 in the final week.
• Aerobic or general stamina: from 6−8 km running at steady speed in the first week to 8−10 km in the final week.

Typical week in the basic cycle, 8−10 weeks in duration, between December and mid-February

Session 1
• Speed endurance: from the first to the third week, 5−8 sprints over 80 m with 2 min. intervals; from the fourth to the final week, 4−6 × 80 m, with intervals of 3 min. and 4 min.
• Aerobic stamina: running from the first to the last week from 12 to 15 km at steady speed.

Session 2
• Running exercises: From 12 to 15 sets from the first to the last week.
• Trunk strengthening: from the first to the last week, carrying out 4−6 sets of exercises.
• Aerobic strength: from the first to the last week, running 4−5 km at steady speed.

Session 3
• Strengthening of the lower limbs: 10−12 exercises to be carried out from the first to the last week.
• Aerobic stamina: running distances of 10−12 km with gentle speed progression.

Session 4
• Running exercises: from 12 to 15 sets, from the first to the last week.
• Speed endurance: from the first to the third week, 3−4 fast sprints over 80 m with intervals of 2−6 min., then 3−4 × 100 m with intervals of 3 min.; from the fourth to the last week, 4 × 100 m, intervals of 3−6 min., 3 × 150 m, intervals of 4−8 min., 2 × 200 m, intervals of 5 min.

Session 5
• Running exercises: 8−10 sets from first to last week.
• Strengthening of lower limbs: from first to last week, 5−6 series of exercises to be performed.
• Aerobic stamina: 12−15 km to be run at steady speed from the first to last week.

Session 6
• Running exercises: 6−8 series from the first to the last week.
• Trunk strengthening: 4−6 series of exercises from the first to the last week.
• Aerobic strength: in the first three weeks, total distance of 4000−5000 m to be run, subdivided into splits of 1500 m, 6 min. interval; 1000 m, 4 min. interval; 1000 m, 4 min. interval; 500 m. From the fourth week to the last, same total distance, broken down into 1000 m, 4 min. interval; 1000 m, 4 min. interval; 800 m, 4 min. interval; 600 m, 3 min. interval; 500 m.

Typical week in the specific phase, 6−8 weeks in duration, between mid-February and mid-April

Session 1
• Running exercises. Move on from 6−8 sets in first week to 4−6 sets in final week.
• Lactic acid stamina. First to last week, total distances of 2500−3000 m to be run, decreasing to 2000−2500 m, subdivided into 800 m to 300 m splits.

Session 2
• Strengthening of lower limbs: 6−8 sets of exercises in the first week only.
• Aerobic stamina: 10−12 km to be run in gentle progression from the first to final weeks.

Session 3
• Running exercises. From 6−8 exercises in the first week to 4−6 in the final week.
• Aerobic strength. Continuous running of 3−4 km at constant speed from first to last week or, still with total 3−4 km, subdivided into splits of 1000 m to 500 m, from first to last week.

Session 4
• Aerobic stamina: from the first to the final weeks, 8−10 km to be run in gentle progression.

Session 5
• Speed endurance. Sprints starting in first week with 3 × 100 m, intervals of 4−10 min. between; 2 × 200 m, interval of 5−10 min. between; 2 × 300 m, interval of 6 min. between, giving total of 1300 m, to arrive at the final week splitting a total of 1000 m into 100 m; 4 min. interval; 150 m, 5 min. interval; 200 m, 5 min. interval, 250 m, 8 min. interval; 300 m.
• Aerobic stamina: from first to last week, 10−12 km to be run in gentle progression.

Session 6
• Strengthening of lower limbs. First week only: 6−8 series of exercises.
• Running exercises: 6−8 series from first to last week.

Typical week in the final phase, 3−4 weeks' duration, between mid-April and May

Session 1
• Running exercises: from 4−6 sets, every week.
• Aerobic stamina: 10−12 km to be run, every week.

Session 2
• Mixed work on aerobic strength/lactic acid stamina: from first to last week, 2500−3000 m to be run, subdivided into stages of between 1000 m and 300 m.

Session 3
• Aerobic stamina: 6−7 km to be run every week, with gentle speed progression.

Session 4
• Mixed work on aerobic strength/lactic acid stamina: from 2500−3000 m to be run every week, subdivided into splits of 1000 m and 300 m.

Session 5
• Every week, series of steady runs to be carried out, possibly on grass. The programme is less onerous than usual as the completion cycle provides for the first races to be run outdoors.

Recommended races
In general, over the year, it is recommended for 4−5 400 m races to be run; 8−10 800 m; 4−5 1500 m; 2−3 3000 m.

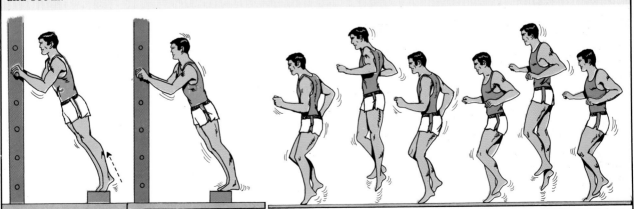

Physiology:
■ What happens in the 800 m ■

In races over middle and long distances (800 m to the marathon), tactical ability is certainly important, but not as much as in other events. However, it is important to have a good final sprint. While this characteristic can be crucial in all middle-distance and long-distance running (and recently even some of the marathons have been won with a 'sprint finish'), it is in the 800 m that this is most likely to be a determining factor.

A good finisher will be recognized in his very first contact with athletics. Alberto Cova, for example, was a master of the sprint finish from a very young age. Anyone naturally having a good number of 'fast-twitch fibres' will immediately have an advantage over someone who has predominantly slow-twitch fibres. Specific training can of course only increase the percentage of fast-twitch fibres to a limited extent, but it can modify the concentration of certain enzymes to a much greater extent. To understand the importance of these enzymes, we need to know what happens during a sprint finish from an energy viewpoint. If two athletes are shoulder to shoulder near the finish line, the one who wins will be the one who manages to take the shortest time for the few metres remaining; this means that, all things being equal, his muscles have available a greater quantity of energy per second: in other words, they must be capable of producing ATP, their fuel, at a faster rate.

In the final stage of a race, even if it is a short one as in the case of the 800 m, the mechanism producing ATP with the aid of oxygen, i.e. the aerobic mechanism, is working at maximum intensity: no increase in energy per unit of time can therefore be hoped for from here. When an increase in running speed is observed in the final stretch of a race, therefore, what happens is that the energy mechanisms in which no oxygen is involved, the anaerobic mechanisms, are increasing in efficiency: these are termed the alactic acid and lactic acid mechanisms.

The fact that these succeed in producing a greater quantity of ATP per unit of time is explained by the fact that certain specific enzymes increase their activity.

Simply, the enzymes are like small machines which assist the biochemical conversion of substances: each machine facilitates the occurrence of a single stage of this conversion.

So, with suitable training, the number of these machines in the muscle fibres is increased. But even with the same number of such machines (i.e. with an identical concentration of enzymes), the production of ATP can be increased still further. Some hormones produced by the adrenal glands are, for example, able to stimulate the functioning of the enzymes.

Sometimes man is capable of performing acts which would normally be beyond him: for example, a man pursued by a tiger can find the strength to run faster and further than ever before. The good finisher, in effect, is able to create in himself the same psychological and neuro-endocrine conditions as someone fleeing from a tiger. The brain sends stimuli which, through various processes, lead to an increase in certain hormones of the adrenal glands in the blood.

There are also other important characteristics at the end of the final sprint. Anyone, for example, who customarily has an extremely broad stride, with the pelvis held high at all times, and with a marked spring in his stride, will often have greater difficulty in increasing the pace in a sprint finish: those who do well on the other hand tend more often to have a normal or rather short and rapid stride, their spring always being in relation to their stride, and giving the impression of always being closer to the ground. There is also the problem of maintaining rhythm when changing speed: a good coach can teach how to continue to thrust in the decisive part of the race, which is usually the section just after the first 400 m, the third quarter.

PERFORMANCE OF THE VARIOUS EXERCISES

Running exercises and exercises to strengthen the foot muscles

- Successive springs with the feet together, knees locked, with a superimposed load of 15–30 kg; 15–45 movements.
- Successive springs on one foot, knee locked, leaning against a wall; 20–50/60 movements.
- Over distances of 15–20 m, up to 30–40, elastic bounding strides, front of foot–sole–front of foot locked and knees locked.
- Carry out bounds of running-on-the-spot and slight-forward-movement types, elastic movement of foot upwards and back; 30–40 to 50–100 movements.
- Long skips over distances from 30–40 to 50–100 m, i.e. alternating hops on the lower limbs, forwards and high.
- Over distances of 60–100 m, start with bound running, progressively changing to sprint running.
- Start with long skip, progressively moving to fast running over distances of 60–100 m.
- For 50–100 m, perform action known as 'circular running', i.e. running in which attention is paid to the circularity of the running action, which is accentuated with the aim of educating the athlete to take advantage of the elastic effect of thrust and to prepare the best situation for the successive elastic thrust.

Exercises to strengthen the trunk muscles

These are designed to strengthen the abdominal muscles, and the flexor muscles of the pelvis above the thighs, when carried out lying on the ground on the back. With the ankles and shoulders fixed, for example, to the base of the wall bars, raise the trunk or lower limbs with the widest possible movements, approaching the support surfaces but without actually touching them. The repetitions to be carried out should be matched to the individual's ability. Similar exercises are recommended also from the same lying position, but on an inclined plane. From the prone position, lying on the ground with the face down, similar exercises serve to strengthen the back muscles, at the same time involving the thigh and gluteal muscles.

Exercises to strengthen the lower limbs

• Striding with successive bending of the thighs (high knee lifts), covering distances of 20−30 to 40−60 m (striding is a forward movement action which is not truly running).
• Striding with successive bending of the thighs against the pelvis and thrusting, recommended distances 20−30 to 40−60 m.
• Further striding with successive swinging of the lower limbs over distances of 20−30 to 40−60 m.
• Gallop running strides over distances of 20−50 m.
• Striding with alternating swinging of the lower limbs over distances of 20−50 m.
• Striding with step and take-off (take-off is the energetic thrusting of the feet with which a jump is started) over distances of 30−60 m.
• Striding with two paces and take-off over distances of 40−60 m.
• Alternating hops upwards, i.e. first on one foot, then on the other, on the spot, or moving forward slightly; 15−30 movements.
• Half-squat or quarter-squat with upward jump: from 15 to 30 movements.
• Forward frog-leaps, i.e. with both feet together, in fives and tens, over the maximum possible distance.
• Successive hops, i.e. jumping on the same leg, in fives and tens, over the maximum possible distance.
• Alternating forward hops, in fives and tens, over 50 m, and also over 100 m and above.
Still to strengthen the lower limbs, other exercises can be carried out consisting of bending and flexing the lower limbs both forwards and to the side. The limb is said to be bent when the limb being moved is bent, and flexed if the limb being moved remains extended.

Training to develop aerobic or general stamina

Continue incorporating bound running or high knee running sessions in the standard week training exercises, or a little of one type of running and a little of the other, as follows.

Week one: every kilometre, cover 100 m running of the type specified above, known as 'special striding';
Week two: every kilometre, 150 m of 'special stride';
Last week: every kilometre, 30 m of 'special stride'.

Training to develop aerobic strength

We should begin by stating that aerobic strength is the characteristic which allows certain portions of the total distance of 2−3 km for the 800 m runner (4−5 km for the 1500 m runner) to be run at sustained speed. In the introduction to the preparatory phase, this characteristic is developed by carrying out a section of hop running at the end of each run. For example:
Week one: 3000 m running with the last 200 m accentuated spring running, i.e. accentuating the bounds.
Week two: 3000 m running with the last 300 m run as above.
Last week: 4000 m run with the last 1000 m run as above.
The suggested variation can be incorporated due to the relatively low level of fatigue required of the athlete during the performance of the introductory phase.

Improved speed endurance training

Speed endurance is the ability to withstand high running speeds for the longest possible period of time. Initially, training is by running shorter distances at gradually increasing intensity as the weeks go by. The increase in efficiency will at a certain point allow development in one of two ways:

(a) keeping the distances short, but running at increasing speed and with slightly longer recovery periods (true speed exercises)

(b) applying to distances of increasing length.

The first variation helps to develop running speed in young runners: the second method is intended to allow the young runner to maintain a higher speed over increasing distances, hence to extend his endurance capability.

Training to develop lactic acid resistance

This is work intended to endow the youngster with the ability to build up and withstand an increasing level of fatigue, via runs of differing intensity, with short recovery intervals. For example:
• 3 × 800 m, with 3−4 min. recovery time.
• 3 × 800 m, with 10−12 min. recovery time.
• 1 × 800 m, with 6−8 min. recovery time/2 × 500 m, with 6−8 min. recovery time/2 × 300 m, with 5−6 min. recovery time.
• 3 × 600 m, with 6−8 min. recovery time/2 × 400 m, with 6−8 min. recovery time.
• 6 × 400 m, 6−8 min. recovery time.
• 4 × 400 m, with 6−10 min. recovery time/4 × 300 m, with 5 min. recovery time.
• 300 m, 2 min. recovery time/400 m, 2 min. recovery time/300 m, 8 min. recovery time/200 m, 2 min. recovery time/300 m, 2 min. recovery time/ 200 m, 8 min. recovery time/300 m.

USE OF EXERCISES IN TRAINING

The examples suggested relate primarily to the 'introductory' part of the phase. In the successive 'basic' and 'special' phases, running exercises will increasingly involve the action most appropriate for racing. The exercises designed to strengthen the feet muscles and trunk should be carried out at increasing speed. Strengthening of the lower limbs is to be done with alternating hops forward over ever-increasing distances. These exercises are to be gradually reduced to the minimum essential for the completion phase. In the final phase, exercises to extend speed endurance, aerobic stamina and strength and lactic acid resistance become more specific, with increasingly intense effort on continuous and interval running, increasing recovery times.

Variations to the racing programme

The annual racing programme is a recommended general outline: modifications should be made to suit particular individuals.

A suggested programme for fit young 1500 m runners would be:
• approximately 5−8 cross-country races and/or 3000 m indoor races;
• approximately 20 outdoor races as follows: 2−3 400 m; 4−5 800 m; 6−8 1500 m; 5−8 3000−5000 m.
Suggested programme for 'sprint'-type young 800 m runners:

• 2−3 km college-type cross-country runs and possible indoor runs of 1500−3000 m to supplement and up-lift the exercises to develop aerobic strength;
• approximately 20 outdoor runs, as follows: 2−3 × 200 m; 6−8 × 400 m; 6−8 × 800 m; 2−3 × 1500 m.

The stars

TED MEREDITH (USA)

To date he is the only athlete to have won an Olympic title in the 800 m while still under 21. This he did at the Stockholm games in 1912, in a race which is among the best in Olympic history, producing a world record of 1 min. 51.9 sec. The organizers had placed a second tape at the 880 yard distance (804.67 m) and Meredith set a new world record for the 880 yards too, at 1 min. 52.5 sec.

In 1916, he improved on his world record in the 880 yards with 1 min. 52.2 sec. and then beat the 440 yard record with 47.4 sec., two marks that remained unbeaten for many years. By the time of the Antwerp Olympics, his form was no longer good enough to win any events, and he subsequently became a coach in Czechoslovakia.

RUDOLF HARBIG (GERMANY)

Rudolf Harbig was an athlete ahead of his time. The most famous of his world records, 1 min. 46.6 sec. for the 800 m set in 1939, was to remain unbeaten for 16 years. A few weeks after this, Harbig took another record, this time in the 400 m, with a time of 46.0 sec.

In 800 m racing, Harbig was un-beaten from August 1936 to September 1940. Despite being called up into the army and no longer having time to train properly, he still managed to take a third world record, running a kilometre in 2 min. 21.5 sec.

From 1934 to 1942, he took part in 233 races, winning 201 of them. His personal records were 10.6 sec. in the 100 m, 21.5 sec. in the 200 m and 4 min. 01.0 sec. in the 1500 m.

MAL WHITFIELD (USA)

Between June 1948 and the end of 1954 he ran 69 races at 800 m or 880 yards, losing only three. At the Olympic Games he was twice gold medallist in the 800 m (1948 and 1952), in both cases clocking 1 min. 49.2 sec. He also won another three Olympic medals: the bronze in the 400 m (1948), the gold (1948) and the silver (1952) in the 4 × 400 m relay.

His temperament often led him to content himself with victory rather than going for a record, but he had an extremely attractive running style, often kicking 200 m from the finish line. He did manage to take two world records for non-Olympic distances: 1 min. 48.6 sec. (880 yards) and 2 min. 20.8 sec. (1000 m).

PETER SNELL (NEW ZEALAND)

One of the most unexpected Olympic victories was that of Peter Snell in the 800 m at the Rome Olympics in 1960. He came to Rome with a personal best of 1 min. 49.2 sec. in the 880 yards but, in the final, he held off the Belgian Roger Moens, the favourite, to win in 1 min. 46.3 sec. Snell was a pupil of Arthur Lydiard, a coach who gave preference to long distance work in the winter and spring, moving on to speed and interval training only in the weeks preceding major events. Using this method, Snell did even better in the 1964 Olympics in Tokyo, where he won the 800 m in 1 min. 45.1 sec. and the 1500 m in 3 min. 38.1 sec., and he is the most recent middle-distance runner to have com-pleted the Olympic double at 800 m/1500 m. Combined with his natural strength, Snell had an excep-tionally fast finish and could manage the last 200 m of a mile race in 24 sec. He held the world records for the 800 m (1 min. 44.3 sec.), the 880 yards (1 min. 45.1 sec.) and the mile (3 min. 54.1 sec.).

STEVE OVETT (GB)

Although only one year older than Sebastian Coe, he appeared on the scene some while earlier than his great rival. In 1973 as an 18-year-old, he won the European Junior champion-ship in the 800 m in 1 min. 47.5 sec. A year later, he finished second in the European Championships in Rome

Peter Snell

Steve Ovett

losing only twice, and the 1500 m/mile 70 times, losing only four times. His attempts at achieving Olympic success at Los Angeles in 1984 were thwarted by a severe respiratory disorder which resulted in him trailing in last in the 800 m final and dropping out on the last lap of the 1500 m final.

However, he appeared to have recovered fully from this problem, and in early 1985 raced in several events including the Paris mile. It was expected that he would move up to the 5000 m distance in top-class competition.

SEBASTIAN COE (GB)

One of the great middle-distance runners of all time, no-one has been more prolific than Sebastian Coe in setting world records. Between 1979 and 1982 he set eight records at distances between 800 m and the mile.

He arrived on the international scene when the successes of men such as Juantorena, Van Damme and Walker seemed to indicate the tall and powerful athlete as the prototype in the world middle-distance class. He trusted in his natural gifts of agility and speed, to which in time he added increased strength, under the guidance of his father, Peter. His smooth stride and change in speed, which enable him to break away from opponents surprisingly quickly, have made him a model runner. However, although he knocked one and a half seconds off Alberto Juantorena's world record at 800 m, it is over this distance that he has suffered the most bitter defeats, having lost two of his three confrontations with his great rival, Steve Ovett. In the third race, it was Coe who won, at the 1500 m Olympic final in Moscow in 1980.

In the 1984 Los Angeles Olympics 800 m final with Ovett obviously in difficulty, Coe was left to provide the only challenge to the young Brazilian, Joachim Cruz, and he ended up with the silver medal in 1 min. 43.64 sec.; Cruz took the gold in a new Olympic record of 1 min. 43 sec. The 1500 m was a repeat of the 1980 Olympics for Coe, as he became the first man to retain the 1500 m title, in a time of 3 min. 32.53 sec., thus smashing Kip Keino's 1968 Olympic record in the event.

Sebastian Coe

As well as holding the world record for the mile at 3 min. 47.33 sec., Coe has also set indoor world records: 800 m, 1 min. 44.91 sec.; 1000 m, 2 min. 18.58 sec.

NINA OTKALENKO (USSR)

Like several other female middle-distance runners, Nina Otkalenko was unlucky to be at her best at the 800 m before this event was included in the Olympic programme for women.

Otkalenko set her first world record in the 800 m in 1951 with 2 min. 12.0 sec. She then succeeded in improving on this six times, reducing the time to 2 min. 05.0 sec. by 1955.

She had an exceptional range of times for an athlete of her era: 12.5 sec. (100 m), 25.4 sec. (200 m), 55.0 sec. (400 m), 4 min. 37.0 sec. (1500 m) and 5 min. dead for the mile.

with a time of 1 min. 45.8 sec. However, he failed to fulfil this early promise when taking part in the Montreal Olympics in 1976.

He finally came to the fore in 1977, when he won the 1500 m in the World Cup with a strong kick on the final lap. Since then he has strongly contested the crown of world middle-distance running with Sebastian Coe. The two shared the honours at the Moscow Olympics, where each won the race in which the other was favourite; Ovett took the 800 m (1 min. 45.40 sec.) and Coe the 1500 m (3 min. 38.40 sec.). This rivalry was seized upon by the media, who have probably contributed to Ovett and Coe avoiding each other a great deal in major competition.

Ovett has taken fewer world records than Coe, but has won more often in major races: added to the Olympic title are two victories in the 1500 m in the World Cup, a first place in the 1500 m and two second places in the 800 m in the European Championships.

In his most successful years (1977–1981) he ran the 800 m 21 times,

NADYEZHDA OLIZARENKO
(USSR)

She began in athletics at the age of 14 in 1967, starting as a sprinter, then moving to middle-distance running. As an 800 m runner, at the age of 17 she recorded a personal best of 2 min. 11.4 sec. She revealed her international class in 1978 at the European Championships in Prague by taking second place in 1 min. 55.82 sec., 2/100 sec. behind her fellow Russian Provodokhina. Her best year has been 1980, when she took the world record before the Olympics with 1 min. 54.85 sec., and gained a great victory in the Olympic final, further lowering the world record to 1 min. 53.43 sec. She also took third place in the 1500 m, making her the best female middle-distance runner of the Moscow games.

Men
min.sec.
1:51.9 Ted Meredith (USA) 1912
1:51.6 Otto Peltzer (Germany) 1926
1:50.6 Seraphin Martin (France) 1928
1:49.8* Thomas Hampson (GB) 1932
1:49.8 Ben Eastman (USA) 1934
1:49.7 Glenn Cunningham (USA) 1936
1:49.6 Elroy Robinson (USA) 1937
1:48.4 Sidney Wooderson (GB) 1938
1:46.6 Rudolf Harbig (Germany) 1939
1:45.7 Roger Moens (Belgium) 1955
1:44.3 Peter Snell (New Zealand) 1962
1:44.3 Ralph Doubell (Australia) 1968
1:44.3 David Wottle (USA) 1972
1:43.7 Marcello Fiasconaro (Italy) 1973
1:43.5 Alberto Juantorena (Cuba) 1976
1:43.44 Alberto Juantorena (Cuba) 1977
1:42.33 Sebastian Coe (GB) 1979
1:41.73 Sebastian Coe (GB) 1981

*actual time 1:49.7

Left: *The young Brazilian, Joachim Cruz, who in 1984 took the Olympic gold medal in the 800 m ahead of Sebastian Coe. The first Brazilian runner to gain an Olympic title, Cruz ran the third fastest 800 m of all time (1 min. 43 sec.) and also took the Olympic record.*
Below: *Nadyezhda Olizarenko (281)*

Women
2:16.8 Lina Batschauer-Radke
     (Germany) 1928
2:15.8 Anna Larsson (Sweden) 1944
2:14.8 Anna Larsson (Sweden) 1945
2:13.8 Anna Larsson (Sweden) 1945
2:13.0 Yedokiya Vasilyeva (USSR) 1950
2:12.2 Valentina Pomogayeva (USSR)
     1951
2:12.0 Nina Pletnyova (USSR) 1951
2:08.5 Nina Pletnyova (USSR) 1952
2:07.3 Nina Otkalenko (USSR) 1953
2:06.6 Nina Otkalenko (USSR) 1954
2:05.0 Nina Otkalenko (USSR) 1955
2:04.3 Lyudmila Shevtsova (USSR) 1960
2:04.3 Lyudmila Shevtsova (USSR) 1960
2:01.2 Dixie Willis (Australia) 1962
2:01.1 Ann Packer (GB) 1964
2:01.0 Judy Pollock (Australia) 1967
2:00.5 Vera Nikolic (Yugoslavia) 1968
1:58.5 Hildegard Falck (FRG) 1971
1:57.5 Svetla Zlateva (Bulgaria) 1973
1:56.0 Valentina Gerasimova (USSR)
     1976
1:54.9 Tatyana Kazankina (USSR) 1976
1:54.85 Nadyezhda Olizarenko (USSR)
     1980
1:53.43 Nadyezhda Olizarenko (USSR)
     1980
1:53.28 Jarmila Kratochvilova
     (Czechoslovakia) 1983

1500m
How it is run

The 1500 m, one of the two fast middle distance races, consists of three laps of a 400 m track, plus 300 m at the start. The race starts at the end of the first bend after the finish, with the runners lining up across the track.

Even in major competitions in which the final is limited to 12 runners, there is often controversy among competitors at the start. In the rush pushing and elbowing often occurs, sometimes even resulting in falls and injuries. A competitor in the 1500 m must therefore try to minimize the risk of being pushed.

Once he has taken up a position, it is best to keep to the inside, or not go farther out than the second lane, especially on a bend, unless tactics dictate otherwise. If he stays on the outside on a bend he will travel farther and waste precious energy.

First World Championships, Helsinki (7–14 Aug. 1983)
This photograph shows the final of the 1500 m with the Spaniard José Abascal (183) in the lead, with the Yugoslav Zdravkovic (943) on his shoulder. The eventual winner of the race, Steve Cram is just visible behind his compatriot, Steve Ovett (341); Cram, the latest in a great tradition of British middle-distance runners, outsprinted the other competitors at the finish.

Moscow Olympics, 1980
Sebastian Coe (254) kicks off the final bend on his way to winning the gold medal in the 1500 m, to avenge his defeat by Steve Ovett (279) in the 800 m final; oddly enough these two athletes each won the event in which the other was favourite.

We have indicated that there is no difference in practice between running the 800 m and the 1500 m. The same training programmes have been suggested for 16- and 17-year olds for both these races. The latest examples of this similarity between the two distances are the Britons Sebastian Coe and Steve Ovett who, in recent years, have run both races with equal success. However, there is a clear distinction between the short (800 m and 1500 m) and the long (5000 m and 10,000 m) distances, while the 3000 m serves as the link for the junior classes (men of 18 and 19 and girls of 17 and 18).

The increased distinction between the two categories of middle-distance race, which has led to the first (800 m and 1500 m) being defined as a 'fast' and the second (5000 m and 10,000 m) as the 'stamina' group, is the result of greater specialization.

Sixty years ago the legendary Finnish runner Paavo Nurmi excelled in the 1500 m, the 5 km and the 10 km, still looking easy even over the longest of these distances. In 1924 he was world champion at all three distances at once. At that time the 1500 m and the more popular British mile were still considered more suitable for athletes with stamina. The fact that Nurmi held world records for the one-hour race and the 20 km showed that he was really a long-distance runner.

More recently, in 1955 and 1956 the Hungarian Sandor Iharos became, like Nurmi, holder of world records for the 1500 m, 5000 m and 10,000 m.

Unlike Nurmi, however, Iharos discarded the customary speed requirement, for which quantitative training was employed, in favour of stamina needed for ever-increasing distances. Nowadays it is no longer possible to pick a short-distance runner as a result of his performance over longer distances, nor is it possible to select a runner with stamina for a short middle-distance race.

However, it is possible to pick a long-distance runner from his performance at shorter distances, as is shown by the West German Thomas Wessinghage, a born 1500 m runner who, when more mature, became a top class 5000 m runner and winner of the European 5000 m championship in 1982.

Consequently, even for the 1500 m, strong specialization is necessary in order to have any chance of success, specialization in speed stamina.

Training for speed stamina takes place gradually when the athlete is young, by compensating between inherent and acquired qualities. For example, the young person with greater than average natural stamina for long-distance races, but lacking the necessary quick reflexes to alter speed (which are vital in the 1500 m), must be trained to overcome this shortcoming.

As in the 800 m, tactics are designed to correlate the objectives as closely as possible with the athlete's qualities and the possible degree of improvement with training. Successful athletes too impose their own tactics, taking the same criteria into account.

Technique has a fundamental role, even at this distance. The suggestions made for acquiring the most functional, least wasteful running technique for the 800 m are also valid for the 1500 m. Since almost double the distance has to be covered it is extremely important to run as 'close to the ground' as possible without any jumping movement, so as not to waste energy in vertical motion which should be used for forward thrust.

■ Training ■

Before suggesting a training programme for 1500 m runners, we should mention that, for this, the second of the two short middle-distance races, the programme suitable for young athletes of 17 and 18 (given in the chapter on the 800 m) will not be repeated since the basic sections are valid for the training of runners at both distances.

For the 1500 m, the suggested week's training programme is designed for a top-class athlete; consequently the work is strenuous and intense, and is for a runner who is specializing in the 1500 m. Training is divided into four stages: introductory, basic, specific and completion spread over seven months.

When the athletics season begins the trainer will adjust the work according to the runner's commitments. Training will become less strenuous and will be designed to maintain the maximum degree of efficiency reached during the previous periods.

Before setting out the daily programme we should explain some of the terms used. 'Slow long distance' means running a minimum of 12–15 km at a relatively easy pace, around 4 min./km. 'Average long distance' means increasing the pace from 3 min. 40 sec. to 3 min. 30 sec. per kilometre, and reducing the distance to 10–12 km. 'Fast long distance' requires a further reduction in pace from 3 min. 15 sec. down to 3 min. 10 sec. per kilometre over a distance of 6–10 km. Generally, before giving the distance, the training time is set out, i.e. one hour slow long distance, 40 min. of average long distance, etc. In addition, exercises are prescribed to strengthen the feet, the legs, the trunk and the abdominal and back muscles. 'Stretching' defines the exercises to be done to improve flexing of the muscles. In the case of running uphill, the gradient chosen should be related to the distance to be run: 200 m at 12–15%, or 600–800 m at 6–7% gradient. 'Variation in pace' involves running different distances at varying speeds, according to the athlete's ability, but at a pace faster than 'fast long distance'. 'Mixed endurance' training consists of running decreasing distances at increased speeds, until race pace has been reached or exceeded.

An athlete will train for two sessions daily during the peak of training, either on the road or in the country. When it is necessary to check on the standard achieved, these sessions will take place on the track since it is then easier to time the performance because the distance can be measured accurately.

Weekly training – introductory stage, lasting 4–6 weeks between October and November

Session 1

- Morning: one hour slow long distance (15 km at 4 min./km).
- Afternoon: muscle-strengthening exercises, non-specific; stretching.

Session 2

- Afternoon: one hour slow long distance.

Session 3

- Morning: one hour slow long distance.
- Afternoon: muscle-strengthening exercises, non-specific; stretching.

Session 4

- Afternoon: one and a quarter hours' slow long distance (18–19 km at about 4 min./km).

Session 5

- Morning: one hour slow long distance.
- Afternoon: muscle-strengthening exercises, non-specific; stretching.

Session 6

- Afternoon: one hour slow long distance.

Session 7

- Afternoon: one hour's running, 40 min. of which should be at varying speeds (equivalent to 12 km at 3 min. 40 sec./km).

Weekly training – basic stage, lasting 8 weeks from December to January

Session 1

- Morning: general muscle-strengthening exercises; stretching.
- Afternoon: one and a quarter hours' slow long distance (18 km at 3 min. 45 sec./km); sprinting 100–120 m ten times.

Session 2

- Morning: one hour slow long distance (15 km at 3 min. 45 sec./km).
- Afternoon: running different distances (2000 m/3000 m/2000 m/3000 m/2000 m) with 3 min. to 3 min. 45 sec. recovery between each.

Session 3

- Morning: muscle-strengthening exercises, specific – feet and legs; exercises on running technique; stretching.
- Afternoon: one and a quarter hours' slow long distance (18 km at 3 min. 45 sec./km); sprinting 100–120 m ten times.

Session 4

- Morning: one hour slow long distance (15 km at 3 min. 45 sec./km).
- Afternoon: one hour's running, 40 min. of which should be of average long distance (12 km at 3 min. 30 sec. to 3 min. 40 sec./kilometre).

Session 5

- Morning: general muscle-strengthening exercises; stretching.
- Afternoon: one and a quarter hours' slow long distance (18 km at 3 min. 45 sec./km).

Session 6

- Afternoon: one and a quarter hours' slow long distance (18 km at 3 min. 45 sec./km); sprinting 100–120 m ten times.

Session 7

- Afternoon: fast long distance (10–12 km at 3 min. 15 sec./km) or, preferably, participation in a 10–12 km cross-country race.

Weekly training – specific stage, lasting 6 weeks from February to mid-March

Session 1

- Morning: one hour slow long distance (15 km at 3 min. 45 sec./km).

- Afternoon: 2 × 200 m uphill ten times (recovery 1 min. 30 sec. to 8 min.).

Session 2

- Morning: specific muscle exercises; stretching.

- Afternoon: one and a quarter hours' running as follows: 15 min. warming up, 45 min. progressively faster (from 3 min. 30 sec. to 3 min. 10 sec. per kilometre), 15 min. 'limbering down'.

Session 3

- Morning: one hour slow long distance (15 km at 3 min. 45 sec.).

- Afternoon: running different distances (1000 m/2000 m/3000 m/2000 m/1000 m) with 3 min. to 3 min. 45 sec. recovery between each.

Session 4

- Morning: specific muscle exercises; sprinting 100–120 m ten times; stretching.

- Afternoon: one and a quarter hours' slow long distance (18 km at 3 min. 45 sec./km).

Session 5

- Morning: one hour slow long distance (15 km at 3 min. 45 sec./km).

- Afternoon: 2 × 2 × 800 m uphill (4–10 min. recovery), then twice 2 × 600 m (3–8 min. recovery).

Session 6

- Afternoon: one and a quarter hours' slow long distance (18 km at 3 min. 45 sec./km); sprinting 100–120 m five or six times.

Session 7

- Afternoon: fast long distance (10–12 km at 3 min./km or under) or, preferably, participation in a cross-country race of a similar distance.

Weekly training – completion stage, lasting 4 weeks in April

Session 1

- Morning: one hour slow long distance (15 km at 3 min. 40 sec./km).

- Afternoon: one hour's running, 30 min. of which should be progressively faster (from 3 min. 20 sec. to 2 min. 50 sec./km).

Session 2

- Morning: one hour slow long distance (15 km at 3 min. 40 sec./km); sprinting 100–120 m ten times.

- Afternoon: 3 × 2000 m with 3 min. recovery, then 5 × 400 m with 2 min. recovery, or 6 × 1000 m with 3 min. recovery, then 5 × 400 m with 2 min. recovery.

Session 3

- Afternoon: one and a quarter hours' slow long distance (18 km at 3 min. 40 sec./km); sprinting 100–120 m ten times.

Session 4

- Morning: one hour slow long distance (15 km at 3 min. 40 sec.).

- Afternoon: 10 × 400 m, repeated once with 5–8 min. recovery between the series, or 6 × 500 m with 8 min. recovery, then 6 × 400 m with 8 min. recovery, then 6 × 300 m with 1 min. recovery.

Session 5

- Morning: one hour slow long distance (15 km at 3 min. 40 sec./km).

- Afternoon: one hour's running, 20 min. of which should be fast long distance (from 3 min. to 2 min. 55 sec./km).

Session 6

- Afternoon: one hour slow long distance (15 km at 3 min. 40 sec./km); sprinting 100–120 m ten times.

Session 7

- Afternoon: endurance training, increasing pace over 3000 m/2000 m/1000 m/500 m/300 m, recovery 800 m in 3 min.

Physiology:
What happens in the 1500 m

The typical 1500 m runner is usually of above-average height, light, long-legged, but with well developed muscles. Although exceptions exist, most of the best athletes at this distance are of this type. Is there a physiological explanation for this?

First of all, their low weight (possibly less than 60 kg (132 lb) for a height of nearly 6 ft (1.80 m), as in the case of some champions) is undoubtedly an advantage. In fact the amount of energy expended on running is approximately directly proportional to body weight: since a runner weighing 66 kg is 10% heavier than a runner of 60 kg, he will expend 10% more energy when running a race. This increase may appear modest, but it may mean the difference between being a top international athlete or a competitor of county standard.

However, middle-distance runners who want to be successful must obviously submit themselves to intensive training as well. This is hardly compatible with carrying body fat which, for a person who does not take part in sport, would be considered merely superfluous, while for a runner it is a real handicap – an extra load which makes him run more slowly than if he were thinner.

Another problem for runners is being big-boned, and the best middle-distance runners therefore have light bones. Also, at the pace at which the 1500 m is run, long-legged runners use slightly less energy than those whose legs are short.

Two more important factors determine the amount of energy expended on running. The first is technique. In the past some people maintained that it was a waste of time for trainers to teach athletes to run since, as soon as they had run many kilometres in training, their style was automatically perfected to the extent of being energy saving. However, today even highly trained 1500 m runners know that those with a good technique save around 10% of effort compared with those whose technique is incorrect – an appreciable amount. It can be difficult to correct errors in technique, but it is worth attempting to do so. The second factor which can influence the effort required is muscular elasticity. Muscles which are stretched are capable of storing energy and releasing it later when they contract, provided that a minimum time elapses between stretching and contraction. This pause occurs even in running, especially in the case of the calf muscles, the muscles of the front part of the thigh and the gluteus muscles. Therefore people with more elastic muscles save more energy than those whose muscles are less elastic.

Another factor to be taken into consideration is the ability to maintain the same pace over the whole distance, especially not making any sudden changes in speed. For this reason, when running to set a record, middle-distance (and even long-distance) runners try to maintain the same pace right through the race. Obviously, in competitions in which it is important to win or obtain a place, tactics dictate that parts of the race are run at speeds often very different from other parts of the same length, and that there are sudden changes in pace. In these cases the final times usually suffer.

However, in addition to expending energy carefully (and therefore expending little effort, having good muscle elasticity and distributing effort uniformly), in order to obtain the best results it is essential to have a large amount of energy. In a 1500 m race more than two thirds of the energy is derived from the aerobic mechanism, which entails a good supply of oxygen to the muscles and a high rate of utilization of that oxygen by muscles. The remaining energy is derived from the anaerobic mechanisms (either alactacid or lactacid); both require specific muscle characteristics. Thus, to excel in the 1500 m, many qualities are required involving technique, tactics, style and physical characteristics.

The stars

WALTER GEORGE (GB)
This tall thin Englishman was one of the great athletes of modern times, and his only real competitor for the title 'Athlete of the 19th Century' was the American Lon Myers. The two met on several occasions, first as amateurs and later as professionals. Myers was best over 880 yards and 1000 yards, but George was the better miler.

As an amateur George set up world records over several distances: 1 mile in 4 min. 18.4 sec., 2 miles in 9 min. 17.4 sec., 3 miles in 14 min. 39.0 sec., 6 miles in 30 min. 21.5 sec., 10 miles in 51 min. 20.0 sec. and 18,555 m in one hour. Soon there were no English runners to touch him, so he therefore wanted to run against the most famous professional at that time, the Scot William Cummings. To do this he had to relinquish his amateur status which he did without hesitation, because he could not afford to spend so much time training without adequate financial reward. The races between George and Cummings drew crowds of up to 30,000 and betting was commonplace.

In one of these races, on 23 Aug. 1886 in London, George ran the mile in 4 min. 12.75 sec., a record which

Gundar Hägg, the great Swedish athlete of the 1940s.

remained unbroken for nearly 30 years. In an unofficial race he was said to have been timed as low as 4 min. 10.2 sec. for the mile.

His training methods were far in advance of those of his time, and some English historians maintain that the Swedish coach Gösta Holmer was able to draw useful ideas from these methods half a century later; Holmer has a place in the history of middle-distance running through having successfully used the well-known 'Fartlek' method of training at varying speeds.

GUNDAR HÄGG (SWEDEN)
Gundar Hägg is undoubtedly the greatest of all Swedish athletes. A woodman from Jämtland who trained in the country and employed methods which were revolutionary at the time, he gained a remarkable number of world records. He broke 15 (ten of them in 1942) over distances between 1500 m and 5000 m between 1941 and 1945.

Few athletes trained in the country in the 1930s and 1940s; at that time most middle- and long-distance runners were governed by the track and the stopwatch. However, the coach Gösta Holmer was of the opinion that running over both flat and hilly country provided variety, which helped to prevent the boredom that arises from a strict training programme. Hägg followed the 'Fartlek' (literally 'speed play') system, after Holmer's theories.

Hägg might not have had success had he not met Arne Andersson, not such a strong runner as Hägg but versatile and with a strong sprint finish. The two fought memorable battles in the middle-distance events in 1944 and 1945. There was such an interest in the two runners that they became a great spectacle, resulting in their receiving unofficial payments from the organizers of athletics meetings. Consequently, at the beginning of 1946 they were disqualified for infringing their amateur status, and their careers ended as they were on the verge of breaking the four-minute mile barrier.

Hägg, a tall, powerful athlete, began his distinguished career over long distances, but from 1940 onwards his favourite race was the 1500 m. At the end of his career his personal bests were: 800 m in 1 min. 52.8 sec., 1500 m in 3 min. 43.0 sec. (world record), 1 mile in 4 min. 1.03 sec. (world record), 2000 m in 5 min. 11.8 sec. (world record), 3000 m in 8 min. 01.2 sec. (world record), 2

Roger Bannister, who made history as the first person to break four minutes for the mile.

miles in 8 min. 42.8 sec. (world record), 3 miles in 13 min. 32.4 sec. (world record), 5000 m in 13 min. 58.2 sec. (world record).

ROGER BANNISTER (GB)
No result has been more widely publicized and acclaimed than the first sub-4-minute mile run by the medical student Roger Bannister on 6 May 1954 at Oxford in a time of 3 min. 59.4 sec.

His mind had been occupied with this goal for several months, but only a month after his achievement, John Landy succeeded in improving on Bannister's time with a record of 3 min. 57.9 sec.

The two met again at the Commonwealth Games in Vancouver in the same year, Bannister finishing faster to win in 3 min. 58.8 sec. He crowned his year by winning the European 1500 m at Berne in 3 min. 43.8 sec.

Bannister, who was tall and slim, had no success in the Olympic Games, however. He had been selected for the 1948 London Games when he was only 19, but declined to take part, saying that he felt too immature. In Helsinki in 1952 he came fourth in the 1500 m in 3 min. 46.0 sec., his best time up until then. During his famous mile-record-breaking run he passed the 1500 m mark in 3 min. 43 sec. (an unofficial time). He gave up athletics at the end of that year (1954).

HERB ELLIOTT
(AUSTRALIA)

One of the world's great middle-distance runners, he was responsible for revolutionary changes in the way the 1500 m and mile races were run.

Athletes had previously tackled these distances in the belief that a final burst of speed was not possible before the final 200–300 m; consequently in races there was generally a waiting stage before the final fight to the line. Elliott, from the Australian outback, had as his adviser Percy Cerutty, who considered that a new attitude towards the 1500 m and the mile was possible if both mental and physical conditions were sound. Elliott improved his physical condition, which was already exceptional, by intense training along the beaches and over the dunes at Portsea, near Melbourne. The results were seen by the public for the first time during a tournament in Europe in 1958, during which Elliott set new world records in the 1500 m (3 min. 36.0 sec.) and the mile (3 min. 54.5 sec.). His most successful meeting was the 1960 Olympic Games in Rome, where he started his

Herb Elliott, the revolutionary miler of the Rome Olympics.

Jim Ryun

finishing burst 700 m from the tape, gradually leaving the field behind him. He gained a world record of 3 min. 35.6 sec., completing the last 800 m in 1 min. 52.8 sec.

Elliott, who was never defeated in the 1500 m and the mile, broke the 4-minute barrier for the mile before he was 20. He even ran the 880 yards in 1 min. 47.3 sec. and the 5000 m in 14 min. 09.9 sec.

JIM RYUN (USA)

No middle-distance runner has had such a meteoric rise to fame as Jim Ryun from Kansas who, at the age of 19, set world records for the 880 yards (1 min. 44.9 sec.) and the mile (3 min. 51.3 sec.). His success continued the following year, 1967, when he broke the world record for the 1500 m (3 min. 33.1 sec.), beating the Kenyan Kip Keino and bringing the mile

record down to 3 min. 51.1 sec. In the latter race Ryun led from start to finish, which had never happened before in the mile.

He often maintained an exceptionally fast pace throughout a race, and in the 1967 West Germany v USA match at Düsseldorf he outclassed the two outstanding German finishers Tummler and Norpoth, who finished 4 seconds behind him in the 1500 m, by winning in 3 min. 38.2 sec. On that occasion Ryun covered the last lap in 50.6 sec., and the last 200 m in 24.8 sec.

However, Ryun had no luck in the Olympics. In the 1964 Games in Tokyo, when only 17, he failed to qualify in the 1500 m heats; in the 1968 Mexico Games he was unable to cope with the rarefied air and was outstripped by his great rival Kip Keino (3 min. 37.8 sec. against 3 min. 34.9 sec.) winning only a silver medal to his great disappointment; in the 1972 Munich Games he fell in heats during some bunching and was eliminated.

As a sprinter in relays and straight races he recorded 21.6 sec. for the 220 yards and 47.0 sec. for the 440 yards. He even ran the 5000 m in 13 min. 38.2 sec.

JOHN WALKER (NEW ZEALAND)

John Walker, a worthy successor to his fellow countrymen Jack Lovelock and Peter Snell, has enjoyed a remarkably long athletics career from 1972 onwards.

A strong man physically and mentally, he was the first miler to break the 3 min. 50 sec. barrier, with a world record of 3 min. 49.4 sec. at Gothenberg in 1975. He broke the world 2000 m record with 4 min. 51.4 sec. at Oslo shortly before the Montreal Olympic Games, where he won the 1500 m after three years'

John Walker (694) takes the gold medal in the 1500 m final at the Montreal Olympics.

hard effort. However, he paid a price for overwork: he began to suffer from chronic tendinitis and was operated on several times. Nevertheless he made a comeback and, despite being overshadowed by the great English pair Ovett and Coe, he has still recorded outstanding times. In 1982, when he was 30, he ran a mile in 3 min. 49.08 sec., faster than his own record seven years earlier. He competed over 5000 m at the 1984 Los Angeles Olympics, but could manage only eighth in the final. Other results obtained by him have been 800 m in 1 min. 44.9 sec., 1500 m in 3 min. 32.4 sec., 3000 m in 7 min. 37.49 sec. and 5000 m in 13 min. 20.89 sec.

LYUDMILA BRAGINA (USSR)

Women have only been competing internationally in middle-distance running for little more than ten years. Its increase in popularity is perhaps due to the Russian Lyudmila Bragina more than anyone else; in the 1970s she reduced the world record time for the 1500 m by more than 8 seconds and the time for the 3000 m by more than 18 seconds.

Like all other Russian middle-distance runners she matured slowly, and was 29 when she reached her

Lyudmila Bragina

peak, setting a new world record of 4 min. 06.9 sec. for the 1500 m at the Russian Championships in 1972, but at the Munich Olympics Bragina did even better. The women's 1500 m was included in the programme for the first time and she improved her own world record three times in five days: 4 min. 06.5 sec. in the heats, 4 min. 05.1 sec. in the semi-finals and 4 min. 01.4 sec. in the final, during which she covered the last two laps in 2 min. 07.4 sec.

In 1976, she concentrated on the 3000 m, an even newer event for women, and in a USA–USSR match she finished in an amazing 8 min. 27.12 sec.

TATYANA KAZANKINA (USSR)

It is largely due to her that there is now a smaller gap between men and women in this event than in any other of athletics.

In 1976 she made a tremendous improvement in performance after some fairly mediocre years. Having set a world record for the 1500 m of 3 min. 56.0 sec., she competed in the Montreal Olympic Games where she won two gold medals: in the 800 m, with a world record time of 1 min. 54.94 sec. and in the 1500 m, where

Tatyana Kazankina

she ran a tactical race to win in 4 min. 05.5 sec.

In the years that followed she combined family and athletics commitments. In 1978 she gave birth to a daughter but was able to regain her Olympic form in 1980 when, at the Moscow Games, she again won the 1500 m (in 3 min. 56.6 sec.).

One of her greatest successes took place at the Zurich Letzigrund on 13 Aug. 1980 when she ran the 1500 m in 3 min. 52.47 sec., faster than the men's record set by Paavo Nurmi in 1924. At the Helsinki World Championships in 1983, she came third in the 3000 m behind Mary Decker and Brigita Kraus.

Maricica Puica

Men (1500 m)
min.sec.
3:55.8 Abel Kiviat (USA), 1912
3:54.7 John Zander (Sweden), 1917
3:52.6 Paavo Nurmi (Finland), 1924
3:51.0 Otto Peltzer (Germany), 1926
3:49.2 Jules Ladoumegue (France), 1930
3:49.2 Luigi Beccali (Italy), 1933
3:49.0 Luigi Beccali (Italy), 1933
3:48.8 Bill Bonthron (USA), 1934
3:47.8 Jack Lovelock (New Zealand), 1936
3:47.6 Gundar Hägg (Sweden), 1941
3:45.8 Gundar Hägg (Sweden), 1942
3:45.0 Arne Andersson (Sweden), 1943
3:43.0 Gundar Hägg (Sweden), 1944
3:43.0 Lennart Strand (Sweden), 1947
3:43.0 Werner Lueg (Germany), 1952
3:42.8 Wes Santee (USA), 1954
3:41.8 John Landy (Australia), 1954
3:40.8 Sandor Iharos (Hungary), 1955
3:40.8 Laszlo Tabori (Hungary), 1955
3:40.6 Istvan Rozsavolgyi (Hungary), 1956
3:40.2 Olavi Salonen (Finland), 1957
3:40.2 Olavi Salsola (Finland), 1957
3:38.1 Stanislav Jungwirth (Czechoslovakia), 1957
3:36.0 Herb Elliott (Australia), 1958
3:35.6 Herb Elliott (Australia), 1960
3:33.1 Jim Ryun (USA), 1967
3:32.2 Filbert Bayi (Tanzania), 1974
3:32.12 Sebastian Coe (GB), 1979
3:32.09 Steve Ovett (GB), 1980
3:31.36 Steve Ovett (GB), 1980
3:31.24 Sydney Maree (USA), 1983
3:30.77 Steve Ovett (GB), 1983
3:29.67 Steve Cram (GB), 1985

Women (1500 m)
4:17.3 Anne Smith (GB), 1967
4:15.6 Maria Gommers (The Netherlands), 1967
4:12.4 Paola Pigni (Italy), 1969
4:10.7 Jaroslava Jehlickova (Czechoslovakia), 1969
4:09.6 Karen Burneleit (E. Germany), 1971
4:06.9 Lyudmila Bragina (USSR), 1972
4:06.5 Lyudmila Bragina (USSR), 1972
4:05.1 Lyudmila Bragina (USSR), 1972
4:01.4 Lyudmila Bragina (USSR), 1972
3:56.0 Tatyana Kazankina (USSR), 1976
3:55.0 Tatyana Kazankina (USSR), 1980
3:52.47 Tatyana Kazankina (USSR), 1980

Steve Ovett (GB) − *See the 800 m.*
Sebastian Coe (GB) − *See the 800 m.*

Men (Mile)
min.sec.
4:14.4 John Paul Jones (USA), 1913
4:12.6 Norman Taber (USA), 1915
4:10.4 Paavo Nurmi (Finland), 1923
4:09.2 Jules Ladoumegue (France), 1931
4:07.6 Jack Lovelock (New Zealand), 1933
4:06.8 Glenn Cunningham (USA), 1934
4:06.4 Sidney Wooderson (GB), 1937
4:06.2 Gundar Hägg (Sweden), 1942
4:06.2 Arne Andersson (Sweden), 1942
4:04.6 Gundar Hägg (Sweden), 1942
4:02.6 Arne Andersson (Sweden), 1943
4:01.6 Arne Andersson (Sweden), 1944
4:01.4 Gundar Hägg (Sweden), 1945 (actual time 4:01.3)
3:59.4 Roger Bannister (GB), 1954
3:58.0 John Landy (Australia), 1954 (actual time 3: 57.9)
3:57.2 Derek Ibbotson (GB), 1957
3:54.5 Herb Elliott (Australia), 1958
3:54.4 Peter Snell (New Zealand), 1962
3:54.1 Peter Snell (New Zealand), 1964
3:53.6 Michel Jazy (France), 1965
3:51.3 Jim Ryun (USA), 1966
3:51.1 Jim Ryun (USA), 1967
3:51.0 Filbert Bayi (Tanzania), 1975
3:49.4 John Walker (New Zealand), 1975
3:49.0 Sebastian Coe (GB), 1979
3:48.8 Steve Ovett (GB), 1980
3:48.53 Sebastian Coe (GB), 1981
3:48.4 Steve Ovett (GB), 1981
3:47.33 Sebastian Coe (GB), 1981
3:46.31 Steve Cram (GB), 1985

Women (Mile)
4:37.0 Anne Smith (GB), 1967
4:36.8 Maria Gommers (The Netherlands), 1969
4:35.3 Ellen Tittel (W. Germany), 1971
4:29.5 Paola Pigni-Cacchi (Italy), 1973
4:23.8 Natalia Marasescu (Romania), 1977
4:22.1 Natalia Marasescu (Romania), 1979
4:21.68 Mary Decker (USA), 1980
4:20.89 Liudmila Veselkova (USSR), 1981
4:17.44 Maricica Puica (Romania), 1982

5000 m
How it is run

Having dealt with the short middle-distance events, we can look at the long middle-distance races, the 5000 m and 10,000 m, otherwise known as the distance, endurance or stamina events.

A stepping-stone is provided between these two events and the 800 m and 1500 m by the 3000 m, an event run only in the women's section of the Olympics. In men's athletics, it is run in youth events and invitation meetings, and is included in the European Junior Championships, which also have a 5000 m event, for boys only. It is also held for schoolgirls of 15−16, schoolboys of 16−17 and juniors of 17−18 and 18−19.

While we intend to concentrate on the 5000 m, we must mention the 3000 m because of the strong links in junior men's athletics between this event and the longer event (not forgetting the 10,000 m), with the 3000 m being used specifically to train and prepare future specialists in longer middle-distance events. The 3000 m begins with a 200 m stretch, followed by seven complete laps of a 400 m track, while the 5000 m begins with 200 m, followed by twelve laps of the track, and the two events share the same starting line. All the unknown quantities of a group start become apparent when starting on the same line rather than with a stagger, including the danger of falling and of being elbowed or spiked. It is therefore advisable for the 5000 m runner to become adept at getting free as quickly as possible from the pack when setting off. It is easier to develop the necessary fast reflex action in a youngster, should he not have it. Especially in the 5000 m, and even more importantly in the 10,000 m, it is best to avoid running the curves on the outside, along the line of the second lane, except for tactical reasons and unless it is strictly necessary − adding any extra on to the distance to be covered means giving an unnecessary advantage to the other competitors.

In the 5000 m, as in all the middle-distance events, race tactics are a compromise between a runner's ability and his objectives in the race. While striving for speed on the one hand and stamina on the other, the main aim in training should be to compensate for a runner's weaknesses by his strengths. So, in a runner who already has natural stamina for long races, it is a good idea to develop a capability to withstand variations in rhythm and changes of speed. A different training method is suggested for a runner with the opposite attributes.

Before dealing with the training, we think it will be useful to the reader if we repeat some of the advice of the Federazione Italiana di Atletica Leggera.

At the beginning. Just because a youngster exhibits the qualities necessary to do well in middle-distance endurance events, his training should not necessarily be directed at specializing in that area.

It is necessary to recognize the need to encourage the development of qualities such as muscle efficiency, lactic acid resistance and speed endurance which, if they are neglected, run the risk of being totally ignored. Experience has shown that, when training, simply running long distances, with no specific goal, does not assist the development of the lower limb muscles, for example.

Towards a second gold medal
The photograph shows the Olympic 5000 m final in Moscow in 1980: the Ethiopian, Yifter (191), is in the lead and went on to win the race, having also won the 10,000 m. Behind him are his compatriot Kedir (178), the Tanzanian Nyambui (649) and Coghlan (403) from Ireland.

When to make a choice. For a youngster who shows promise in middle-distance running, the choice of an event in which to specialize can be made, without too much danger of making a mistake, when he has reached psychological and physical maturity; this obviously occurs at different times for different individuals.

In the case of a youngster of 17–18, decisions can be made by considering to what extent the developing athlete can still attain equally satisfactory times at 1500 m and 5000 m, but it is too early to make definite decisions about whether he should concentrate on speed events or stamina events. In this case, the recommendations of the experts of the Federazione Italiana di Atletica Leggera are that the greatest possible use should be made of all the exercises generally designed for training runners. All this is conditional on a clear understanding of what must be done over the subsequent four or five years, during which more emphasis will need to be placed on the effort to specialize in the chosen event.

Objectives. We now consider the different characteristics to be developed through training, and the exercises to be undertaken to achieve this development.

In the particular age group we are discussing, 17–18 year olds, the main aims are to improve aerobic and general strength, muscular efficiency and technical expertise. This grounding will in future years assist the development of aerobic power, lactic acid resistance and speed endurance.

In order to develop aerobic endurance, two types of exercise are recommended: (a) continuous running at a constant speed; (b) continuous running at increasing speed. In the case of (a), the distance run can be from a minimum of 12 km to a maximum of 18 km. For a young runner who can manage 3000 m in 8 min. 30 sec. and 5000 m in 14 min. 30 sec., speeds of 3 min. 25 sec./km over a 12 km course and 3 min. 45 sec./km over an 18 km course are recommended. This type of exercise should be undertaken in natural surroundings (roads or cross-country) and over varied and uneven courses. Continuous running at a con-

stant speed is especially designed to accustom the young athlete's mind and body to withstand fatigue over a long period and the tendons to the difficulties of racing and to sustained effort. There is the additional advantage of learning 'economy of movement' during a race and how to lengthen stride. In the case of (b), the course distance should be between a minimum of 10 km and a maximum of 16 km at a speed of between 3 min. 50 sec./km and 3 min. 15 sec./km over 10 km, and 4 min./km and 3 min. 30 sec./km over 16 km. Continuous running at increasing speed, particularly over reduced distances, is remarkably effective in forming the link during training between general or aerobic endurance and the aerobic power mentioned above.

Some of the terms used in the training programme suggested for middle-distance endurance runners of 17–18 are explained below.

Aerobic power. This is the ability to cover all sections of the course at a constant speed, even when this distance is extensive. Aerobic power is developed through three basic types of work: continuous running at a constant speed (from 5 km to 7 km at 3 min. 10 sec./km); continuous running at increasing speed (from 5 km to 7 km, at speeds of 3 min. 25 sec./km to 2 min. 50 sec./km); continuous running with variations in speed (overall distance of 12–15 km at an average speed of 3 min. 45 sec./km, but every 3–4 min. running a section at a higher speed for 3–6 min.).

All of these running exercises are carried out after a suitable muscle warm-up. It should also be stressed that the recommendations given should not be taken as gospel, but should be interpreted sensibly with regard to the youngster concerned and to his physical condition as an athlete before each training session.

Lactic acid resistance. We have already explained in the section on short middle-distance running, that this means the ability to endure high levels of exertion, covering trial runs, with short breaks of 2–4 min. between. It means the ability to tolerate ever-increasing concentrations of lactic acid in the muscles during pro-

tracted effort, lasting over 40 sec. As workloads are increased, this ability or technique becomes progressively more linked with general or aerobic endurance (required for marathon running) and aerobic power (which is a specific requirement for middle-distance running, whether sprint or endurance).

In view of the close correlation between lactic acid resistance, aerobic power and aerobic or general endurance, highly-trained athletes often use combinations of exercises which allow all of these to be included in the course of one exercise period. For example, practice can be carried out over different distances during the course of one session. The young runner is advised not to subject himself to extreme exertion during training, as it is preferable for him to concentrate on a build-up of fixed distances.

Lactic acid resistance is developed in two ways:
1. Spaced runs over distances of 1000–2000 m, repeated to give an overall distance of 5–7 km, with breaks of between 3 and 5 min. between runs moving at a walking pace, building up to a slow run, using running speeds comparable with those suggested for aerobic power training, aimed at creating significant accumulations of lactic acid in the muscles.
2. A series of runs over distances of 300–600 m, repeated until a total distance of 3–4 km has been covered, with 2–5 min. breaks between, 8 min. intervals between each session and speeds over 300 m, 400 m, 500 m and 600 m gradually rising and, in any case, much higher than an overall racing speed.

Speed endurance. This means the ability to raise the running speed for the race-distance for as long a period as possible. The theoretical objective is the greatest speed possible over the whole course of the race, within the limits of the individual's personal best time. Speed endurance must naturally be related to each middle-distance event. Because of that, we also come across 'specific endurance'.

Training for this consists of running distances of 80–200 m, totalling a maximum of 1000/1500 m in each session, with breaks of 1–3 min. between runs.

The typical weekly training programme set out by the middle-distance section of the Federazione Italiana di Atletica Leggera as recommendations for use by runners between 17 and 18 years of age with an inclination towards endurance racing, should be used as a general checklist, to be reconciled with the demands of schoolwork, leisure activities and family life. Up to the age in question, the role of parents remains paramount, but the youngster's willingness to make sacrifices for the sake of training is also very important.

Physiology:
discovering the mitochondria

In order to perform well in a 5000 m or 10,000 m race, the muscles which are most used in the race have to be fed with a large amount of oxygen each second, and the fibres which make up those muscles have to be efficient in using this large amount. The problem of oxygen supply calls for great efficiency in a wide variety of tissues, organs and body mechanisms; utilization, however, is essentially a localized problem involving the muscles.

The oxygen which must be supplied to the muscles is only present in the blood in small quantities; the rest is in the air around, of which it makes up around a fifth by volume. From the air, oxygen goes first to the lungs, by means of external respiration. Once it has entered with the air into the pulmonary alveoli in the lungs, it then passes into the blood; the pulmonary alveoli can actually be imagined as a small balloon, whose surface is covered with blood capillaries, tiny tubes with a very small diameter and fairly thin walls, thin enough for oxygen to pass through them. In this way the oxygen is able to enter the blood and to combine with the haemoglobin, in a molecule which is contained in the red corpuscles. However, these red corpuscles are not capable of moving around on their own; they are suspended in the blood and have to be pumped round by the heart – the greater the quantity of blood being pumped around at any one time, the greater the amount of oxygen being carried from the lungs to all parts of the body. So it should always be borne in mind that when activity is increased in one part of the body (and thus the need for oxygen in that part), the body supplies it with a

quantity of blood many times greater than when it is at rest. In fact, when an athlete is running, his heart not only pumps a greater quantity of blood, but also a larger percentage of that blood reaches those muscles which are working hardest.

It is important that there should not be wastage so that, for example, too much blood should not be used up by groups of muscles which are doing little work, while only a little is being supplied to where it is most needed. It is essential that there should be optimum distribution of the blood, and there are various factors which ensure that this happens. The arteries carrying blood to those muscles most used in running dilate, while those carrying it to other muscles or organs, which do not usually function (or function minimally) during running, contract. For instance, the stomach, intestines and kidneys will all be supplied with a much reduced quantity of blood in a person running a 5000 m or 10,000 m race.

Training has the effect of causing many new blood capillaries to develop in those muscles most active at the various stages of a race, so that a network of these is created around each muscle fibre, and it is through the capillaries that the oxygen can pass out into the fibres. This is how the supply of that gas to the muscles takes place.

Utilization of the oxygen is linked to certain characteristics of the fibres and, in particular, to the presence of many organisms called mitochondria, which have been defined as the 'cell's energy generators'. In the mitochondria – due to certain enzymes working in a precise sequence – the oxygen

is combined with glucose produced from stores of glycogen to be found in the fibres. During the 5000 m and 10,000 m, there also occurs – although not to any great extent – a combining of the oxygen with fatty acids delivered to the muscles with the blood. This joining of the oxygen with glucose and fatty acids (the 'aerobic energy process') causes the manufacture of ATP, the fuel which allows the muscles to function, and to perform those movements upon which the running action depends. The fibres where production of ATP with the aerobic energy process is most active are the slow-twitch ones, in which the mitochondria are also more abundant; 5000 m and 10,000 m runners have a higher percentage of slow-twitch fibres compared with other people. In addition, their fast-twitch fibres too possess a somewhat larger quantity of mitochondria than is usual and they are therefore able to produce a great deal of ATP using the aerobic energy process. However, it is in the slow-twitch fibres that, through training, these increases in mitochondria and aerobic activity become most marked.

In the 5000 m and 10,000 m specialist, the production of 'fuel' by the other energy processes (the anaerobic lactic acid process and the anaerobic alactic acid process) is very important, especially at the end of that main part of the race, which is marked by the final sprint.

This is why so many athletes put a lot of effort during their preparations into raising their aerobic capacity in this way (to raise both the supply of oxygen to the muscles and its utilization by them) and also into improving their anaerobic performance.

WEEKLY TRAINING SCHEDULE

Typical week's training in the introductory period lasting for 6–8 weeks from October to November

Session 1

• Practice runs: from a series of 6–8 runs in the first week, rising to 10–12 in the last (for all practice runs, see explanation on p. 153.).

• Exercises to strengthen the trunk: 3–4 sets in the first week, rising to 6–8 in the last (for these exercises, see explanation on p. 153.).

• Aerobic resistance: 6–8 km in the first week, rising to 8–12 km in the last, at a constant speed.

Session 2

• Exercises to strengthen the lower limbs: 5–6 sets in the first week, rising to 6–8 in the last (for all these exercises for strengthening the lower limbs, see explanation on p. 153.).

• Aerobic resistance: from 8–10 km at increasing speed in the first week, rising to 10–16 km, still at increasing speed, in the last.

Session 3

• Exercises for strengthening the trunk: from 4–6 sets in the first week rising to 6–8 in the last.

• Practice runs: from a series of 6–8 in the first week, rising to 10–12 in the last.

• Aerobic resistance: 6–8 km in the first week, rising to 8–12 km in the last, at a constant speed.

Session 4

• Aerobic power: 4–5 km in the first week, rising to 5–7 km in the last, at a constant speed.
Note: On alternate weeks, you could also practise running over a similar distance at increasing speed.

Session 5

• Practice runs: from a series of 6–8 in the first week, rising to 10–12 in the last.

• Aerobic resistance: 10–12 km in the first week, rising to 15–18 km in the last, at a constant speed.

Session 6

• Practice runs: a series of 4–5 from the first to the last week.

• Trunk strengthening: 3–4 sets in the first week, rising to 4–5 in the last.

• Strengthening of the lower limbs: 3–4 sets in the first week, rising to 5–6 in the last.

• Aerobic resistance: 8–10 km in the first week, rising to 10–12 km in the last, at a constant speed.

Typical week's training in the basic period lasting for 8–10 weeks from December to mid-February

Session 1

• Speed endurance: 80 m run 6–7 times, with pauses of 1 min. 30 sec., in the first week, rising to 150 m run 6–7 times, with pauses of 2 min., in the last week.

• Aerobic resistance: 15–18 km from the first week to the last, run at a constant speed.

Session 2

• Practice runs: a series of 6–8 from the first week to the last.

• Trunk strengthening: 4–6 sets from the first week to the last.

• Aerobic power: 5–7 km from the first week to the last, at a constant speed.

Session 3

• Strengthening of the lower limbs: 10–12 sets from the first week to the last.

• Aerobic resistance: 10–16 km from the first week to the last, at a constant speed.

Session 4

• Practice runs: a series of 6–8 from the first week to the last.

• Trunk strengthening: 4–6 sets from the first week to the last.

• Aerobic resistance: 15–18 km from the first week to the last, at a constant speed.

Session 5

• Aerobic power: from the first week to the last, split runs for a total distance of 5–7 km (1500–1000–800–600 m, with pauses of 6 min. to 4 min.).

Session 6

• Practice runs: a series of 6–8 from the first week to the last.

• Trunk strengthening: 4–6 sets from the first week to the last.

• Aerobic resistance: 10–16 km from the first week to the last, run at increasing speed.

Typical week's training during the special period lasting for 6–8 weeks from February to March

Session 1

• Practice runs: a series of 6–8 in the first week, falling to 4–6 in the last.

• Lactic acid resistance combined with aerobic power: continuous running with variations in pace alternating with trial runs, over a total distance of 4–6 km in the first week, falling to 3–5 km in the last week.

Session 2

• Strengthening of lower limbs: 6–8 sets in the first week only.

• Aerobic resistance: 10–16 km from the first week to the last, at increasing speed.

Session 3

• Practice runs: a series of 6–8 in the first week, falling to 4–6 in the last.

• Aerobic resistance: 5–7 km from the first week to the last, at increasing speed.

Session 4

• Aerobic resistance: 10–14 km from the first week to the last, at increasing speed.

Session 5

• Speed endurance: 6 × 200 m, with pauses of 3 min., in the first week, changing to 5 × 300 m, with 4 min. pauses, by the last week.

• Aerobic resistance: 10–14 km from the first week to the last, at a constant speed.

Session 6

• Strengthening of the lower limbs: 6–8 sets in the first week only.

• Practice runs: a series of 6–8 in the first week, falling to 4–6 in the last.

• Aerobic resistance: 10–14 km from the first week to the last, at a constant speed.

Typical week's training in the advanced period lasting for 6–8 weeks from April to May

Session 1

• Practice runs: a series of 4–6 every week.

• Aerobic resistance: 10–14 km at constant speed every week.

Session 2

• Lactic acid resistance combined with aerobic power: running at varied pace alternating with trial runs over a total distance of 3–5 km every week.

Session 3

• Aerobic resistance: 12–16 km at a constant speed every week.

Session 4

• Lactic acid resistance combined with aerobic power: every week, as in session two, over a total distance of 3–5 km.

Session 5

• Work based on stretching exercises, following a long warm-up.

Athletic programme for the year

• Advisable to run 5–8 cross-country races and/or 3000 m indoor races.

• About 20 outdoor races over varying distances: 2–3 over 800 m; 4–5 over 1500 m; 6–8 over 3000 m; 4–6 over 5000 m.

◼ The stars ◼

HANNES KOLEHMAINEN (FINLAND)

He is classed as the 'First of the Finns' and the great tradition of Finnish distance runners began with him.

At the time of his first Olympic successes, at Stockholm in 1912, Finland was still a Grand Duchy of Tsarist Russia, but it was allowed to enter its own team under its own flag.

In these Olympics he won three gold medals, in the 10,000 m, the 5000 m and in cross-country running. His duel with the Frenchman Jean Bouin in the 5000 m was particularly memorable, and the two of them ended up by improving on the world record by almost half a minute, Kolehmainen coming in first in 14 min. 36.6 sec. His victory inspired the 15-year-old Paavo Nurmi to take up a career in athletics.

Kolehmainen then spent a large part of his life in the USA, where he dominated distance running for many years. In 1920, now 30, he went back to running for Finland in the Antwerp Olympics and won the marathon in a world record time of 2 hr 32 min. 35.8 sec.

PAAVO NURMI (FINLAND)

The most famous of all the Finnish champions, he marked the 1920s by dominating all distances from 1500 m to the one-hour run. In his brilliant career he won nine gold medals and three silvers in Olympic competition between 1920 and 1928 and set 20 world records.

Nurmi set the first of his world records in 1921 and the last ten years later. His best year was 1924, when he made history at the Paris Olympics by winning two gold medals (1500 m and 5000 m) in the space of an hour.

In 1925 he went on a triumphant tour of the USA, taking part in 55 races over a period of five months and winning all but two. In 1932, now 35 years old, his ambition was to finish his career with a victory in the Los Angeles Olympic marathon, but on the eve of the Games he was disqualified for 'infringing amateur rules', by claiming excessive expenses for some meetings. However, Nurmi was able to compete in his homeland as an

Paavo Nurmi dominated the middle-distance events in his day. The photograph shows him in 1928 in Berlin, where he set the world record for the one-hour run at 19.210 km.

amateur member of the national team for several more years. In 1933, he won his last Finnish title, in the 1500 m. A devotee of even pace, Nurmi used to run with a stopwatch, which he would consult from time to time. The most important of his many world records are: 3 min. 52.6 sec. (1500 m), 4 min. 10.4 sec. (mile), 5 min. 24.6 sec. (2000 m), 8 min. 20.4 sec. (3000 m), 14 min. 28.2 sec. (5000 m), 30 min. 06.1 sec. (10,000 m), 19.210 km in an hour. Also he completed the 800 m hurdles in 1 min. 56.3 sec. and the 3000 m steeplechase in 9 min. 30.8 sec.

SANDOR IHAROS (HUNGARY)

The most famous of the three great Hungarian athletes of the 1950s,

Iharos managed quantities of training which were unheard of in his time. In the twelve months between 1954 and 1955, he underwent 700 training sessions, an average of nearly two a day. The reward for such work was seen in the records he held over seven distances, both metric and imperial, from the 1500 m to the 10,000 m. His most notable results were 3 min. 40.8 sec. (1500 m), 13 min. 40.6 sec. (5000 m) and 28 min. 42.8 sec. (10,000 m). This last record bettered Zátopek's time by more than 11 sec.

However, Iharos did not have the satisfaction of any great athletics victories, perhaps because his excessive commitment right through the year meant that he was psychologically exhausted when it came to international competitions, and he managed only two sixth places in the European Games. He might perhaps have expected to do well at the Melbourne Olympics, but he was unable to compete because of the 1956 Hungarian uprising.

RON CLARKE (AUSTRALIA)

The largest producer of world records in the post-Nurmi era, he set them for all distances, both metric and imperial, including the 3 miles and the one-hour run. He achieved this in the second half of the 1960s, when competition in distance running was much stiffer than in Nurmi's time.

A tall and powerful athlete, he improved the world record for the 5000 m by more than 18 sec., taking it from 13 min. 35 sec. to 13 min. 16.6 sec.; and for the 10,000 m by nearly 39 sec., from 28 min. 18.2 sec. to 27 min. 39.4 sec. However, he was denied the satisfaction of an Olympic gold medal. In the 1964 games in Tokyo, he finished third in the 10,000 m; four years later, in Mexico City, he suffered the effects of high altitude and was well outside his normal times. Even in the Commonwealth Games, he managed only four silver medals from 1962–70.

Many years later, he was diagnosed as having a heart disorder (for which he was successfully operated on) which, according to an Australian doctor, would have made it impossible for him to withstand sudden changes in pace in a race, while not preventing him from sustaining long periods of running at a steady speed.

KIPCHOGE 'KIP' KEINO (KENYA)

Athletics first achieved prominence in Kenya in the 1950s, and the first Kenyan distance runner to distinguish himself in international competition was Nyandika Maiyoro, who was seventh in the 5000 m at the 1956 Olympic Games, and sixth over the same distance at the 1960 Games. After him came a fine crop of champions, whom the Europeans called 'high-altitude runners' because they lived mostly in mountainous areas. Among these, the ablest and most versatile was Kipchoge Keino. He had four Olympic medals to his credit: in Mexico City in 1968, a gold in the 1500 m (3 min. 34.91 sec.), beating the great Jim Ryun, and a silver in the 5000 m; in Munich in 1972, he won a gold in the 3000 m steeplechase (8 min. 23.6 sec.) and a silver in the 1500 m.

Keino was capable of running the 800 m in 1 min. 46.41 sec. and the

Kipchoge Keino followed by Vasala and Foster.

Henry Rono

10,000 m in 28 min. 06.4 sec., thus displaying an extraordinary range of ability. He held world records in the 3000 m (7 min. 39.6 sec.) and the 5000 m (13 min. 24.2 sec.). However, his best result was in the 1500 m in the 1968 Olympic Games, with an outstanding 800 m split time of 1 min. 55.3 sec.

HENRY RONO (KENYA)

Like his compatriot, Keino, he too was born in the mountainous region of Kenya at an altitude of around 2000 m. In his great year, 1978, he made the mistake of overdoing things by running 52 races in eleven months, but in the space of 80 days from 8 April to 27 June he set four world records: 13 min. 08.4 sec. in the 5000 m, 8 min. 05.4 sec. in the 3000 m steeplechase, 27 min. 22.5 sec. in the 10,000 m and 7 min. 32.1 sec. in the 3000 m. He thus became the first distance runner in history to hold world records in both hurdle and flat events at the same distance.

That tremendous season must have left its mark, for Rono never subsequently regained such tremendous form, although in 1981 he reduced the world record for the 5000 m to 13 min. 06.20 sec.

Rono achieved notable successes at the Commonwealth Games (golds in the 5000 m and steeplechase in 1978) and the African Championships, but was unable to take part in the Olympic Games in 1976 and 1980.

Lasse Viren on his way to winning the 5000 m in the 1972 Munich Olympics.

LASSE VIREN (FINLAND)

Paavo Nurmi, great as he was, never managed to win the 5000 m and 10,000 m in the same Olympic competition, but another Finn succeeded in completing this double twice.

On the first occasion, at Munich in 1972, Lasse Viren's most impressive performance was in the 10,000 m. Involved in a fall just before the halfway stage, he lost precious ground, but did not panic and gradually managed to pull back the deficit. With his long sprint finish he completed the race in a world record time of 27 min. 38.35 sec.

Four years later, in Montreal, having beaten such class athletes in the 5000 m as Dick Quax and Rod Dixon, he made the mistake of overdoing things by lining up less than 24 hours later for the first competitive marathon of his career. He had set his sights on equalling another prestigious first, held by the Czech, Emil Zátopek, the legendary winner of the 5000 m, 10,000 m and marathon at the 1952 Helsinki Games. Unfortunately, Viren came fifth, in 2 hr 13 min. 11 sec., but it was still one of the greatest feats of his career. He was dehydrated for hours afterwards and vowed never to do it again.

DAVID MOORCROFT (GB)

For many years Dave Moorcroft concentrated on the 1500 m and the mile as his main events, achieving good success in them, including a victory at the 1978 Commonwealth Games (3 min. 35.48 sec.) and a third place in the European Games the same year.

However, with the rise of Seb Coe and Steve Ovett he decided to change to the 5000 m, which he had already attempted previously. In his first year of international competition at the new distance, he was dogged by recurrent injuries and could not do himself justice (he was eliminated in the semi-final at the Olympic Games in Moscow). In 1981, however, he ran the distance in 13 min. 20.51 sec. and won an important tactical race in the final of the European Cup in Zagreb. The year 1982 was the peak of his achievement, because he established a new world record of 13 min. 00.41 sec. for the 5000 m, one of the most memorable records ever recorded, improving Henry Rono's record by almost 6 sec. In the same season he also improved his personal best for the 1500 m (3 min. 33.79 sec.) and in the mile (3 min. 49.34 sec.) and came close to a world record in the 3000 m

Dave Moorcroft

with 7 min. 32.79 sec. Finally, he ran the 800 m in 1 min. 46.64 sec.

Recently he has again been dogged by injury, and was unable to compete effectively in the final of the 5000 m at the Los Angeles Olympics in 1984.

◼ WORLD RECORDS ◼

Men
min.sec.
14:36.6 Hannes Kolehmainen (Finland) 1912
14.35.4 Paavo Nurmi (Finland) 1922
14.28.2 Paavo Nurmi (Finland) 1924
14.17.0 Lauri Lehtinen (Finland) 1932
14.08.8 Taisto Máki (Finland) 1939
13:58.2 Gundar Hägg (Sweden) 1942
13:57.2 Emil Zátopek (Czechoslovakia) 1954
13:56.6 Vladimir Kuts (USSR) 1954
13:51.6 Chris Chataway (GB) 1954
13:51.2 Vladimir Kuts (USSR) 1954
13:50.8 Sándor Iharos (Hungary) 1955
13:46.8 Vladimir Kuts (USSR) 1955
13:40.6 Sándor Iharos (Hungary) 1955
13:36.8 Gordon Pirie (GB) 1956
13:35.0 Vladimir Kuts (USSR) 1957
13:34.8 Ron Clarke (Australia) 1965
13:33.6 Ron Clarke (Australia) 1965
13:25.8 Ron Clarke (Australia) 1965
13:24.2 Kipchoge Keino (Kenya) 1965
13:16.6 Ron Clarke (Australia) 1966
13:16.4 Lasse Viren (Finland) 1972
13:13.0 Emiel Puttemans (Belgium) 1972
13:12.9 Dick Quax (New Zealand) 1977

13:08.4 Henry Rono (Kenya) 1978
13:06.20 Henry Rono (Kenya) 1981
13:00.41 Dave Moorcroft (GB) 1982
13:00.40 Said Aouita (Morocco) 1985
Women (3000 m)

8:52.8 Lyudmila Bragina (USSR) 1974
8:46.6 Grete Andersen (Norway) 1975
8:45.4 Grete Andersen-Waitz (Norway) 1976
8:27.12 Lyudmila Bragina (USSR) 1976
8:26.78 Svetlana Ulmasova (USSR) 1982
8:22.62 Tatyana Kazankina (USSR) 1984

10,000 m
How it is run

The 10,000 m, the longest of the two endurance middle-distance races, is suitable only for athletes who have been training thoroughly in every way for several years. They are physically and psychologically mature runners for whom training has developed the characteristics required for a race of this type, namely technical and muscular efficiency, 'aerobic endurance', lung capacity, lactic acid resistance and speed endurance. The importance and significance of these have already been explained in the section on the 5000 m.

Training for the 5000 m and 10,000 m is almost identical, and runners who specialize in the middle-distance endurance races are likely to do well at both distances. The same occurs with the fast middle-distance races, where there is little difference in approach between the 800 m and the 1500 m.

Specialization in endurance. The continuous effort over about half an hour which is necessary for the 10,000 m calls for an adaptation from the 5000 m. For this reason the 10,000 m does not feature in meetings for young athletes and successful competitors are physically mature runners only. Specialized training must involve a programme covering several years, taking into account the characteristics of the athlete so that they can be developed together rationally paying particular attention to improving any weak points.

Cross-country running as an aid. Cross-country running has always been one of the most important items in the long-term training of 5000 m and 10,000 m runners. Almost all the great middle-distance endurance runners have used it to help maintain their fitness at its peak.

It is an exhausting activity since it is carried out in the winter period, over muddy or frozen ground, and often in inclement weather conditions. Because of this it requires great endurance and stamina, and therefore improves the ability to tolerate the discomforts of track running.

The longest track race. The 10,000 m consists of 25 complete laps of a 400 m track. The runners start in line across the track, as in the 1500 m and 5000 m, finishing at the same place. The 5000 m and 10,000 m track races, which are approximately equivalent to 3 and 6 miles (4828.032 m and 9656.064 m respectively), have only been officially recognized as Olympic distances since the 1912 Stockholm Games.

Since the 10,000 m is only for mature specialists, there is no point in giving advice and suggestions about running technique and the tactics to be adopted. At the start provisions will have already been made for training by any good coach who, with the runner, will periodically decide on the best tactics to be employed, taking into consideration the opponents, the runner's state of training and the conditions. Instead it is more interesting to recall how some of the great runners have run the 10 km race.

How the great athletes ran it. The first athletes to have a profound effect on the history of the race were two Finns: Hannes Kolehmainen, who has been universally recognized as the pioneer of a more ordered training programme; and Paavo Nurmi. Both athletes employed a steady pace throughout the race, which was designed to tire their opponents well before the finish. As a result of their training they were able to run at a pace that few athletes of that time could match, and no other athletes have ever gained as many Olympic titles and records as they did. In the most important races Nurmi ran according to a schedule which he prepared from the best times of his opponents, often wearing a stopwatch to check their pace against the times he had anticipated in his schedule. Neither Kolehmainen nor Nurmi considered speed and changes of pace were particularly important; the steady pace at which they ran was sufficient to kill off challenges from other competitors.

After the Second World War Emil Zátopek appeared, and he was responsible for a revolutionary concept in training, based on the relationship between quantity and quality, and taken to extremes never considered before. He used the Fartlek method, in which running takes place in a natural environment and includes repeated sections run alternately fast and slow, the difference with Zátopek being that he never gave in to exhaustion. When he felt exhausted, instead of stopping, he just carried on, thus raising his threshold of tolerance. In addition he ran 60 × 400 m fast, followed by 60 × 200 m at a slow pace, a total of 36 km in one session. As a result of this training Zátopek not only excelled at the 10,000 m and the 5000 m, but was also able to win the marathon at the 1952 Olympics at Helsinki, having won the 5000 m and the 10,000 m. Zátopek trained himself to vary his pace, especially at the finish of a race.

The Russian Vladimir Kuts, whose training was as tough as that of Zátopek, made more use of variations in speed, thus destroying his opposition. These tactics won him a memorable double victory in the 5000 m and 10,000 m at the 1956 Melbourne Olympics. Another famous middle-distance endurance runner is Lasse Viren, double champion at 5000 m and 10,000 m at successive Olympic Games, in 1972 and 1976. Viren achieved his four Olympic victories using the same tactics as Kuts. He maintained a close watch on the pace from near the front, and took the lead

The great runners

These two photos show the 10,000 m finals at two Olympics, 1972 (top) and 1980 (bottom). In the top photo, the Briton Dave Bedford (274) is in the lead, but he later dropped back and Viren (228) came through to win. In the bottom photo, Miruts Yifter (191) is shown on his way to victory, with Viren (223) apparently still in contention. Also visible are the Ethiopian Kotu (179) and the German Jorg (320).

to increase or stabilize the pace to his maximum endurance, making a final burst from the bell on the last lap.

The Ethiopian Miruts Yifter, whose familiarity with high altitude helped in giving him stamina for maintaining his pace over long distances, had the ability to maintain pretty well any speed without feeling it in the final stages, setting a killing pace. Yifter, who always employed the same tactics, won the 5000 m and 10,000 m in the 1977 and 1979 World Cup competitions and the 1980 Moscow Olympics.

An example of yet another tactic in the 10,000 m is that of the Italian, Alberto Cova, who runs a defensive race until half-way through the last lap, and then puts in a devastating sprint finish.

Since it is assumed that young runners will not take part in the 10,000 m, we will give the training programme followed by Alberto Cova when he was preparing for the 1982 European Games in Athens, the 1983 Helsinki World Championships and the 1984 Olympic Games in Los Angeles.

The weekly programme is divided into four periods. The first, the introduction, involves 10 or 11 sessions during the week, some in the morning and some in the afternoon. For about three weeks Cova also undertook joint-movement exercises with a physiotherapist in order to improve muscle tone. This was repeated in the subsequent periods, but to a lesser degree.

During the second period Cova took part in cross-country races and was tested on roads over 30 km or a half-marathon (21 km), in 12 sessions weekly.

The third, specific, period (the 'speed–quantity' period) involved 13 sessions weekly, the athlete competing in races as well.

In the fourth period, also a 'speed–quantity' period, Cova took part in the first demanding races as a trial for the important meetings.

The term 'recovery' in the following refers to a speed of approximately 4 min./km.

Cova's sprint finish at the end of the 10,000 m final in the 1983 World Championships.

WEEKLY TRAINING PROGRAMME

Introductory stage, lasting for 8 weeks from November to December.

Session 1

• Morning: one hour's running at 3 min. 50 sec./km.

• Afternoon: 40 min. running at 3 min. 40 sec./km, and some sprints on grass.

Session 2

• 15 min. warming up, gymnastics; one hour's running on hilly terrain.

Session 3

• Morning: one hour's running at 3 min. 50 sec./km.

• Afternoon: 40 min. running at 3 min. 40 sec./km, then some sprints.

Session 4

• 20 min. warming up, 'aerobic power'. On alternate weeks: (a) 12 km at 3 min. 20 sec. to 3 min. 15 sec./km, recovery from 1 to 4 km, then 6 km at 3 min. 05 sec./km; (b) 10 km at 3 min. 15 sec. to 3 min. 10 sec./km, recovery from 1 to 4 km, then 5 km at 3 min. 05 sec./km; (c) 8 km at 3 min. 10 sec./km, recovery from 1 to 4 km, then 3 km at 3 min. 00 sec./km.

Session 5

• Morning: one hour's running at 3 min. 50 sec./km.

• Afternoon: 40 min. running at 3 min. 40 sec./km, then some sprints.

Session 6

• 15 min. warming up, gymnastics, one hour's running on hilly terrain.

Session 7

• One and a half hours' running.

Basic stage – lasting for 12 weeks
from January to the end of March

Session 1

- Morning: one hour's running at 3 min. 50 sec./km.

- Afternoon: one hour's running at 3 min. 40 sec./km, then some sprints.

Session 2

- Running 20 km on hilly terrain at 3 min. 30 sec. to 3 min. 20 sec./km.

Session 3

- Morning: 40 min. running.

- Afternoon: 'Aerobic power'. On alternate weeks, cross-country: (a) 5 × 2000 m in 5 min. 55 sec. to 6 min. 00 sec. per 2000 m, 400 m recovery; (b) 8 × 1200 m in 3 min. 30 sec. to 3 min. 33 sec. per 1200 m, 400 m recovery; (c) 10 × 800 m in 2 min. 18 sec. to 2 min. 20 sec. per 800 m, 400 m recovery on the track; (d) 5 × 2000 m in 5 min. 40 sec. to 5 min. 45 sec. per 2000 m, 800 m recovery; (e) 8 × 1200 m in 2 min. 14 sec. to 2 min. 15 sec. per 800 m, 400 m recovery.

Session 4

- Morning: running one hour at 3 min. 50 sec./km.

- Afternoon: one hour running at 3 min. 40 sec./km, then some sprints.

Session 5

- Morning: 14 km over hilly terrain.

- Afternoon: 40 min. running, gymnastics.

Session 6

- Morning: breathing exercises, 15 min. warming up, 6–8 km running at 3 min. 05 sec. to 3 min. 10 sec./km.

- Afternoon: first period cross-country or uphill: (a) 15–20 × 300 m, 300 m recovery; (b) 15–20 × 400 m, 400 m recovery. Second period on track: (c) 15–20 × 300 m in 47–48 sec., 100 m recovery; (d) 15–20 × 300 m, 200 m recovery.

Session 7

- Running for one-and-a-half hours.

Special stage, lasting for 8 weeks
from April to May

Session 1

- Morning: one hour's running.

- Afternoon: 40 min. running, gymnastics, some sprints.

Session 2

- Morning: one hour's running on hilly terrain.

- Afternoon: 40 min. running.

Session 3

- Morning: breathing exercises, 15 min. warming up, 5–8 km at 3 min. 00 sec. to 3 min. 10 sec./km.

- Afternoon: training over parts of the distance: (a) 3 × 3000 m in 8 min. 30 sec. to 8 min. 25 sec. per 3000 m, 1200 m recovery; (b) 5 × 2000 m in 5 min. 35 sec. to 5 min. 40 sec. per 2000 m, 800 m recovery; (c) 6 × 1500 m in 4 min. 08 sec. to 4 min. 10 sec. per 1500 m, 900 m recovery; (d) 8 × 1000 m in 2 min. 43 sec. to 2 min. 45 sec. per 1000 m, 600 m recovery; (e) 10 × 800 m in 2 min. 10 sec. to 2 min. 12 sec. per 800 m, 400 m recovery.

Session 4

- Morning: one hour's running.

- Afternoon: 40 min. running, gymnastics, some sprints.

Session 5

- 15 min. warming up, gymnastics, one hour's running over hilly terrain.

Session 6

- Morning: breathing exercises, 15 min. warming up, 10–12 km at 3 min. 15 sec. to 3 min. 20 sec./km.

- Afternoon: lactic acid endurance: (a) 15–20 × 400 m in 64–65 sec. per 400 m, 200 m recovery; (b) 15–20 × 300 m in 45–46 sec. per 300 m, 100 m recovery; (c) 15–20 × 200 m in 28–29 sec. per 200 m, 200 m recovery; varied distances as follows: (d) 1 × 3000 m in 8 min. 15 sec., 8 min. recovery, 1 × 800 m in 1 min. 58 sec., 8 min. recovery, 4 × 400 m at 58–59 sec. per 400 m, 2 min. recovery; (e) 1 × 2000 m in 5 min. 25 sec., 8 min. recovery, 1 × 600 m in 1 min. 26 sec., 8 min. recovery, 5 × 300 m in 42–43 sec. per 300 m, 1 min. 30 sec. recovery.

Session 7

- Morning: one and a half hours' running.

Finishing stage – during June and July

Session 1

- Morning: one hour's running.

- Afternoon: one and a half hours' running, gymnastics, some sprints.

Session 2

- Breathing exercises, one hour's running at 3 min. 10 sec./km.

Session 3

- Morning: Running one hour.

- Afternoon: 40 min. running, 10–15 × 100 m at 80% of maximum speed.

Session 4

- Morning: breathing exercises, running 8–10 km at 3 min. 15 sec. to 3 min. 20 sec./km.

- Afternoon: training over part of the distance and lactic acid endurance: 15 min. warming up: (a) 5 × 2000 m in 5 min. 30 sec. per 2000 m, 800 m recovery; (b) 6 × 1500 m in 4 min. 03 sec. to 4 min. 04 sec. per 1500 m, 900 m recovery; (c) 8 × 800 m in 2 min. 06 sec. to 2 min. 08 sec. per 800 m, 400 m recovery; (d) 6 × 1000 m in 2 min. 33 sec. to 2 min. 34 sec. per 1000 m, 1000 m recovery.

Session 5

- Morning: one hour's running.

- Afternoon: 40 min. running.

Session 6

- Morning: breathing exercises, 15 min. warming up, running 5–6 km at 3 min. 00 sec./km.

- Afternoon: lactic acid endurance: (a) 20–25 × 400 m in 62–63 sec. per 400 m, 200 m recovery; (b) 4 × 500 m in 1 min. 17 sec. per 500 m, 6 min. recovery; 5 × 400 m in 61 sec. per 400 m, 6 min. recovery, 5 × 300 m in 45 sec. per 300 m, 6 min. recovery, 10 × 200 m in 28 sec. per 200 m, 100 m recovery; (c) 1 × 600 m in 1 min. 26 sec., 6 min. recovery, 10 × 300 m in 43–44 sec. per 300 m, 1 min. 30 sec. recovery, 1 × 600 m in 1 min. 25 sec.; (d) training test for race finals: 1 × 3200 m in 8 min. 10 sec., 10 min. recovery, last 800 m in 2 min., 1 × 1000 m in 2 min. 33 sec., last 300 m in 41 sec.

Session 7

- 1 hr 20 min. running.

The stars

ALF SHRUBB (GB)

Alf Shrubb was the first great long-distance runner of the 20th century. Between 1903 and 1904 he set up nine world records over a wide range of distances: 2 miles in 9 min. 09.6 sec., 3 miles in 14 min. 17.6 sec., 6 miles in 29 min. 59.4 sec., 10,000 m in 31 min. 02.4 sec., 10 miles in 50 min. 40.6 sec. and 18.742 km in an hour. The last four were obtained in Glasgow on one day, 5 Nov. 1904.

During the month preceding this incredible feat he ran 286 km in training. Since he would have had ten days' rest in this period, his training would have been carried out in 20 days and was, therefore, compara-tively modern in character, consisting of long distances at a not very fast pace, such as used by Paavo Nurmi 20 years later. Shrubb's performance aroused the suspicions of the athletic authorities, who then banned him from amateur athletics. Having been disqualified Shrubb ran for several years as a professional.

VILLE RITOLA (FINLAND)

In the 1920s, Ritola was known as the 'second Nurmi', as he won eight Olympic medals during his career. He was not very popular in Finland and the rest of Europe, partly because he lived in the USA most of the time, only coming to Finland for the Olym-pic Games. Consequently he and Nurmi rarely competed against each other, the only occasions really being at the Olympics. He always did well in the Games but was beaten by Nurmi on every occasion except one, the 5000 m in Amsterdam in 1928 on their last encounter. Four years earlier in Paris Ritola won two races (the 10,000 m and the steeplechase) when Nurmi was not participating.

However, Ritola managed to set a record in the USA for the 5000 m indoors, in 14 min. 23.2 sec., better-ing Nurmi's official outdoor record. He held the world record for the 10,000 m in 1924, although only for a few months.

TAISTO MAKI (FINLAND)

He was one of the many top-class athletes who was unlucky enough to reach his peak just before the outbreak of the Second World War. On 16 June 1939 he ran the 5000 m in 14 min. 08.8 sec., having passed the three-mile mark in 13 min. 42.4 sec., both of these times being world records. A few weeks later on the same track he set up a new record of 8 min. 53.2 sec. for the two miles. He ended this highly successful season by being the first man to break the 30 min. barrier in the 10,000 m, with a time of 29 min. 52.6 sec., again in Helsinki. During this race he covered the first half in 14 min. 58.2 sec. and the second in an amazing 14 min. 54.4 sec.

EMIL ZÁTOPEK (CZECHOSLOVAKIA)

Emil Zátopek has left a lasting impression on long-distance running. Between 1948 and 1954 he was the most prominent figure in the field, creating new records at all distances between 5 km and 20 km. His early development was hindered by wartime conditions, but the turning point in his career was the visit to Czechoslovakia, at the end of 1945, of the Swede

Emil Zátopek

Arne Andersson, Gundar Hägg's great rival. Zátopek followed his theories and paid more attention to speed work and training over repeated short distances.

On his first appearance in an international event, the European Games in Oslo in 1946, Zátopek finished fifth in the 5000 m, which was won by the Englishman Sidney Wooderson, one of the few great athletes who enjoyed success both before and after the war. Two years later, at the London Olympic Games, Zátopek won the 10,000 m gold medal and the 5000 m silver medal, when he made the mistake of allowing the Belgian Reiff to get away. He reached the peak of his career at the 1952 Olympic Games in Helsinki where he won the 5000 m, 10,000 m and the marathon, a feat still unequalled today.

As far as records were concerned, however, Zátopek did not achieve his best until 1954, when he was 32. It was also the year in which he lost his supremacy. In Paris in May he broke a world record that had always eluded him, the 5000 m, in a time of 13 min. 57.2 sec. Only two days later, in Brussels he broke the 10,000 m record by dipping below 29 minutes for the first time with 28 min. 54.2 sec. The same year, at the European Games in Berne, he was defeated in the 5000 m by the up and coming Vladimir Kuts. Zátopek ran in his third Olympic Games in 1956 in Melbourne, finishing sixth in the Marathon. In addition to these achievements he was the first man to break the 20 km barrier in the one-hour race.

VLADIMIR KUTS (USSR)

Kuts emerged as the world's best in 1954, the year in which Zátopek obtained the best times of his career in the 5000 m and the 10,000 m. At the 1954 European Games in Berne, he won the 5000 m in a new world record of 13 min. 56.6 sec.

Kuts used the same tactics in all the major races in his career – tiring his opponents by his consistently fast pace and occasionally putting in a burst of speed. On two occasions in the 5000 m, when running against the Englishman Christopher Chataway in London in 1954, and against Gordon Pirie at Bergen in 1956, this tactic failed and he was beaten by a narrow

Vladimir Kuts

margin. However, in the two most important races, the finals of the 5000 m and the 10,000 m at the 1956 Olympics at Melbourne, he managed to win gold medals.

His finest achievement took place at the Olympic Stadium in Rome in 1957, where he took the 5000 m world record for the fourth time in 13 min. 35 sec., much of the time out on his own. He had held the world record for the 10,000 m since the previous year with a time of 28 min. 30.4 sec.

DAVE BEDFORD (GB)

Dave Bedford was an athlete who won very few international championships, but who nevertheless formed an important part of the period between the end of the 1960s and the beginning of the 1970s because of his spirit and extraordinarily strenuous training.

When training during the winter of 1971–1972 for the Olympic Games in Munich, Bedford managed as much as 200 miles (more than 300 km) in training each week. He divided his programme into three sessions: a short one first thing in the morning, a much longer session about mid-day and a short one in the evening. This training schedule led to his condition being envied, but he had weakened his tendons and medical treatment failed to effect a cure. In spite of his gifts, Bedford could not win important races: he only came sixth in the 10,000 m at the 1971 European Games and at the 1972 Olympic Games. His best achievement was a world record for the 10,000 m, set at the 1973 AAA Championships in London, when he covered the first 5000 m in an amazing 13 min. 39.4 sec. and survived to cover the second half in 13 min. 51.4 sec., giving a time of 27 min. 30.80 sec., breaking the record set by Lasse Viren in Munich in 1972 by almost 8 sec. His bold 'front running' contributed to raising the standard of long-distance running.

MIRUTS YIFTER (ETHIOPIA)

There is some doubt about the exact age of this Ethiopian, a small solidly built man who has created a name for himself in long-distance running by winning three doubles at prestige meetings – the 5000 m and the 10,000 m in the 1977 and 1979 World Cup competitions and the 1980 Moscow Olympic Games.

It is known that Yifter has spent most of life at an altitude of around 2000 m. He appeared on the international scene between 1970 and 1971 when he was at least 25, but first became known as much for his blunders as for his victories. In a USA–Africa athletics match in 1971 he went on a long sprint on what he thought was the last lap of the 5000 m, when in fact it was the penultimate one, an error which handed victory to Steve Prefontaine. The following year, at the Munich Olympic Games, he began well, winning the bronze medal in the 10,000 m (in 27 min. 40.96 sec.), which was won by Viren, then missed his heat of the 5000 m because he had supposedly been delayed by a call of nature.

After the African boycott of the 1976 Games, it seemed that Yifter's career would end, but in the 1980 Moscow Games he finally reaped the reward for his hard work by winning first the 10,000 m (in 27 min. 42.69 sec.) then the 5000 m (in 13 min. 20.91 sec.). In both races he demonstrated his trade mark – a deadly kick about 250 m out, and a sprint finish.

ALBERTO COVA (ITALY)

Despite being only 22nd on the all-time list of 10,000 m times, Cova has emerged as one of the great distance athletes of the 1980s, having won this race at the European Championships in 1982, the World Championships in 1983 and the Los Angeles Olympics in 1984. Perhaps his most spectacular victory has been at the 1984 Olympics, where he was involved in a tremendously exciting second half of the race with Martti Vainio of Finland. Vainio, despite having a good sprint finish himself, was well aware of Cova's devastating kick and tried to open up a gap between himself and the Italian. However, although he was 90 m in front of the pack after 9000 m, he could not lose Cova, and the Italian sped past on the final bend to win by 20 m in 27 min. 47.54 sec. The most impressive figure was the time for the second 5000 m, which Cova completed in an astonishing 13 min. 26.98 sec.; this is nearly 2 sec. faster than Eamonn Coghlan's winning time for the 5000 m in the 1983 World Championships.

Lasse Viren (Finland) – *See the 5000 m.*

Fernando Mamede, who struggles in all-out competition but is 10,000 m world record holder.

◼ WORLD RECORDS ◼

min.sec.

30:58.8 Jean Bouin (France), 1911
30:40.2 Paavo Nurmi (Finland), 1921
30:35.4 Ville Ritola (Finland), 1924
30:23.2 Ville Ritola (Finland), 1924
30:06.2 Paavo Nurmi (Finland), 1924
30:05.6 Ilmari Salminen (Finland), 1937
30:02.0 Taisto Maki (Finland), 1938
29:52.6 Taisto Maki (Finland), 1939
29:35.4 Viljo Heino (Finland), 1944
29:28.4 Emil Zátopek (Czechoslovakia), 1949
29:27.2 Viljo Heino (Finland), 1949
29:21.2 Emil Zátopek (Czechoslovakia), 1949
29:02.6 Emil Zátopek (Czechoslovakia), 1950
29:01.6 Emil Zátopek (Czechoslovakia), 1953
28:54.2 Emil Zátopek (Czechoslovakia), 1954
28:42.8 Sandor Iharos (Hungary), 1956
28:30.4 Vladimir Kuts (USSR), 1956
28:18.8 Pyotr Bolotnikov (USSR), 1960
28:18.2 Pyotr Bolotnikov (USSR), 1962
28:15.6 Ron Clarke (Australia), 1963
27:39.4 Ron Clarke (Australia), 1965
27:38.4 Lasse Viren (Finland), 1972
27:30.8 Dave Bedford (GB), 1973
27:30.5 Samson Kimobwa (Kenya), 1977
27:22.4 Henry Rono (Kenya), 1978
27:13.81 Fernando Mamede (Portugal), 1984

100m/110m hurdles

Technique

Hurdling has its origins in Great Britain in the 19th century. Sports pages of the time give little information on the subject, but it is believed that the first races over hurdles took place around the mid-19th century at the famous English school Eton, near London.

THE DISTANCES

Originally, distances were measured in yards and the races were classified as follows: 120 yards, 220 yards, 440 yards, with ten hurdles for each distance, a rule which has remained unchanged up to the present time. With the conversion of the distances into metres, the races became 110 m, 200 m, 400 m hurdles.

THE HURDLES

The height of the hurdles was fixed as follows: 'high' hurdles 3 ft 6 in. high (106.7 cm), 'intermediate' hurdles 3 ft high (91.4 cm) and 'low' hurdles 2 ft 6 in. high (76.2 cm). The 200 m hurdles was included only in the Olympics of 1900 and 1904, but was then replaced by the 400 m hurdles.

FIXED HURDLES

Initially, barriers were fixed firmly to the ground, so the athlete had to avoid hitting the barrier. This resulted in an exceedingly clumsy technique. The athletes were forced to slow down at each hurdle to take a leap upwards, keeping the leading leg completely bent and the torso nearly straight.

Towards the end of the 19th century, British and American trainers tried out new methods for eliminating the discomfort of the fixed hurdles. They thought of stretching a rope across the track at the desired height, so that the obstacle to be cleared was the same for everybody. They also studied the possibility of adopting a horizontal bar, finally deciding on movable wooden hurdles similar to those of today, in the shape of an upside-down T.

PENALTIES

The introduction of light movable wooden barriers standardized the race and, to avoid abuse in knocking over the hurdles, the time of an athlete knocking over two of the ten barriers was not ratified; if three barriers were knocked over the athlete was disqualified. These days, with weights at the base of the hurdles, these rules have been abolished; knocking over a hurdle only means losing time, because the athlete is thrown off balance by the resistance from the barrier at the moment of impact. International rules stipulate that the hurdles must be constructed so that, to knock them over, a force of at least 3.6 kg has to be applied to the centre of the upper edge of the horizontal bar.

WOMEN

Women first took part in hurdles races during the 1920s. Races of 120 yards were run in Great Britain, and then, when women were admitted to the Olympics in the 1928 Games, the 80 m hurdles was introduced, a distance which continued until 1968 when it was replaced by the 100 m hurdles over barriers 84 cm high.

How to run between hurdles. Because both the 100 m and 110 m hurdles demand high speed, the athlete has only to adopt the techniques of sprinting, and move forward with his hips raised in order to enable him to attack the barrier better. Also when racing, the athlete leans forward more than a sprinter would, in order to aid dynamism at the moment of attacking and clearing the hurdle.

The first eight steps. From the start to the first hurdle, the athlete must travel 13.72 m in the 110 m and 13 m in the 100 m women's hurdles, and has to assume the correct sprinting position in the first strides after the start. To prevent the athlete from 'rising' after only the first five strides and from not getting into the correct running position as soon as possible, various methods can be tried out, even in taking up the 'set' position on the starting blocks, which lead to an optimal start to this crucial part of the race. Clearly the runner will not reach his top speed, but will try to check himself in order to make a good start to clearing the first hurdle. Athletes normally cover the distance to the first hurdle in eight strides.

The 'leading' leg. The first, or 'leading', leg is the one which clears the hurdle first. The leading action of the first leg towards the hurdle always begins thigh–knee, never leg–foot. By attacking with the thigh–knee, the athlete 'penetrates' in the direction of the race; by attacking with the leg–foot, there is an inevitable tendency to rise, as in jumping. The attack by the leading leg is prepared with high elevation of the thigh–knee, thrusting forward.

The knee directs the entire action forward from the pelvis towards the hurdle, and this position facilitates the drive of the foot towards the ground.

The leading leg has a fast action in the direction of the race; on attacking the hurdle the knee is slightly bent, and the foot is pointed forwards. The moment the foot clears the hurdle, drive carrying the foot towards the ground begins, 'seeking' a firm foothold in order to be able to kick off and resume running.

This action is defined as 'in balance' because it effectively imitates the swing of a pair of scales, with the pelvis acting as the pivot. The athlete lands fairly close to the hurdle, between 1.05 m and 1.15 m from it. The leading leg is not allowed to travel very far forward; instead thrusting the line of the hips forward is favoured. It is extremely important to avoid slowing down so that, on landing, the foot is not forward of the line of centre of gravity, opposing the drive forward of the pelvis. If the

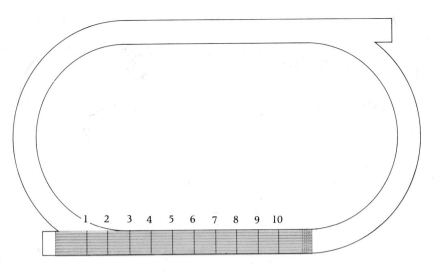

pelvis is thrust forward correctly the foot, on touching the ground, gives the impression of going backwards.

The faster the drive of the pelvis on the foot which is landing, the quicker running is resumed.

Landing. The leading foot makes contact with the ground with the outer front part, while the leg is fully extended; then the whole of the metatarsus touches the track, seeking a better foothold, while the heel descends in order to form a lever which helps thrust and is required in order to take the first stride.

The effort of leverage for this thrust is taken almost completely by the ankle; the knee does not have time to form a spring, permitting it to bring into play the greatest leverage by the knee–thigh.

Spring at the knee would bring about a 'lowering' of the line of the hips, impairing the correct line of running. The leading leg serves as a support with a spring at the base; a support which 'transports' forward the pelvis and the trunk which are, at the moment of landing, perfectly aligned with the 'fulcrum'.

The task of the leading leg is therefore to 'resist' the load which it receives, without giving way, conveying the pelvis forward to assist the inertia of the hips after clearing the hurdle.

The second 'trailing' leg. The trailing leg, generally the right one, is the one which allows, with its powerful thrust, clearance of the hurdle in a beneficial way, and the time taken to clear the hurdle depends on its drive.

Clearing the hurdle
When the athlete approaches the hurdle he must think of it as part of the running action and not as a high-jump. He will leave the ground approximately 2.20 m (7 ft 3 in.) before the hurdle and touch down again about 1.1 m (3 ft 7 in.) after it.

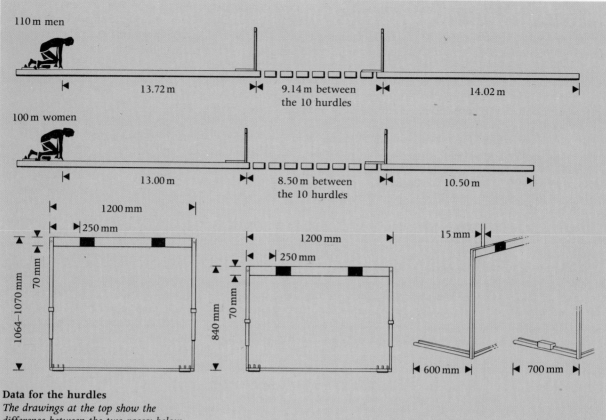

110 m men

13.72 m

9.14 m between
the 10 hurdles

14.02 m

100 m women

13.00 m

8.50 m between
the 10 hurdles

10.50 m

1200 mm

250 mm

70 mm

1064–1070 mm

1200 mm

250 mm

70 mm

840 mm

15 mm

600 mm

700 mm

Data for the hurdles

*The drawings at the top show the
difference between the two races; below
these are the hurdles. Those in the 110 m
are 106.7 cm high and 120 cm wide; the
central bar is made from wood and is
7 cm deep. The hurdles in the 100 m
women's race are 84 cm high, while the
other measurements remain unchanged.
The base of the hurdle is weighted so that
a force of at least 3.6 kg must be applied
with momentum in order to knock it over.*

	Race	Height of the hurdles	Distance from start to the first hurdle	Distance between hurdles	Distance from the last hurdle to the finish line
Men	110 m	106.7 cm	13.72 m	9.14 m	14.02 m
Women	100 m	84.0 cm	13.00 m	8.50 m	10.50 m

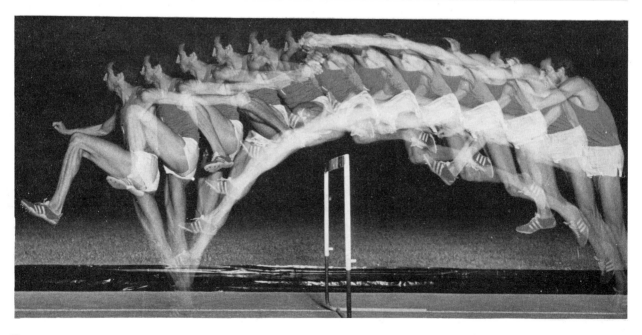

This is one of the most important factors in that correct drive by the 'trailing' leg makes it possible to control deceleration on clearing the hurdle. However, many beginners do not consider the importance of this factor and end up forming running habits which do not permit them to achieve their top speed. An incorrect take-off not only affects the flight over the hurdle, but also subsequent resumption of running on the flat.

Many athletes mistakenly overwork the leading leg, but it should be remembered that movement forward of the centre of gravity is the result of drive from behind, not traction.

We see how the leg comes into play as soon as the drive for the ground has finished. The foot is drawn towards the upper part of the gluteus and, together with the knee, performs a semi-circular movement out and up. When the knee is fully extended and the thigh is parallel to the hurdle, the entire bent limb must be parallel to the ground at all points, to make the hips move forward, following the trajectory of running on the flat as closely as possible. Then the trailing leg will start to clear the hurdle with the front of the thigh, moving forward and up, and this will be completed when the foot of the leading leg has touched the ground and the drive has finished. At this moment the leg will begin to stretch downwards seeking contact with the ground, in order to continue the running action.

The trunk and the arms. The action of the trunk at the time of clearing the hurdle is different in the 110 m men's hurdles and the 100 m women's hurdles. In the first case the trunk leans forward considerably, while the opposite arm to the leading leg is thrown forward to balance the action of the leg. In the 100 m hurdles the position of the trunk does not alter much with respect to the position it assumes during running, and may be 'leaned' forward slightly when the trailing leg has finished its drive.

During flight over the hurdle the opposite arm to the leading leg, while bent, will be held out and back, until it returns to its position for running when the athlete is again in contact with the ground. The other arm swings in a similar manner to that during normal running, except for the elbow which is held distinctly outwards during attack of the hurdle. In order to facilitate the correct direction of drive when attacking the hurdle, the athlete's chest must face in the direction of running, with the chest square on.

It is very important for the line of the pelvis always to be facing in the direction of running.

The hip on the same side as the leg which kicks last must not remain back because then the thrust would be incomplete and would compel the athlete to resort to a 'pulling' action, which is always damaging to speed and fluency.

Rhythm. A basic element of a hurdles race is the rhythm which the athlete has to achieve in order to perform this discipline correctly.

LENGTH OF FLIGHT
100 m hurdles
distance of attack: 1.90 m approx.
landing distance: 0.90 m approx.
length of flight over hurdle: 2.80 m approx.
distance between hurdles: 8.50 m
$(8.50 - 2.80 = 5.70$ m$)$
distance which the athlete actually runs: 5.70 m approx.

110 m hurdles
distance of attack: 2.20 m approx.
landing distance: 1.10 m approx.
length of flight over hurdle: 3.30 m approx.
distance between hurdles: 9.14 m
$(9.14 - 3.30 = 5.84$ m$)$
distance which the athlete actually runs: 5.84 m approx.

STRIDE LENGTH
100 m hurdles
1st stride: 1.60 m approx.
2nd stride: 2.15 m approx.
3rd stride: 1.95 m approx.

110 m hurdles
1st stride: 1.60 m approx.
2nd stride: 2.20 m approx.
3rd stride: 2.05 m approx.

INCORRECT CLEARANCE
The drawings show the correct way to clear a hurdle (a) and the incorrect way (b). As the first drawing clearly shows, the second leg (trailing leg, which is clearing the hurdle while the first is already nearly in contact with the ground) passes over the bar. In drawing (b), however, the foot passes over the side of the hurdle, which is against the rules. This occurrence is rare in the 100 m and 110 m hurdles; in order to make use of it, the athlete must be in the outside lane if he leads with his right leg, or in the inside lane if he leads with his left leg, because the hurdles are all side by side. However, it occurs more frequently in the 400 m hurdles.

In the 100 m and 110 m hurdles, it is essential to remember how important exercises are, especially learning the technique for clearing the hurdles. Here Edwin Moses demonstrates the basic exercises. Rhythm is one of the essential factors which make a good hurdler. It must be attended to right from the start, because mistakes made in the basic learning stage risk becoming long term and therefore difficult to eradicate. The technical action of the second leg, the trailing leg, is fundamental, because it permits rapid clearance of the hurdle, and attention must be concentrated on this detail since the entire race is affected by correct performance of this stage.

For training, we recommend a typical week of preparation for teenagers of 16–17 years, because this represents the basis for subsequent stages.

■ Training ■

OUTLINE OF WEEKLY TRAINING
Exercises for learning and perfecting the hurdling technique of runners in the 110 m and 100 m hurdles are divided into three groups:

basic technical exercises
rhythm exercises
rhythmic racing exercises

Basic technical exercises
Basic technical exercises make it possible to learn and perfect clearing hurdles, regardless of the number of strides used to 'attack' the hurdle. These comprise:
• lateral exercising of the leading leg
• lateral exercising of the trailing leg
• exercises for central hurdling.

The number of barriers cleared must be between 6 and 8 and the number of tests in each exercise must be sufficient to ensure effective tuition. The distance between the hurdles varies depending on the height of the hurdles, the capacity of the hurdler and their sex, and ranges from 3 m to 3.50 m permitting one stride between the hurdles.

Technique–dynamism requirements of exercising
(a) Exercise of the leading leg
The hurdle must be approached with the pelvis raised, driven by the leg used as a pivot, co-ordinated with flexing of the thigh of the leading leg forwards and up (therefore the foot must be under the knee).
The trailing leg, after the thrust, will move forward with the knee bent and fairly low with the heel at the gluteus, in order to prevent the pelvis from staying back.

During the attack, the arm opposite the leading leg is extended forward, towards the knee, while the other arm is bent backwards slightly.

It is emphasized that during the attack the feet must pivot with the metatarsus outside of the foot, with the ankle greatly stressed.

As the athlete becomes acquainted with the action, the overall dynamism of execution must increase.

(b) Exercise of the trailing leg
The hurdle must be approached with a rapid powerful drive of the trailing leg, less flexed than the leading one. Consequently, the trailing leg is flexed outwards, guided by the opening out of the foot–knee and carried forward, bent, with the knee raised high, to complete the 'rotation'.

Without disruption of continuity, it continues the drive downwards in anticipation of the next powerful drive.

Rhythmic continuity can thus be paraphrased as: short thrust time, long rotation time for clearance, short subsequent drive downwards.

The upper limbs are held almost in line in the first exercise, with variation of the position of the arm opposite the trailing leg, which flexes back slightly away from the trunk, to balance the 'eccentric' mass of the opposite leg.

The powerful drive of the trailing leg after clearing the hurdle is made to prepare for clearance of the following hurdles.

It is emphasized that flexing of the free leg (which passes outwards), even though less marked than in the previous exercise, must be such as to carry the corresponding hip in the same line as the other, driven by the movement of the trailing leg.

Also in this exercise, the feet are highly tensed, and the overall dynamism of the action increases with the improved ability of the athlete. Complete co-ordination of the arm and leg as a result of training must never be forgotten.

(c) Exercise for central clearance
This is carried out with the same distances and the same number of hurdles, and brings together the two foregoing technical exercises in a single more complete one.

Care must be taken for the trunk not to flatten forward towards the leading leg, preventing it from flexing greatly, and bending as a result of hurling the leading leg towards the trunk.

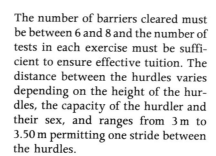

Height of the hurdles

Depending on the stage of preparation, the ability of the athletes and their sex, the height of the hurdles may vary from 76 cm to 1 m for men and up to 84 cm for women.

Organization of the training cycle

The range of basic technical exercises is performed a great deal in the first part of the preparatory period, and is almost the only technical training at this time. The amount of exercise is then gradually reduced, although without ceasing altogether, in the subsequent stages of preparation.

RHYTHM EXERCISES

Rhythm exercises are those which make it possible to define precisely and combine the technique for clearing the hurdle and the technique of rhythmic running between the hurdles.

Therefore these provide for tests with the stipulated number of strides (four steps) over shorter distances and with the barriers at heights lower than or equal to those applicable to races.

When both the distance and the height of the hurdles correspond to racing conditions, rhythmic racing exercise will be discussed.

The distances between the barriers may vary from 6 m to 8.50 m for women, and 7 m to 9.14 m for men.

The height of the hurdles is always between 76 cm and 84 cm for women and 91 cm and 106 cm for men.

Naturally, for the group of exercises (rhythmic ones), race heights and distances are never combined. The number of hurdles may vary from a minimum of 6 to a maximum of 12.

Requirements

It is taken for granted that the technique for clearing the barrier is controlled, in order to produce the most beneficial patterns, but attention should be paid particularly to a rhythmic stride pattern and the technique for developing this.

The rhythmic pattern which the athlete and trainer must strive for, particularly as the distances get longer and the barriers are raised, may be outlined as follows:

tan ___ tan ___ tan ___ tan

with the sound 'tan' beating out the steps while the lines represent the various times when these occur (and not the distance travelled with each stride).

Therefore the steps take place with an accelerated rhythm. The most common error of rhythm is as follows:

tan ___ tan _____ tan ___ tan

with a much longer time in the middle phase of the four steps.

A useful method for correcting any incorrect rhythmic performance is to ask the athlete to bend the knee of the second leg, his heel to his gluteus, immediately after touching the ground, and then during the next drive and 'flight'.

Another practical method relates to carrying out the rhythmic exercises over shorter distances than during racing (6 m for women, 7 m for men).

In order to permit rapid strides, in view of the short distance, the athlete must develop 'skip'-type running, that is, bringing his knees up high. Preparatory to this, a running exercise between 30–40 cm high hurdles (about 10–12) approximately 2 m apart must be considered.

Many combinations of the various distances and heights are possible. As preparation progresses, both aspects must be increased in order to comply with competition conditions in the exercise cycle before the racing period, thus becoming 'rhythmic racing exercises'. In fact, before this competition period begins, the rhythmic exercises must be eliminated almost completely, and only be resumed when necessary.

RHYTHMIC RACING EXERCISES

Rhythmic racing exercises are performed using the starting blocks, with and without the starter, so that the athlete learns to develop acceleration which must, with eight steps, achieve the requirements of: (a) developing increasing speed; (b) running in the best position for attacking the first hurdle.

They must be performed using a number of barriers which may vary from 1 up to 11–12.

Exercises for training and improving acceleration and suppleness.

(1) Squats (by folding the legs and rising with weights) with a load of 60–100% of the body weight.

(2) Squat jumps (by folding the legs and jumping) with a load of 20–25% of the body weight.

(3) A series of springs on the balls of the feet, with a load of 50–60% of the body weight.

(4) Walking with legs apart, with a load of 40–60% of the body weight.

(5) Stretches on the balls of the feet from a sitting position, with a load of 60–100% of the body weight.

(6) Kicking jogging with ankle weights of 1.2–1.5 kg.

(7) Swinging the legs up from a prostrate position (with ankle weights).

(8) Flexing the leg on the thigh from a prostrate position (with legs bowed).

(9) Flexing of the thigh on the pelvis (with 5–6 kg shoes or weights).

(10) Springy jumps with both feet together, with or without hurdles.

(11) Springy trot with the foot touching the ground ball–heel–ball.

(12) Leaping upwards.

(13) Long leaps forwards.

(14) Trotting with springy bounces of the foot up and back.

(15) As for 14, progressing into a run.

(16) Progression from alternating leaps forward into a run.

(17) Bouncing run.

(18) Skip (fast running with knees brought up high) on the spot.

(19) Progression from running backwards (2–3 strides) to running forward at speed.

(20) Short leaps forwards.

(21) Long skips forward.

(22) Progression from skipping on the spot to a long skip, to running.

(23) Running up a slope.

(24) Running pulling a load.

(25) Acceleration exercises from a standing start and from the blocks.

Note:
6–10 of the above exercises may be selected to be carried out at any one time, constituting a set to be used during the first part of the training session.
   Here are some combinations:

(a) 1, 3, 18, 21, 20, 13, 25.

(b) 2, 5, 8, 12, 16, 22.

(c) 11, 19, 18, 22, 16, 24.

(d) 10, 11, 21, 16, 14, 15.

(e) 7, 8, 9, 12, 20, 17, 14, 15.

WEEKLY TRAINING SCHEDULE

A typical week in the introductory exercise cycle for hurdlers of 16–17 years of age (duration 90 days)

Session 1

• Basic technical exercises.

• Rhythmic exercises.

• Leaps: 3 leap-frogs, 4 successive sets of five, 3 alternating sets of ten, 3 × 50 m alternating leaps (alternating meaning alternate feet).

• Repetition runs: distances between 400 m and 1000 m, over a total of approx. 3000 m. E.g.: 5 × 600 m, 4–5 min. rest between each, or 1000 m/800 m/600 m/600 m with breaks of 7, 6, 5 min. respectively; not at great speed.

Session 2

• Basic technical exercises.

• Running technique, acceleration and suppleness.

• Cross-country: 3000–4000 m at constant speed, not very fast.

Session 3

• Repetition runs on a slope, gradient of 18%: distances 30 m and 50 m, maximum 500 m; 2 min. rest between runs over 30 m and 3 min. between runs over 50 m; break between sets of exercises of 10 min.

Session 4

• Basic technical exercises.

• Leaps: 6 successive sets of three, 4 alternating sets of three, 2 alternating sets of five, 1–2 × 50 m with alternating leaps.

• Repetition runs: distances from 400 m to 1000 m over a maximum total of 3000 m. E.g.: 800 m/800 m/800 m/800 m/600 m with breaks of 7, 6, 6 min.; not very fast.

Session 5

• Running technique, acceleration and suppleness.

• Repetition runs up a slope, gradient of 18%: distances 30 m and 50 m over a maximum of 500 m; 2 min. rest between 30 m runs and 3 min. between 50 m runs, with break between sets of runs of 10 min.

Session 6

• Basic technical exercises.

• Leaps: 4 alternating sets of three, 4 alternating sets of five, 4 alternating sets of ten alternating leaps.

• Cross-country: 4000–5000 m at increasing speed; medium effort.

A typical week in the basic exercise cycle for hurdlers of 16–17 years of age (duration 90 days)

Session 1

- Basic and rhythmic technical exercises.

- Leaps: 3 leap-frogs, 4 successive sets of five, 2 alternating sets of ten, 2–3 × 50 m of alternating leaps.

- Resistance to speed: 2 series of 5 × 60 m, with 2–2 min. 30 sec. rest between tests, 8 min. between the series, or 2 series of 2 × 60 m with 2–2 min. 30 sec. rest between runs and 8 min. between the series, plus 2 × 80 m with pauses of 3–4 min. between runs and 10 min. between series.

- Specific resistance (relating to the race distance): 3–5 × 200 m with hurdles, with 10–12 min. rest between the tests.

Session 2

- Running technique.

- Sprinting with weights: 2 series of 4 × 30 m with weight of 10–12 kg; 3 min. rest between runs and 8 min. between series.

- Repetition runs: distance of 30–60 m, 3 min. rest between 30 m runs and 5 min. between the 60 m runs.

- Cross-country: 4000–5000 m building up speed.

Session 3

- Repetition runs up a slope, gradient of 18%: distances of 30 m and 50 m, with a maximum of approximately 500 m, with 2 min. rest between the 30 m and 3 min. between the 50 m runs, and 10 min. rest between the series.

Session 4

- Basic technical exercises.

- Leaps: 4 successive sets of three, 2 alternating sets of five, 2–3 × 50 m alternating leaps.

- Resistance to speed: 2 series of 3 × 60 m with 2–2 min. 30 sec. rest between tests and 8 min. between the series, plus 2 × 80 m with breaks of 3–4 min. between runs and 10 min. between series.

- Specific resistance (over race distance), runs repeated over distances of 200–400 m, with a maximum of 1200 m, with breaks of 12–15 min. after 400 m, 10–12 min. after 300 m, 8–10 min. after 200 m.

Session 5

- Running technique.

- Sprinting with weights: 2 series of 4 × 30 m with 10–12 kg load, with 3 min. rest between runs and 8 min. between series.

- Repetition runs: distances of 400–1000 m, with a total of 3000 m approximately. E.g.: 5 × 600 m or 1000 m/800 m/600 m/600 m with 7–5 min. rest between.

Session 6

- Basic technical exercises.

- Rhythmic exercises.

- Leaps: 3 alternating sets of three, 3 alternating sets of five and 3 alternating sets of ten.

- Resistance to speed over hurdles: 3 × 5 hurdles, plus 3 × 6 hurdles with 3–4 min. rest between tests and 10 min. between the series.

A typical week in the intensive basic exercise for hurdlers of 16–17 years of age (duration 30 days)

Session 1

• Basic technical exercises.

• Rhythmic exercises.

• Leaps: 3 leap-frogs, 4 successive sets of five, 3 alternating sets of ten, 3 × 50 m alternating leaps.

• Rhythmic racing exercises.

• Repetition runs: distances of 400–1000 m, with a total of 3000 m. E.g.: 800 m/800 m/800 m/600 m, with 5–6 min. rest between.

Session 2

• Running technique and acceleration and suppleness.

• Repetition runs: distances of 30–60 m from blocks. E.g.: 3 × 30 m plus 3 × 60 m, with 3–5 min. rest between the runs.

• Repetition runs over hurdles: 3–5 × 200 m; distance from the start to the first hurdles and between the other barriers is 18.28 m: the hurdles are 76 cm high.

Session 3

• Leaps: 4 successive sets of three, 2 alternating sets of three, 2 alternating sets of five, 2–3 × 50 m in alternating leaps.

• Series of repeats over hurdles: distances of 50–60 m. E.g.: 3 × 5 hurdles plus 3 × 6 hurdles, with 5 min. rest between runs and 10 min. between the series.

• Repetition runs: distances of 200–400 m, with a maximum of 1200 m. E.g.: 400 m/300 m/300 m/200 m with 8–15 min. rest between.

Session 4

• Sprinting with weights: 2 series of 4 × 30 m with load of 10–12 kg, with 3 min. rest between runs and 8 min. between series.

• Repetition runs: distances of 30–60 m from blocks. E.g.: 60 m/80 m/60 m with breaks of 6–8 min.

Session 5

• Leaps: 3 alternating sets of three, 3 alternating sets of five, 3 alternating sets of ten.

• Series of repeats: distance of 60–80 m, with a maximum of 600 m. E.g.: 3 × 60 m plus 3 × 80 m, with 3–5 min. rest between runs and 10 min. between series.

• Repetition runs with 76 cm high hurdles: 35 × 200 m: distance between hurdles of 18.28 m, the same as from the start to the first hurdle.

Session 6

• Running technique and acceleration and suppleness.

• Basic technical exercises.

• Rhythmic racing exercises.

• Repetition runs: 2 series of 80 m/100 m/150 m with breaks of 15–20 min.

■ The stars ■

ALVIN KRAENZLEIN (USA)
At the turn of the century this American of Austrian extraction dominated the high hurdles (120 yards) and the low hurdles (220 yards), as well as being outstanding as a sprinter and a long-jumper.

He reached his peak at the 1900 Olympics in Paris, where he won four gold medals: 60 yards sprint (7.0 sec.), 110 yards hurdles (15.4 sec.) and 200 yards hurdles (25.4 sec.), and the long-jump (7.18 m).

As a specialist in the high hurdles, he began the technique of holding the leg outstretched when 'attacking' the hurdles, a style which is the only method today, but which had until then only been tried out by the Englishman Croome at Oxford during the 1880s. Kraenzlein set the record for the 120 yards hurdles at 15.2 sec. at the end of the 19th century.

FORREST TOWNS (USA)
The world record of 13.7 sec. achieved by Towns in the 110 m hurdles on 27 Aug. 1936 at Oslo cut an enormous margin for such a short distance. A few weeks earlier he became Olympic Champion in Berlin with 14.2 sec., after recording 14.1 sec. in the semi-finals.

Towns' career was a relatively short one, but in the couple of years he was at the top he achieved 14 results between 14.1 and 14.2 sec. plus the famous 13.7 sec. world record. He was also a world-class sprinter over 100 yards, with a personal best of 9.7 sec.

HARRISON DILLARD (USA)
Between 1946 and 1948 Dillard became firmly established in the USA as undisputed number one high and low hurdler, achieving 82 consecutive wins in outdoor and indoor races. However, this sequence was broken at the American Championships in 1948. A week later, in the Olympic trials in Evanston, he attempted to qualify for the 100 m sprint and 110 m hurdles. On the first day he finished third in the 100 m sprint, thus guaranteeing his ticket to the Olympics in London, but in the 110 m hurdles he hit three barriers, lost his balance and

had to drop out. He was therefore unable to defend the reputation he had gained in April of that year with a world record of 13.6 sec. over 120 yards (= 109.73 m).

In the 1948 Olympic 100 m final, he took the gold medal in 10.3 sec. in this, his second event.

Four years later, at the Helsinki Games, he made up for his previous failure to qualify, by taking the gold in the 110 m hurdles with a time of 13.7 sec.

As well as holding the world record for the 220 yards hurdles, 22.3 sec., at 19 years of age he had run the 400 yards hurdles in 53.7 sec.

LEE CALHOUN (USA)
He is the only athlete to have won the Olympic title at the 110 m hurdles twice (1956/1960). This is an extraordinary achievement over such a short distance. In his first success the margin of victory was 3/100 sec., while in his second win the margin was a mere 1/100 sec.

Calhoun had started out as a high-jumper, moving on to the hurdles in

1951. It took him five seasons to reach world class, and his peak form was in 1960 in Berne when he took the world record for the 110 m hurdles to 13.2 sec.

Although he rarely ran other events, he managed the 100 yards sprint in 9.7 sec. and the 220 yards hurdles in 22.8 sec.

ROD MILBURN (USA)
One of the great hurdles specialists, he reached world class in 1969, running the 120 yards in 13.7 sec. Fourteen years later he was still capable of 13.60 sec. in the 110 m hurdles.

His golden period, during which time he earned the nickname 'Hot Rod', stretched from 1971 to 1973. In these three years, despite strong competition, he suffered only two defeats. In 1971 he put together 28 consecutive wins and achieved the first 13 sec. dead over 120 yards. In Munich in 1972 he won the Olympic title in 13.24 sec., a new world best for the metric distance.

After 1973 he joined Mike O'Hara's professional group, but after requali-

Rod Milburn

fying as an 'amateur' when 30, he ran the 110 m hurdles in 13.40 sec. in 1980. Very tall, he is a fast sprinter and has a very fast action of the leading leg.

GUY DRUT (FRANCE)

Initially he preferred the pole vault, but then discovered his ability at the high hurdles. He first distinguished himself with fourth place in the European Games in 1969 in Athens, and at the Munich Olympics in 1972 he came second in 13.34 sec., a new European record. In 1974 he won the European title in Rome and in 1975 he established a new world record in Berlin in 13.0 sec. A few weeks before, he had set the automatically timed European record at 13.28 sec., which still stands. He crowned his career at the Montreal Olympics in 1976 by winning in 13.30 sec., beating Alejandro Casañas into second place (13.33 sec.).

RENALDO NEHEMIAH (USA)

One of the greatest talents ever in athletics, Renaldo Nehemiah had only one goal; to break the 13.0 sec. barrier in the high hurdles. In 1977, at 18 years of age, he achieved this over hurdles 3 ft 3 in. (99 cm) high, as used in American high schools, running a time of 12.9 sec. On that occasion he declared that, one day, he would repeat the feat over the hurdles used by senior hurdlers, which are 106.7 cm high. In 1979 he came very close to this when he twice bettered the world record, first with 13.16 sec. and then with 13.00 sec. In that year he also clocked a wind-assisted time of 12.91 sec. and a manually clocked time of 12.8 sec. with permissible wind assistance of 1 m/sec. He ended

that marvellous season with a win in the World Cup at Montreal.

In 1980 the US boycott of the Moscow Olympics deprived him of a gold medal, but the following year he finally achieved his goal, against his great rival, Greg Foster. With a slight headwind, he won in a time of 12.93 sec.

In 1982 he gave up athletics to play professional American football with a San Francisco team, the 'Forty-Niners'. He then tried unsuccessfully to requalify for amateur races. As well as being a hurdler, Nehemiah is also a superb sprinter, having run the 100 m in 10.24 sec., the 200 m in 20.37 sec., and the 400 m in 44.3 sec. in a leg of the relay. At 19 years of age he cleared 7.60 m in the long-jump.

KARIN BALZER (GDR)

For most of her career she ran the distance used for women, 80 m, at which she was joint holder of the world record in 1964 with 10.5 sec. The move up to the 100 m came when she was already 31 years old, and yet she was still able to improve the world record six times from 13.3 sec. in 1969 to 12.6 sec. in 1971. She competed in three Olympics, coming first in the 80 m hurdles in Tokyo, fifth over the same distance in Mexico in 1968, and third in the 100 m hurdles in 1972 when she was 34.

At the European Games she won on three occasions (1966, 1969 and 1971).

The first sub-13 sec. time
Renaldo Nehemiah, the first athlete ever to record less than 13 sec. for the 110 m hurdles. These photos demonstrate his exceptional technique in the hurdling event.

ANNELIE ERHARDT (GDR)

She began her career as a hurdler in 1967 over 80 m, but came to the fore after the 100 m distance was introduced.

For three seasons she remained in Balzer's shadow, but at the 1972 Olympics in Munich she won the 100 m hurdles title in 12.59 sec., the first official world record which was timed automatically. In 1976 an injury to her back prevented her from reaching the finals of the Montreal Olympics.

She was also a world-class 100 m sprinter, with a personal best of 11.3 sec.

Guy Drut, on the right, in the 1976 Olympic final; in the centre is Greg Foster, and the Cuban Casañas is on the left.

GRAZYNA RABSZTYN (POLAND)

Although she achieved superb results against the clock, this Polish girl came below expectations in many of the major competitions in which she took part,

She was twice holder of the world record in the 100 m hurdles, with 12.48 sec. in 1978 and 12.36 sec. two years later in Warsaw. Her technique over the hurdles, which she cleared by a hair's breadth, tended to become disjointed in races of high stress. Only this can explain her relative lack of success. At the Olympics she finished eighth in 1972, fifth in 1976 and fifth in 1980 when her times made her the favourite. However, she did have two wins in the World Cup (1977 and 1979).

■WORLD RECORDS■

Men (110 m hurdles)
sec.
15.0 Forrest Smithson (USA) 1908
14.8 Earl Thomson (Canada) 1920
14.8 Sten Petterson (Sweden) 1927
14.6 Geo. Weightman-Smith (S. Africa) 1928
14.4 Erik Wenneström (Sweden) 1929
14.4 Bengt Sjöstedt (Finland) 1931
14.4 Percy Beard (USA) 1932
14.4 Jack Keller (USA) 1932
14.4 George Saling (USA) 1932
14.4 John Morriss (USA) 1934
14.3 Percy Beard (USA) 1934
14.2 Percy Beard (USA) 1934
14.2 Al Moreau (USA) 1935
14.1 Forrest Towns (USA) 1936
13.7 Forrest Towns (USA) 1936
13.7 Fred Wolcott (USA) 1941
13.6 Dick Attlesey (USA) 1950
13.5 Dick Attlesey (USA) 1950
13.4 Jack Davis (USA) 1956
13.2 Martin Lauer (Germany) 1959
13.2 Lee Calhoun (USA) 1960
13.2 Earl McCullouch (USA) 1967
13.2 Willie Davenport (USA) 1969
13.2 Rodney Milburn (USA) 1972
13.1 Rodney Milburn (USA) 1973
13.1 Guy Drut (France) 1975
13.0 Guy Drut (France) 1975

Automatic times
13.24 Rodney Milburn (USA) 1972
13.21 Alejandro Casañas (Cuba) 1977
13.16 Renaldo Nehemiah (USA) 1979
13.00 Renaldo Nehemiah (USA) 1979
12.93 Renaldo Nehemiah (USA) 1981

Women (80 m hurdles)
11.6 Ruth Engelhard (Germany) 1934
11.6 Trebisonda Valla (Italy) 1936
11.6 Barbara Burke (S. Africa) 1937
11.6 Lisa Gelius (Germany) 1938
11.3 Claudia Testoni (Italy) 1939
11.3 Fanny Blankers-Koen (Netherlands) 1942
11.0 Fanny Blankers-Koen (Netherlands) 1948
11.0 Shirley de la Hunty (Australia) 1952
10.9 Shirley de la Hunty (Australia) 1952
10.9 Maria Golubnichaya (USSR) 1954
10.8 Galina Yermolenko (USSR) 1955
10.6 Kreszentia Gasti (Germany) 1956
10.6 Galina Bystrova (USSR) 1958
10.6 Norma Thrower (Australia) 1960
10.6 Rimma Koshelyeva (USSR) 1960
10.6 Gisela Birkemeyer (Germany) 1960
10.6 Irina Press (USSR) 1960
10.5 Gisela Birkemeyer (Germany) 1962

10.5 Betty Moore (Australia) 1962
10.5 Karin Balzer (Germany) 1964
10.5 Irina Press (USSR) 1964
10.5 Draga Stamejčić (Yugoslavia) 1964
10.5 Pamela Kilborn (Australia) 1964
10.4 Pamela Kilborn (Australia) 1965
10.4 Irina Press (USSR) 1965
10.3 Irina Press (USSR) 1965
10.3 Vera Korsakova (USSR) 1968
10.2 Vera Korsakova (USSR) 1968

Women (100 m hurdles)
13.3 Karin Balzer (GDR) 1969
13.3 Teresa Sukniewicz (Poland) 1969
13.0 Karin Balzer (GDR) 1969
12.9 Karin Balzer (GDR) 1969
12.8 Teresa Sukniewicz (Poland) 1970
12.8 Chi Cheng (Taiwan) 1970
12.7 Karin Balzer (GDR) 1970
12.7 Teresa Sukniewicz (Poland) 1970
12.6 Karin Balzer (GDR) 1971
12.5 Annelie Erhardt (GDR) 1972
12.5 Pamela Kilborn (Australia) 1972
12.3 Annelie Erhardt (GDR) 1973

Automatic times
12.59 Annelie Erhardt (GDR) 1972
12.48 Grazyna Rabsztyn (Poland) 1978
12.48 Grazyna Rabsztyn (Poland) 1979
12.36 Grazyna Rabsztyn (Poland) 1980

400 m hurdles

How it is run

The 400 m hurdles was rather ignored during the 19th century, because it was considered to be a specialist event which was extremely tiring and difficult to tackle.

Newspapers of the time first mention a race with 12 hurdles over a quarter of a mile in Oxford in 1860 at a university meeting, but the 400 m hurdles was only introduced into the official programme of English, Swedish and American championships in 1914. However, the race had previously flourished in France, the first French title being awarded in 1893.

Features

In this race a full circuit of the track is run with 10 hurdles, 91.4 cm high, placed 35 m apart. The distance from the start to the first hurdle is 45 m, while the last hurdle to the finish line measures 40 m.

In the 440 yards hurdles the distance between the hurdles was the same as in the 400 m hurdles, the final sprint being 2.34 m longer, equal to the difference between the metric and imperial distances. Even though snubbed at national level by the great athletics powers of the time, the 400 m hurdles was included in the Olympic programme as early as 1900.

Women, who began to run this distance only in the 1970s (European Cup in 1977, European Games 1978 and the Olympic programme for 1984), have to clear 10 hurdles 76.2 cm high.

Physical ability

In the 110 m hurdles it is almost essential to have long legs, because the height of the hurdles also presupposes sufficient height of the person tackling this discipline; in the 400 m hurdles, however, it is possible for shorter athletes to do well. In fact there have been many finalists in the European Championships and Olympic Games who have been no taller than 5 ft 11 in. (1.80 m).

Qualities required

An athlete attempting the 400 m hurdles who intends to achieve good results must be able to run the 400 m well, and also have sufficient strength to enable him to obtain good times over 600 m. The difference between a time achieved in a 400 m hurdles race and that recorded in a 400 m flat race must be around 2.6 sec. for an athlete of international standard, while for an average hurdler it should be around 4 sec. It is important that the running action of the athlete be flowing and balanced, following an exact rhythm, enabling him to attack the hurdles in a composed manner.

In addition, the ability to lead with either the left or the right leg is required when clearing a hurdle, because in this way the athlete may easily change his rhythm, varying his stride pattern between hurdles without 'jumping'.

The start

The athlete leaves the blocks and in the first 8–10 strides must accelerate as in a sprint race, thus settling into the pattern which provides slight acceleration again in the five strides before the hurdles, as a prelude to the 'flight' phase. The distance from the start to the first hurdle is 45 m, and the exceptional Ed Moses covers this in 20 strides.

The number of strides in the initial phase has an effect on the rhythm between hurdles; in fact, experience has led to a table being drawn up, which forecasts a successive stride pattern of 13, or at the least 12 after the first 20–21, of 14–13 after the first 22, or 16–17 after the first 23 strides to the first hurdle.

The strides

We have discussed stride pattern between hurdles. As we have seen, 20–23 strides may be taken to cover the 45 m from the start to the first hurdle. As a rough estimate, Moses, who requires only 20 strides, must cover 2.25 m with his leg extended, while athletes using 21 strides cover approximately 2.15 m.

Between the hurdles, athletes such as Moses, for example, who use 13 strides, have a stride length of 2.40–2.50 m, while for 14 strides, the length varies from 2.22 to 2.30 m, for 15 strides from 2.15 to 2.20 m, for 16 strides, from 2.10 to 2 m, and for 17 strides, from 1.85 to 1.80 m.

When there is an even number of strides between hurdles, the athlete must alternate his leading leg.

Only Ed Moses can keep the pat-

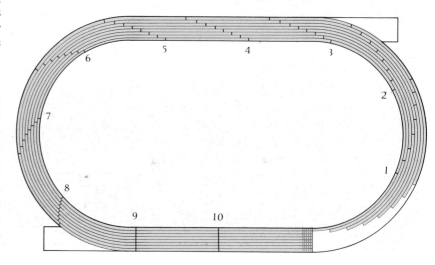

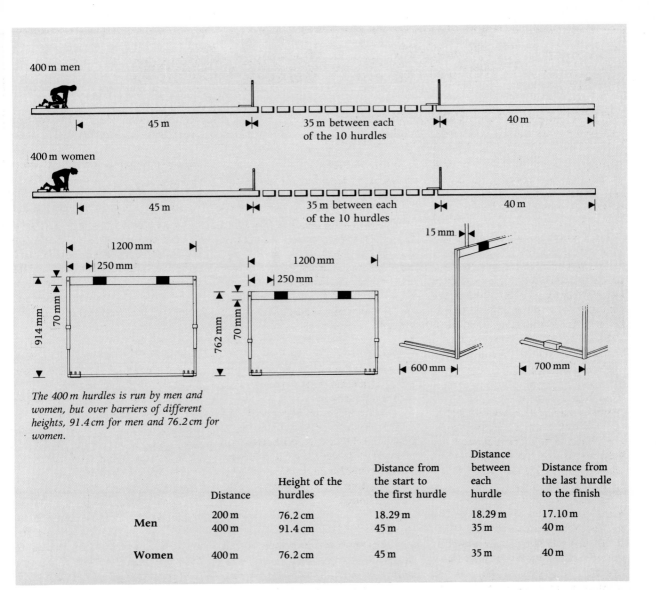

400 m men

45 m

35 m between each
of the 10 hurdles

40 m

400 m women

45 m

35 m between each
of the 10 hurdles

40 m

1200 mm

250 mm

914 mm

70 mm

1200 mm

250 mm

762 mm

70 mm

15 mm

600 mm

700 mm

*The 400 m hurdles is run by men and
women, but over barriers of different
heights, 91.4 cm for men and 76.2 cm for
women.*

	Distance	Height of the hurdles	Distance from the start to the first hurdle	Distance between each hurdle	Distance from the last hurdle to the finish
Men	200 m	76.2 cm	18.29 m	18.29 m	17.10 m
	400 m	91.4 cm	45 m	35 m	40 m
Women	400 m	76.2 cm	45 m	35 m	40 m

The stride patterns (strides between hurdles) of the greatest hurdlers

	from the start to first hurdle	between hurdles	from last hurdle to finish line	final time
Hemery	21	13 to 6th 15 from 6–10th	18	48.1
Akii-Bua	21	13 to 5th 14 from 5–9th 15 from 9–10th	18	47.82
Moses	20	13 for entire race	16	47.02

Ideal intermediate times for 400 m men hurdlers

				hurdles						final dash	final time
1	2	3	4	5	6	7	8	9	10		
5.8	9.5	13.2	17.0	20.8	24.7	28.7	32.9	37.3	41.8	5.2	47.0
5.9	9.7	13.5	17.4	21.3	25.3	29.5	33.8	38.8	42.7	5.3	48.0
6.0	9.9	13.8	17.7	21.7	25.8	30.1	34.5	39.1	43.6	5.4	49.0
6.0	10.0	14.0	18.1	22.2	26.4	30.8	35.3	39.9	33.4	5.5	50.0
6.1	10.2	14.3	18.5	22.7	27.0	31.4	35.9	40.6	45.9	5.6	51.0

Ideal intermediate times for 400 m women hurdlers

				hurdles						final dash	final time
1	2	3	4	5	6	7	8	9	10		
6.1	10.3	14.5	18.8	23.1	27.5	32.0	36.7	41.4	46.3	5.7	52.0
6.3	10.7	15.1	19.6	24.1	28.7	33.4	38.2	43.2	48.2	5.8	54.0
6.5	11.1	15.7	20.3	25.0	29.8	34.7	39.7	44.9	50.1	5.9	56.0
6.7	11.5	16.3	21.1	25.9	30.8	35.9	41.1	46.2	51.8	6.2	58.0
6.9	11.9	16.9	21.9	26.8	31.9	37.2	42.6	47.9	53.4	6.6	60.0

The fastest Olympic finals: intermediate times over ten hurdles

	1	2	3	4	5	6	7	8	9	10	Final
Mexico 1968 D. Hemery (GB)	6.1	9.8	13.6	17.5	21.5	25.4	29.6	33.9	38.3	42.8	48.12
Munich 1972 J. Akii-Bua (Uganda)	6.1	9.8	13.6	17.4	21.3	25.4	29.5	33.7	38.1	42.6	47.82
Montreal 1976 E. Moses (USA)	6.0	9.8	13.5	17.4	21.4	25.4	29.6	33.9	38.2	42.6	47.63

tern of 13 strides from the start to the finish and between the first hurdles, and it is very exhausting to maintain such a rhythm. He can even manage 12 strides for at least four hurdles.

As the table shows, world record holders before him used a different race tactic: in 1968 David Hemery ran from the first to the sixth in 13 strides, then used 15 to the finish. John Akii-Bua followed this rhythm: 13 strides to the fifth, then 14 to the ninth and 15 for the final stretch from the ninth to the tenth.

Youngsters

Those who tackle this discipline must immediately try to acquire an accurate technique for clearing the hurdle, because only in this way can they achieve good results. This is not to say that a good 400 m runner can become a good hurdler because he can run around the track; in addition to the technique for clearing the hurdles, it is essential to acquire a specific race rhythm.

It is not actually sufficient to run fast, because bad technique can lead to deceleration and a lack of fluidity of action, thus significantly affecting the final time. This explains why only rarely have good 400 m runners succeeded to the same extent in the hurdles.

Furthermore, it should be remembered that clearing the hurdles must not interrupt the running action, but should be thought of as a longer stride and not as an actual jump.

Having given the preparation for 16–17 year old hurdlers tackling the 110 m hurdles, we now give the guidelines for training drafted by the Federazione Italiana di Atletica Leggera for youngsters of 18–19 years of age applying themselves to the 400 m hurdles. The schedule also applies to athletes of a high standard, because the basis of work is the same; the difference lies in the loads which athletes of different ages can bear.

On pages 106–107 Ed Moses illustrates the basic exercises.

■ Training ■

WEEKLY TRAINING SCHEDULE
Exercises for learning and perfecting the technique of 400 m hurdlers

These are divided into three groups:
Basic technical exercises
Rhythmic exercises
Rhythmic racing exercises

Basic technical exercises make it possible to learn and perfect the technique for clearing the hurdles, regardless of the number of strides used to 'attack' the hurdle. These include: lateral exercising of the leading leg; lateral exercising of the trailing leg; exercising for central clearance of the hurdle.

The number of hurdles to clear must be between six and eight and the number of runs in each exercise must be such as to guarantee efficient learning. The distances vary with the height of the hurdle, with the ability of the person and their sex, and are between 3 m and 19 m; these distances permit a number of steps of between two and nine (respectively one stride and eight strides) to be made, so as to provide for clearance with the leading leg and the trailing leg. The height of the hurdles, depending on the stage of preparation, the ability and sex of the athlete, may vary from 76 cm to 91 cm for men and from 76 cm to 84 cm for women. This height (84 cm) can be useful in planning the possible participation of the athlete in the 100 m hurdles.

Rhythmic exercises: these make it possible to pinpoint and consolidate the technique for clearing the hurdle and the rhythm of running between the hurdles. They provide for runs over hurdles at the distances and heights applicable to races, with the number of strides used by the athlete, even if this is not carried out at racing speed, given that the athlete's conditioning and skill do not allow high speed and keeping to the number of strides to be reconciled at this point. When the athlete is able to perform at speeds very close to those applicable in competitions, exercising will obviously become more specific and similar to the racing pattern. In this case rhythmic racing exercises will be discussed.

Rhythmic racing exercises: the best time for introducing these exercises is during the race period, when the athlete naturally is in the best position to be able to perform with acceptable dynamism.

Exercises for training and improving speed and suppleness

1. By means of squats (lifting weights with the legs half bent): (a) This must be carried out fairly fast from the start of the preparatory period and therefore the weights are to be chosen accordingly and are to be proportionate to the strength and physical build of the athlete: as the exercise cycles progress, the speed of performance must be stressed more and more; this is to be as fast as possible in relation to the number of repetitions to be carried out. The times for carrying out the exercise may also be recorded, while ensuring that the extent of the movements is not less than that required.

(b) It is advisable to carry out adjustment exercises without weights, of a different type between the series of repetitions of each exercise and moving from one exercise on to the next, as will be seen later.

(c) It is advisable to include exercises systematically without any load on the spine during and at the end of the exercises with weights;
3−4 series of 4−6 repeats with a break between series of approximately 2 min.
2. By means of squat jumps (with folding of the legs and jumping) with a weight belt: see provisions made for exercise 1:
2−4 series of 4−6 repeats with a break between of approximately 2 min.
3. A series of springs on the balls of the feet:
2−4 series of 15−20 repeats with a break between series of approximately 2 min.
4. Walking with the legs in a split position:
2−4 series of 8−10 steps with a break between series of approximately 2 min.
5. Stretches on the balls of the feet from a sitting position:
2−4 series of 10−15 repeats with a break of approximately 2 min. between series.
6. Back-kicking jogging with ankle weights of 1.2−1.5 kg: this exercise develops the strength of the back muscles of the thigh, if the number of movements per leg is of the order of 80−100. Series of considerably fewer movements (e.g. 20−40) can also be used, permitting faster performance of the exercise, thus developing (in particular) speed of action:
2−4 × 30−40 m with a break between repetitions of approximately 3 min.
7. Swinging the legs up from a prostrate position:
2−3 series of 10−15 repeats with a break of approximately 3 min. between series.
8. Flexing of the leg on the thigh from a prostrate position: slow, continuous performance:
2−4 series of 10−15 repeats with a break of approximately 3 min. between series.
9. Flexing of the thigh on the pelvis:
2−4 series of 15−20 repeats with a break of approximately 3 min. between series.
10. Springy jumps with both feet together, with and without hurdles: in the first stage of preparation it is advisable to carry out the jumps emphasizing the height to reach,

regardless of the time of contact with the ground, which may be slightly longer than will be striven for in later phases of preparation, characterized by stress on bouncing in much shorter times:
3−5 series of 6−10 jumps with a break between series of approximately 1 min. 30 sec.; if using hurdles: height of 50−85 cm in the first part of the preparatory period and 30−40 cm in the cycle of exercises for the race.
11. Springy trot with the foot touching the ground ball−heel−ball: during this the legs must be held stretched at the knee so as to exploit the work of the sural triceps and the other muscles of the leg and foot:
3−5 × 40−50 m, to be included in the warm-up phase.
12. Leaps upwards on alternate legs: these are a preliminary to leaps forward. In fact, by directing the leaps upwards the problems of co-ordination are less, but above all the athlete is able to perceive and exploit better the use of the driving leg; the free leg, however, remains rather low.
3−4 series of 10−20 leaps with breaks of approximately 2 min. between series, to be included at the end of the warm-up.
13. and **20.** Leaps over 'long' and 'short' distances forward: these exercises have been included in this group because they constitute a very effective way of training and improving the capacity for speed and suppleness of the legs.
14. Trotting with springy bounces of the foot up and back: this exercise, used well, permits considerable progress in running technique. In particular, it makes it possible to perfect the 'springy use' of the feet and the resulting rise of them up and back, finished off by the back muscles of the thigh (which are contracted):
3−5 × 50 m approximately with a break of a couple of minutes between the 50 m repetitions.
15. Trotting with springy bounces of the foot up and back, progressing to running: it should be added that progression to running at speed must take place by means of increasingly powerful kicks by the feet and not 'pulling' of the free leg which, on the contrary, must be kept rather low:
2−3 × 100 m with a short break between the 100 m repetitions.

16. Progression from leaps forward on alternating legs to running: the same applies as for the preceding exercise. In addition it should be stated that the link between the two exercises (alternating leaps and running) is really a springy run:

3−4 × 50−60 m with a break between tests of approximately 2 min., to be included at the end of the warm-up.

17. Springy run: in this exercise the difficulties of co-ordination are far greater than in alternating leaps where length is the aim, in that it is necessary to bring together ef-ficiently and at the right time the action of the leg in contact with the ground and that of the free leg, without the latter being brought into play too early with respect to the leading leg, thus causing a reduction in the effectiveness of the exercise both as regards development of the back muscles of the leg and with respect to technical training. Exercise not recommended for this age group.

18. Skipping on the spot: during this the athlete must hold his hips 'high' and work his legs like pistons, enabling him to perform the exercise in a sufficiently 'bouncy' manner.

3−4 series of 50−70 kicks (25−35 per leg) with a break of approximately 2 min. between series, to be included at the end of the warm-up.

19. Progression from running backwards to running at speed forwards: see comments for exercises under 25: 3−4 × 15−20 m.

21. 'Long' skips (forward): progression from skipping on the spot to long skips must be by means of increasing thrust; however, in the event of movement forward being 'guided' by the free leg being drawn forward, the athlete will end up with his hips too low and his shoulders back, and

---

Typical week in the introductory preparatory period for hurdlers of 18−19 years (duration 60 days)

Session 1

• Repetition runs on a slope: gradient 18%, distances 50 m and 100 m, maximum: 5 × 50 m with breaks of 4 min.; 5 × 100 m with breaks of 6−8 min.; break between series of 10 min.

• Adjusting stretching and sprinting: dashes of at least 30 m at near maximum effort.

• Cross-country: 6000 m at increasing speed.

Session 2

• Leaps over short and long distances.

• Adjusting stretching and sprinting.

• Running technique and capacity for speed and suppleness (see example on page 94).

Session 3

• Leaps over short distances.

• Hurdling technique.

• Cross-country: 4000−6000 m at constant speed.

Session 4

• Repetition runs on a slope: gradient 18%, distances 50 m and 100 m, maximum: 5 × 50 m with breaks of 4 min. between the runs; 5 × 100 m with breaks of 6−8 min.; breaks between series of 10 min.

• Adjusting stretching and sprinting on the flat.

• Repetition runs on the flat: distances between 500 m and 1200 m with a maximum total of 5000 m. Examples of combinations: 1200 m/ 1000 m/800 m/600 m/500 m/500 m with breaks of 7, 6, 5, 4, 4 min. Speed is to correspond to not too high a level of effort.

Session 5

• Running technique and capacity for speed and suppleness.

• Hurdling technique.

• Cross-country: 4000−6000 m at constant speed.

Session 6

• Leaps over short and long distances.

• Adjusting stretching and sprinting.

• Running technique and capacity for speed and suppleness.

therefore with his centre of gravity behind the perpendicular to the foot in contact with the ground. In this way, rotation backwards would be created; in other words, the body would not be able to make full use of the thrust from the leg in contact with the ground:

3–4 series of 20–30 m with a break between the series of approximately 2 min., to be included at the end of the warm-up.

22. Progression from skipping on the spot to long skips to running: 2–3 × 50–60 m with a break between tests of 2–3 min.

23. Running up a slope: the same applies as for exercises 13 and 20 on p. 103.

24. Running pulling a load: the load to be pulled may be made of an inner tube filled with sand or a car tyre (with or without any additional ballast) or a small box with or without weights inside, or a weight on its own. However, the first two suggestions are preferable. The extent of the weight depends on the type of ground and the capacity and speed of the athlete, but must also be such as to bring about a deterioration of the time over 30 m of about 0.7–0.8 sec.

25. Acceleration exercises from a standing start and from the blocks: these serve as training; in particular the athlete must attend to the leaning of the trunk, the use of the driving foot in co-ordination with use of the free leg: 8–12 tests to be selected from:

starting from an upright position, feet together, with body weight forward;

starting in motion, with body out of balance;

starting on all fours, without blocks;

starting from the blocks.

Typical week in the basic preparatory period for hurdlers of 18–19 years (duration 60 days)

Session 1

• Hurdling technique.

• Rhythmic tests with hurdles: distances of 400–200 m: over 400 m the first part is run on the flat; the second with 5–6 hurdles; the 300 m tests use 8 hurdles, the 200 m tests comprise 5 hurdles; Example: 3–4 × 200 m; or 2 × 300 m, plus 2 × 200 m; or 5–6 × 200 m.

• Cross-country: 6000 m at increasing speed.

Session 2

• Leaps over short and long distances.

• Repetition runs: distances 60–80–100 m. Example: 3 series of 5 × 60 m with breaks of 1 min. 30 sec.–2 min. between tests and 8 min. between series; or 3 series of 4 × 80 m with breaks of 2–2 min. 30 sec. between tests and 8 min. between series.

• Cross-country: 4000 m at constant speed.

Session 3

• Repetition runs on a slope: gradient 18%, distances 50 m and 100 m, maximum: 5 × 50 m with breaks of 4 min.; 5 × 100 m with breaks of 6–8 min.; break between series of 10 min.

• Adjusting stretching and sprinting.

• Hurdling technique.

Session 4

• Repetition runs on the flat: distance of 60–80–100 m. Examples: 3 × 60 m with breaks of 5 min., plus 3 × 80 m with breaks of 6 min., plus 2 × 100 m with breaks of 8 min.; or 4 × 60 m with breaks of 5 min., plus 4 × 80 m with breaks of 6 min.

• Rhythmic exercises on the flat and using hurdles: distances 60–80–100 m. Examples: 3 × 60 m with breaks of 6 min., plus 2 × 100 m with breaks of 8 min.; or 4 × 60 m with breaks of 5 min., plus 4 × 80 m with breaks of 6 min.

• Rhythmic exercises on the flat and with hurdles: distances from 500 m to 200 m with breaks of 10–15 min.

Session 5

• Running technique and capacity for speed and suppleness.

• Repetition runs: distances of 500–1200 m. Example: 3 × 1000 m plus 2 × 800 m with breaks of 6 min. and 5 min. between the exercises; or 800 m/800 m/600 m/600 m/500 m/500 m with breaks of 5, 5, 4, 4, 4 min.

Session 6

• Leaps over short and long distances.

• Sets of repetitions: distances 60–80–100 m. Example: 3 series of 5 × 60 m with breaks of 1 min. 30 sec.–2 min. between exercises and 8 min. between series; or 5 × 60 m with breaks of 1 min. 30 sec.–2 min. between exercises, plus 4 × 80 m with breaks of 2–2 min. 30 sec. between exercises, plus 3 × 100 m with breaks of 3–3 min. 30 sec. between exercises.

• Sets of repetitions: distances 200–250–300 m, maximum: 1800 m. Example: 300 m/300 m/300 m/200 m/300 m/200 m; or 300 m/300 m/250 m/250 m/200 m/200 m with breaks of 5 min.

Typical week in the basic intensive period for hurdlers of 18–19 years (duration 30 days)

Session 1

- Hurdling technique.

- Rhythmic exercises with hurdles: distances from 400 m to 200 m: over 400 m the first part is run on the flat; the second part with 5–6 hurdles; the 300 m exercise used 8 hurdles; the 200 m exercise comprises 5 hurdles. Example: 3–4 × 200 m; or 2 × 300 m, plus 2 × 200 m; or 5–6 × 200 m.

- Repetition runs on the flat: distances from 500 m to 1200 m (maximum total 5000 m). Example: 1200 m/1000 m/800 m/600 m/500 m/500 m, breaks of 7, 6, 5, 4, 4 min.

Session 2

- Running technique and capacity for speed and suppleness.

- Leaps over short and long distances.

Session 3

- Sets of repetitions: distances 80–100 m. Examples: 3 series of 4 × 80 m with breaks of 3 min. between exercises and 8 min. between series; or 4 × 80 m and 4 × 100 m with breaks of 3–4 min. between exercises and 10 min. between series.

- Repetition runs on the flat: distances of 500–200 m. Examples: 3 × 500 m with breaks of 12–15 min.; or 5–6 × 300 m with breaks of 12–15 min.; or 500 m/400 m/300 m/300 m with breaks of 12–15 min.

Session 4

- Repetition runs on the flat: distances of 60–80–100 m. Examples: 2–3 × 60 m with breaks of 5 min., plus 2–3 × 80 m with breaks of 6 min., plus 1–2 × 100 m with breaks of 8 min.; or 8–10 × 60 m with breaks of 5 min.; or 5–6 × 100 m with breaks of 8 min.

- Leaps over short and long distances.

- Running technique and capacity for speed and suppleness.

Session 5

- Sets of repetitions: distances 80–100 m. Examples: 3 series of 4 × 80 m with breaks of 2–2 min. 30 sec. between exercises and 8 min. between series.

- Rhythmic exercises and repetition runs on the flat: distances of 500–200 m. Examples: 3 × 200 m with hurdles, plus 3 × 300 m with breaks of 8 min.; or 1 × 300 m with hurdles, plus 1 × 200 m with hurdles, plus 1 × 500 m.

Session 6

- Repetition runs on the flat: distances 60–80–100 m. Examples: 2–3 × 60 m, plus 2–3 × 80 m, plus 1–2 × 100 m with breaks of 6–8 min.; or 4 × 60 m, plus 4 × 80 m; or 6–7 × 80 m.

- Repetition runs: 3–4 × 150 m with breaks of 8–10 min.

- Cross-country: 3000–4000 m at increasing speed.

Typical week in the pre-race period for hurdlers of 18–19 years (duration 60 days)

Session 1

• Rhythmic exercises with hurdles: distances from 400 m to 200 m. Examples: 3–4 × 200 m with breaks of 10 min.; or 2 × 300 m, plus 2 × 200 m with breaks of 10–12 min.; or 5–6 × 200 m with breaks of 10 min.

Session 2

• Leaps over short and long distances.

• Repetition runs on the flat: distances 60–80–100 m. Examples: 2–3 × 60 m, plus 2–3 × 80 m, plus 1–2 × 100 m with breaks of 5–8 min; or 8–10 × 60 m with breaks of 5 min.; or 5–6 × 100 m with breaks of 8 min.

• Repetition runs: 5–6 × 150 m with breaks of 8–10 min.

Session 3

• Running technique and capacity for speed and suppleness.

• Hurdling technique.

Session 4

• Rhythmic exercises and repetition runs on the flat: distances from 500–200 m. Examples: 2 × 200 m with hurdles, plus 1 × 500 m, plus 1 × 300 m with breaks of 15–20 min.

• Cross-country: 3000–4000 m at increasing speed.

Session 5

• Running technique and capacity for speed and suppleness.

• Leaps over short and long distances.

Session 6

• Sets of repetitions: distances 80–100 m. Examples: 5 × 80 m, plus 4 × 100 m with breaks of 3–4 min. between exercises and 10–12 min. between series.

• Repetition runs on the flat: distances from 500–200 m. Examples: 3 × 500 m; or 5–6 × 300 m; or 4 × 400 m; or 500 m/400 m/300 m/300 m; or 8–9 × 200 m with breaks of 12–20 min.

■ The stars ■

MORGAN TAYLOR (USA)

To gain a medal in an event at three Olympics is an extraordinary achievement and the only person to have done this in the 400 m hurdles is the American Morgan Taylor. Although in his day relatively few athletes attempted this event, in nine seasons (1924–32) he ran the distance no more than 25–30 times, a schedule which these days takes three seasons at the most.

In 1924, barely 21 years of age, Taylor went to the Paris Olympics as the favourite, having run the 400 m hurdles in 53.0 sec. and 52.6 sec. on consecutive days. The latter result would have been a world record, but it was not ratified. At the Olympics he won in 52.6 sec., but as he had struck the last hurdle his time was not recognized because of the rules applicable at the time. The gold medal was his, but the Olympic record went to the Finn Vilen, second in 53.8 sec. Four years later, in Amsterdam, Taylor was again favourite, thanks to a world record of 52.0 sec., achieved in the Olympic trials and officially recognized. However, he could manage only third place in the final. In the Olympic final in 1932 in Los Angeles he again finished third, equalling his personal best of 52.0 sec.

Lord Burghley (centre of picture) in a 120 yards hurdles race.

LORD BURGHLEY (GB)

This titled Englishman played an important role in athletics throughout his adult life. After being one of the best hurdlers in the world, he was President of the IAAF for 30 years, from 1946 to 1976.

He was introduced to the hurdles during his time at Cambridge University. He entered the Olympic arena in Paris in 1924 as an unknown, falling in a heat of the 110 m and being eliminated. He won his first and only world record at the British Championships in London in 1927, running the 440 yards hurdles in 54.2 sec.

He won the 400 m hurdles at the Olympic Games in Amsterdam in 53.4 sec., beating the American favourites Cuhel and Taylor. He ended his career with fourth place in the 1932 Olympic final in Los Angeles with 52.2 sec. At the same Games he came fifth in the 110 m hurdles and contributed to the British silver medal in the 4 × 400 m relay, running his leg in 46.7 sec. A complete hurdler, he had personal bests of 14.5 sec. (120 yards), 24.3 sec. (220 yards) and 52.2 sec. (400 m).

GLENN HARDIN (USA)

On 26 July 1934 in Stockholm, in the 400 m hurdles, Hardin set a world record of 50.6 sec., a time which stood for 19 years. In his greatest year, 1934, he was number one in America on the flat as well, running the 440 yards in 46.8 sec., about 46.5 sec. over 400 m.

Hardin had won a silver medal at the Olympic Games in Los Angeles in 1932, finishing second to the Irishman Tisdall in 51.9 sec. Because the winner had struck a hurdle, the Olympic and world record was attributed to Hardin, rounded-up to 52.0 sec. Four years later, in Berlin, Hardin won the gold in 52.4 sec.

He also excelled at the 220 yards hurdles, which he ran in 22.7 sec. At the University Championships (NCAA) in 1935 he was beaten over this distance by Jesse Owens.

GLENN DAVIS (USA)

An extremely solid athlete, until Ed Moses in 1984 he was the only man to have won the 400 m hurdles twice at the Olympics. He is also the last 400 m runner to have led the world on the flat and over hurdles. He did this in his best year, 1958, when he ran less than 46 sec. half a dozen times, with times of 45.5 sec. (400 m) and 45.7 sec. (440 yards), the latter being a world record. He also bettered the world record at 400 m hurdles, which he already held, taking it to 49.2 sec.

Davis successfully defended his Olympic title in the 1960 Olympics at Rome, winning in 49.3 sec. He also contributed to the American 4 × 400 m victory. Other personal bests were 9.7 sec. (100 yards), 10.3 sec. (100 m), 21.0 sec. (220 yards), 14.3 sec. (120 yards hurdles), 1.92 m (high-jump) and 7.32 m (long-jump).

Glenn Davis, twice Olympic gold medallist at the 400 m hurdles.

DAVID HEMERY (GB)

Although born in England, he grew up in the USA, first attending high school and then college in Massachusetts. His first attempts as a hurdler were in 1963, and he achieved success straight away both in the 'highs' and 'intermediates'. Over the first of the two he won the Commonwealth Games in 1966 with a time of 14.1 sec. In 1968 he began to perform well in the 400 m hurdles, ending the season with a marvellous win at the Mexico Olympics, where he bettered the world record by nearly a second with 48.12 sec. He then turned to the 110 m hurdles, placing second in the Athens European Games of 1969 in 13.7 sec. and first at the Commonwealth Games in Edinburgh in 1970 with 13.67 sec. (this latter time was with the wind over the limit).

After a virtual absence in 1971 he competed in the Munich Olympics, finishing third in the 400 m hurdles behind Akii-Bua and Mann in 48.52 sec. At the same Games he won a silver medal with the British 4 × 400 m relay team. He was also capable of running the 200 m in 21.8 sec., the 400 m in 47.1 sec. and the 110 m hurdles in 13.72 sec.

JOHN AKII-BUA (UGANDA)

By winning the Olympic title for the 400 m hurdles in 1972, this Ugandan put his country on the athletics map. Running in the disadvantageous inside lane, he achieved a new world record of 47.82 sec. His effort was well distributed, with 23.0 sec. in the first 200 m and 24.8 sec. in the second 200 m.

Born into a family of 43 children (his father had eight wives), he was introduced to athletics just before he was 18. In 1970 he finished fourth in the 400 m hurdles at the Edinburgh Commonwealth Games in 51.1 sec.

Ed Moses, undefeated in the 400 m hurdles for seven years

His big break came in the USA–Africa match in 1971, when he won in a time of 49.0 sec.

After his Olympic success in Munich he was caught up in the unhappy events in his country under the regime of Idi Amin. He was forced to flee Uganda and with his family took refuge in the German Federal Republic, where he resumed preparation for the 1976 Olympic Games. He looked capable of doing well in Montreal, having taken his personal best for the 400 m flat to 45.82 sec., but the boycott by the African countries prevented him from competing.

In 1980 he again participated and reached the semi-finals in the 400 m hurdles at the Moscow Olympics.

EDWIN MOSES (USA)

These days competition in athletics is so intense as to make it extremely difficult to be unbeatable for very long. The longest chain of consecutive successes strung together to date by a male champion is 116, achieved in the shot-put by the American Parry O'Brien between 1952 and 1956. One present-day athlete who is not far from exceeding this total is Edwin Moses, who has been unbeatable in the 400 m hurdles for over seven years. From the end of August 1977 to the end of 1984 he completed more than 90 consecutive wins, not including wins in heats.

Initially, Moses was a fairly average competitor but, in 1976, Moses suddenly specialized in the event and in a few months was one of the best in the world, an unusual achievement for a beginner. In Montreal he won the Olympic title with ease and gained a new world record of 47.63 sec.

Since then Moses has bettered the record on three occasions: 47.45 sec. in 1977 at Westwood, 47.13 sec. in 1980 in Milan and 47.02 sec. in Koblenz in 1983. As late as 1956 this last time would have given him a medal in a 400 m flat race. He was unable to regain the Olympic title in 1980 because of the boycott by the USA of the Moscow Olympics, but he has won the World Cup three times, 1977, 1979 and 1981, the World Championships in 1983 and the Olympic gold in 1984.

Gifted with a good physique and long legs, Moses has shown his great ability at other distances too, running the 400 m flat in 45.60 sec. (and 44.1 sec. in the relay), the 110 m hurdles in 13.64 sec. and the 800 m, in his only attempt at the distance, in 1 min. 48.98 sec.

KARIN ROSSLEY (GDR)

The 400 m hurdles is one of the most recent additions to women's athletics. The first experiments over this distance took place in 1971, but the first official world record was that of

John Akii-Bua

Krystyna Kacperczyk, the Polish girl: 56.51 sec. in 1974. It was not an international event until the European Cup in 1977. The winner was the East German girl named Karin Rossley, in 55.63 sec., and a new world record. In 1980, with an Olympic race not yet scheduled over this distance, the IAAF organized a separate world championship for the 400 m hurdles. In preparation she took the world record to 54.28 sec., but had the misfortune to injure herself shortly afterwards and was unable to take part.

WORLD RECORDS

Men

sec.
55.0 Charles Bacon (USA) 1908
54.2 John Norton (USA) 1920
54.0 Frank Loomis (USA) 1920
53.8 Sten Pettersson (Sweden) 1925
52.6 John Gibson (USA) 1927
52.0 Morgan Taylor (USA) 1928
52.0 Glenn Hardin (USA) 1932
51.8 Glenn Hardin (USA) 1934
50.6 Glenn Hardin (USA) 1934
50.4 Yuri Lituyev (USSR) 1953
49.5 Glenn Davis (USA) 1956
49.2 Glenn Davis (USA) 1958
49.2 Salvatore Morale (Italy) 1962
49.1 Rix Cawley (USA) 1964
48.8 Geoff Vanderstock (USA) 1968
48.1 David Hemery (GB) 1968
47.8 John Akii-Bua (Uganda) 1972
47.6 Edwin Moses (USA) 1976

Automatic times
47.82 John Akii-Bua (Uganda) 1972
47.64 Edwin Moses (USA) 1976
47.45 Edwin Moses (USA) 1977
47.13 Edwin Moses (USA) 1980
47.02 Edwin Moses (USA) 1983

Women
56.51 Krystyna Kacperczyk (Poland) 1974
55.74 Tatyana Storozhewa (USSR) 1977
55.63 Karin Rossley (GDR) 1977
55.44 Krystyna Kacperczyk (Poland) 1978
55.31 Tatyana Zelencova (USSR) 1978
54.89 Tatyana Zelencova (USSR) 1978
54.78 Marina Makeyeva (USSR) 1979
54.28 Karin Rossley (GDR) 1980
54.02 Anna Ambrosiene (USSR) 1983
53.58 Margarita Ponomaryova (USSR) 1984

3000 m steeplechase

How it is run

Various theories exist on the origins of hurdles races. It is clear, however, that the name 'steeplechase', by which this long-distance hurdle event came to be known, was inherited from horse racing over jumps. On a cold and rainy autumn afternoon in 1850, at Exeter College, Oxford, several students were commenting on a hard 'steeplechase' race on horses, in which they had just competed. One of them, Halifax Wyatt, had been thrown out of his saddle by a temperamental animal, and his reaction was to declare, 'Rather than climb back on to that damned 'camel' I should prefer to run those two miles on foot!'. His colleagues took him at his word and the idea of setting up a steeplechase race on foot was born.

The first official experiment took place towards the end of the same year over an extremely hard two-mile course scattered with 24 jumps, in a marshy area of Binsey near Oxford, the winner being Halifax Wyatt himself. A race of this kind was included in the programme of the first 'match' between the universities of Oxford and Cambridge, held at Christ Church Ground, Oxford, in 1864. Later on, however, the event faded into obscurity for a number of years.

The early years. The 1920s can be considered as the basis of steeplechasing as we know it today. There were few countries at that time where attention was devoted to the event, which was not recognized at that time by the IAAF. The courses were not particularly defined: in some places, e.g. Scandinavia, the race was run over a total of 37 jumps; elsewhere there were only 36 or 35; often there were no water jumps. In the USA there was for several years a 3000 m indoor hurdle event.

The modern hurdler. The modern competitor in the 3000 m steeplechase must be a perfect cross between the fast middle-distance runner and agile hurdler.

The event includes the crossing of 28 solid barriers and the clearing of 7 water jumps. The barriers are 91.7 cm high and 3.96 m wide, and the upper wooden bar is 12.7 cm wide, so that the athlete may place his foot on it to help himself over if necessary. The water jump consists of an obstacle which has the same features as the others, but it is placed right on the edge of a trench 3.66 m square, full of water. The bottom slopes down from the track towards the obstacle in the direction opposite to that of the race, so that the athlete can land on an inclined mat, therefore breaking the force of his impact on the ground after the jump.

The themes. The main themes involved in this discipline may be summarized as follows: in order to obtain good performances in the 3000 m steeplechase, what qualities does an athlete need in addition to those typical of a middle-distance runner? Apart from being capable of a good time in the 3000 m on the flat, what characteristics should the athlete exhibit?

First of all, it is very important that the athlete knows how to cross the water jump and the barriers with a good technique. It is also clear that a middle-distance runner becomes a complete hurdler only by crossing the hurdles with reasonable style. The hurdling aspect cannot be isolated from the rest of the event, and the presence of the water jump and of the obstacles also has a great influence on the flat stretches of the 3000 m steeplechase.

Thinking initially of the 3000 m flat event, the best performance is usually obtained when the pace is as fast and even as possible. In the 3000 m steeplechase, because of the presence of the jumps, this uniformity of pace is clearly not achievable.

Loss of time. Crossing the barriers and water jumps naturally slows down the pace, and it has been calculated that top-ranking hurdlers lose 0.4–0.7 sec. in clearing each of the hurdles. When jumping the barrier, the pelvis must stay above a certain height for a given distance which is always equal at any speed; when one runs slowly, therefore, in order to be able to remain above this height for this fixed interval, one must necessarily form a different parabola, with a higher apex; consequently, the push-off must be stronger.

For this reason, as he nears the barrier, the hurdler increases his speed; if he were to go too slowly, he would have to push off very strongly with considerable muscular effort and high expenditure of energy concentrated in a short time; therefore he increases his speed so that the clearing of the jump is due to the kinetic energy of the race. The increase in speed must be that much greater according to the extent to which the athlete raises his pelvis, or smaller depending on the length of his lower limbs, and also depends on the effectiveness of his hurdle clearance technique.

A similar approach can be adopted for the water jump. In this case the increase of speed in the approach allows the athlete to touch ground a fair distance away without expending much energy in the push-off performed by the foot which is in the water jump.

The athlete must try to find the right balance between the increase in speed in the lead-up to each jump and the increase in power of the push-off in order to clear the barrier and to pass beyond a good proportion of the trench; neither the increase in running speed, nor the push-off, must be excessive, otherwise there is likely to be a sharp increase in energy expenditure.

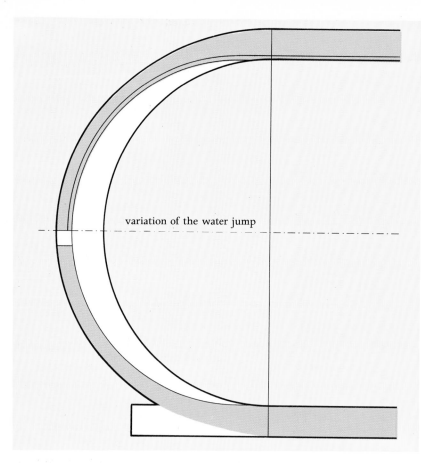

variation of the water jump

HURDLE DATA

The 3000 m steeplechase event allows for $7\frac{1}{2}$ laps of the track with 28 barrier jumps and 7 water jumps, while in the 2000 m for juniors there are 5 laps with 18 barriers and 5 water jumps.

The water jump forms the fourth obstacle on each lap.

The International Regulations recommend that in the 2000 m the water jump should be the second obstacle of the first lap, and after that the fourth. It is situated at the apex of the bend.

There must be sufficient distance from the starting line to the first barrier in order to prevent overcrowding of competitors, and there must be approximately 68 m from the last barrier to the finish line.

Measurements. The measurements listed in the table are supplied as a guide and any necessary variation may occur because of the lengthening or shortening of the distance from the starting point of the event. A lap of 400 m will be shortened or lengthened depending on whether the trench has been constructed inside or outside the track.

In the 3000 m, the distance from the starting point to the beginning of the first lap must not include any jump and the barriers must be set up after the competitors have completed the section which precedes the start of the first lap.

The barriers. These must be 91.4 cm high ± 3 mm, and be at least 3.96 m wide. The section of the upper bar of the barriers, including that of the water-jump, must be square with 12.7 cm sides. The weight of each obstacle must be between 80 and 100 kg. Every barrier must have on each side a base between 1.20 m and 1.40 m in length.

Arrangement of the barriers	390 m lap	410 m lap
Distance from the start to the beginning of the first lap, to be run without barriers	270 m	130 m
From the start of the first lap to the first barrier	10 m	10 m
From the first to the second barrier	78 m	82 m
From the second to the third barrier	78 m	82 m
From the third barrier to the water jump	78 m	82 m
From the water jump to the fourth barrier	78 m	82 m
From the fourth barrier to the finish	68 m	72 m
	7 × 390 m = 2730 m	7 × 410 m = 2870 m
	3000 m	3000 m

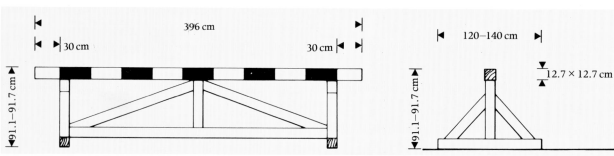

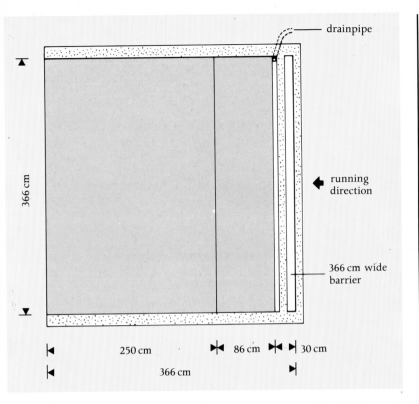

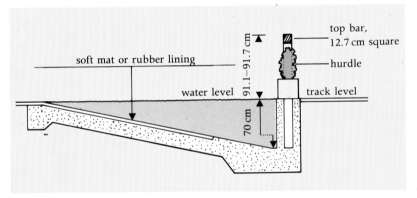

The barrier must be placed on the track so that 30 cm of the top bar, measured from the inside border of the track, is inside the field.

The trench. Including the barrier, it must be a square of 3.66 m sides, filled with water level with the surface of the track. Immediately on the other side of the barrier it must be 70 cm deep for a distance of 30 cm. From this point the bottom must rise until it reaches the level of the track at the opposite end of the trench.

The barrier in front of the trench must be firmly fixed and of the same height as the others.

The jumps and the water jump
At the top on the opposite page, the position of the pit is shown, on the outside of the track. Opposite left are the measurements of the hurdles. Top, the measurements of the trench or water jump are given. Above, the lateral section of the trench is shown.

Push-offs. In clearing the jumps the muscles of the lower limbs must push much more than in running, and this leads to an increase in energy expenditure which is of short duration but which is considerable even when the technique is good; in clearing the ordinary barriers there is only one push-off; in crossing the water jump, however, there are two push-offs; firstly that of one limb to raise the body over the jump, then that of the other limb to allow the body to clear a good part of the trench.

Sometimes when nearing the jump the hurdler increases his speed by more than is really necessary so that he can clear the jump with greater ease, arriving with the jump the right distance away and having fewer competitors and more space around him; this too increases energy expenditure. In relation to the 3000 m flat, these continuous variations of energy expenditure which occur in the 3000 m steeplechase would correspond to 35 variations of speed for several metres each, certainly not the most suitable method for obtaining the best performance.

We said earlier that the way to obtain the best performance in middle-distance flat events (especially the 1500 m upwards) is to maintain a constant pace, and thus constant energy expenditure. In the 3000 m steeplechase, however, the expenditure of energy is not constant; in fact, proportionately speaking, the difference between a 3000 m flat race at even pace and the 3000 m steeplechase is equivalent to the difference between training at a steady pace and Fartlek training.

Advice. In order to cross the hurdles and water jumps correctly, it is vital that:
(a) the jump, just like the running action, must take place with a fluid action, relaxed without useless waste of energy;
(b) one should avoid slowing down in front of the obstacle so as not to reduce the action (crossing) to a sort of 'leap' with consequent loss of speed and difficult resumption of running pace;
(c) one should be able to pass over the hurdles leading just as easily with either leg; dangerous hesitations

would be avoided in the case of several athletes crossing the same obstacle simultaneously.

For crossing the water jumps, the advice for the ordinary barriers applies, but the following should be remembered:

(a) the athlete must try to reduce to a minimum the reduction in pace which results from the long parabola which he executes in order to carry himself over the jump and clear the water jump (about 5 m);

(b) the point of 'attack' of the obstacle must be about 1.40–1.50 m;

(c) the contact with the top part of the barrier must be in such a way as to allow a jump-support and a subsequent effective push-off towards the ground in front;

(d) the landing must occur in a state of perfect balance and the athlete must point his body in the direction of the push-off; in order to do this the entire limb remains taut without bending at knee height, hence avoiding a lowering of the hips and thus a further decrease in speed;

(e) it is wrong to land beyond the water because, to do this, the athlete would have to effect a rather strong push-off which would consume a great deal of energy.

The hurdles. The most economical and practical way of clearing the barriers is to think of the crossing as a true and proper passing of an obstacle, with a technique reduced to essentials, avoiding violent and tiring movements.

When the athlete gets near to an obstacle he should speed up his strides to give him sufficient inertia for clearing the beam without having to make a strong push off from the track. For the crossing to be successful the action of passing over should be thought of from the top towards the bottom preceded by a brief period of suspension.

The water jump. To tackle this obstacle, the athlete should be nearer to it than for the other barriers. The leading leg must not be completely extended, while that used to push off does not press as hard as in the 400 m hurdles. The chest is sloped slightly forward so that the centre of gravity remains as low as possible. When the

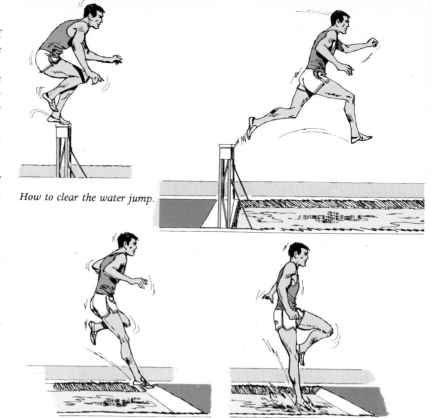

How to clear the water jump.

take-off is completed the athlete rests the foot of the forward leg on the top part of the barrier. The knee is bent by up to 90°, the centre of gravity remaining low over the obstacle. Greater bending than this is not advisable, since the push-off stage which follows is then too prolonged. The leg remains bent and, while the trailing leg goes forward, the arms are carried forward and out to balance the body during the leap.

At the moment of crossing the barrier, the leading leg is extended and opened completely in order to land slightly inside the trench. In this manner the body will be projected towards the lower part of the front of the trench with a rather flattened trajectory.

The landing is perfectly balanced and running is resumed thanks to the co-ordinated actions of the lower and upper limbs and to the remaining inertia.

Tactics. Quite frequently, experienced hurdlers will run the first few laps tactically at the back of the field, in order to stay clear of crowded groups at the barriers and thus run the risk of being spiked or falling; also they remain unaffected by continuous changes of pace which force

wasteful accelerations to be made in order to catch up later on. Those athletes who prefer to retain a position at the front try to avoid these problems by changing the line of running when confronting the obstacles, i.e. spreading out towards the outside. This creates difficulties for their fellow competitors, who are obliged to break up the pace. In the 1983 Helsinki World Championships, the first obstacle consisted of two barriers placed side by side which cut off the whole track; the aim was to allow the compact group to disperse while clearing the first hurdle, thus minimizing the risk of a pile-up.

■ Training ■

Training for the 3000 m steeplechase obviously does not differ greatly from that for the classic middle-distance runner. Naturally, from the time when the athlete has to tackle obstacles and water jumps, a large proportion is dedicated to the technique of clearing obstacles. The weekly work plan has been drawn up by Giorgio Rondelli, who has helped to prepare schedules in previous chapters on the middle-distance events.

WEEKLY TRAINING SCHEDULE

Typical week of the first cycle of winter training (from October to December)

Session 1

• Morning: 40 min. running at a speed of 3 min. 50 sec.–4 min. per kilometre. Sprints: 10–15 × 100 m at a pace dictated by the coach.

• Afternoon: 40 min. of running at a speed of 3 min. 50 sec.–4 min. per kilometre on hilly ground.

Session 2

• Morning: 10–15 min. of warming up. 30 min. running at a speed of 3 min. 20 sec./km.

• Afternoon: warming up, 15 min. of running. 15–20 min. of stretching (muscular strengthening of lower limbs). Abdominal and dorsal gymnastics. 3–4 repetitions of circuit training in a gymnasium based on bar clearances, crossbar, stretches of walking, strengthening of the upper limbs, exercises of co-ordination and dexterity.

Session 3

• Morning or afternoon: 1 hour 15 min. of running at 3 min. 50 sec.–4 min. per kilometre.

Session 4

• Morning: 40 min. of running. Gymnastics and technical runs. Runs: 10–15 × 100–150 m at a pace controlled by the trainer.

• Afternoon: 40 min. of slow long distance at 3 min. 50 sec.–4 min. per kilometre, on hilly ground.

Session 5

• Morning: 15 min. of warming up. 30 min. of running at a speed of 3 min. 20 sec./km.

• Afternoon: 15 min. of warming up. Stretching. Abdominal and dorsal gymnastics. 3–4 repetitions of the training already dealt with previously in Session 2.

Session 6

• Morning and afternoon: 1 hour 15 min. of slow long distance at 3 min. 50 sec.–4 min. per kilometre.

Session 7

• Morning or afternoon: 15 min. of warming up. Aerobic power: running 12 km at a speed of 3 min. 30 sec./km, on hilly ground.

Typical week of the second cycle of winter training (from January to March)

Session 1

• Morning: 40 min. of warming up. Gymnastics and crossbar technique. At the end of training, technical runs controlled by the trainer.

• Afternoon: 40 min. of running at 3 min. 45 sec.–3 min. 50 sec. per kilometre.

Session 2

• Morning: 30 min. of slow long distance.

• Afternoon: warming up. Aerobic power: about 10 km at 3 min. 30 sec./km on the track, with five jumps per lap, at the regular height of the hurdles.

Session 3

• Morning or afternoon: 1 hour 15 min. of running at 3 min. 45 sec.–3 min. 50 sec. per kilometre.

Session 4

• Morning: 40 min. of warming up. Gymnastics. Technical runs, at the end of training, of 100–150 m.

• Afternoon: 40 min. of running at 3 min. 40 sec.–3 min. 50 sec./km.

Session 5

• Morning: 30 min. of slow long distance.

• Afternoon: warming up. Mixed work of aerobic power: 12 km at 3 min. 15 sec./km, recovery 1 km, 4 min./km; 3–5 km at a speed of 3 min. 5 sec.–3 min. per kilometre.

Session 6

• Morning or afternoon: 40 min. of running at 3 min. 50 sec./km. 10–15 × 100 m in not particularly demanding speed: recovery with gentle looseness (easy running); conclude with 20 min. of looseness at the preceding pace, 3 min. 40 sec.–3 min. 50 sec. per kilometre.

Session 7

• Morning or afternoon: 1 hour 20 min. of running, on hilly ground, the last 20 min. at 3 min. 20 sec./km.

Typical week of the third cycle of winter training in preparation for track events (from April to mid-May)

Session 1

• Morning: 30 min. of warming up. Gymnastics and technical runs.

• Afternoon: aerobic power with obstacles: 6–8 km at 3 min. 20 sec./per km (the work will be done on the track).

Session 2

• Morning or afternoon: 1 hour of slow long distance at 3 min. 50 sec./km.

Session 3

• Morning: 15 min. of warming up. Running: 6 km at 3 min. 20 sec./km

• Afternoon: 15 min. of warming up. 3 × 2000 m at 5 min. 30 sec–5 min. per kilometre, with 800 m of recovery with looseness of about 3 min.–3 min. 30 sec.; or 5 × 1000 m at a pace of 2 min. 20 sec.–2 min. 45 sec. per kilometre, with 600 m of recovery with looseness of about 2 min.–2 min. 30 sec.; or 8 × 800 m in 2 min. 8 sec.–2 min. 10 sec. with 400 m of recovery with looseness of about 2 min.

Session 4

• Morning: 30 min. of looseness. Gymnastics and spurts.

• Afternoon: 40 min. of running at 3 min. 40 sec./km.

Session 5

• Morning: 15 min. of warming up. Aerobic power: 30 min. of running at 3 min. 30 sec./km.

• Afternoon: 15 min. of warming up. Gymnastics. 15 × 400 m with five barriers in times of 1 min. 6 sec.–1 min. 8 sec., with 200 m of recovery of about 1 min.

Session 6

• Morning or afternoon: 1 hour 10 min. of slow long distance at about 3 min. 50 sec.–4 min. per kilometre.

Session 7

• Morning or afternoon: 15 min. of warming up. 3 × 500 m in 1 min. 15 sec., recovery 100 m; pause 5 min.; 5 × 300 m in 43–44 sec., recovery 100 m; pause 5 min., 5 × 200 m in 27–28 sec., recovery 100 m.

Typical week of the fourth cycle or typical competitive weeks (from mid-May onwards)

Session 1

• Morning: 40 min. of slow long distance at 3 min. 50 sec.–4 min. per kilometre. Gymnastics.

• Afternoon: 40 min. of slow long distance. Technical runs. Varied runs (basing the work on frequently varying the breadth and frequency of the pace).

Session 2

• Morning: warming up. Aerobic power: 5 km at 3 min. 10 sec.–3 min. 5 sec. per kilometre.

• Afternoon: 15 min. of warming up. 2000 m steeple with obstacles, jumps and the water jump as in a race, pause of 8–10 min.; or 600 m with obstacles at a speed similar to that of event finals; pause 6–8 min.; 5 × 300 m with very fast obstacles (here too as in the event finals) with recovery of 100 m; or 4 × 600 m with obstacles, pause of 200 m or 5 min.; 5 × 400 m with obstacles in 60–62 sec., recovery of 400 m in 5–6 min.

Session 3

• Morning or afternoon: 1 hour of slow long distance at will.

Session 4

• Morning: 30–40 min. of slow long distance.

• Afternoon: 15–20 min. of warming up. 2 × 400 m in 58 sec.; recovery of 200 m with looseness; 4 min. pause; 3 × 300 m in 42–43 sec.; recovery of 100 m; pause 4–5 min.; 5 × 200 m in 27–28 sec.; recovery of 100 m.

Session 5

• Morning: 40 min. of slow looseness.

• Afternoon: 30 min. running with the last 10 min. in a continuously increasing rhythm.

Session 6

• Morning or afternoon: 50 min. of slow long distance. Gymnastics and runs.

Session 7

• Morning: 15–20 min. of preliminary warming up.

• Afternoon: competition.

■ The stars ■

TOIVO LOUKOLA (FINLAND)
The first of the great modern 'steeplechasers', Loukola was Finnish champion in the event for five consecutive years (1928–32), but his best victory was at the Amsterdam Olympic Games, where he won in 9 min. 21.8 sec. from Nurmi and Andersen.

For Loukola the steeplechase was a consolation for the fact that on the flat he was invariably beaten by Nurmi and Ritola. Nevertheless he was a first-class runner with personal bests of: 3 min. 58.4 sec. (1500 m), 8 min. 36.6 sec. (3000 m), 14 min. 48.1 sec. (5000 m) and 31 min. 12.9 sec. (10,000 m).

VOLMARI ISO-HOLLO (FINLAND)
One of the greatest long-distance runners following Paavo Nurmi, he divided his time between flat races and steeplechases, achieving notable successes in both events. Iso-Hollo showed his class in two different Olympiads. In 1932 he took second place in the 10,000 m, finishing a short distance behind the Pole, Janusz Kusocinski. Then he made a name for himself in the '3450' m steeplechase. Through a disgraceful error in the lap-counting the athletes ran one more lap than they should have done. When the event was finished the athletes decided unanimously to leave things as they were, not wanting to have a re-run. Iso-Hollo won in 10 min. 33.4 sec.

Iso-Hollo also obtained significant results in the period between the Los Angeles and Berlin Games. In 1933 he ran the 3000 m in 9 min. 09.4 sec., second fastest ever at the time. In the Berlin Olympics he was third in the 10,000 m (30 min. 20.2 sec.) behind two Finnish team-mates, and won the steeplechase in 9 min. 03.8 sec., the best time of the pre-war period.

His range of times included 51.6 sec. for 400 m, 3 min. 54.3 sec. for 1500 m, 8 min. 19.6 sec. for 3000 m, and 14 min. 18.3 sec. for 5000 m. Unlike many of his compatriots, he did not subject himself to severe training. At a time when very few athletes made long journeys, he competed in Brazil and the USSR.

ZDZISLAW KRZYSZKOWIAK (POLAND)
In the Olympic Games in 1956 at Melbourne he was fourth in 29 min. 05.0 sec. in the 10,000 m won by Vladimir Kuts. He also qualified for the final of the 3000 m steeplechase, but an accident prevented him from participating in them. Two years later, at the European Championships in Stockholm, he won first the 10,000 m in 28 min. 56.0 sec., then the 5000 m in 13 min. 53.4 sec.

In 1960 Krzyszkowiak concentrated on the 3000 m steeplechase with his sights on the Olympic Games. In June he took the world record with 8 min. 31.4 sec. In Rome he contested the 10,000 m, finishing seventh in 28 min. 52.4 sec., then won the 3000 m steeplechase in 8 min. 34.2 sec. In 1961 he claimed a new world record of 8 min. 30.4 sec.

GASTON ROELANTS (BELGIUM)
Having finished fourth in 1960 at the Rome Olympics, he easily won the European title in 1962 at Belgrade. His greatest triumph was at the Olympic Games of 1964 in Tokyo, winning in 8 min. 30.8 sec. having left everyone behind from the second kilometre. His tactic was to force the pace in the hope of destroying his opponents. From August 1961 to September 1966 he lost only once, in a heat of the Tokyo Games. His run of success was ended at the European Games at Budapest in 1966, when the Russians Kudinski and Kuryan succeeded in overhauling him in the final stages, and he finished the race in third place.

He was an excellent runner on the flat too: European record-holder at 10,000 m with 28 min. 10.6 sec. in 1965, and world record-holder at 20,000 m (58 min. 06.2 sec. in 1966 and 57 min. 44.4 sec. in 1972) and for the hour run (20,664 m in 1966 and 20,784 m in 1972). As a marathon runner he placed well at the European Games of 1969 and 1974.

AMOS BIWOTT (KENYA)
When Amos Biwott collected his gold medal at the 1968 Mexico Olympics, he sent many experts hurrying to consult their record books because he was so unknown. In 1968 Biwott had finished second in the East African championships with 8 min. 44.8 sec.,

Amos Biwott and Ben Jipcho (574) at the Munich Olympics in 1972.

Anders Gärderud

behind his compatriot Benjamin Kogo who was already famous internationally. At the Mexico Olympics the young Kenyan attracted immediate attention through his unorthodox style and ease with which he won his heat in 8 min. 49.4 sec. In the final he won in 8 min. 51.0 sec. ahead of Kogo.

Four years later, at the Munich Olympics, Biwott appeared with little improvement in his technique. He won his heat in a personal best of 8 min. 23.8 sec., but in the final he had to content himself with sixth place (8 min. 33.6 sec.). After these Games he disappeared just as suddenly as he had arrived, and returned to live in anonymity in his own country.

ANDERS GÄRDERUD (SWEDEN)

As a teenager in Sweden he was labelled as 'a new Hägg'. When this sort of prediction is made of someone it is fairly rare for the person concerned to fulfil it, but Anders Gärderud was an exception. He revealed his precocious talent in the 1500 m steeplechase at the first European Junior Games, held in 1964 in Warsaw. Only 18 years old, he shot away from the start and after two laps he had a lead of 100 m over the next competitor, finally winning in 4 min. 08.0 sec. A year later he ran the same distance in 4 min. 00.6 sec. On graduating to senior level and tackling the 3000 m steeplechase, he obtained creditable times but was disappointing in big races, and remained in obscurity for the Olympic Games of 1968 and 1972.

In September 1972, he gained the world 3000 m steeplechase record for the first time in 8 min. 20.8 sec. At the 1974 European Games in Rome, he was defeated by only 0.37 sec. by the Pole Bronislaw Malinowski, who was to be his greatest rival. In 1975 Gärderud began to establish himself as number one in the event, and recaptured the world record from the Kenyan Jipcho, running 8 min. 10.4 sec. at Oslo and 8 min. 09.70 sec. at Stockholm in the space of six days. At the 1976 Olympic Games in Montreal, Gärderud defeated Malinowski again with the last of his world records in 8 min. 08.02 sec., which is still a European and Olympic record. Besides his success at the 3000 m steeplechase, Gärderud also proved he was a top-class middle-distance athlete on the flat with times of 1 min. 47.2 sec. (800 m), 3 min. 36.73 sec. (1500 m), 3 min. 54.45 sec. (mile), 7 min. 47.8 sec. (3000 m), 13 min. 17.59 sec. (5000 m) and 28 min. 59.2 sec. (10,000 m).

BRONISLAW MALINOWSKI (POLAND)

This Pole was one of those athletes who gains Olympic success at the third attempt. Initially he did well in the European Games, in 1974 beating the Swede Gärderud with a time of 8 min. 15.04 sec. Four years later in Prague, he won in 8 min. 15.08 sec. However, he did not perform so well

at the Olympic Games: fourth in 1972 at Munich, and second in 1976 behind Gärderud. In 1980, in Moscow, his strongest rival was the Tanzanian Filbert Bayi who several years before had held the world record for the 1500 m (3 min. 32.16 sec.) and the mile (3 min. 51.0 sec.). Bayi went from the gun in the final, but it was clear that he had gone off too fast. After 2 km he had a considerable lead, but by the bell it was reduced to 20 m. Malinowski caught up and passed his exhausted rival over the last hurdle and went on to win in 8 min. 09.70 sec. At the age of 29 he was finally an Olympic champion. Tragically, he died in a car accident in the autumn of 1981, having decided to settle in Great Britain.

Henry Rono (Uganda) — *See the 5000 m.*

▬▬ WORLD RECORDS ▬▬

(from 1954, the year of IAAF recognition of the event)

min. sec.
8:45.4 Horace Ashenfelter (USA) 1952*
8:44.4 Olavi Rinteenpaa (Finland) 1953*
8:49.6 Sandor Rozsnyoi (Hungary) 1954
8:47.8 Pentti Karvonen (Finland) 1955
8:45.4 Pentti Karvonen (Finland) 1955
8:45.4 Vasili Vlasenko (USSR) 1955
8:41.2 Jerzy Chromik (Poland) 1955
8:40.2 Jerzy Chromik (Poland) 1955
8:39.8 Semyon Rzhishchin (USSR) 1956
8:35.6 Sandor Rozsnyoi (Hungary) 1956
8:35.6 Semyon Rzhishchin (USSR) 1958
8:32.0 Jerzy Chromik (Poland) 1958
8:31.4 Zdzislaw Krzyszkowiak (Poland) 1960
8:31.2 Grigori Taran (USSR) 1961
8:30.4 Zdzislaw Krzyszkowiak (Poland) 1961
8:29.6 Gaston Roelants (Belgium) 1963
8:26.4 Gaston Roelants (Belgium) 1965
8:24.2 Jouko Kuha (Finland) 1968
8:22.2 Vladimir Dudin (USSR) 1969
8:22.0 Kerry O'Brien (Australia) 1970
8:20.8 Anders Gärderud (Sweden) 1972
8:19.8 Benjamin Jipcho (Kenya) 1973
8:14.0 Benjamin Jipcho (Kenya) 1973
8:10.4 Anders Gärderud (Sweden) 1975
8:09.8 Anders Gärderud (Sweden) 1975
8:08.0 Anders Gärderud (Sweden) 1976
8:05.4 Henry Rono (Kenya) 1978

* The two results before 1954 constituted the authentic best world performances.

High jump
Evolution

The high-jump as we know it today first became popular in the 19th century, when professionals performed for payment and were able to clear over 6 ft (1.83 m). The Scotsman William Tivendale managed to clear 1.85 m as long ago as 1861. At that time, the cross-bar or rope stretched between uprights was cleared with the feet together and with the trunk almost erect, so the head was a comparatively long way from the horizontal obstacle.

Subsequent perfecting of the jumping technique took place in stages, but it has depended particularly on the modification of the rules for the event and on the elimination of some restrictive conditions. For example, at one time the jumper was not permitted to touch the pit with his hands before his legs had touched down, nor could his head pass over the cross-bar before his legs. Also, the improvement in performance owes a great deal to the use of mattresses, which have replaced sand in the landing area; mattresses have also helped the adoption of the arched-back method of clearing the bar, the 'Fosbury flop', which is very fashionable at present.

Jump from standstill. The high jump, through its close relationship with gymnastics, was practised at the beginning of the 20th century either with a run-up or from a standstill. Four versions of the jump from a standstill were included in the Olympics from 1900 to 1912, and it remained in sporting programmes until the early 1930s.

The technical evolution of the high jump with a run-up has taken place on the basis of experiments to ascertain the most suitable bodily stance

for the greatest exploitation of the height which may be reached from the centre of gravity of the athlete's body in relation to the height to be cleared. This has resulted in a change from the body clearing the cross-bar in an almost vertical position, to the inclination of the body to a horizontal position, with arching of the back.

The scissors. Towards the end of the 19th century, an American named Mike Sweeny proposed the 'scissors' jump as an alternative to the frontal clearance. The scissors involved passing one leg over after the other at the same time bending the trunk towards the knees when clearing the bar.

Sweeny's technique was successfully taken up by Frenchman Pierre Lewden who, being small, adapted it to his physique. Thus emerged the style named 'scissors with return inside', a scissors kick with internal overturning. It consisted of the following movement: while the forward leg was above the cross-bar, the other one kicked upwards, causing the

chest to rotate towards the direction of jumping and a landing on the feet.

Horine. Lewden's double scissors kick survived for the whole period between the two world wars, but the advantages of another technique were already being put forward by a Californian called George Horine during this time; this technique involved approaching the cross-bar in the air on his side with his body parallel to it, while completing a rotation. Hence the definition of 'rolling', known as the 'western roll'; this name was derived from the fact that Horine was from the west coast of the USA. As a result of this technique Horine was the first man to jump above 2 m (6 ft 7 in.), on 18 May 1912 at Palo Alto in California. Later the 'western roll' simply took the name of its inventor.

With the use of this style, the world record began to rise gradually, as high-jumpers introduced minor adjustments to the technique according to their physical characteristics and talents.

Dick Fosbury clears the height which gave him the gold medal at the Mexico City Olympics in 1968; the success of his style of jumping led to the technique being called the 'Fosbury flop'.

WHAT THE RULES SAY

Here is an extract from the International Rules.
• The competitor must take off with one foot only.
• A competitor commits a foul if:
– he causes the cross-bar to drop from the supports;
– he touches the ground, including the landing area beyond the uprights, either inside or outside them, with any part of the body, without having first cleared the cross-bar. (But if, in the opinion of the judge, he does not derive any advantage from touching the landing zone with his foot, the jump must not be considered void for this reason).
• The order of jumping must be decided by drawing lots.
• Before the event, the judges must announce to the competitors the starting height and the heights at which the cross-bar will be placed at the end of each heat, until no competitors remain in the event or there is a tie.
• Each competitor must be placed according to the best of his jumps, including the jumps performed in a decider in the event of a tie for first place.
• A competitor may begin to jump at any height from the minimum height and can jump at his discretion at any later height. Three consecutive faults, irrespective of the height at which each fault has occurred, exclude him from further attempts.

The effect of this rule is that a competitor may give up his second or third attempts at a certain height (having failed a first or a second time) and try instead at a greater height.

If a competitor renounces an attempt at a certain height, he cannot make any further attempt at that height, except in the case of a tie.

• A new height must be measured before the competitors attempt that height. In the case of a record the judges must check the height after it has been cleared, so that the record may be approved.
• Even after all the other competitors have failed on three consecutive attempts, a competitor can continue to jump until he has lost the right to compete further.

Once a competitor has won the event, the height at which the cross-bar is placed will be established after the principal judge or the referee responsible for that event has heard from the competitor.
• The uprights must not be moved during the competition unless the referee considers that the take-off or run-up area has become unusable. In this case, the change must be made after a round has been completed.
• MARKERS. A competitor may place

The straddle
Towards the middle of the 1930s another American, Dave Albritton, proposed a radical new technique for clearing the cross-bar, involving the body being parallel to the bar, but with the stomach downwards rather than with the body sideways. Thus the 'straddle' was born, which was clearly demonstrated by the Soviet trainer Vladimir Mihailovic Dyachkov and put to good effect by Valeri Brumel, who took the world record to 2.28 m in 1963.

Fosbury
An entirely original and revolutionary method of high-jumping was provided by Dick Fosbury, the most recent of the North American inventors, who used his technique to win the high-jump in the 1968 Olympics. It involves a curved run-up, which places the athlete side-on to the bar from where he jumps and rotates his body so that he crosses the bar on his back before landing on his shoulders. However, although this new technique proved to be highly successful, the straddle still showed itself to be a very effective method when Vladimir Yaschenko jumped 2.35 m in 1978, thus keeping alive the discussions as to the relative merits of the Fosbury flop and straddle.

Fosbury's technique makes it possible to use technically in flight all the force produced by the take-off.

markers (supplied by the organizers) to assist him in the run-up and in the take-off, and a small handkerchief or similar object on the cross-bar so that he is able to see it better.
• The length of the run-up is unlimited.

In the Olympic Games and in the world, Continental or Group Championships, the run-up area must be at least 20 m long.
• UPRIGHTS. Uprights or supports of any type may be used, provided that they are rigid. The supports for the cross-bar must be firmly fixed to them. The distance between the two uprights must not be less than 4.00 m or greater than 4.04 m.
• CROSS-BAR. The cross-bar must be made of wood, metal or other suitable material, with triangular or circular section. Its length must be between 3.98 m and 4.02 m. The maximum weight of the cross-bar must be 2 kg.

• SUPPORTS FOR THE CROSS-BAR. The supports for the cross-bar must be flat and rectangular, 40 mm wide and 60 mm long. They must be fixed steadily to the uprights during the jump and each of them must face the opposite upright. The ends of the cross-bar must rest in such a way that, if it is touched by a competitor, it may fall to the ground without difficulty either in front or behind. The supports may not be covered with rubber or with any other material which might increase the friction between the two surfaces of the cross-bar and of the supports. They may not even have any type of springs.
• There must be a space of at least 10 mm between the ends of the cross-bar and the uprights.
• The landing zone must measure not less than 5 × 3 m.
• TIES. The competitor with the smaller number of jumps at the height

at which the tie is confirmed shall be awarded the placing. If there is still a tie the competitor with fewer faults during the entire event shall be awarded the best placing. If after this there is still a tie, if it concerns first place, the competitors involved must perform another jump at the lowest height at which either of the tied athletes has failed, and if this is not conclusive then the cross-bar shall be lowered or raised to the heights which shall be announced by the judge in charge; they shall perform a jump at each height until the tie is decided; competitors concerned must make all the attempts required; if it concerns any other placing, the competitors must be classified equal.

Styles of high jumping in use today

THE STRADDLE
The straddle jump is still in use, although in recent years it has been mostly displaced by the Fosbury flop.

Here are the features of the straddle.

The run-up. For top-ranking athletes the run-up is angled at 30°–40° in relation to the uprights.

This inclination is necessary to carry out the beneficial 'kicking' action of the limb which is projected upwards at the moment of take-off from the ground. In this way, through the simultaneous rotation by more than 30°–40° of the take-off foot, caused by the kicking action of the free (swinging) limb, an optimal flight parabola follows. This technique is

also called 'orthodox', but outstanding results have also been obtained by athletes who practise the so-called 'diving straddle', involving a run-up with a greater angle, from 40° to 60°, which obliges the athlete to take off further from the plane of the uprights with an action of the free limb called 'kicking with leg flexed'. This action involves a subsequent difficulty in

The style of Vladimir Yaschenko
Vladimir Yaschenko as he clears 2.35 m at the Indoor European Championships of 1978 in Milan. That measurement gave him the indoor world record. The sequence sketched shows the style of the Soviet athlete who in 1978 took not only the indoor world record, but also the outdoor one, which he raised to 2.34 m.

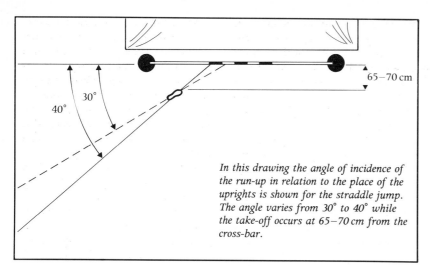

40° 30°

65−70 cm

In this drawing the angle of incidence of the run-up in relation to the place of the uprights is shown for the straddle jump. The angle varies from 30° to 40° while the take-off occurs at 65−70 cm from the cross-bar.

This photo shows Sara Simeoni at the moment of take-off; note the difference between her technique and the one shown below. The arm nearest the bar anticipates the flight phase.

clearing the bar by the take-off leg, because of the longer parabola which the athlete's body describes over the cross-bar. Usually the run-up is of 8−10 strides. The maximum speed which a jumper reaches before take-off is about 7.5 m/s (27 km/h or 17 mph). The technique of the run differs appreciably from that of the sprinter, since the object is to attain a horizontal speed which will enable the 'entry−take-off' action to transmit the maximum vertical speed to the centre of gravity of the athlete. In order to achieve this the athlete has to acquire speed without causing excessive vertical movement of the centre of gravity with each step. The result is a more skimming jump which seems like a succession of leaps with short pauses on each foot.

The last three strides. The grounding for completing an effective take-off is made from the third from last stride onwards. After the first stage (acceleration), in which he has his trunk sloping forward slightly, the athlete must bring the trunk into a perfectly vertical position in the penultimate two strides, then straighten up, and establish contact on the last stride (charging) closely and with a marked bending of the leg (about 110°−120°). Next comes the positioning of the take-off foot with the leading foot pushing at the ankle joint.

The drawings at the side represent each detail of the arched-back clearance. In comparison with Simeoni's technique, the athlete shown does not anticipate the flight with the arm opposite to that of the take-off leg.

This action permits a rapid movement of the pelvis which, at the moment it passes the upright, will receive a thrust upwards caused by the extension of the take-off foot and assisted by the kicking movement of the free limb and of the arms.

From the third from last stride the upper limbs prepare for the final action with a simultaneous oscillation, a semicircular movement of outside−backwards−down−forwards−up.

The crossing. Having completed the take-off stage, the athlete continues towards the cross-bar, attacking it with the free leg and the corresponding arm. The jumper should remember that, after take-off, it is not possible to change the trajectory of the centre of gravity. He raises one part of the body by lowering another through reaction, or else twists the shoulders in one direction, offsetting it by twisting the pelvis in the opposite direction. Thus he completes a rotation of the body along its longitudinal axis and clears the cross-bar.

The maximum vertical speed has been reached by Brumel with about 4.5 m/s, equal to 16.20 km/h.

The drop. The landing used to take place on sand or wood shavings, so the athlete had to be careful of the impact he would sustain. Now, with mattresses, there is no longer any problem for straddle jumpers.

Advice to the young. For boys who intend to take up high-jumping they should practise both the straddle and arched-back techniques. Those who plan to specialize in the straddle must realize that the development of technique is closely bound up with the improvement of the physical quality of 'force'. For this reason the straddle requires a longer period of maturation in the learning stage in comparison with the arched-back technique, which makes particular use of speed and elasticity which are already present at a young age and do not therefore require a long period of

training in order to obtain adequate development. From the time when the action of entry—take-off appears somewhat difficult in the straddle, it is advisable to repeat the last three strides several times before stopping and then progressively adding 2—4—6 run-up strides.

A useful piece of equipment for assimilating the clearance technique is the vaulting-horse (without pommels) at suitable heights; with the development of the athlete this will be exchanged for the 'roller', a cylinder mounted on two supports of variable height, able to rotate on itself and on which the athlete, having moved off the ground after a normal run-up, is helped to perform the rotation along the longitudinal axis by leaning on it.

THE ARCHED-BACK TECHNIQUE

The Fosbury flop was introduced by Dick Fosbury, who won the high-jump at the Mexico Olympics in 1968.

Apart from his technique for clearing the bar, his run-up was also very notable because it was in the form of a semi-circle, and he took off with his foot at an angle of about 20° relative to the plane of the uprights. He suddenly appeared to have more speed on take-off than the best exponents of the straddle; in fact it was more than 8 m/s (28 km/h).

At the point of take-off Dick Fosbury, with a vigorous bending action and driving up of the free leg, supported by an alternated movement of the upper limbs, rose completing a rotation on the longitudinal axis of the body and then prepared for flight with his back to the cross-bar. Next he performed a rotation on the transverse axis of the body and, at the extreme point of the parabola, he arched himself and continued his trajectory in this position until, so as not to knock down the cross-bar, he straightened his legs and landed on his back, bowing his head on to his trunk so that the impact was taken by

the top part of the back, thus avoiding unpleasant injuries to the cervical part of the spinal column.

Fosbury's innovative technique has now become the accepted one for the high-jump, and in the first World Championships, in Helsinki in August 1983, all the high-jump competitors both male and female, adopted the arched-back method.

The run-up. This is curved, because it has been ascertained that, by running in a curve, the jumper's centre of gravity falls inside, in relation to the support of the feet, because of the inclination on the longitudinal axis of the body. This permits the athlete to maintain a higher horizontal speed at the moment of the entry–take-off phase, since at that stage he benefits from a natural loading due to the position of the centre of gravity. At the moment of take-off the centre of gravity is lifted as a result of the athlete straightening his body; he can then complete the upwards thrust, benefiting from the higher run-up speed and from the centrifugal action caused by the circular trajectory, which, if properly directed by the take-off force, increases the vertical speed, making greater use of the elastic qualities of the human muscular system.

The speed in the run-up can easily be as much as 8 m/sec. The usefulness of a curved run-up becomes apparent only at the end of it, so Fosbury's curved run-up has been modified; this is also because of the difficulties in maintaining the inclination of the body in the final part of the run-up when the athlete is still moving on a curved trajectory.

Following Dwight Stones' example, many top-class high jumpers of today run the first 4–6 strides in a straight line, and then continue the last 5 strides towards the take-off on a curve of variable radius, which allows them to arrive at the take-off point ready to transform as much of the horizontal speed as possible into vertical speed and to allow inclination towards the inside of the curve and inclination backwards in the direction of jumping.

The number of strides in the run-up varies between 9 and 11, excluding the initial walking steps.

The last three strides. In this style of jumping also, although pretty imperceptibly, loading takes place on the next to last stride in order to assist the athlete to take off. Unlike the straddle, where the loading consists of a penultimate step which is much longer than the last one, in the Fosbury flop this does not necessarily happen, but it is sufficient to carry out a more marked landing on the penultimate step, followed by complete extension of the leg; this stride is therefore different from the normal running action and enables the take-off leg to establish contact well in front of the projection of the centre of gravity on to the ground and to carry out an effective take-off.

The arm action has also undergone development compared with the original Fosbury flop. The alternating action has changed to a synchronized action of the arms, which helps to give greater lift to the body. Nowadays there are two variations of the Fosbury flop: the first adheres to Fosbury's standards while the second type is much more similar to the straddle with regard to the movements and the kicking action of the free leg. This allows athletes who are not very fast and supple to use longer pauses on each stride, which favour the application of a greater force in time and therefore to obtain more vertical movement which will nevertheless reduce the forward speed. However, when the horizontal speed is reduced too much, the athlete, possibly bringing the centre of gravity very high, is unable to complete a sufficiently broad parabola in order to clear the cross-bar with all parts of the body.

Very tall athletes (from 1.90 m to 2.03 m) who at first find it difficult to use the straddle because of the excessive force necessary for elevation which, developed over such long segments of the body, results in an unfavourable weight–power ratio, might do better trying out the Fosbury flop.

Training for the young

It is important to emphasize that this training is completely different from that for a mature athlete. The programme is laid out to cover each school term, one work period for each one. We advise four training sessions per week of an hour's duration, with up to 1½ hours for 14–15 year olds.

FIRST WORK PERIOD

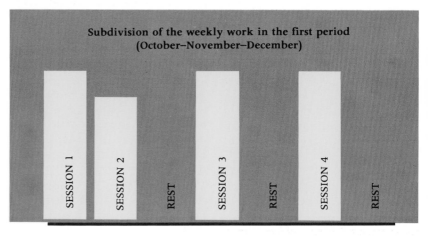

Subdivision of the weekly work in the first period
(October–November–December)

SESSION 1 — SESSION 2 — REST — SESSION 3 — REST — SESSION 4 — REST

Session 1
Warming up: imitative paces (alternated step–take-off, alternated jumps, two steps–take-off, etc.); these exercises perform a double function, technical and conditional, since they trace the principles of the take-off thrust and, if repeated as a series, lead to useful muscular strengthening. These exercises must also be repeated on a slight slope, with small overloads: ankle-supports of about 500 g each and ballasted belts weighing 2–3 kg; 3–4 spurts of 70–80 m at progressive speed.

Jumps: both single and multiple jumps are carried out. For example: long jump and triple and quintuple jump with start from standstill and landing in sand. A total of 20−25 jumps are recommended for each session.

Hill sprint: these are carried out on slopes which vary from 10% to 15%; the recommended distances are of 30 m and 40 m to be repeated 6−8 times with a recovery of 3−4 min.

Games: chosen from those which involve jumping (volley-ball and basket-ball).

Session 2

Warming up: the exercises which affect the lower limbs, and in particular the paces for the feet, are directed at improving ankle-joint mobility and the reaction of the feet to impulses (rolling paces and all the running exercises of the sprinter).

Reactivity: series of jumps with both feet together to be performed over 6−8 small obstacles placed at intervals of 60−80 cm and others at 40−60 cm; carry out 8−10 series.

Strengthening: exercises for learning the technique of lifting with the balance; but it will certainly result in a development of the speed force since the loads must be very light.

Principal exercises: swinging to the chest, the high lift jerk, half-squat or crouch, scissor jumps as in drawing 4.

During and after the exercises with the overload a series of general muscle-strengthening exercises is performed, which affect the scapulo-humeral girdle, the abdominal and back muscular system. N.B.: the exercises with the overload must be carried out in 4−6 series of 6−10 repetitions, with a pause of 3−4 min. between one series and the next. It is inadvisable to perform more than 2−3 exercises with overload per session.

Session 3

Warming up: flexibility and stretching exercises; 3−4 runs of 60−80 m at progressive speed.

Technique: carrying out several basic elements of jumping styles. Examples: technique of running in a curve for the 'flop'; take-off exercises using the long-jump runway with short run-ups (4−6 strides); combinations of successive jumps starting from standstill and with several launching steps; exercises with the rigid pole on the runway.

General exercises: a series of 40−50 throws with iron balls or 3−5 kg medicine balls in all directions for development of the athlete's instantly available power.

Session 4

Warming up: exercises of flexibility and mobility of the hip joints; technical exercising over obstacles; bar clearances with first and second leg and runs over 3−5 obstacles at suitable distances and heights.

Aerobic power: continuous running at a steady speed with heart rate of about 150−160 beats per minute over distances of 2−3 km. The exercises serve to improve the general organic qualities and contribute to the development of the cardio-circulatory system. Exercising is included in the first half of the first period, while in the second half it is replaced by training for speed resistance. Repetitions are carried out over distances of between 60 m and 200 m with recoveries sufficient to ensure reasonable speed in all the runs. Examples: 2 series of 2 × 60 m, with a pause of 2 min. between tests, and pause between series of 8 min., so 10 min. altogether; 2 × 80 m with pause between tests of 2 min. 30 sec., 12 min. pause; 1 × 150 m.

Games: see the games suggested in the first session. When necessary, this training may be replaced by elementary free-standing or large-apparatus acrobatics.

◼ SECOND WORK PERIOD ◼

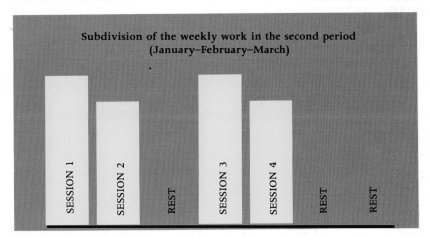

Subdivision of the weekly work in the second period (January−February−March)

SESSION 1 | SESSION 2 | REST | SESSION 3 | SESSION 4 | REST | REST

The subdivision allows greater recovery compared with that of the preceding cycle and, by lightening the work on the fourth day, allows for indoor competitions in the case of jumping, on the sixth or seventh days.

Session 1

Warming up: paces for the feet (the exercises are identical to those performed by sprinters); two or three runs.

Reactivity: series of jumps with both feet together to be carried out over 6−8 small obstacles placed at intervals of 60−80 cm and others at 40−60 cm: complete 8−10 series.

Sprint: 6−8 series of accelerations starting from a standing position and from starting-blocks.

Exercises in technique: series of imitative paces: the same exercises of the first period must be performed with several run-up steps which will allow a higher speed of execution. Examples: 3−5−7 steps and take-off in a continuous series; several complete run-ups imitating the take-off of the high jump; several entry−take-off exercises.

General exercises: series of throws (20−30) of a medicine ball from behind and bottom−forwards−up.

Session 2

Warming-up: exercises of flexibility and stretching; 3−4 spurts of 60−80 m; exercises in technique and runs repeated over 5 obstacles at suitable heights and distances.

Jumps: 6–8 long jumps from a standstill; 10–12 multiple jumps with 2–4 run-up strides (double-triple-quintuple) in successive and alternate form.

N.B.: in this period the jumps may be carried out alternately using a light overload (2–3 kg belt).

Speed resistance: runs of 60–200 m at intensity greater than that of the first period. In order to obtain this speed in all the tests it will be necessary to reduce the amount of the work and to lengthen the recovery periods slightly.

Session 3

Warming-up: exercises of flexibility and stretching; 3–4 spurts of 60–80 m in progression.
Reactivity: see first session.
Technique: series of jumps, in the various disciplines, with shortened run-ups; towards the end of the period use complete run-ups as well.

Particular attention should be paid to the technique and the most obvious mistakes corrected; 15–20 jumps in all are recommended.

Strengthening: exercises directed at maintaining strength acquired in the first period through a more limited number of series and repetitions. The following will be undertaken: swings to the chest (4 series with 2–3 repetitions with medium–high load and brief pauses for recovery between the series); high lift jerk (with the same method quoted above); rapid half squat (3–4 series of 4–6 repetitions with heavy load) or alternated scissors jumps on the sagittal plane (4 series per 4–6 repetitions).

Session 4

Warming up: imitative technical paces in intensive form; 2–3 accelerations for 30–40 m.
Training: sprint dragging a load of 8–10 kg; 1 series of 4 × 20 m; 1 series

of 4 × 30 m; 3–8 min. pauses.
Compensation sprint: stretches of running of about 30 m are carried out both with start from a standstill and when moving. This form of exercising is typical in the first half of the second period. In the second half, it will be replaced by exercises to improve speed. Examples: 2–3 tests are completed over 80–120 m with long recovery periods and at almost maximum speeds.
Games: see preceding periods. If necessary, this part can be exchanged for a series of general muscle-strengthening exercises (preparatory athletics).

TRAINING FOR THE COMPETITION PERIOD (from mid-April to mid-June)

Session 1
Warming up: exercises of flexibility

THIRD WORK PERIOD

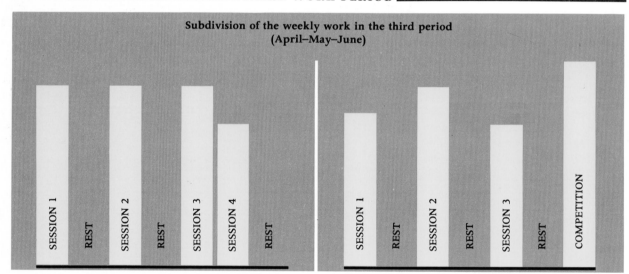

Subdivision of the weekly work in the third period
(April–May–June)

The 'special' period is given that name because 'special' training is introduced which puts the finishing touches to the preparation allowing the athlete to take part in competitions.

After a break of about 15 days for recuperation (in the last fortnight of March), training is resumed with a third work period.

In this period of training, there are two possible divisions of the work of building up and technique characteristic of the second part of the second

Competitive period: typical of the second part and there is a considerable reduction in the work since, especially in the high jump, the efficiency of the nervous system plays a large part.

period; however, the intensity will vary and several new means of training will be included. As for the jumps, the main special system of exercises is called 'pliometry'. It consists of a series of jumps from a height to the ground and a successive jump upwards or forwards and up. It may be

carried out on both the limbs or on only one (generally that used for take-off). Because of the intensity of the exercises it is advisable for the 'young' to fall from heights no greater than 40–50 cm, not vertically, but 1–1.50 m forwards in order to avoid too severe stresses on the tendons.

and elongation (stretching); 3–4 spurts of 80–100 m in progression; exercises over the obstacles and runs repeated over 5 obstacles.

Reactivity: see training session of the preceding periods.

Polycompetition: series of throws (20–30) for maintaining strength and speed.

N.B.: this training is not heavy because it is on the day following competition.

Session 2

Warming-up: intensive running paces; 3–4 spurts of 60–80 m; 3–4 accelerations of 30–40 m.

Pliometry: complete 10–15 drops alternating the exercises with thrust upwards with others having thrust forwards and upwards according to the particular event and the requirements.

Technique: series of 10–15 jumps with shortened and complete run-ups. Generalized strengthening: exercises affecting the abdominal and back muscular system of the upper limbs.

Session 3

Warming up: exercises of flexibility and stretching, several exercises of swinging and jerks with the balance.

Speed: (1) variation of speed: run distances from 80 m to 120 m with deceleration. Repeat 2–3 tests with long periods of recovery (12–15 min.); (2) tests of speed: they are carried out over distances from 40 m to 60 m timing the first stretches of 20–30 m. In this way both the capabilities of acceleration and those of starting can be tested. Alternate exercises 1 and 2.

Training for mature jumpers

The training schedules given below are those followed by Sara Simeoni, and there are two important points to note: (a) a wide range of exercises is employed and these help to provide interest in training sessions; (b) the aim is to learn strength and how to use it.

The athlete should also note that the sessions are for women, and that the potential for the muscles is less than that of men.

THE BASIC EXERCISES

Weights 1, 3, 5

1: Half-squat: 4 series of 6 repetitions to be carried out quickly and rhythmically. The load should be increased gradually to 80% of body weight, with 3 min. pauses between the series.

3: Alternated scissors jumps on the sagittal forward plane: 4 series of 8 repetitions with a load increasing from 50% to 80% of body weight.

5: Stretching exercises for the feet: 4 series of 30 stretches with a load of 20–30 kg.

Weights 2, 4

2: Alternated scissors jumps on the sagittal plane. Similar to no. 3, but they can be carried out more slowly because of the increased weight, 4 series of 6 repetitions; starting with no load increasing to 80–100% of body weight.

4: Half-squat with jump; 4 series of 5 repetitions; initial load of 20 kg increasing to 70% of body weight.

General strengthening: Various throws

	Typical week in the introductory cycle (from 15 Oct. to 10 Nov.)
Session 1 • Weights 1,3,5 (see this page). • Basket-ball. • Progressive stretches: 10 × 100 m, recovery of 3 min. between the tests.	**Session 5** • Weights 1,3,5. • Basket-ball. • Generalized strengthening with acrobatic exercises.
Session 2 • Exercises in running technique with and without obstacles. • Special paces. • Generalized strengthening.	**Session 6** • Running uphill (slope 15%): 3 series of 3 × 30 m. • Progressive stretches: 10 × 100 m, recovery of 3 min. between the tests. • Generalized strengthening with acrobatic exercises.
Session 3 • Weights 2,4,5 (see this page). • Basket-ball. • Jumps: 5 triple, 5 quintuple. • Spurts: 8 × 100 m, recovery of 4 min. between the tests.	**Session 7** • Rest.
Session 4 • Active rest. • Basket-ball or volley-ball.	

with both hands; behind and forwards with a 4 kg weight, total of 30–50 throws in each training session.

Elasticity: In the special cycle execute jumps with feet together between hurdles of 30–50 cm high (it is suggested that the athlete does not bend his knees on contact with the ground) in the shortest time possible: 3 series of 3 × 8 hurdles 80–90 cm apart.

Sprinting: To improve acceleration and strength and the capacity to activate the nervous system as quickly as possible: 3 series of 3 × 30 m.

Method: In the introductory and basic cycles, the training with weights is by a series of repetitions, with the difference that in the basic cycle the load is increased by 15–20%.

In the special cycle, the system is a

pyramidal one with the number of repetitions being reduced as the load is increased. Most of the repetitions will be with the least overload (80% of max. force) while the maximum load will be applied in one go.

Useful advice: Training with overload can be dangerous; the main problem is damage to the joints, particularly the knees and the base of the spine. To avoid this risk, the following precautions can be taken:
(a) the improvement in technique in carrying out the movements;
(b) the use of special shoes to raise the heels 5 cm from the ground;
(c) the use of a rigid belt to limit the movement of the base of the spine.

JUMPS AND PACES

Exercising with jumps and paces enriches the training of the jumper, aiming to give a structure to the muscular system for the purpose of jumping. From a biomechanical point of view, the parts of the body which contribute to jumping – bones, joints, muscles – are stimulated in the stretching–absorption–push-off phase in a similar manner to the action of jumping true and proper.

The paces are a preparatory means of learning the high jump. In fact, in the way they are carried out, some technical elements of exercises of this kind are very like some movements in competition jumping, such as the penultimate stride, the positioning of the take-off leg, the action of the free leg, the arm action. In short, the exercises suggested in the paces combine to allow completion of the take-off thrust at maximum speed.

Jumps: alternate the triple, quintuple and decuple jumps with and without belt. Complete successive triple and quintuple forward jumps.

Methodology: in the basic work stage alternate and successive jumps are performed with and without a belt, in a ratio of 1:1 thus influencing, by means of the light load, strength more than the speed. Later on, as specific work approaches, the light overload can be eliminated and a brief run-up of 4 strides included, in order to help the stretching of the muscular system of the lower limbs. The ideal weight of the belt is 5% of the athlete's body weight.

Paces: they consist of the alternate step–take-off; always landing back on the same limb; executing three steps and take-off.

Methodology: in the basic work stage paces are carried out with and without a belt in the ratio of 1:1. In the period of special work, light overload is eliminated and obstacles of variable height (30–50 cm) are included when executing the step–take-off exercises and the 3 steps–take-off.

NOTE: Because a detailed training schedule for the young has been given, we have omitted some of the sessions for the mature high jumper. The typical week in the basic cycle (Oct.–Nov.) is broadly similar to the introductory cycle; that of the special cycle (Dec.–Jan.) is similar to the basic intensive cycle; and that of the basic cycle in preparation for outdoor events (Mar.–Apr.) is similar to the introductory cycle.

How to perform the exercise on the sagittal plane

Session 1
• Technique: 10 run ups, 10 jumps with half run-up.
• Paces: step–take-off landing back on the same leg: 3 series of 3 × 5 take-offs; 3 steps–take-off; 3 series of 3 × 5 obstacles.

Session 2
• Weights 1,3,5.
• Jumps: 4 triple; 4 quintuple.
• Spurts: 8 × 100 m, recovery of 4 min. between the tests.

Session 3
• Sprint: 3 series of 3 × 30 m, recovery of 3 min. between the tests.

Session 4
• Technique: 10 run-ups; 10 jumps with half run-up.
• Paces: step–take-off landing back on the same limb; 3 series of 3 × 5

In this three-week cycle, the training with weights will be carried out pyramidally and each session must not last longer than 30 min. It is important to carry out stretching exercises every day, during warming up.

Session 1
• Technique: 20 jumps.
• Sprint: 3 series of 3 × 30 m.
• General exercises: 30 throws, especially dorsal.
• Progressive stretches: 8 × 100 m, recovery of 4 min. between the tests.

Session 2
• Weights 2,4.
• Paces: 3 steps–take-off; 3 series of 3 × 3 obstacles.

Session 3
• Running exercises (running with obstacles, skipping, sprinting, run-

take-offs; 3 steps–take-off; 3 series of 3 × 5 obstacles.

Session 5
- Weights 1,3,5.
- Jumps: 4 triple; 4 quintuple.
- Spurts: 8 × 100 m, recovery of 4 min. between the tests.

Session 6
- Paces: step–take-off landing back on the same leg: 3 series of 3 × 5 take-offs; 3 steps–take-off; 3 series of 3 × 5 obstacles.
- General exercises: 40 throws.
- Progressive stretches: 8 × 100 m, recovery of 4 min. between the tests.

Session 7
- Rest.

Typical week in the special cycle (from 6 May to 26 May)

ning kicking forwards and backwards, running in a curve).

Session 4
- Technique: 20 jumps.
- General exercises: 30 throws.

Session 5
- Paces: 3 steps–take-off: 3 series of 3 × 3 obstacles.
- Progressive stretches: 8 × 100 m, recovery of 4 min. between the tests.

Session 6
- Technique: 20 jumps.
- Sprint: 3 series of 3 × 30 m.
- General exercises: 30 throws, especially back.
- Progressive stretches: 8 × 100 m, recovery of 4 min. between the tests.

Session 7
- Rest.

The special cycle has a particular importance for the high intensities which are achieved in view of the top competitions; therefore, it is advisable to give the athlete ample chance to recuperate and to modulate the work loads in the space of the weekly microcycle as follows: a high level of work on the first day, reducing to the third day, with an increase to a peak on the sixth day and rest on the seventh.

The stars

GEORGE HORINE (USA)
The first jumper to bring the sport up to date with modern times was George Horine. At the start of his career in 1910 he used a modified version of the scissors, but he invented the western roll and increased the record by 20 cm to 1.75 m. However, his trainer persuaded him to retain the previous method; he still made progress though, clearing 1.93 m in 1911. Eventually, Horine returned to his invention and on 18 May 1912 he became the first man ever to clear 2 m (6 ft 7 in.). His technique was rather rudimentary and he could manage only 1.89 m for third place at the 1912 Olympic Games in Stockholm. Horine was American champion only once, in 1915. At the end of his career, he had cleared 6 ft (1.83 m) no fewer than 57 times in official competitions, with 17 results between 1.905 m and 2.005 m.

VALERI BRUMEL (USSR)
The USSR entered high jumping for the first time in 1937, but 20 years passed before another Russian emerged of world class: Yuri Styepanov. Three years later, at the Olympic Games of 1960 in Rome, their emergence was confirmed by 18-year old Valeri Brumel, who took second place with 2.16 m. For Brumel it was only the beginning of a great international career. Before the end of 1960 he raised the European record to 2.20 m and the following year he took it to 2.25 m. Altogether he held the world record six times, with a maximum of 2.28 m in 1963 in Moscow, during the USSR–USA match.

His great rival was the American, John Thomas, and one of the closest battles between the two took place at the 1964 Olympic Games in Tokyo, where both men cleared 2.18 m and Brumel won on the basis of fewer faults. In 1965 Brumel suffered a motorcycle accident, in which he received numerous serious fractures. After many operations he returned to high-jumping in 1969, but his best height was 2.13 m in 1970. Brumel

Valeri Brumel

was one of the pioneers of training with weights, and was also capable of 10.5 sec. for the 100 m and 7.65 m in the long jump.

DICK FOSBURY (USA)

The Americans have always played a prominent part in the technical development and discovery of new high-jump styles. One of the most recent inventors was Dick Fosbury. Even though he had made the first experiments with his style at the age of 16, success did not come to him until the 1968 Olympic Games in Mexico, where he won with a new personal best of 2.24 m. The new style was named after him and was called the 'Fosbury flop'. After the Olympics he faded into obscurity and ended his career following a period with the Mike O'Hara professional circus. For many years the 'Fosbury flop' was regarded with scepticism by the older experts, especially in East European countries, but 17 years after Mexico Fosbury's style has conquered the world, almost completely supplanting the straddle.

DWIGHT STONES (USA)

He emerged at world level in 1972 when he was 19, winning the bronze medal at the Munich Olympic Games. Eleven years afterwards he was still capable of taking sixth place at the World Championships in Helsinki. He had an incredibly long career for a high-jumper, and was much talked about. He was the first to clear 2.30 m (1973), later improving on this on two occasions with 2.31 m and 2.32 m.

He uses the Fosbury flop, approaching the cross-bar from the right and taking off with the left foot. He has nevertheless tried the straddle, managing to clear 2.14 m.

VLADIMIR YASCHENKO (USSR)

Capable of jumping 2.03 m at the age of 15, 2.12 m at 16 and 2.22 m at 17, Yaschenko broke the world record on 3 July 1977 during the match between American and Russian juniors. The 18-year old cleared the bar at 2.33 m, thus succeeding Dwight Stones as world record-holder. The rise of this precocious talent continued in 1978, when he jumped 2.35 m in Milan and 2.34 m in June at Tbilisi. Many people

considered him capable of 2.40 m, but the harshness of his training began to take its toll. Injuries began to trouble him in 1978, when he won the European title in Prague with 2.30 m. Afterwards he underwent various operations to a knee which have kept him out of the sport. He is the most recent exponent of the straddle jump to hold the world record.

ZHU JIANHUA (PEOPLE'S REPUBLIC OF CHINA)

In the high-jump China has had three world-record holders: Cheng Feng-yung in the women's event (1.77 m in 1957), Ni Chi-chin in the men's event (2.29 m in 1970, not recognized because at that time the People's Republic of China did not form part of the IAAF) and finally Zhu Jianhua, who on 11 June 1983 in Peking jumped 2.37 m. On 22 Sept. of the same year in Shanghai he broke the record again, taking it to 2.38 m and, in 1984, he increased it by a further centimetre.

In 1973, just ten, he cleared 1.10 m. At the age of 16 he cleared 2 m for the first time with 13 cm to spare. In 1980 he did not participate in the Moscow Games, but jumped 2.25 m at a meeting in Mexico. Internationally, Zhu has not had as much success as he might, and he has entered two major competitions in consecutive years (World Championships 1983, and Olympics 1984) as world record holder and favourite and come away with only the bronze medal.

Zhu Jianhua

IOLANDA BALAS (ROMANIA)

Few athletics champions have dominated the world in their event for as long as Iolanda Balas in the high jump from 1958 to 1966. Using a modified version of the scissors she succeeded in taking the world high-jump record 14 times between 1956 and 1961. This last record remained unbeaten for 10 years. Between December 1956, when she was classified fifth at the Melbourne Olympics, and June 1967, she put together an amazing series of 140 consecutive victories.

At the peak of her career, when she had cleared 1.91 m, the second best height in the world was 7 cm below hers. Balas confirmed her superiority with two victories at the Olympic Games (1960 and 1964) and two at the European Games (1958 and 1962).

SARA SIMEONI (ITALY)

Her world record of 2.01 m in 1978 was the culmination of 13 years of work from the age of 12. At first she used a frontal jump, then the scissors and finally the Fosbury flop from 1969 onwards. Among her many successes in competition she has won the silver medal in the 1976 Olympics, the gold in Moscow in 1980, and the silver in the 1984 Games at Los Angeles. The third medal was particularly rewarding, as Simeoni has been plagued with injuries since the 1980 Olympics. She also took the bronze medal at the 1982 European Championships in Athens.

ROSEMARIE ACKERMANN (GERMAN DEMOCRATIC REPUBLIC)

Between 1974 and 1977 she reigned supreme in the world in the women's high jump, winning an Olympic title (Montreal, 1976) and a European one (Rome 1974). She gained the world record for the first time in 1974 with 1.94 m and improved on it several times, finally clearing 2 m on 26 Aug. 1977 in West Berlin.

Her greatest rival has been Sara Simeoni, but the German girl began to lose competitions after an Achilles' tendon operation.

Their most memorable encounter was at the European Games in Prague in 1978, where Simeoni (who a few days before had succeeded Acker-

Rosemarie Ackermann

mann as world record-holder with 2.01 m) defeated her by equalling the record of 2.01 m, while Ackermann jumped 1.99 m.

The German girl turned the tables in the 1979 European Cup in Turin, beating Simeoni with 1.99 m, but, like many champions, Ackermann too was a victim of stress fractures caused by overwork, and she never regained this level of performance. Her subsequent best was fourth place at the 1980 Games in Moscow.

ULRIKE MEYFARTH (FEDERAL GERMAN REPUBLIC)

Olympic champion and world-record holder (1.92 m) in 1972 at the age of 16, she excelled right at the start but then seemed to lose her way. Only in 1978 did she begin to recover, clearing 1.95 m and being placed fifth in the European Games in Prague.

A new Meyfarth, mature and determined, re-emerged in 1981, when she won the World Cup with 1.96 m. Meyfarth jumped 1.99 m at the 1982 European Indoor Games in Milan, establishing a new world record for indoor events, and finally beat the 2 m mark in July of that year. One month later, at the European Games in

Tamara Bykova

Athens, she succeeded Sara Simeoni as world-record holder with 2.02 m, and had thus once again reached the peak of her discipline after a gap of 10 years. Since 1981, she has had a great rivalry with Tamara Bykova, and added a further centimetre to her best height in 1983.

TAMARA BYKOVA (USSR)

For almost 30 years the world record eluded the efforts of female jumpers from the USSR, but in 1983 Tamara Bykova regained this for the Soviets.

In 1983, Bykova beat the 2 m barrier for the first time, won at the World Championships with 2.01 m and afterwards improved twice on the world record: 2.03 m in the final of the European Cup in London, along with Ulrike Meyfarth, then 2.04 m in Pisa. In the 1952 games in Helsinki, Walt Davis won the Olympic men's event with precisely this height. There is in this connection a difference which says a great deal about the progress of the women's high jump: with his leap of 2.04 m, Davis jumped his own height, whereas Bykova, 1.79 m tall, went 25 cm more than her own height. In 1984, she improved on that record by a further centimetre.

WORLD RECORDS

Men
m

2.00 George Horine (USA) 1912
2.01 Edward Beeson (USA) 1914
2.03 Harold Osborn (USA) 1924
2.04 Walter Marty (USA) 1933
2.06 Walter Marty (USA) 1934
2.07 Cornelius Johnson (USA) 1936
2.07 David Albritton (USA) 1936
2.09 Mel Walker (USA) 1937
2.11 Lester Steers (USA) 1941
2.12 Walter Davis (USA) 1953
2.15 Charles Dumas (USA) 1956
2.16 Yuri Styepanov (USSR) 1957
2.17 John Thomas (USA) 1960
2.18 John Thomas (USA) 1960
2.22 John Thomas (USA) 1960
2.23 Valeri Brumel (USSR) 1961
2.24 Valeri Brumel (USSR) 1961
2.25 Valeri Brumel (USSR) 1961
2.26 Valeri Brumel (USSR) 1962
2.27 Valeri Brumel (USSR) 1962
2.28 Valeri Brumel (USSR) 1963
2.29 Pat Matzdorf (USA) 1971
2.30 Dwight Stones (USA) 1973
2.31 Dwight Stones (USA) 1976
2.32 Dwight Stones (USA) 1976
2.33 Vladimir Yaschenko (USSR) 1977
2.34 Vladimir Yaschenko (USSR) 1978
2.35 Jacek Wszola (Poland) 1980
2.35 Dietmar Mogenburg (West Germany) 1980
2.36 Gerd Wessig (German Democratic Republic) 1980
2.37 Zhu Jianhua (People's Republic of China) 1983
2.38 Zhu Jianhua (People's Republic of China) 1983
2.39 Zhu Jianhua (People's Republic of China) 1984

Women
1.65 Jean Shiley (USA) 1932
1.65 Mildred Didrikson (USA) 1932
1.66 Dorothy Odam (GB) 1939
1.66 Esther Van Heerden (S. Africa) 1941
1.71 Fanny Blankers-Koen (The Netherlands) 1943
1.72 Sheila Lerwill (GB) 1951
1.73 Aleksandra Chudina (USSR) 1954
1.74 Thelma Hopkins (GB) 1956
1.75 Iolanda Balas (Romania) 1956
1.76 Mildred McDaniel (USA) 1956
1.76 Iolanda Balas (Romania) 1957
1.77 Cheng Feng-yung (China) 1957
1.78 Iolanda Balas (Romania) 1958
1.80 Iolanda Balas (Romania) 1958
1.81 Iolanda Balas (Romania) 1958
1.82 Iolanda Balas (Romania) 1958
1.83 Iolanda Balas (Romania) 1958
1.84 Iolanda Balas (Romania) 1959
1.85 Iolanda Balas (Romania) 1960
1.86 Iolanda Balas (Romania) 1960
1.87 Iolanda Balas (Romania) 1961
1.88 Iolanda Balas (Romania) 1961
1.90 Iolanda Balas (Romania) 1961
1.91 Iolanda Balas (Romania) 1961
1.92 Ilona Gusenbauer (Austria) 1971
1.92 Ulrike Meyfarth (West Germany) 1972
1.94 Yordanka Blagoeva (Bulgaria) 1972
1.94 Rosemarie Witschas (GDR) 1974
1.95 Rosemarie Witschas (GDR) 1974
1.96 Rosemarie Witschas-Ackermann (GDR) 1976
1.97 Rosemarie Witschas-Ackermann (GDR) 1977
2.00 Rosemarie Witschas-Ackermann (GDR) 1977
2.01 Sara Simeoni (Italy) 1978
2.02 Ulrike Meyfarth (West Germany) 1982
2.03 Ulrike Meyfarth (West Germany) 1983
2.03 Tamara Bykova (USSR) 1983
2.04 Tamara Bykova (USSR) 1983
2.05 Tamara Bykova (USSR) 1984
2.07 Lyudmila Andonova (Bulgaria) 1984

Pole vault
Technique

The first pole-vaulting competitions were in Ireland over 2000 years ago and, round about the middle of the 19th century, they were again included in the Caledonian Games, in the northern region of the British Isles, corresponding to present-day Scotland.

Both in the USA and in Britain, the first pole-vaulting events date back to about the middle of the 19th century, too. The first North American champion, Hugh H. Baxter, used a pole weighing about 30 lbs, (13.6 kg). The pole used in the same period in England by the 'flying men' of Ulverston, in Lancashire, was even heavier. The athlete could then move up the bottom grip to above the top one, in other words to climb up before clearing the bar. In those days the poles were made of ash, walnut or fir and had at the bottom end a triangular iron cap, 5 cm long. The vault was performed by planting the pole at about 90 cm from the line of the uprights. After the take-off, the athlete swung his body forwards, remaining suspended from the pole, in order to bring himself up while the pole reached a vertical position and to pass over the rope (later replaced by a cross-bar) in a sitting position.

The Ulverston technique was abandoned when new rules prohibited the moving of the grip during the airborne stage, and this led athletes to seek a greater pendular oscillation of the body suspended from the pole.

The age of bamboo. With the use of bamboo, lighter in weight, there was immediately an appreciable improvement in the results. In 1883, Baxter rose above 11 ft (3.65 m), just through using a bamboo pole.

An American, William Hoyt, was the first Olympic winner in 1896 in Athens. Also from the USA were the first innovators of alternatives to the techniques in use at that time; one example was the bringing of the gripping hand at the bottom closer to that at the top at the moment the pole was inserted in the ground, perfected by Raymond Clapp, this technique helping him to a world record of 3.62 m.

Bamboo poles gained universal use in the first years of the 20th century, thanks to instruction from the Frenchman Fernand Gonder, who used to train by also performing long jumps with a pole. With a bamboo pole the jumping technique settled down to a long pendular swinging of the body, also described as 'single action', since it eliminated any superfluous movements.

The run-up, also, stabilized over a length of about 32 m, and preparation for insertion in the hole took place between the final two steps. In the 1930s the Japanese and the Soviet Ozolin adopted very flexible bamboo poles, which they tried to load like the present-day glass-fibre ones.

The age of steel. In the period after the Second World War the steel pole was introduced which was an improvement on aluminium initially tested in the USA; aluminium had the advantage of being light, but the disadvantage of rigidity. Steel poles, although slightly heavier, already possessed a fair degree of elasticity, which continued to improve until they could bend up to 3 ft (0.914 m) without breaking. The credit for the improvement goes to the American engineer Richard Ganslen, who made a great contribution to the development of this event.

The age of metal poles practically ended towards the middle of the 1960s with the widespread adoption of glass-fibre equipment, introduced experimentally just after the Second World War. With the adoption of synthetic poles, competition results increased dramatically until the world record was beaten by over a metre, compared with heights obtained with a bamboo pole by the American Cornelius Warmerdam (4.769 m in 1942) and with a metal pole by the American Robert Gutowski (4.819 m in 1957).

The age of glass-fibre. The pole made of glass-fibre, a mixture of strands of glass filaments twisted and intertwined according to a precise design, held together by plastic resins, possesses great tensile strength. With glass-fibre, the athlete can grip the pole higher up and transfer the horizontal speed of the run-up to the pole, which bends a few feet below the grip and provides the impulse when it returns to a vertical position, coinciding with the athlete releasing his grip to clear the cross-bar.

The methods of clearing the crossbar have also undergone significant development, resulting in two basic styles known as 'jack-knife' and 'flyaway'.

With the jack-knife method the athlete flexes his body markedly, projecting his legs beyond the crossbar, usually outstretched, while with the 'fly-away' method the body tends to keep the flag position and carry out a faster clearance of the bar.

The 'fly-away' method
The athlete in action is Konstantin Volkov, one of the best vaulters of current years. The first picture depicts him in the final stage of planting the glass-fibre pole, which, starting from (2), begins to provide the accumulated energy, catapulting the athlete's body upwards. In picture (5), the athlete includes the clearing stage in which he keeps his body in a flag position with rapid crossing of the bar.

REGULATIONS (POLE VAULT)

1. The order in which the competitors take part is to be decided by drawing lots.

2. Before the competition begins, the judges/officials must tell the competitors what the starting height will be and the heights at which the bar will be placed at the end of each round, no-one remains in the competition or there is a tie.

3. Each competitor must be placed according to his best jump, including jumps performed in a decider in the event of a tie for first place.

In the case of a tie, the same rules apply as in the high jump.

4. A competitor can begin jumping at any height from the minimum height and can jump at his discretion at any later height. Three consecutive faults, irrespective of the height at which each fault has occurred, exclude a competitor from further attempts.

The effect of this rule is that a competitor may give up his second or third attempts at a certain height (having failed the first or second time) and instead try a greater height.

If a competitor renounces an attempt at a certain height, he cannot make any further attempts at that height, except in the case of a tie.

5. Each new height must be measured before the competitors attempt that height.

In the case of a record the judges must check the height after it has been cleared, so that the record may be ratified. In the case of a height exceeding a record, an official must measure the height (before and after the attempt) in addition to the other two judges.

Before the competition begins the judges must ensure the underneath and front edges of the bar can be clearly distinguished and that, if the bar comes down, it is replaced with the edges facing the same way as before.

6. Even after all the other competitors have failed on three consecutive jumps, a competitor can continue to jump until he has lost the right to compete further.

Once a competitor has won the event, the height at which the bar is placed will be established after the main judge or the referee responsible for that event has heard from the competitor.

7. A competitor may have the uprights moved to either side for his attempt, but not by more than 60 cm from the extension of the inside of the upper part of the stopping-board in the take-off box.

8. To get a better grip, a competitor can spread a suitable substance on the pole or his hands.

He is allowed to protect his forearm to help prevent injury.

A competitor is not allowed to use any sticky tape or plaster on his fingers or hands unless it is to cover an open wound.

9. A competitor commits a foul if:
- he knocks the bar from the supports;
- leaves the ground during his attempt but does not clear the bar;
- having left the ground he moves the lower hand on the pole above the other one, or moves the upper hand higher up the pole;
- at the take-off he touches, with the pole or his body, the ground including the landing area on the other side of the vertical plane above the stopping board.

10. If the pole breaks during a competitor's attempted vault, this does not constitute a foul.

11. No-one other than a competitor may touch the pole, except to take it away from the crossbar or the uprights. If, however, someone does touch it and the referee considers that the bar might have fallen anyway without interference, then the jump is considered to be void.

12. A competitor is allowed to use his own pole. No competitor can use another competitor's pole without the consent of the person concerned.

The pole can be made from any material or combination of materials, and can be of any length and diameter, but the surface must be smooth. The pole can have a covering of not more than two layers of sticky tape of uniform thickness.

This restriction is not applicable to the protective covering made from strips of tape at the lower end of the pole, for a length of about 30 cm, to reduce the risk of damaging the pole when pushing against the bottom of the take-off box.

13. The length of the run-up track is unlimited; the minimum length is 40 m. The width of the track must be at least 1.22 m.

14. The maximum slope across the track should be 1:100, and along the track 1:1000.

15. No indicator can be placed on the runway itself, but a competitor may place a marker (provided by the organizers) by the side of the runway. No indicator may be placed in the landing area. After the start of the competition no competitor may use the run-up track for training attempts.

16. The take-off for the pole-vault must be from a take-off box made from a suitably rigid material, which must be sunk level with the ground.

17. The landing area must be at least 5 × 5 m.

18. THE UPRIGHTS. Any uprights can be used as long as they are rigid.

The distance between the uprights or between the extension arms when used, must be not less than 4.30 m and not more than 4.37 m.

19. THE BAR. The bar must be made from wood, metal or other suitable material, and be of triangular or circular section. Its length must be 4.48–4.52 m. The maximum weight of the bar should be 2.25 kg.

Each side of the triangular bar should be 28–30 mm. To avoid dangerously sharp edges, the triangular bar should be made so that the edges are slightly rounded. The circular-section pole should be at least 25 mm in diameter but not more than 30 mm. The ends of the circular bar must be made so that a flat surface 25–30 × 150–200 mm is obtained, in order to rest the bar on the supports fixed to the uprights. The parts of the bar which rest on the supports must be smooth and not covered with any substance which might increase the friction with the supports.

20. SUPPORTS FOR THE BAR. Supports must be used to keep the bar up; they must have no notches or indentations of any kind, be of uniform thickness and of a diameter of not more than 13 mm. They must not jut out from the uprights by more than 75 mm, and the bar must rest on these so that, if touched by a competitor or the pole, it can fall easily in the direction of the landing area.

The supports must not have a rubber covering or covering of any other material which would help to increase the friction between them and the bar.

21. THE TAKE-OFF-BOX. This must be made from a suitable rigid material and sunk level with the ground, the sloping internal surface being 1 m long, 60 cm wide at the front narrowing at the end to 15 cm at the bottom of the stopping-board. The length of the take-off-box at ground level and the depth of the stopping-board depend on the angle formed between the sloping bottom and the stopping board, which must be 105°.

The bottom of the take-off-box must slope from ground level away from the front of the box to a depth of 20 cm where it joins with the stopping-board. The take-off-box must be made in such a way that the sides slope inwards and join the stopping-board at an angle of ~120°.

If the take-off box is made of wood, the bottom must be lined with a layer of metal 2.5 cm deep and 80 cm long from the front part of the take-off box.

Below and to the right are drawings of the landing zone and of the take-off-box with the relevant dimensions specified in the regulations.

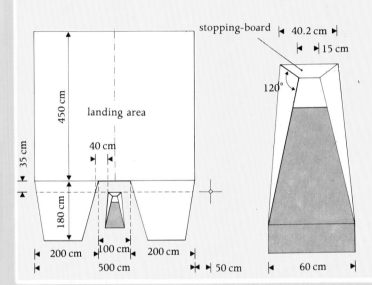

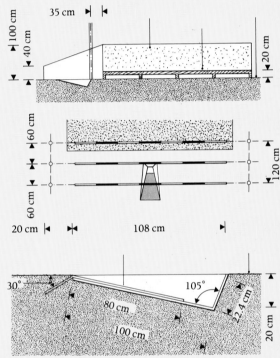

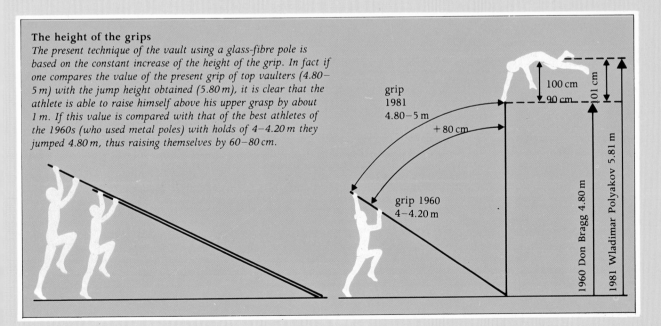

The height of the grips
The present technique of the vault using a glass-fibre pole is based on the constant increase of the height of the grip. In fact if one compares the value of the present grip of top vaulters (4.80– 5 m) with the jump height obtained (5.80 m), it is clear that the athlete is able to raise himself above his upper grasp by about 1 m. If this value is compared with that of the best athletes of the 1960s (who used metal poles) with holds of 4–4.20 m they jumped 4.80 m, thus raising themselves by 60–80 cm.

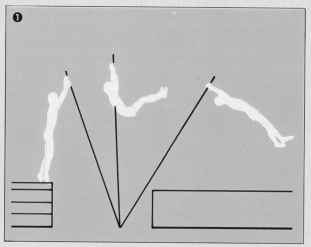

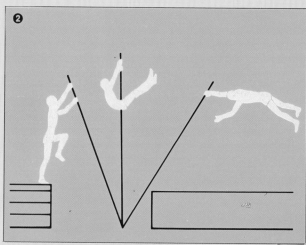

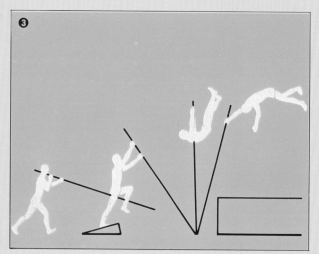

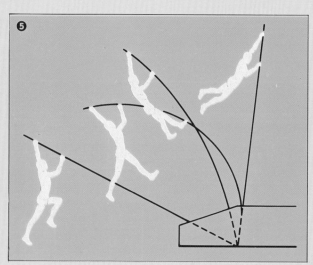

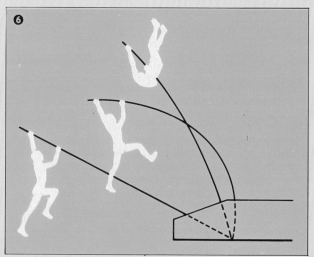

Instruction

From the teaching point of view it is advisable to proceed by carrying out a series of exercises which present ever-increasing difficulties, naturally being aware of the gradual nature of the task.

With this aim, we suggest the sequence represented below: drawings 1–2–3–4–5–6.

It may be observed that first contact with the equipment takes place with the use of a rigid pole (drawings 1–2–3).

Later on, one will pass (drawings 4–5–6) to a flexible pole, making use of some simplified situations in order to accustom the young athlete to flexing the pole.

Training in technique for the young

Although defined as an elevated jump, the pole vault presents several peculiarities bound up with the equipment which cause it to be considered a jump up to the moment of the take-off, after which the athlete becomes a gymnast. The ideal competitor for this jump should be long-limbed, have a good muscular system, with strong upper limbs and trunk, and be gifted with courage and acrobatic talents. This will allow the athlete to grasp the pole higher up and, consequently, when his run-up speed and his take-off capacities are suited to the pole, he will be able to achieve greater heights.

This athletic event includes a long period of coaching, in which the youth must acquire all the technical and acrobatic basics necessary for mastering the pole. It is therefore advisable more than ever to bring the person who is suited to this event into it right from adolescence.

As the pole vault is a cross between gymnastics, acrobatics and athletics, the discipline will therefore be assimilated through a large number of repetitions and a progressive scale of difficulty. In fact between the ages of 7 and 11 the youngster should be directed to diverse athletic activities, thus stimulating new and increasingly complex schemes of movement. It is during the same period that the young man will begin the basic exercises of the pole vault, which between 12 and 14 years of age must become more specific. As we shall see later on, it will be necessary to follow a graduated programme.

Initially, the boy will be coached with a rigid pole and then he will be gradually accustomed to the use of flexible glass-fibre equipment. Obviously, his physical structure will probably not allow him to utilize the flexibility straightaway and, consequently, for a short time he may handle the glass-fibre pole as if it were rigid. By using suitable methods, it will be possible later on to make up for his initial lack of ability in order to bring him gradually to bend the pole in the way which is of most use and most functional for gaining the most height. At the present time, there are some fibre poles on sale which are particularly suited, through length, weight and gripping diameter, for the young. By taking advantage of these junior poles, beginners will very soon be able to experience the sensations of the flexible pole.

The various steps of the technique

How the pole is gripped
For athletes who take off with the left foot, the pole must be carried on the right-hand side; the left arm, half-bent, supports the pole with the palm of the same hand turned downwards), while the right arm grips about 60–70 cm higher with the hand lightly turned out. It is advisable to begin with these gripping exercises, and then go on to those of running with the pole, using a pole which is not too long (about 3 m), then raising the holding heights gradually.

The run-up
On account of its length and technique, the run-up in the pole vault is not very different from the run-ups for the long and triple jumps; nevertheless the appreciable loss of speed is due to carrying the pole which enforces a slightly asymmetrical running attitude and prevents the use of the upper limbs.

How the pole is planted
Having arrived close to the take-off box, and on the third from last step of the run-up, the athlete must direct the pole into the box itself.

Take-off and loading the pole
The athlete will then perform a take-off forwards and upwards, beginning the loading of the pole, which depends on:
(a) speed of the run-up at the moment of take-off;
(b) height of the hold;
(c) direction of the push-off in the take-off;
(d) greater or lesser hold of the front arm at the take-off stage;
(e) varying degree of oscillation of the athlete below the pole.

Somersault and follow-through
Having completed the swing under the pole, the athlete, using his arms as hinges, must complete a rocking-back action, at the same time drawing his knees up to his chest.

When the rock-back is achieved, allowing for the time taken for the pole to straighten, he will begin the 'follow-through', completing a quarter of a turn towards the left and bringing his body above the level of grip.

Clearance and landing on to the falling area
The jumper continues his action towards the cross-bar with the final thrust of the upper limb. This last action will enable him to clear the cross-bar with his stomach, with the head bent. Clearance will be achieved with a rapid bending towards the shoulder of the upper limb. As already stated, there are two styles for clearing the cross-bar: the jack-knife and the fly-away methods. There are no particular advantages with either technique so, as a result, athletes are advised to apply the one best suited to their acrobatic and physical qualities.

In the fall, since the height is considerable, the athlete must worry only about establishing contact with the mattresses on his back in order to prevent injury to himself.

One of the purposes of dividing the training into periods is to place the athlete in a state for reaching competition fitness. The training may be divided up into periods of one year or several years. The appearance of special cycles or periods within the division has introduced the term 'cyclization', which has come increasingly into current use.

More generally the cyclization of the training process includes periods of varying length. Within the limits of the jumps may be distinguished:
– the macrocycle lasting from six months to a year;
– the medium-cycle lasting from one and a half months to two months;
– the microcycle lasting from one to three weeks.

This subdivision is particularly important for the microcycle, since the cycle of one week will be seen as an organizational unit, while the three-week cycle constitutes a functional unit which acts through the cumulative effect of the training load.

In particular, in the pole vault the macrocycle lasts for six months since the double division into periods which provides two competitive cycles in the year is preferable: the cycle of indoor and outdoor competitions. In this work we have taken as an example the preparation leading to indoor competition.

Within the sphere of the first macrocycle are three periods of training: the introductory period, the basic preparatory period and the special completion period in preparation for the 'indoor' events. Then follows the period of winter competitions lasting one month, ending with the European Indoor Championships.

Viktor Drechsel is the demonstrator of some exercises which pole vaulters carry out during training and which appear on these pages.

Session 1
• Afternoon: warm-up. Stretching. Technique: 20–30 jumps with medium run-up (8–12 paces). Weights:
(a) snatch;
(b) scissors jumps;
(c) bench-press.

General exercises: 60 throws divided into two sets of 30.

Session 2
• Morning: warm-up. Uphill sprint: 5 × 40 m, recovery 3 min., 10 min. pause, 5 × 50 m.

• Afternoon: warm-up. Stretching. Jumps: 15 long, 15 triple, 10 quintuple. Gymnastics on apparatus. Specific exercises for the pole in gymnasium. Weights: 1/2 quick-squat, 1/4 squat-jump. 4 series x 5 repetitions.

WEEKLY TRAINING SCHEDULE

Typical week of the introductory cycle (from 24 Oct. to 15 Nov.)

Session 1
- Warm-up.
- Spurts: 5–6 × 80–100 m.
- Sprints: 8–10 × 20–30 m with flying and standing starts.
- General exercises (series of throws in all directions with iron ball weighing 6–7 kg).

Session 2
- Warm-up.
- Technical paces with the aim of stretching.
- Localized muscular exercises (flexors of the thighs, ischio-crural, gluteus, abdominal and back muscles).
- Jumps: slope 10–15%. 2 series of 4–5 repetitions of 30–40 m, pause of 2–3 min. between the runs and 6 min. between the series.

Session 3
- Sporting games: 1–1½ hours.

The games which offer the greatest affinity with jumping are chosen: (basket-ball, volley-ball, field hand-ball).

Session 4
- Warm-up.
- Stretching exercises.
- Weights:
(a) exercises of turning, snatching and throwing;
(b) squat or half-squat, 6 series of 6 repetitions with suitable load, pause between one series and the next 3–4 min.
(c) weight-lifting from the bench: 4 series with 6 repetitions.

Session 5
- Warm-up.
- Jumps:
(a) 6 triple with start from a standstill;
(b) 4 quintuple with start from a standstill;
(c) 2 decuple.
- Sprints 6–8 × 20–30 m.
- General exercises.

Session 6
- Warm-up.
- Technical paces with the aim of stretching.
- Hill runs: slope 10–15%, 2 series of 4–5 repetitions of 30–40 m, pause of 2–3 min. between the runs and 6 min. between the series.
- Exercises with springy mat.

Typical week of the cycle of basic preparation (from 16 Nov. to 15 Jan.)

Session 3
- Warm-up.
- General stretching paces and special ones for the pole.
- Technique: 20–30 jumps with short run-ups (4–6 paces).
- Short fast cross-country (3 km at a heart rate of 170–180 beats per minute).

Session 4
- Warm-up.
- Stretching.
- Sprint exercises.
- Track capacity: 1 × 150 m, recovery 8 min.; 1 × 200 m, recovery 8 min.; 1 × 250 m, recovery 10 min.; 1 × 250 m.
- General exercises: 80 throws, divided into two sets of 40.

Session 5
- Morning: warm-up. Pliometry: 3–4 × 6–8 falls, 2 min. recovery. Jumps: 5 triple, 5 quintuple, 5 decuple.
- Afternoon: warm-up.

Technique: 20–25 jumps with medium run-up. Apparatus. Special exercises for the pole in gymnasium. Weights: 1/2 quick squat, 1/4 squat-jump, 4 × 5 repetitions.

Session 6
- Warm-up.
- Sprint exercise: 10–12 × 30 m with start, recovery 3 min.
- Mixed capacity: 3 × 3 × 60 m, recovery 2 min., pause 8 min., 2 × 3 × 80 m, recovery 3 min., pause 10 min., 1 × 150 m, recovery 10 min.; 1 × 200 m.
- Weights: exercises for the upper limbs.

Session 7
- Morning: warm-up.

Circuit-training: 3 times with 10 min. recovery. General exercises, 80 throws: 40 back and 40 from below. Short fast cross-country (3 km at heart rate 170–180 beats per minute).

Week of the special completion cycle in preparation for the indoor events (from 16 Jan. to 7 Feb.)

Session 1

- Warm-up.

- Stretching.

- Normal and specific track capacity: 6 complete run-ups (18–20 strides) with the pole, recovery 4 min. between the runs and pause of 15 min.; 1 × 60 m, recovery 8 min. 1 × 80 m recovery 12 min.; 1 × 100 m. Polycompetition.

Session 2

- Morning: warm-up. Sprint exercises with 2 kg belt. 5 triple jumps, 5 quintuple with 2–4 run-up paces. Pliometry: 4 × 6 falls from 60 cm.

- Afternoon: warm-up. Stretching. Technique: 15–20 jumps with medium run-up (14 strides). Specific exercises for pole vaulting. Dynamic strengthening: 1/4 quick squat (load = 70% of the body weight); 4 series × 5 repetitions.

Session 3

- Warm-up.

- Technique: 10–15 jumps with complete run-up (16 strides first three weeks; 18 strides last three weeks).

- Strengthening the upper limbs.

Session 4

- Warm-up.

- Stretching.

- Sprint exercises.

- Mixed power: 1 × 100 m, recovery 10 min.; 1 × 50 m, recovery 15 min.; 1 × 150 m, recovery 10 min.; 1 × 100 m, or 4 × 100 m, recovery 12 min.

- General exercises.

Session 5

- Morning: warm-up. Jumps as in Session 2. Sprint: 3 × 3 × 40 m, 2 min. recovery and pause of 5 min. between the series.

- Afternoon: warm-up. Technique: 15–20 jumps with medium run-up (14 strides). Special exercises for the pole at the apparatus. Dynamic strengthening: 1/4 squat-jumps (load 50% body weight); 4 series × 5 repetitions.

Session 6

- Warm-up.

- Technique: 10–15 jumps with complete run-up (16 paces in the first three weeks, 18 in the last six weeks).

- Pliometry: 2 series × 4 falls before jumping and 3 × 4 falls after the technique.

- Strengthening the upper limbs.

The stars

HUGH BAXTER (USA)

The most important vaulter of the 19th century was the American Hugh Baxter of the New York Athletics Club. In 1878 he used a bamboo pole for the first time, but the following year he returned to a much heavier pole, made of white ash. Baxter is credited with modernizing the vaulting style, very effectively using both hands for the purposes of propulsion, whereas his predecessors were accustomed to 'pull' with only one hand, using the other as a prop.

Baxter was American champion for four consecutive years (1883–86) and improved on the world record until he brought it to 3.48 m in 1887, when he was 25 years old. In a paper on the pole vault which appeared in the 1920s ('Pole vaulting', by Henry F. Schulte), the author considered that Baxter's 3.48 m, obtained with a heavy and non-flexible pole, should be considered more or less equal to 4.11 m (13 ft 6 in.) in the 1920s, when such a measurement was good enough to win medals at the Olympic Games.

Baxter maintained that he was beaten only once in the period 1881–1895, by the English 'climber' Tom Ray. Baxter was a versatile athlete, showing good ability in the high jump, the hammer and the tug-of-war, and he organized and led the famous encounter between the athletics clubs of New York and London in 1895.

CHARLES HOFF (NORWAY)

The Americans dominated the world pole-vault scene for many decades, winning all the Olympics from 1896 to 1968. In the first half of the 20th century only one foreigner succeeded in breaking their monopoly in the world-record lists: the Norwegian Charles Hoff. He began with cross-country races and then passed on to the pole-vault. In 1921 he broke the Norwegian record with 3.87 m: up to that time there had only been two 'four-metre vaulters', the first being the American Mark Wright, with 4.02 m in 1912. In 1922 Hoff also cleared that height and before the end of the season he took the world record with 4.12 m. Later on he broke the record on several occasions, until he increased it to 4.25 m in 1925. Unluckily for him he was unable to participate in his event at the 1924 Olympic Games in Paris because of an ankle injury; instead he competed on the track, reaching the semis of the 400 m and the final of the 800 m.

In 1926 the American AAU invited Hoff to go on a 'tour' in the USA, and on several occasions Hoff beat the US all-comers record with a maximum of 4.17 m indoors and 4.19 m outdoors.

Hoff's commercial sense led him to capitalize financially on his talent, but the AAU subsequently disqualified him for infringing his amateur status, cancelling his American records. This was confirmed by the IAAF, who nevertheless let him retain his world record set the year before. Hoff introduced the fly-away method of pole-vaulting.

CORNELIUS WARMERDAM (USA)

He is considered by many as the most important name in the history of the pole vault. He was the first to clear 15 ft (4.57 m) in 1940 at Berkeley, and managed to raise the world record to 4.77 m, in 1942 at Modesto, a measurement never reached afterwards with bamboo poles. Indoors he did even better: 4.78 m in 1943.

At the time of his retirement in 1944, he had completed over 43 vaults of 15 ft. It was 1950 before another jumper, the American Don Laz, conquered that height.

He had begun to vault at the age of 14, clearing 9 ft (2.74 m). At 19 he cleared 14 ft (4.26 m) for the first time, which was then world class. In 1944, he was enlisted in the American Navy; had the Olympiads of 1940 and 1944 been held he would have had an excellent chance of winning two gold medals.

BOB RICHARDS (USA)

He never managed to hold the world record in this event, but he gained three Olympic medals from 1948 to 1956. He was also US champion nine times from 1948 to 1957. Although clearing 15 ft (4.57 m) 126 times, he never succeeded in surpassing the 4.77 m of Warmerdam. He ended with personal records of 4.70 m outdoors and 4.72 m indoors. For a good part of his career he jumped using metal poles, which bridged the gap between the age of bamboo and glass-fibre. Richards was versatile enough to be American decathlon champion three times.

BOB SEAGREN (USA)

One of the most important men of the age of glass-fibre was the American Bob Seagren, who gained the world record four times, beginning with 5.32 m in 1966 and finishing with 5.63 m in 1972.

An athlete of great competitive ability, he won a gold in the 1968 Olympics and a silver in Munich. On this last occasion he suffered from the fact that the pole of the new type used

by him a few weeks before for the last of his records was not among those allowed by the IAAF for Olympic competition. Any new equipment, even if in accordance with the rules, has to be on the market for at least a year in order to be approved by the IAAF.

WOLFGANG NORDWIG (WEST GERMANY)

Although his personal best of 5.50 m is not particularly outstanding, Wolfgang Nordwig is possibly the best pole vaulter that Europe has ever had. He was master of long-endurance competitions, in which the athletes are obliged to remain around the pole-vault runway for five hours or more, thus being subjected to a tremendous psycho-physical stress.

Nordwig won two Olympic medals: a bronze in 1968 in Mexico with 5.40 m (the same height with which Bob Seagren won the title) and a gold in 1972 at Munich with 5.50 m, the best result of his career.

In Europe he was dominant, winning outdoors in 1966, 1969 and 1971, and four victories at the European Indoor Games.

He began to pole-vault at the age of 15, clearing 2.80 m. He was familiar with the first glass-fibre poles as a junior and with one of them went up to 5.01 m in 1964. He was also outstanding at the decathlon.

WLADYSLAW KOZAKIEWICZ (POLAND)

His greatest victory was at the 1980 Olympic Games in Moscow, when he beat an exceptional field with the best result of his career, 5.78 m (also a new world record).

Kozakiewicz had begun to vault with a pole before the age of 11. He conquered 5 m for the first time at the age of 19. He became European record-holder in 1975 with 5.60 m and took the world record for the first time in the spring of 1980 in Milan with 5.72 m: he lost it during the course of the season, but recaptured it in Moscow.

Already in 1976, at the Montreal Games, he was among the favourites for the Olympic gold, but he suffered an accident in the early part of the event which prevented him from placing higher than eleventh. At the

Bob Seagren

European Championships he obtained his best placing (second) when he was young, in 1974 in Rome. He twice won the European Cup finals and in 1977 was placed second in the World Cup. He also scored a total of 7683 points in the decathlon.

KONSTANTIN VOLKOV (USSR)

In 1979, when he was still a junior, Volkov caused a sensation by coming first in the final of the European Cup and third in the World Cup. In 1980 he tied second in the Olympic event in Moscow; in 1981 he won again in the European Cup final and in the World Cup, although tying with the Frenchman Bellot. At the Helsinki World Championships he won the silver behind his young compatriot Sergei Bubka.

Thierry Vigneron

Sergei Bubka, the young Russian pole vaulter, who in 1984 raised the world record four times

His wins include two victories at the University Games (1981 and 1983), and his personal record is 5.75 m.

THIERRY VIGNERON (FRANCE)

Between 1980 and 1983 French athletes took the world pole-vault record no fewer than six times: one each by Philippe Houvion and Pierre Quinon, and four times by Thierry Vigneron. After a third place at the junior European Games of 1979 (where he was favourite), Vigneron finished seventh at the Moscow Olympic Games, tied fifth at the 1982 European Games and tied eighth at the 1983 World Championships. Like his compatriots, Vigneron usually gives his best performance in events of short duration, but tends to tire in those which last for a long time. Nevertheless his victories include two fairly important ones indoors: the 1981 European Championships and the US Championships of the same year.

WORLD RECORDS

m
4.02 Mark Wright (USA) 1912
4.09 Frank Foss (USA) 1920
4.12 Charles Hoff (Norway) 1922
4.21 Charles Hoff (Norway) 1923
4.23 Charles Hoff (Norway) 1925
4.25 Charles Hoff (Norway) 1925
4.27 Sabin Carr (USA) 1927
4.30 Lee Barnes (USA) 1928
4.37 Bill Graber (USA) 1932
4.39 Keith Brown (USA) 1935
4.43 George Varoff (USA) 1936
4.54 Bill Sefton (USA) 1937
4.54 Earle Meadows (USA) 1937
4.60 Cornelius Warmerdam (USA) 1940
4.72 Cornelius Warmerdam (USA) 1941
4.77 Cornelius Warmerdam (USA) 1942
4.78 Bob Gutowski (USA) 1957
4.80 Don Bragg (USA) 1960
4.83 George Davies (USA) 1960
4.89 John Uelses (USA) 1962
4.93 Dave Tork (USA) 1962
4.94 Pennti Nikula (Finland) 1962
5.00 Brian Sternberg (USA) 1963
5.08 Brian Sternberg (USA) 1963
5.13 John Pennel (USA) 1963
5.20 John Pennel (USA) 1963
5.23 Fred Hansen (USA) 1964
5.28 Fred Hansen (USA) 1964
5.32 Bob Seagren (USA) 1966
5.34 John Pennel (USA) 1966
5.36 Bob Seagren (USA) 1967
5.38 Paul Wilson (USA) 1967
5.41 Bob Seagren (USA) 1968
5.44 John Pennel (USA) 1969
5.45 Wolfgang Nordwig (GDR) 1970
5.46 Wolfgang Nordwig (GDR) 1970
5.49 Christos Papanicolau (Greece) 1970
5.51 Kjell Isaksson (Sweden) 1972
5.54 Kjell Isaksson (Sweden) 1972
5.55 Kjell Isaksson (Sweden) 1972
5.63 Bob Seagren (USA) 1972
5.65 Dave Roberts (USA) 1975
5.67 Earl Bell (USA) 1976
5.70 Dave Roberts (USA) 1976
5.72 Wladyslaw Kozakiewicz (Poland) 1980
5.75 Thierry Vigneron (France) 1980
5.77 Philippe Houvion (France) 1980
5.78 Wladyslaw Kozakiewicz (Poland) 1980
5.80 Thierry Vigneron (France) 1981
5.81 Vladimir Polyakov (USSR) 1981
5.82 Pierre Quinon (France) 1983
5.83 Thierry Vigneron (France) 1983
5.85 Sergei Bubka (USSR) 1984
5.88 Sergei Bubka (USSR) 1984
5.90 Sergei Bubka (USSR) 1984
5.94 Sergei Bubka (USSR) 1984
6.00 Sergei Bubka (USSR) 1985

Long jump
Technique

The long jump is one of man's most natural exercises.

In prehistoric times it was practised as a necessity of life, then it became a sport and an opportunity for athletics contests in Ancient Greece, where it was included in the Olympic Games. In those days long jumpers used light weights which they discarded by throwing them backwards when taking off, in order to make use of the reaction derived from this.

The long jump with a run-up was included in the first modern Olympic Games in 1896 in Athens. It is important to mention that the jump was with a run-up, because in the four subsequent Olympics there was also a long jump from a standstill.

This standing jump, which was abandoned some time ago, was probably performed best by an American athlete, Ray Ewry, who trained to jump from a standstill in the high jump, the long jump and the triple jump, to cure the polio which confined him to an invalid carriage when he was a child.

Unlike the high jump, in the case of the long jump not as much research has been done on the most effective techniques for achieving longer and longer jumps. Since studies have revealed that, once in the air, it is impossible to give additional propulsion to that resulting from the take-off, the theories about the advantages of strides in the air (one, two or even three-and-a-half), which used to be in vogue, have been discarded. The hang jump, i.e. the forward projec-

Bob Beamon jumps his astonishing world record of 8.90 m (which still stands) in the 1968 Olympics.

tion of the lower limbs with the body in an aerodynamic position, used to be the most favoured technique, but the hitch-kick is now the most popular among top athletes.

In order to be a successful long jumper, it is essential to be a good sprinter and to possess excellent reactive capacity in the muscles used in the take-off. In fact, the theoretical distance of the jump depends on the initial speed of the jump (v_0), the angle of projection of the centre of gravity (angle α) and the height of the jump itself. The movements which the athlete makes during the jump only help him to keep his balance and to assume the best position for landing so as to make as long a jump as possible. The speed of the run before the jump mainly determines the distance and this is confirmed by its correlation with performance (coefficient of correlation, $r = 0.943$). The study of the run-up is therefore very important for obtaining an increasingly high controllable speed at the take-off and almost perfect automatic movement so that the take-off occurs along the centre-line of the foot's striking action on the board. The length of the run-up varies from 12–14 strides in the case of beginners (24–30 m) up to 20–24 strides (40–50 m) for top athletes.

According to analyses carried out at recent Olympic Games, the best athletes use a run-up from 37 m to 50 m in length (33–40 m in the case of women). In some cases the run-up is preceded by 2–6 strides consisting of walking steps or short running steps.

The length of the run-up is determined by the height of the jumper and his ability to accelerate in the run.

However, while in the high jump the height of the jumper plays a decisive role, in the long jump even athletes of normal build (i.e. who have a good balance between the torso and the lower limbs and are 5 ft 9 in. (1.75 m) to 6 ft 3 in. (1.85 m) tall) can obtain top results.

Stability in the run-up. During the athletics season, the length of the run-up is gradually modified as the jumper becomes fitter, and it also depends on the weather, the composition of the surface of the jumping track, the direction of the wind and the importance of the competition.

For most jumpers and their coaches, precision and stability, speed and skill in the run-up represent the main problems as far as technical improvement is concerned. Therefore, in every competitive event, the athlete must take note of the likely weather conditions well in advance so that he can make the appropriate adjustments during the permitted warm-up and his proper attempts, also taking into account his psychological state.

The starting position and the beginning of the run-up should ensure a smooth rhythm in the strides.

The development of speed in the run-up depends on the increase in the length and frequency of the strides. Usually the jumper distributes his efforts so that the last strides before the take-off are taken with more controlled speed and greater readiness.

The horizontal speed of some champions at take-off is as follows:
(1) Ter-Ovanesyan (8.35 m jump) 10.4 m/s;

(2) Beamon (world record jump of 8.90 m) 10.7 m/s;
(3) Lewis (8.72 m jump, Zurich 1981) 10.73 m/s.

Despite differences in the build-up of speed in the run-up, jumpers reach maximum speed not at the take-off but in the last two strides preceding it.

The take-off. The length of the jump depends not only on horizontal speed but also on the speed and power of the take-off. In the preparation for the take-off (last three strides) about 10% of the run-up speed is taken away. The last step is executed more quickly and the whole foot is placed on the ground, ahead of the projection of the centre of gravity.

The vertical speed of the take-off (V_y) and the horizontal speed (V_x) of the run-up transmit an impulse to the centre of gravity. This impulse makes a parabola (AB) whose angle (α) varies in the best athletes between 15° and 24° (see diagram). The optimum ratio between V_x and V_y is around 2.6–2.8:1.

The jump. Jumping styles vary according to the development of the athlete and his muscular characteristics and bone structure. The most common are:
(1) the hitch-kick (1–2–3 strides and a half in the air);
(2) the sail (common among beginners);
(3) the hang (or extended jump or glide).

The landing. A good landing technique will allow complete utilization of the push which the centre of gravity received at the point of take-off.

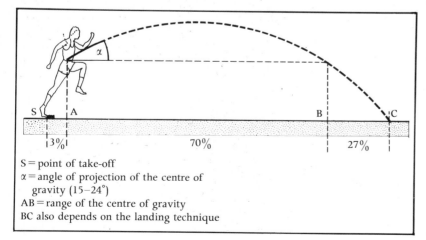

S = point of take-off
α = angle of projection of the centre of gravity (15–24°)
AB = range of the centre of gravity
BC also depends on the landing technique

Lewis's jump at the world championships
This sequence shows Carl Lewis's first attempt in the final at the 1983 World Championships in Helsinki, resulting in an 8.55 m jump which brought him victory. The American made his jump soon after he had led his team to victory in the second semi-final of the 4 × 100 m relay. On the same afternoon they won the World Championship in the record time of 37.86 sec.

Bouncing runs
These should be carried out taking care to accentuate the sprinting and bouncing actions. Apart from developing the muscles, these exercises also improve the functioning of the feet.

■Useful hints for youngsters■

With youngsters who have an inclination for the long jump and who have already received some guidance from their coach on how it is performed, it is important to start concentrating immediately, albeit gradually, on developing the take-off capacity and co-ordination of the movements which characterize this jump. Therefore some basic exercises are recommended, such as running

Alternating hops with hurdles
These can also be performed without hurdles and with complete extension of the sprinting limb accompanied by accentuated swinging, either in synchrony or alternating, of the upper limbs.

with accentuated bouncing on the feet, in order to develop the muscular reaction of the lower limbs; these are demonstrated in photos 1–3.

In photos 4–6, he demonstrates the so-called alternating take-off step with compensatory swinging of the upper limbs. This is followed by the take-off step (always taking-off on the take-off limb) which is a more specific exercise; it is also carried out with 3–5 run-up strides and with hurdles in between.

Photos 7–10 show a long jump from a standstill, starting with the feet together from the edge of the take-off board and landing on the sand. The maximum extension of the

upper limbs upwards and forwards (photo 8) should be noted. This pulls the athlete's whole body forward.

Photos 11–13 show exercising with low hurdles (for youngsters a height of 20 cm is recommended) known as running with alternating hops, in this case with synchronized arms, but this can also be done without hurdles and with alternating arm movements.

Constant correct repetition of these exercises combined with other exercises for developing impetus, together with training to increase speed, create the prerequisites for achieving proficiency in the long jump.

The take-off stride

This exercise, more than the others, resembles the basic part of the long jump in that it develops the automatic motion required for performing the take-off in the most effective manner.

The long jump from a standstill

The long jump from a standstill, which was a speciality in its own right in the past, is now a valuable aid which helps to increase take-off power and to improve landing methods.

REGULATIONS FOR THE LONG JUMP

1. The order in which the competitors make their attempts must be decided by drawing lots.

2. Each competitor will be placed according to his best jump.

3. When there are more than eight competitors, each one is given 3 attempts and the 8 competitors with the best jumps are given a further three jumps. In the case of a tie for the eighth position, each competitor involved in the tie has three additional attempts. When there are eight or less competitors, each one is allowed six attempts.

4. A competitor commits a foul if he: touches the ground beyond the jumping board with any part of his body before the main jumping action is carried out; to help determine this, a plasticine indicator must be placed right at the front edge of the take-off board;

takes off from beyond the take-off line extended either side of the take-off board;

touches the landing area during the landing at a point behind the footprint;

walks back through the sand pit having made the jump;

uses an illegal style of jump;

uses a weight or aid of any kind;

exceeds the time allowed to make his attempt.

5. If a competitor takes off before the board or the line this does not constitute a foul.

6. The runway must be 1.22 m wide. Its length is not fixed but must be a minimum of 40 m.

7. The maximum slope across the runway must not be more than 1:100, and along it not more than 1:1000.

8. No mark or indicator must be placed on the runway, but a competitor can put one (supplied by the organizers) at the side of the runway. No indicator can be placed in the landing area.

9. Once the competition is under way, competitors are not allowed to use the runway for trial attempts.

10. The take-off boundary must be marked by a board embedded level with the run-up track and the surface of the landing area.

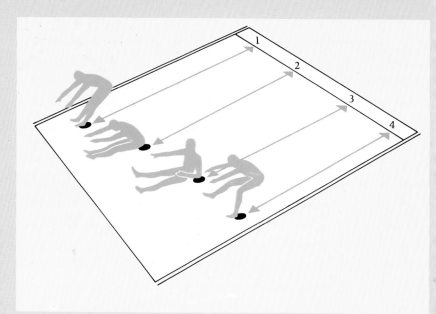

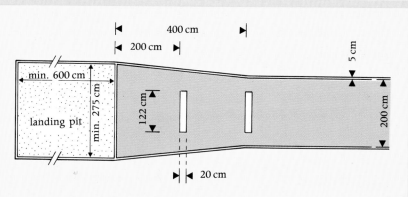

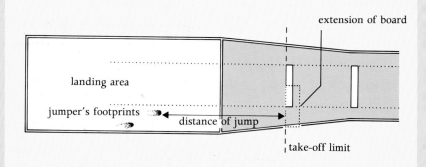

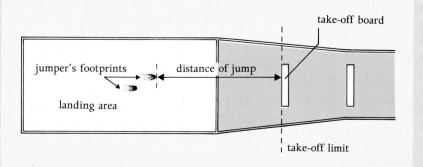

The edge of the board nearest to the landing area is called the take-off line. Immediately beyond the take-off line there must be a layer of Plasticine or other material suitable for preserving an athlete's footmark in the event of a fault.

The Plasticine layer must have its front edge at an angle of 30° in the direction of jumping, and must be a maximum of 10–13 mm.

If it is not possible to provide such a layer, the following method can be used: the ground immediately beyond the take-off line and along its entire length over a width of 10 cm should be covered with earth or sand at an angle of 30°.

11. The distance between the take-off line and the end of the landing area should be at least 10 m.

12. The take-off board should not be less than 1 m from the edge of the landing area.

13. The take-off board must be made of wood or other suitable hard material and must be 1.21–1.22 m long, 19.8–20.2 cm wide and no more than 10 cm from front to back. It must be painted white.

14. The Plasticine marker support must be a rigid block which should be 98–102 mm from front to back and 121–123 cm wide.

The surface of the Plasticine must slope upwards from the take-off board at an angle of 30° up to a maximum of 7 mm above the board. The marker support should be inset in the runway to the width of the take-off board and on the landing area side of it. When these are in position they must be sufficiently strong to take the full weight of an athlete. The surface below the Plasticine must be made from a material on which the spikes of the athlete's running shoe can grip. The layer of Plasticine must be able to be smoothed by a roller or by scraping in order to get rid of any mark made in it by a competitor who has made a no-jump.

15. The landing area must be at least 2.75 m wide and the run-up track must be positioned so that its centre, if extended, would coincide with the centre of the landing area.

16. All jumps must be measured from the nearest mark in the landing area made by any part of the body or limbs of the athlete to the take-off line or its extension and at right angles with the take-off line.

17. To ensure that each jump is measured correctly, the surface of the sand in the landing area must be perfectly level with the surface of the take-off board.

The take-off and measurement
The picture at the top shows a valid jump from the take-off board, and the second picture shows a no-jump where the athlete's shoe has made a mark in the sand (or plasticine). Above left are four examples of landings in the long-jump pit; the jump is measured from the mark nearest to the take-off board. The three drawings to the left show all the measurements relevant to the final section of the runway and the landing area. It is worth noting that if the jump is made at an angle to the runway, then the distance is measured from an extension of the take-off board.

Training

The training programme for a top long-jumper is particularly complex because sprinting and jumping skills have to improve at the same time.

For this event also, the double-period system is preferred, starting with the usual introductory cycle which lasts only 3–4 weeks. This training cycle is practically the same for all four jumping events.

The basic preparatory cycle in the training programme for top jumpers consists of 10–11 training units per week so that on some days there are two training units, one in the morning and one in the afternoon.

In the second part of the cycle (as a guide, from 28 Nov. to 18 Dec.), some parts of the preparation will be replaced by other special exercises. For example, aerobic power will be dis-

continued on the second day and ball games will stop on the fifth day, being replaced by two sessions designed to improve reactions. At this stage training becomes much more intensive.

A typical week in the special preparatory cycle consists of eight training units. The structure of this cycle, which precedes indoor competitions, is characterized by the use of several special techniques (e.g. landing practice), by an increase in technical work and more emphasis on the intensity rather than the quantity of training.

During the second part of this cycle (as a guide, from 9 Jan. to 22 Jan.), some parts of the preparatory training (for example, sprinting with a trailing weight) and some strength exercises, such as the jerk and the snatch, will be discontinued.

The periods of work in the basic and special cycles will be divided in a ratio of 2:1, which means that for two weeks the full training programme will be followed accurately, while during the third week (the release week) the athlete does only 50–60% of the work.

The second part of the special cycle corresponds to the completion period in preparation for indoor events, and some competitions are included in order to check the technical condition of the athlete.

In the subsequent indoor competitive cycle, the amount of training should be reduced to allow the athlete to compete in important events with his nervous energy intact, which is of paramount importance if the athlete is to achieve top performance in jumping events.

There will now be four training sessions per week. The last but one session will act as a release (i.e. it will not be intensive).

At the end of the indoor season, after a transition period during which the work is more general and may include other sports (games such as tennis, volley-ball, basket-ball, etc.), preparation is resumed with a second four-week cycle which is the same as the second part of the first basic winter cycle.

This is followed by a second special cycle lasting four weeks, which precedes the actual completion cycle, and this includes a few trial events, during which the athlete will gradually reach top form for the most important outdoor events.

WEEKLY TRAINING PROGRAMME

Typical week in the introductory cycle (as a guide, from 15 Oct. to 6 Nov.)

Session 1
- Warm-up.
- Runs: 5–6 × 80–100 m.
- Sprints: 8–10 × 20–30 m with a flying start and from a standstill.
- Medicine ball training: series of thrusts in all directions with an iron ball weighing 6–7 kg.

Session 2
- Warm-up.
- Extensive technical paces.
- Localized muscle exercises (thigh, ischial and femoral, gluteal, abdominal and dorsal flexors).
- Uphill sprints: 10–15% gradient, two series of 4–5 repetitions of 30–40 m, 2–3 min. rest between exercises and 6 min. rest between series.

Session 3
- Ball games: 1–1½ hours.
Those games which have the greatest affinity with jumping should be chosen (e.g. basket-ball, volley-ball and hand-ball).

Session 4
- Warm-up.
- Stretching exercises.
- Weights: (a) turning, snatching and jerking exercises; (b) squat or half-squat, 6 series of 6 repetitions with suitable weight, 3–4 min. break between one series and the next; (c) stretching with the bench: 4 series of 6 repetitions.

Session 5
- Warm-up.
- Jumps: (a) 6 triple from a standstill; (b) 4 quintuple from a standstill; (c) 2 decuple (tenfold).
- Sprint: 6–8 × 20–30 m.
- Medicine ball training.

Session 6
- Warm-up.
- Extensive technical paces.
- Uphill springs: 10–15% gradient, 2 series of 4–5 repetitions of 30–40 m, 2–3 min. rest between exercises and 6 min. rest between series.
- Exercises on the sprung mat.

Session 1
- Morning: warm-up. Extensive interval running (also using weighted ankle bands or belts). 2–3 stretches of 60–80 m. Uphill sprint: 5 × 40 m, recovery 3 min.; recovery 10 min.; 5 × 50 m, recovery 4 min.
- Afternoon: warm-up. Stretching exercises and muscular extension. Jumps: 6 long bunny jumps from a standstill, 6 double from a standstill, 6 triple from a standstill. Speed endurance: 1 × 100 m, recovery 5 min.; 1 × 150 m, recovery 6 min., 1 × 200 m, recovery 8 min., 1 × 150 m, recovery 6 min., 1 × 100 m.

Session 2
- Morning: warm-up. Aerobic power: alternate fast short cross-country (3 km, heart rate 170–180 beats per minute), or 4–5 × 500 m on the track, 5–6 min. breaks, 3–4 repetitions (circuit training).
- Afternoon: warm-up. Strength: (a) chest turns; (b) normal jerk and with splits; (c) fast half-squat on the sliding trolley, maximum of 5 × 5 repetitions; (d) general and localized muscle exercises.

Session 3
- Afternoon: warm-up. Stretching. Technical exercises for agility and speed with hurdles at a suitable distance and height. Speed endurance: 6–8 × 100 m, 4 min. recovery. Medicine ball training: 40–60 backward and low–forward–high thrusts.

Typical week in the basic cycle (as a guide, from 7 Nov. to 18 Dec.)

Session 4
• Morning: warm-up. Uphill sprint as first exercise.
• Afternoon: warm-up. Technical paces. Technique: 10−15 jumps with short run-up. Strength: step test: 4 × 20 repetitions max., 4 min. recovery; (b) stretching on the ball of the foot on the trolley: 3 × 20 repetitions max. with heavy load; (c) general and localized muscle exercises.

Session 5
• Morning: 45−60 min. of games. Medicine ball training: 40−60 thrusts.
• Afternoon: warm-up. Stretching. Extensive interval training (also using weighted ankle bands or belts). Cramp-resisting exercises: 3 series of 3 × 30 m, 2 min. recovery between exercises and 5 min. between series; 2 series of 2 × 40 m, recovery as above; 2 series of 2 × 50 m, recovery as above; 2 series of 2 × 50 m, 3 min. recovery between exercises and 6 min. between series. Long bunny jumps: (a) 4 quintuple starting from a standstill; (b) 3 tenfold from a standstill.

Session 6
• Afternoon: warm-up. Technical exercises and agility and speed exercises with hurdles. Mixed standing jumps: (a) 6 long from a standstill; (b) 6 triple from a standstill; (c) 4 quintuple from a standstill; (d) 3 tenfold from a standstill. Strength: (a) chest turns; (b) snatch; (c) fast half-squat: 5 × 5 repetitions max. (d) stretching on the ball of the foot on the trolley: 3 × 20 repetitions max. with heavy load.

Session 7
• Morning: warm-up. Technical paces. Technique: 10−15 jumps with short run-up. Medicine ball training: 40−60 thrusts.

Typical week in the special cycle (as a guide, from 19 Dec. to 22 Jan.)

Session 1
• Afternoon: warm-up. Muscle stretching and extension exercises. Intensive interval running exercises. Reaction: 6 × 10 hurdles placed 3 ft apart and 50−60 cm high. Mixed jumps with 2−4 run-up strides: (a) 6 double, (b) 6 triple, (c) 4 quintuple. Speed endurance: 2 series of 2 × 60 m, 3 min. break between exercises and 8 min. between series; 1 series of 2 × 80 m, 3 min. recovery, 10 min. break; 1 × 100 m, 12 min. break; 1 × 150 m.

Session 2
• Morning: warm-up. Stretching. Agility exercises with hurdles. Sprint with trailing weight: 4 × 30 m with 3 min. recovery and 10 min. break; 4 × 40 m, 3 min. recovery and 8−10 min. break. Compensatory sprints: 5 × 30−40 m with 3−4 min. recovery.
• Afternoon: warm-up. Strength: (a) jerk or snatch; (b) fast half-squat: 5 × 3 repetitions max.; (c) $\frac{1}{4}$ squat-jump with load equivalent to 50−70% of the body weight; (d) general muscle exercises.

Session 3
• Afternoon: warm-up. Stretching exercises. Landing practice: (a) 3 × 6 falls of 60−80 cm; (b) 3 × 6 falls with subsequent long jump with feet together falling 50−60 cm; (c) 2 × 6 falls on one limb only with subsequent long jump falling from 40−50 cm (alternate the limbs). Technique: (a) 6−8 complete run-ups on the main or jumping track; (b) jumps with complete medium length run-ups. Medicine ball training: 20−30 thrusts.

Session 4
• Afternoon: warm-up. Extending and stretching exercises. Intensive interval training exercises. Reaction: 6 × 10 hurdles placed 3 ft apart and 50−60 cm high. Jumps: (a) 6 long bunny jumps from a standstill; (b) 6 triple with 2−4 run-up strides. Speed endurance: 2 series of 3 × 60 m with 3 min. recovery between exercises and 8 min. break between series; 2 series of 2 × 80 m with 3 min. recovery between exercises and 10 min. rest between series, 12 min. break; 1 × 120 m.

Session 5
• Morning: warm-up. Stretching. Landing: (a) 3 × 6 falls from 60−80 cm; (b) 2 × 6 falls on one limb only with subsequent long jump falling from 40−50 cm (take-off limb only). Sprint: 4 × 30 m with 3 min. recovery and 5 min. break; 3 × 40 m with 3 min. recovery and 8 min. break; 2 × 50 m with 4 min. recovery.
• Afternoon: strength: (a) jerk or snatch; special step for long jump with 40−50 kg; (c) $\frac{1}{4}$ squat jump (load same as in second session); (d) general muscle training.

Session 6
• Afternoon: warm-up. Stretching exercises. Reaction: see first and fourth session. Technique: (a) complete run-up, same as third training session; (b) jumps with medium length and complete run-up. Medicine ball training: as per third training session.

Session 1

If the athlete competed on the previous Sunday, the first day of the week is devoted to recuperation by means of massages and a short stretching session preceded by a full warm-up.

Session 2

• Warm-up.
• Muscle stretching and extending exercises.
• Intensive technical running exercises.
• Reaction: 4 series of hops with feet together with 5 hurdles placed at an adequate distance and height.
• Jumps: 2 triple with 6 run-up strides; 2 quintuple with 4 run-up strides.
• Speed: 1×60 m (time the first 30 m and the total time), 8 min. rest; 1×80 m (time the last 30 m and the total time), 8–10 min. rest; 1×60 m as above.
• Medicine ball: 10 back-throws with 6 kg iron ball.

Session 3

• Warm-up.
• Agility exercises with hurdles.
• Runs: $3-4 \times 80$ m.
• Technique: jumps with medium length run-up (8–10 strides), then 4–6 jumps with full run-up.
• Strength: (a) $\frac{1}{4}$ squat jump with load equivalent to 70% of the body weight; 3×5 repetitions; (b) special step for long jump with 50 kg load; 3×3 repetitions.

Session 4

• Warm-up.
• Stretching.
• Limited amount of technical running exercises.
• Runs: $3-6 \times 80-100$ m.
• Medicine ball training: 10–20 thrusts with 6 kg iron ball.

Session 5

• Warm-up.
• Muscle stretching and extending exercises.
• Reaction: 4 series of hops with feet together with 5 hurdles placed at a suitable distance and height.
• Jumps: 3 long bunny jumps from a standstill; 1 triple with 4 run-up strides; 1 quintuple with 2 run-up strides.
• Run-ups: 4–6 complete run-ups as if preparing to take off.
• At the end of the session a 120–150 m trial at almost maximum speed can be run but this is optional.

Session 6

Omitted in view of the competition on the seventh day.

The stars

WILLIAM DEHART HUBBARD (USA)

The first black athlete to win an Olympic gold medal, in the long jump in the Paris Games of 1924, he also began the tradition of great American sprinters/long jumpers.

Hubbard dominated the world long-jumping scene for several seasons, winning the American title in six consecutive years (1922–27). His margin of superiority over his rivals was about 30 cm, and he reached his peak in 1925 with a world record of 7.89 m. Two years later in Cincinnati he jumped 7.98 m, but the result was not approved because the jumping track was on a slight slope. He was the first long-jumper to jump around 25 ft (7.62 m) consistently. As a sprinter, he was one of the best in the USA and in 1925 he ran the 100 yards in 9.6 sec., equalling the world record.

EULACE PEACOCK (USA)

Although most people know of Jesse Owens' exploits, very few people are aware that he had a tough rival in Eulace Peacock; however, there was great rivalry between them in 1935, the year of Owens' great records.

Like Owens, Peacock came from Alabama and was black but, despite being muscularly more powerful than Owens, his running action was less smooth. He emerged internationally in 1934 when, still only 19, he finished third in the 100 m in the American Championships behind Ralph Metcalfe and Owens. In the summer he came to Europe and in Oslo equalled the world record in the 100 m in addition to jumping 7.44 m in the long jump.

His best year was 1935. He had already fought hard with Owens in indoor events over 100 m and 200 m, but their toughest battle was on 4 July in the American outdoor championships. Peacock finished in 10.2 sec., almost a metre ahead of Metcalfe and Owens, with an excessive wind of 3.4 m/sec. In the long jump Owens, whose performance was always con-

Ralph Boston

and was not able to compete effectively that year.

Peacock continued to compete for many years but never returned to his glorious days of 1935. Very versatile, his victories included the American title in the pentathlon no less than six times between 1933 and 1945.

RALPH BOSTON (USA)

The world record of 8.13 m established in 1935 by Jesse Owens was one of the longest-lasting records in the history of athletics. It was beaten 25 years later when Ralph Boston jumped 8.21 m in a pre-Olympic trial on 12 Aug. 1960.

Boston, who was slower than Owens but extraordinarily agile, was a prominent figure in the long jump for many years. He was considered the world number one long-jumper for eight seasons (1960–67), an unusually long period in this type of jump which, apart from being very taxing on the legs, requires a great deal of nervous energy.

He won three Olympic medals and this is also a record for a long-jumper: the gold medal in Rome in 1960 (8.12 m), the silver medal in Tokyo in 1964 (8.03 m) and the bronze medal in Mexico in 1968 (8.16 m). During his best years his main opponent was Igor Ter-Ovanesyan, with whom he alternated in improving the world record several times up to 8.35 m in 1965. He once even cleared 8.49 m but with an excessive wind of 2.6 m/sec. He was a versatile athlete capable of very respectable figures in the high-jump, triple jump, pole vault and 120 yards hurdles.

IGOR TER-OVANESYAN (USSR)

Although over 20 years have passed since his great days, Igor Ter-Ovanesyan remains the greatest ever European long-jumper owing to his international successes and the length of his career.

At the age of 18 in 1956, he was already considered good enough for the Olympic team. At the Melbourne Games he qualified for the finals, but made three no-jumps. After this failure, he became a model of consistency, and in 1959 he was the first European to clear 8 m with 8.01 m. In 1960 he won the bronze medal in the Olympic final in Rome (won by Ralph Boston) with a new personal best of 8.04 m. He broke the world record for

sistent, had three jumps over 7.90 m, with a best of 7.98 m, but in his final attempt Peacock cleared 8 m and took his second title. He followed this with a successful tour of Europe, unfortunately getting injured in the last meeting in Milan.

In 1936 he began by beating Owens in an indoor sprint event, but then he suffered from the effects of his injuries at the end of the previous season

Igor Ter-Ovanesyan

the first time in 1962 at Yerevan with 8.31 m. At the 1964 Olympic Games in Tokyo he was third again, behind Lynn Davies and Boston, with 7.99 m. In 1967 he regained the world record, even though it was shared with Boston, by jumping 8.35 m in Mexico. At his fourth Olympic Games in 1968 he came fourth with 8.12 m.

He dominated the European scene: in the European Championships he collected three golds (1958, 1962 and 1969) and one silver (1966). At the first European Indoor games (Dortmund, 1966) he established a European record with an 8.23 m jump. When his career ended he became a coach in the USSR.

BOB BEAMON (USA)
This athlete holds the greatest and most talked-of record ever: 8.90 m in the long jump, achieved on 18 Oct. 1968 in Mexico City.

It happened in the Olympic final. Beamon, a tall American (1.90 m and 75 kg) was the fourth to jump of 17 finalists. It was an amazing leap, and in fact the length of the jump was beyond the limits of the optical device used for measuring and it was necessary to use a steel tape.

His jump beat the world record held by Ralph Boston and Igor Ter-Ovanesyan by a massive 55 cm, equivalent to 0.35 sec. in the 100 m. In a single leap the world long-jump record had risen further than it had over the previous 40 years.

How could such an explosive jump be explained? Certainly, Beamon was known as a man of great talent, 'capable', as Ralph Boston once said, 'of exceptional things if and when he manages to combine all his strong points in a well executed jump'. Also, to explain his progress of over half a metre, two factors in particular were put forward: the rarefied air in Mexico, which is advantageous in contests requiring efforts of short duration, and the favourable wind, which according to official measurements was at the maximum permitted limit (2.0 m/sec.). It has been calculated that these two factors would have helped Beamon by 4%. An equally powerful jump at sea level and without wind assistance would have been around 8.56 m, which is still 21 cm better than the previous record.

It is interesting that, the previous day in the qualifying rounds, Beamon had reached the required measurement (7.65 m) only at the third and last attempt after two no-jumps. In this third jump he gave away at least 30 cm at the take-off board and then recorded 8.19 m.

Beamon was really great only in 1968, when he also established a world indoor record of 8.30 m, and after his triumph in Mexico he never exceeded 8.20 m.

HEIDE ROSENDAHL (WEST GERMANY)
To win three medals at the same Olympics is a great achievement, but Heide Rosendahl managed this feat in the 1972 Olympic Games in Munich. She began by winning the long jump with 6.78 m, then finished second in the pentathlon only 10 points behind the Northern Irish girl Mary Peters, both of them breaking the world record. She finished with an excellent anchor leg in the 4 × 100 m relay, in which she managed to stay ahead of the East German Renate Stecher, considered the fastest woman in the world at that time.

Daughter of a leading national discus-thrower, Heide began to shine when she was 19, winning the silver medal in the pentathlon at the European Championships in Budapest. In her first Olympics, in 1968 in Mexico, she was injured, finishing eighth in the long jump, and had to give up the pentathlon. At the World University games in Turin in 1970, she broke the world record for the long-jump with 6.84 m, and in Helsinki the following year she won the European pentathlon title.

Some of her best results include: 11.45 sec. (100 m), 22.46 sec. (200 m), 13.28 sec. (100 m hurdles) and 4791 points in the pentathlon.

VILMA BARDAUSKIENE (USSR)
This Lithuanian was the first to jump over 7 m in the history of women's

Heide Rosendahl

athletics; she achieved this on 18 Aug. 1978 in Kishinyov, with 7.07 m. A few days later in the European Championships in Prague, she did better still with 7.09 m in the qualifying rounds, but in the final she had to be content with a 6.88 m leap for victory.

After the 1978 European Championships, Igor Ter-Ovanesyan predicted that she would reach 7.50 m but this did not happen because she finally succumbed to the injuries through overwork which afflict present-day champions. In 1980 she managed to jump no further than 6.68 m. Excluded from the Olympic team for the Moscow Games, she decided to give up athletics.

ANISOARA STANCIU (ROMANIA)

Romania had a top female long-jumper in the 1960s: Viorica Viscopoleanu, who won the Olympic title in Mexico with a world record jump of 6.82 m. This tradition has been carried on in the 1980s by Vali Ionescu and Anisoara Cusmir (now Stanciu), who have alternately improved the world record established in 1978 by Vilma Bardauskiene (7.09 m).

Anisoara Stanciu, the younger of the two, began jumping at the age of 11, when she reached 3.80 m. At the age of 18 she cleared 6 m for the first time. In 1981, while still a junior, she jumped 6.91 m. In 1982 she had some close contests with Ionescu, two in particular standing out: the first in August in Bucharest when Stanciu broke the world record with 7.15 m and Ionescu outjumped her with 7.20 m, and the second at the European Championships in Athens, where Ionescu beat her rival with 6.79 m against 6.73 m.

In 1983 Stanciu got the upper hand, breaking her compatriot's world record three times with 7.21 m, 7.27 m and 7.43 m. However, she received a setback at the World Championships in Helsinki when the East German Heike Daute responded to her 7.15 m with 7.27 m. Stanciu's most recent triumph was at the 1984 Olympics in Los Angeles, when she won the gold medal with 6.96 m, ahead of Ionescu's 6.81 m.

Carl Lewis (USA) – *See the 200 m.*

Anisoara Stanciu

WORLD RECORDS

Men
m
7.61 Peter O'Connor (GB) 1901
7.69 Edwin Gourdin (USA) 1921
7.76 Robert LeGendre (USA) 1924
7.89 William DeHart Hubbard (USA) 1925
7.90 Edward Hamm (USA) 1928
7.93 Sylvio Cator (Haiti) 1928
7.98 Chuhei Nambu (Japan) 1931
8.13 Jesse Owens (USA) 1935
8.21 Ralph Boston (USA) 1960
8.24 Ralph Boston (USA) 1961
8.28 Ralph Boston (USA) 1961
8.31 Igor Ter-Ovanesyan (USSR) 1962
8.31 Ralph Boston (USA) 1964
8.34 Ralph Boston (USA) 1964
8.35 Ralph Boston (USA) 1965
8.35 Igor Ter-Ovanesyan (USSR) 1967
8.90 Bob Beamon (USA) 1968

Women
5.98 Kinue Hitomi (Japan) 1928
6.12 Christei Schulz (Germany) 1939
6.25 Fanny Blankers-Koen (Netherlands) 1943
6.28 Yvette Williams (New Zealand) 1954
6.28 Galina Vinogradova (USSR) 1955
6.31 Galina Vinogradova (USSR) 1955
6.35 Elzbieta Krzesinska (Poland) 1956
6.35 Elzbieta Krzesinska (Poland) 1956
6.40 Hildrun Claus (Germany) 1960
6.42 Hildrun Claus (Germany) 1961
6.48 Tatyana Shchelkanova (USSR) 1961
6.53 Tatyana Shchelkanova (USSR) 1962
6.70 Tatyana Shchelkanova (USSR) 1964
6.76 Mary Rand (GB) 1964
6.82 Viorica Viscopoleanu (Romania) 1968
6.84 Heide Rosendahl (West Germany) 1970
6.92 Angela Schmalfeld-Voigt (GDR) 1976
6.99 Sigrun Thon-Siegl (GDR) 1976
7.07 Vilma Bardauskiene (USSR) 1978
7.09 Vilma Bardauskiene (USSR) 1978
7.15 Anisoara Stanciu (Romania) 1982
7.20 Vali Ionescu (Romania) 1982
7.21 Anisoara Stanciu (Romania) 1983
7.27 Anisoara Stanciu (Romania) 1983
7.43 Anisoara Stanciu (Romania) 1983

Triple jump
Technique

The triple jump originated in the 19th century in Ireland, where it was performed as two hops on the same leg, generally the stronger one, and a jump. This version was performed at the first Olympic Games in Athens in 1896 and was won by James Connolly, with 13.71 m.

In the 'hop, step and jump' version (i.e. a hop on the take-off leg, a step on the other leg, and a jump bringing up both legs and landing on sand in the landing area), the triple jump was performed with or without a run-up at the end of the 19th century, like the long jump and the high jump. It was performed from a standstill only in three Olympic Games, in Paris in 1900, in St Louis in 1904 and in London in 1908.

Although it was a recognized Olympic speciality, the triple jump remained on the fringe of athletics in leading countries such as the USA, who were slow to include it in their national Championships. In Germany, it was even excluded from the national Championships in the early 1940s.

The main contributions towards the promotion of the triple jump were made in the 1930s by the Japanese and, after the Second World War, by a talented Brazilian, Adhemar Ferreira da Silva, as well as the Soviets, who created a true school of triple jump specialists.

Professor Vitold Kreer, the Soviet expert in the triple jump, has said that the ideal triple jumper must be a jumper, a sprinter and a weight-lifter, so it follows that his qualities of speed, jumping ability and strength will be equally developed. However, many athletes with different combinations of these qualities achieve jumps of considerable standard, and they can be classified into three groups.

(1) sprinter + jumper + strength: Saneyev, 17.44 m; Perez Duenas, 17.40 m; Valyukyevich, 17.29 m; Gentile, 17.22 m; Connor, 17.57 m;

(2) sprinter + jumper: de Oliveira, 17.89 m; Prudencio, 17.27 m; Livers, 17.15 m; Banks, 17.23 m; Hoffman, 17.42 m; Schmidt, 17.03 m; Lorraway, 17.12 m;

(3) sprinter + strength: Drehmel, 17.31 m; Piskulin, 17.07 m; Dudkin, 17.09 m; Butts, 17.24 m.

The age at which athletes obtain the best results in this jump is between 23 and 25 bearing in mind, however, that they generally begin to specialize around the age of 16 or 17.

It is precisely at the age of 16 to 17 that the young athlete begins to learn the basics of the technique through numerous exercises centred on 'multiple hops'. A distinction is made between alternate hops and successive hops (or hops on the same leg).

The triple jump is a combination of these two: the first hop and a successive hop, i.e. a hop on the same leg, the second hop (step) and an alternate hop, while the third (jump) is a long jump which concludes the exercise.

As far as the run-up is concerned, the basic concepts are more or less the same as in the long jump.

However, there are some differences, particularly in the take-off action, since the triple-jumper, being conscious of the fact that he has to perform three jumps, will endeavour to snatch less horizontal speed when performing the first hop (as compared with the take-off of the long-jumper), which results in a lesser load and a flatter parabola (16°–17° in the initial hop), so that he can retain sufficient kinetic energy to achieve the best possible performance in the second and third jumps, whose parabolas have angles of 14° and 17°–18° respectively. That is the basic concept of this multiple jump – rhythmical distribution of the three jumps.

During specialization, in order to achieve top results, a great deal of attention is paid to the rhythmical analysis of the jump.

Hop ⟶ | ⟵ Step ⟶ | ⟵ Jump

Hop, step and jump
This is the English definition of the triple jump. The hop must be executed on the same leg which was used for the take off (right-right or left-left). In the step the support is transferred to the other leg and, in this phase, if the foot of the inactive leg touches the jumping track, this constitutes a fault. The final jump is a proper long jump.

The results obtained are largely dependent on the length of the 'hop + jump' rather than on the length of the 'step'. Therefore, the 'hop + jump' has an influence on the total length of the jump, which is greater than that of the 'step + jump'.

The theoretical proportion in percentage terms suggested by Prof. Kreer (for the three jumps) in order to achieve optimum performance, should be 37%/30%/33%. This depends on many factors, such as full use of the run-up speed, the force exerted in the jumps and co-ordination of movements.

However, the ratios for the two greatest jumpers of all time in their best jumps were as follows:

de Oliveira (world record-holder with 17.89 m)

1. hop	35%	6.26 m
2. step	31%	5.54 m
3. jump	34%	6.09 m
		17.89 m

Saneyev (European record-holder and former world record-holder with 17.44 m)

1. hop	37.5%	6.50 m
2. step	28.5%	4.93 m
3. jump	34%	6.01 m
		17.44 m

It is worth remembering that, during training, there are various concepts of rhythmical distribution. In fact, what beginners find most difficult is holding back the first jump and trying to lengthen the second one in order to have sufficient speed and equilibrium to carry out the third one.

During this stage of training, some reference marks on the jumping track are certainly a useful aid to the young athlete, who will find it easier to control the distribution of his efforts and, above all, will avoid excessive injuries, which are particularly likely to occur during heavy landings as a result of the first jump being too strong.

Jumpers are also subdivided according to their arm movements.

Some athletes swing their arms alternately and others use synchronized arm movements.

The latter method is characteristic of the Soviet school, while the alternate arm technique has been adopted by the Polish school, starting with Jozef Schmidt.

In recent years great progress has been made in the triple jump by black athletes, who possess natural qualities for this jump, such as speed and agility.

Zdzislaw Hoffmann

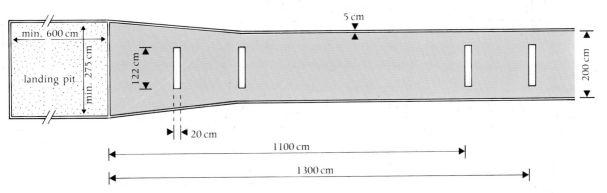

The diagram above shows the last part of the run-up track used for both long and triple jumps which are distinguished by the different positions of the take-off boards. The boards which are further away from the landing pit, at a distance of 11 m and 13 m, are the boards used for the triple jump.

THESE ARE THE RULES GOVERNING THE TRIPLE JUMP

1. The order in which contestants attempt their jumps is determined by drawing lots.
2. Each contestant must be placed according to his best jump.
3. If there are more than 8 competitors, each one is given 3 attempts and the 8 competitors with the best results are given 6 further attempts. In the event of a draw for eighth position each tied competitor is given 3 further attempts. If there are 8 competitors or less, each one is given 6 attempts.
4. The first jump (hop) must be executed in such a manner that the contestant touches the ground with the same foot which he used for the take-off. In the second jump (step) he must land on the other foot, from which the final jump is subsequently executed.
5. If the contestant touches the ground with the foot of the inactive leg during the jump, this constitutes a fault.
6. In all other aspects, the regulations for determining faults are the same as those for the long jump.
7. The jumping runway must be at least 1.22 m wide. The length of the run-up is unlimited. The minimum required length of the track is 40 m.
8. The maximum permitted tolerance for the inclination of the run-up track must not exceed 1% laterally and 1% in the direction of the run-up.
9. No markers may be placed on the jumping track but contestants may place markers (if supplied by the organizers) alongside the track. No markers may be placed in the landing area. After the start of the competition, contestants may not use the jumping track for training purposes.
10. The take-off boundary must be marked by a board embedded level with the run-up track and the surface of the landing area and placed at least 13 m from the landing area. The edge of the board which is nearest to the landing area is called the take-off line. Immediately beyond the take-off line there must be a layer of plasticine or other suitable material to preserve the athlete's footprint in the event of a fault. If it is not possible to provide such a layer, the following method can be used: the ground immediately beyond the take-off line and along its entire length over a width of 10 cm should be covered with earth or sand at an angle of 30°.
11. The distance between the take-off line and the end of the landing area should be at least 21 m.
12. The take-off board should not be less than 13 m from the edge of the landing area in international events.
13. The take-off board must be made of wood or other suitable hard material and must be 1.21–1.22 m long, 19.8–20.2 m wide and no more than 10 cm deep. It must be painted white.
14. As far as the centre-line of the layer of plasticine is concerned, this should be in accordance with the regulations given for the long jump.
15. The landing area must be at least 2.75 m wide and the run-up track must be positioned so that its centre, if extended, would coincide with the centre of the landing area.
16. All jumps must be measured from the nearest mark in the landing area made by any part of the body or limbs of the athlete to the take-off line or its extension and at right angles with the take-off line.
17. To ensure that each jump is measured correctly, the surface of the sand in the landing area must be perfectly level with the surface of the take-off board.

■Training■

The following typical training weeks are for triple-jumpers of national standard. The recommendations which follow are along the same lines as those for the long jump. As in the training programme for the long jump, in the second part of the basic cycle (as a guide, from 28 Nov. to 18 Dec.) some of the preparatory exercises are replaced by other, more specific exercises. For example, the exercises devoted to aerobic power are replaced by exercises to develop reactions or, in the fifth training session, games are replaced by reaction exercises. During this cycle, the preparatory work should gradually become more intensive.

Likewise, in the second part of the special cycle (as a guide, from 19 Dec. to 22 Jan.) sprinting is replaced by trailing objects and some strength exercises (jerk and snatch). The second part of the special cycle corresponds to the completion period in preparation for indoor events, during which the technical and physical condition of the jumper will be tested.

In the subsequent indoor competitive cycle, it is advisable to reduce the workload in order not to use up the nervous energy which will be expended in the competition.

The weekly training sessions will be cut down to four and the last but one session should be a light one (half the amount of work). At the end of the indoor season, after a period of more general work supplemented by other sports (tennis, volley-ball, basketball, etc.), the four-week basic preparation follows the first basic cycle.

This is followed by a second special cycle lasting four weeks leading up to the actual completion cycle during which, through a series of trials, the athlete will reach peak condition for outdoor events.

In the triple jump, it is advisable for jumpers not to take part in too many competitive events so that they do not sustain too many injuries to the muscles, and particularly to the joints, caused by the intense stresses produced by this exercise. Furthermore, in indoor events, the run-up is often shorter (16–18 steps) partly owing to the shorter length of the track. This explains the difference between indoor and outdoor results.

WEEKLY TRAINING PROGRAMME

Typical week in the introductory cycle (as a guide, from 15 Oct. to 6 Nov.)

Session 1
- Warm-up.
- Runs: 5–6 × 80–100 m.
- Sprint: 8–10 × 20–30 m with a flying start and from a standstill.
- Medicine ball exercise (series of thrusts in all directions with a 6–7 kg iron ball).

Session 2
- Warm-up.
- Extensive technical paces.
- Localized muscle exercises (thigh, ischial and femoral, gluteal, abdominal and back flexors).
- Uphill sprints: 10–15% gradient, 2 series of 4–5 repetitions of 30–40 m, 2–3 min. rest between exercises and 6 min. between series.

Session 3
- Games: 1–1½ hours. Games which include jumping are chosen (basketball, volley-ball and hand-ball).

Session 4
- Warm-up.
- Stretching exercises.
- Weights: (a) turning exercises, snatch and jerk; (b) squat or half-squat, 6 series of 6 repetitions with suitable load, 3–4 min. rest between one series and the next; (c) stretching exercises with the bench: 4 series of 6 repetitions.

Session 5
- Warm-up.
- Jumps: (a) 6 triple from a standstill; (b) 4 quintuple from a standstill; 2 decuple (tenfold).
- Sprint: 6–8 × 20–30 m.

Session 6
- Warm-up.
- Extensive technical paces.
- Uphill sprints: 10–15% gradient, 2 series of 4–5 repetitions of 30–40 m, 2–3 min. rest between exercises and 6 min. between series.
- Exercises on the sprung mat.

In photos 1–3 Dario Badinelli demonstrates correct execution of the first leap (the hop), using a teaching expedient (the hurdle), placed about half way along the trajectory of the same jump. Notice that the action is accompanied by a co-ordinated movement synchronized with the arms and the optimal positioning of the trunk. However, notice the coresponding circular action of the free leg, most noticeable in photo 2.

Photos 1–3 show a typical alternating leap. In photo 1 the positioning of the heel in landing is evident as is the raising of the free knee (the right). The thigh of the same leg, parallel to the ground (photo 2), helps the positioning of the knee under the thigh (photo 3). This action helps the athlete to move forward as much as possible before making contact with the ground again and performing the jumping stage as actively as possible.

Typical week in the basic cycle (as a guide, from 7 Nov. to 18 Dec.)

Session 1
- Morning: warm-up. Extensive interval running (also using weighted ankle bands or belts). 2–3 runs of 60–80 m. Uphill sprints: 5 × 40 m, 3 min. rest, 10 min. break; 5 × 150 m, 4 min. rest.
- Afternoon: warm-up. Muscle stretching and extending exercises. Jumps: 6 long bunny jumps from a standstill; 6 double jumps from a standstill; 6 triple jumps from a standstill. Speed endurance: 1 × 100 m, 5 min. rest; 1 × 150 m, 6 min. rest; 1 × 200 m, 8 min. rest; 1 × 150 m, 6 min. rest; 1 × 100 m.

Session 3
- Afternoon: warm-up. Stretching. Technical exercises for agility and speed with 4–5 hurdles placed at a suitable distance and height. Speed endurance: 6–8 × 100 m, 4 min. rest. Medicine ball exercises: 40–60 thrusts backwards and low–forwards–high.

Session 5
- Morning: games 45–60 min. Medicine ball exercises: 40–60 thrusts.
- Afternoon: warm-up. Stretching. Extensive technical running exercises (also with weighted ankle bands or belts). Cramp-resisting exercises: 3 × 3 × 30 m, 2 min. rest between exercises and 5 min. between series; 2 × 2 × 40 m, rest as above; 2 × 2 × 50 m, 3 min. rest between exercises and 6 min. between series. Long bunny jumps: (a) 4 quintuple from a standstill; (b) 3 decuple (tenfold) from a standstill.

Session 7
- Morning: warm-up. Technical paces. Jumping exercises with short run-ups: (a) double jump (e.g. Lx-Lx and close); (b) double jump (e.g. Lx-

Session 2
- Morning: warm-up. Aerobic power: alternate fast short cross-country (3 km, heart rate 170–180 beats per minute) or 4–5 × 500 m on the track, 5–6 min. rest or 3–4 repetitions (circuit training).
- Afternoon: warm-up. Strength: (a) chest turns; (b) normal jerk and with the splits; (c) squat or half-squat (6 × 6 repetitions max.); (d) general and localized muscle exercises.

Session 4
- Morning: warm-up. Uphill sprint as in Session 1.
- Afternoon: warm-up. Technical paces. Jumping exercises with short run-ups (x means together): (a) double jump (e.g. Lx-Lx and close; (b) double jump (e.g. Lx-Rx and close); (c) quadruple jump (1st e.g. Lx-Lx-Rx-Lx and close; 2nd e.g. Lx-Lx-Lx-Rx and close).

Session 6
- Afternoon: warm-up. Technical exercises for agility and speed with hurdles. Mixed standing jumps: (a) 6 long jumps from a standstill; (b) 6 triple jumps from a standstill; (c) 4 quintuple jumps from a standstill; (d) 3 decuple (tenfold) jumps from a standstill. Strength: (a) chest turns; (b) snatch; (c) fast half-squat (5 × 5 repetitions max.); (d) stretching on the ball of the foot on the trolley (3 × 20 repetitions max. with heavy load).

Rx and close); (c) quadruple jumps (1st e.g. Lx-Lx-Rx-Lx and close; 2nd e.g. Lx-Lx-Lx-Rx and close). Medicine ball exercises: 40–60 thrusts.

Session 1
- Afternoon: warm-up. Muscle stretching and extending exercises. Intensive interval running. Reaction: 6 × 10 hurdles placed 3 ft apart and 50–60 cm high. Mixed jumps with 2–4 run-up strides (a) 6 double; (b) 6 triple; (c) 4 quintuple. Speed endurance: 2 × 2 × 60 m, 3 min. rest between exercises and 8 min. between series; 1 × 2 × 80 m, 3 min. rest (10 min. break); 1 × 100 m (12 min. break); 1 × 150 m.

Session 3
- Afternoon: warm-up. Stretching exercises. Landing practice: (a) 3 × 6 falls from 60–80 cm; (b) 3 × 6 falls with subsequent long jump with feet together falling from 50–60 cm; (c) 2 × 6 landings on one leg with subsequent long jump falling from 40–50 cm (alternate the legs). Technique: (a) 6–8 complete run-ups on the main track or the jumping track; (b) jumps with medium length and complete run-up. Medicine ball exercises: 20–30 thrusts.

Session 5
- Morning: warm-up. Stretching. Landing practice: (a) 3 × 6 falls from 60–80 cm; (b) 2 × 6 falls on one leg with subsequent long jump falling from 40–50 cm (take-off leg only). Sprint: 4 × 30 m, 3 min. recovery (5 min. break); 3 × 40 m, 3 min. recovery (8 min. break); 2 × 50 m, 4 min. recovery.
- Afternoon: strength: (a) jerk or snatch; (b) special step for long jump with 40–50 kg; (c) $\frac{1}{4}$ squat-jump (as per Session 2); (d) general muscle exercises.

Typical week in the special cycle (as a guide from 19 Dec. to 22 Jan.)

Session 2
• Morning: warm-up. Stretching. Agility exercises with hurdles. Sprint with a trailer: 4 × 30 m, 3 min. recovery (10 min. break); 4 × 40 m, 3 min. recovery (8−10 min. break). Adjustment sprints: 5 × 30−40 m, 3−4 min. recovery.
• Afternoon: warm-up. Strength: (a) jerk or snatch; (b) fast $\frac{1}{4}$ squat (5 × 3 repetitions max.); (c) $\frac{1}{4}$ squat-jump with load equivalent to 50−70% of the body weight; (d) general muscle exercises.

Session 4
• Afternoon: warm-up. Stretching and extending exercises. Interval training. Reaction: 6 × 10 hurdles placed 3 ft apart and 50−60 cm high. Jumps: (a) 6 long bunny jumps from a standstill; (b) 6 triple jumps with 2−4 run-up strides. Speed endurance: 2 × 3 × 60 m, 3 min. recovery between exercises and 8 min. between series; 2 × 2 × 80 m, 3 min. recovery between exercises and 10 min. between series (12 min. break); 1 × 120 m.

Session 6
• Afternoon: warm-up. Stretching exercises. Reaction: Sessions 1 and 4. Technique: (a) full run-up as per Session 3; (b) jumps with medium length and full run-up. Medicine ball exercises: as Session 3.

Typical week in the competitive cycle (as a guide, from 23 Jan. to 10 Mar.)

Session 1
• If the athlete competed on the previous Sunday, the first day of the week is devoted to recuperation through massages and a brief stretching session, preceded by a thorough warm-up.

Session 3
• Warm-up.
• Agility exercises with hurdles.
• Runs: 3−4 × 80 m.
• Techniques: some jumps with a medium length run-up (8−10 strides), then 4−6 jumps with a full run-up.
• Strength: (a) $\frac{1}{4}$ squat jump with a load equivalent to 70% of the body weight, 3 series of 5 repetitions; (b) special step for the long jump with a 50 kg load, 3 repetitions 3 times.

Session 5
• Warm-up.
• Muscle stretching and extending exercises.
• Reaction: 4 series of hops with the feet together with 5 obstacles at a suitable distance and height.
• Jumps: 3 long bunny jumps from a standstill; 1 triple jump with 4 run-up strides; 1 quintuple jump with 2 run-up strides.
• Run-ups: 4−6 complete run-ups as if about to take off.
• At the end of the session a 120−150 m trial can be run at maximum speed but this is optional.

Session 2
• Warm-up.
• Muscle stretching and extending exercises.
• Intensive interval running.
• Reaction: 4 series of hops with feet together with 5 obstacles placed at a suitable distance and height.
• Jumps: 2 triple jumps with 6 run-up strides; 2 quintuple jumps with 4 run-up strides.
• Speed: 1 × 60 m (time the first 30 m and the total time); 8 min. recovery; 1 × 80 m (time the last 30 m and the total time); 8−10 min. recovery and then again 1 × 60 m as above.
• Medicine ball exercises: 10 back thrusts with 6 kg iron ball.

Session 4
• Warm-up.
• Stretching.
• Limited amount of interval running.
• Runs: 3−4 × 80−100 m.
• Medicine ball exercises: 10−20 thrusts with a 6 kg iron ball.

Session 6
• Cancelled in view of the competition on the seventh day.

Day 7
• Competition or rest.

■ The stars ■

VILHO TUULOS (FINLAND)

The first European to jump over 15 m consistently was the Finn, Vilho Tuulos. He began his career as a triple-jumper and long-jumper very early so that by the age of 18 he was the Finnish record-holder with 14.71 m. Six years later, in 1919, he became the European record-holder with 15.30 m. At the 1920 Olympic Games in Antwerp he won with 14.50 m against the Swedish jumper, Folke Jansson (14.48 m).

In 1923 Tuulos showed great consistency in his performance with 15.39 m in the triple jump, then a splendid double victory in the long jump and triple jump at the Swedish games in Gothenburg: 7.31 m (Finnish record) and 15.39 m, respectively. A few days later he raised the European record to 15.48 m. In 1924 he went to the Olympic Games in Paris with high hopes of defending his title, but he could manage only the bronze medal. Tuulos made this third appearance in the Olympics in 1928 when he was 33, and again he won the bronze medal. During his long career, Tuulos won twelve titles in the Finnish championships, one of which was in the high jump in 1923, when he jumped 1.80 m.

MIKIO ODA (JAPAN)

Mikio Oda was the first athlete from an Asian country to win an Olympic gold medal, which he did with his victory in the triple jump at the 1928 Olympic Games in Amsterdam.

Oda embarked upon his first Olympic venture at the age of 19 in 1924 at the Paris Games. In a close contest he finished sixth with 14.35 m, a new personal best, and subsequently continued to improve: 14.80 m in 1925, 15.34 m and 15.35 m in 1927 and finally 15.41 m in the spring of 1928, the year of his Olympic victory in Amsterdam, which he won with 15.21 m.

Between 1929 and 1931, Oda improved his national triple jump record several times and finally succeeded in breaking the world record with 15.58 m on 27 Oct. 1931 in Tokyo. That year, he also obtained his best result in the long jump (7.52 m)

Adhemar Ferreira da Silva

but, unfortunately, an injury prevented him from doing well at the Los Angeles Games in 1932, where he managed only twelfth place with 13.97 m in the triple jump.

NAOTO TAJIMA (JAPAN)

At the 1936 Olympic Games in Berlin, athletes from the Far East won three of the six available medals in the triple jump and long jump. Two of these were won by Naoto Tajima, who was placed third with 7.74 m in the famous long jump contest between Owens and Long, and then won the triple jump. In this last event, on his fourth attempt Tajima landed at 16 m exactly and with this new world record also secured the Olympic title.

Until 1936 Tajima was better known as an excellent long-jumper. Already in 1932, in Los Angeles, he had finished sixth in the Olympic event with 7.15 m. In 1935, in Osaka, he had jumped 7.74 m. In the summer of the same year he had competed successfully in Europe, winning against the German Long at the University Games in Budapest and then finishing behind another German, Leichum, at the five-nations competition between Germany, Sweden, Hungary, Italy and Japan in Berlin, again in the long jump. As a triple-jumper he exceeded 15 m for the first time in 1933. Three years later he went to Berlin with a personal record of 15.40 m.

ADHEMAR FERREIRA DA SILVA (BRAZIL)

The first star of the post-war period came from a country which was almost a newcomer to the world of athletics. Although Brazil had a couple of 15 m triple-jumpers in the 1940s, Adhemar Ferreira da Silva soon proved his great ability.

His progress in the triple jump began with 13.05 m in his first competitive event (1947) and reached its peak with his last world record of 16.56 m in his one hundredth competition (1955). During the second year of his career, Adhemar made an almost anonymous début at the Olympics, finishing eleventh with 14.31 m, but in 1950 he equalled Tajima's old world record with 16 m exactly; the following year he jumped 1 cm further.

Adhemar began to display his extraordinary athletic gifts at the 1952 Olympic Games in Helsinki, breaking his own record in four of the six jumps and winning with 16.22 m. The Russian, Leonid Scherbakov, took the silver medal with 15.98 m, and in 1953 Scherbakov broke the world

Józef Schmidt

record with 16.235 m. To win it back, Adhemar took advantage of the rarefied air of Mexico where he jumped 16.56 m, at the Pan-American Games in 1955. The following year, at the Olympic Games in Melbourne, Adhemar succeeded in beating tough opposition with 16.35 m. He carried on for several years and in 1960, at the age of 33, he took part in the Olympic Games in Rome where he was placed 14th with 15.07 m.

JÓZEF SCHMIDT (POLAND)

Between 1958 and 1964 he won all the major triple-jump titles. He began to show himself in 1956 with 15.10 m. Two years later, he won the European Championships in Stockholm with 16.43 m, a new personal best, despite the fact that the cinder jumping runway was drenched with rain. In 1960 he took part in the Rome Olympics, having recently broken the world record, and beat the Russians and Americans with 16.81 m. In 1962 in Belgrade he successfully defended his European title with 16.55 m. In 1964 he underwent a knee operation, but he still managed to return to peak form at the Olympics in Tokyo, with a new Olympic record of 16.85 m. This was his last great victory, but Schmidt carried on successfully for several years: he was fifth at the European Championships of 1966 (16.45 m) and seventh at the 1968 Olympics in Mexico (16.89 m).

He broke the world record only once but with a result which marked a new milestone – the first jump of over 17 m. His actual distance was 17.03 m, achieved on 5 Aug. 1960.

VIKTOR SANEYEV (USSR)

Few athletes have left such a mark on the history of their discipline as Viktor Saneyev in the triple jump. In the Olympic Games he won three gold medals and one silver, nearly equalling the absolute record for the greatest number of victories in a single event (four, by the American Al Oerter in the discus).

His career as a triple-jumper began almost accidentally, when he decided to give up his main event, the high jump, owing to a knee injury, and took up horizontal jumping. In 1964, when he was only just 19, he took two second places in the long jump and

Viktor Saneyev

the triple jump at the European Junior Championships. He continued in both events until 1967, obtaining 7.90 m and 16.67 m, after which he decided to specialize in the triple jump. In the memorable 1968 Olympic Games in Mexico, Saneyev won his first Olympic gold medal with a leap of 17.39 m. In 1969 he won his first European title (17.34 m) in Athens, but two years later in Helsinki, he was beaten by the East German, Jörg Drehmel, after a very close contest. They fought another close battle at the 1972 Olympic Games in Munich, where Saneyev beat his German rival with 17.35 m against 17.31 m. At the end of the season he won back the world record, which had been taken

from him the previous year by the Cuban, Pedro Pérez Duenas, by jumping 17.44 m.

His supremacy lasted another four years with victories at the 1974 European Championships (17.23 m) and the 1976 Olympic Games (17.29 m). Inevitably, with the stresses of training and of so many competitive events, his legs finally suffered injuries, but even after several operations on his tendons Saneyev refused to give up. At the European Championships in Prague in 1978 he was beaten by the Yugoslavian Milos Srejović by one centimetre (16.93 m against 16.94 m). After some ups and downs he was selected for his fourth Olympic Games in Moscow in 1980. For most of the competition he was in the middle of the placings, but his final jump (17.24 m) gave him the silver medal.

Saneyev was the world number one triple-jumper for nine consecutive years (1968–76), an unequalled record.

JOAO CARLOS DE OLIVEIRA (BRAZIL)

After Adhemar Ferreira da Silva, Brazil has had two more triple-jumpers of world standard: Nelson Prudencio and Joao Carlos de Oliveira.

Joao jumped over 16 m for the first time in 1974 with 16.34 m. The following year, at the Pan-American Games in Mexico, he astounded the athletics world by winning the long jump with 8.19 m, ahead of the American Arnie Robinson, who was to become the Olympic champion in Montreal the following year. At the same Games he won the triple jump with a new world record of 17.89 m, beating the record established in 1972 by Viktor Saneyev by 45 cm. Undoubtedly, Joao benefited from the rarefied air of Mexico but, unlike Beamon in his famous 8.90 m jump, he did not have the advantage of any wind.

At the beginning of 1976, the Brazilian suffered from sciatica for a long time, and competed in the Olympic Games in Montreal after little preparation. However, he still managed fifth in the long jump (8.00 m)

Joao Carlos de Oliveira

and third in the triple jump (16.90 m). In 1980 Joao went to Moscow as a dubious favourite, but had to be content with the bronze medal, this time with 17.22 m.

Even if Joao was unlucky in the Olympics, he was certainly successful in the World Cup events, which he won three times: 1977 in Düsseldorf (16.68 m), 1979 in Montreal (17.02 m) and 1981 in Rome (17.37 m). This Brazilian, who was probably the most gifted of all the great triple-jumpers, has run 100 m in 10.1 sec. and has jumped 8.36 m in the long jump. Tragically, he suffered a serious car accident in 1981 and subsequently had to have his right leg amputated.

KEITH CONNOR (GB)

Keith Connor is one of the large group of coloured athletes who have considerably strengthened the potential of British athletics in recent years. He has achieved this in the triple jump, an event in which Great Britain has been rather average until now. After recurrent muscular injuries he reached world standard in 1978, winning the Commonwealth Games (17.21 m with the wind over the limit) and then finishing sixth in the European Championships in Prague.

In 1980, at the Moscow Olympics, he was placed fourth with 16.87 m, but his best year so far has been 1982; finally able to train and compete without major interruptions, he established the new European record of 17.57 m. However, he has jumped over 17 m on several occasions, winning at the European Championships in Athens (17.29 m) and at the Commonwealth Games in Brisbane, where he reached 17.81 m with wind assistance of 4.6 m/sec.

In 1983 injuries began to affect him again and at the World Championships in Helsinki Connor got no further than the qualifying rounds. The Los Angeles Games in 1984 saw him back in good form, and he took the bronze medal with 16.87 m.

ZDZISLAW HOFFMAN (POLAND)

The Polish athlete who has succeeded in equalling Schmidt is Zdzislaw Hoffman, winner of the World Championships in Helsinki. Up to a few months before no-one would have

thought of him as a likely candidate for the title; from 1979 to 1982 he had remained between 16.40 m and 16.58 m, which are barely reasonable results by the international standards of the 1980s. He began to aim higher in the spring of 1983 at the three-nation event between Italy, West Germany and Poland in Turin where he won with 17.04 m. Shortly afterwards he beat the Polish record with 17.19 m and 17.20 m, and he also jumped 8.09 m in the long jump. In Helsinki, he achieved an extraordinary sequence of results in the final: 16.74 m, 16.98 m, 17.00 m, 17.18 m, 17.35 m and 17.42 m. It is rare for competitors to improve with every jump, especially in competitions of this kind.

■■■ WORLD RECORDS ■■■

m
15.52 Daniel Ahearn (USA) 1911
15.52 Anthony Winter (Australia) 1924
15.58 Mikio Oda (Japan) 1931
15.72 Chuhei Nambu (Japan) 1932
15.78 Jack Metcalfe (Australia) 1935
16.00 Naoto Tajima (Japan) 1936
16.00 Adhemar Ferreira da Silva (Brazil) 1950
16.01 Adhemar Ferreira da Silva (Brazil) 1951
16.12 Adhemar Ferreira da Silva (Brazil) 1952
16.22 Adhemar Ferreira da Silva (Brazil) 1952
16.23 Leonid Scherbakov (USSR) 1953
16.56 Adhemar Ferreira da Silva (Brazil) 1955
16.59 Olyeg Ryakhovskiy (USSR) 1958
16.70 Olyeg Fedoseyev (USSR) 1959
17.03 Józef Schmidt (Poland) 1960
17.10 Giuseppe Gentile (Italy) 1968
17.22 Giuseppe Gentile (Italy) 1968
17.23 Viktor Saneyev (USSR) 1968
17.27 Nelson Prudencio (Brazil) 1968
17.39 Viktor Saneyev (USSR) 1968
17.40 Pedro Perez Duenas (Cuba) 1971
17.44 Viktor Saneyev (USSR) 1972
17.89 Joao Carlos de Oliveira (Brazil) 1975
17.97 Willie Banks (USA) 1985

Background to throwing

The throwing events form a separate and not universally popular category in the world of athletics. Many people maintain that the most natural event is the javelin, even though today it is only a relative of the weapon once used to strike at an enemy. It was originally a precision weapon too: now the competitor who throws the farthest wins the competition, but in real life the one who hit the target won the battle.

Then there is the discus. In olden times when a warrior had to cross a watercourse he was obliged to rid himself of the weight of his shield by hurling it on to the opposite bank. The shields of lightly armed soldiers were either oval or round, but for the competitive exercise of throwing, the shield was made into a perfect disc. And it requires the utmost style to throw this disc as far as possible.

Discus throwing makes use of centrifugal force, and so does the hammer, except that this requires strength whereas the discus primarily demands style. The javelin is thrown by linear force, as is the shot, which also needs strength.

The requirement common to all the throwing events is preparation. Only if the body is loosened up beforehand can the throw exploit all the power created by these preparatory movements of the body. It is therefore essential to perform a perfect sequence of preparatory movements before the actual throw.

The most simple to throw is the javelin, but it requires great concentration and violent delivery. For a long time the Finns led the world in the event. The discus undoubtedly needs close study, great commitment and extremely good concentration in order to make the movements automatic.

The hammer is the least elegant and least appreciated event. It requires remarkable strength to propel the implement and absolute precision to choose the moment of release, which is not easy. It is an event that demands complex training, particularly for the rotations, which require complete control of the competitor's effort and balance.

Putting the shot demands great application and the adoption of complementary sporting activities such as sprinting and weight lifting. It was the American Parry O'Brien who revolutionized the mechanics of the shot put by working out how to add speed to strength. In addition athletes need to be tall as well as strong in order to perform the shot at world level.

Holding the discus
The discus is held as shown in photos 1 and 2; the hand rests in a relaxed manner on the implement, with the fingers cradling the edge. Photo 1 shows the hold adopted as the athlete picks up the discus, and photo 2 shows how the discus is held when the swinging of the arm is about to begin.

Discus

The origins

Discus throwing is the most ancient of the competitive throwing events; it was included in the pentathlon contested at the Olympic Games in Ancient Greece. The implement then used was both larger in diameter and heavier than the modern one. The discus used in 1896 in Athens was a wooden lens shape edged with iron, weighted in the middle with lead and weighing 1.923 kg, and the athletes stood in a throwing area 2.5 m square. Not until the London Olympics of 1908 was the weight fixed at 2 kg, which it is today, together with the throwing circle 2.5 m in diameter.

In the early versions of the Games the style of throwing was free, as it is today, but the techniques then were still rudimentary. In these same Olympics, there was a discus competition in the 'Ancient Greek style' using an undulating movement instead of spinning round; this was revived for the one occasion and has not been used since. At the Stockholm Olympics of 1912 it was replaced by a two-handed competition judged on the aggregate of throws first with one arm then with the other. This ambidextrous throwing was practised up to the end of the 1920s, but has not been included in the Olympics since 1912.

Technique. The discus thrower turns around the axis of his body. The movement takes place within a circle 2.5 m in diameter; the discus must fall within a 40° sector from the middle of the circle. The throwing action can be described as follows. The thrower stands at the back edge of the circle with his back to the direction of the throw. The body remains erect and the thrower holds the discus resting on the palm with the edge on the end finger-joints of his throwing hand (photos 1 and 2, p. 165). The perpendicular through the centre of gravity of the discus must be between the index and middle fingers of the throwing hand. The upper edge of the discus is in contact with the forearm. The legs should be astride with the toes slightly turned out (photo 1, p. 168). To start with, the athlete swings his throwing arm several times, following the orbit it will describe on delivery (photos 1 and 2, p. 168). Having carried out these preliminary swings the athlete immediately begins the setting-up phase, bringing his legs and feet into action, transferring his weight on to the leg opposite to the throwing arm, bending the knee and turning the leg itself outwards, keeping the foot flat. The throwing arm with the discus describes an outer orbit and the discus remains behind the axis of the pelvis (photo 6, p. 169) while the other arm acts as a counterweight relative to the axis of the shoulders. When the left foot finds itself pointing in the throwing direction it gives a thrust which enhances the initial rotary effect (photo 7, p. 168). From this moment the real pivot begins, with both feet leaving the ground. During this phase the upper part of the body remains independent of the movement of the legs, which make contact with the ground again somewhat ahead of the trunk. The foot on the same side as the throwing arm comes down approximately in the centre of the circle, while the other one lands near to the front rim (photos 8 and 9, p. 168). The throwing arm is extended backwards and the body is very twisted with the shoulder axis further back than the pelvic axis. The drive or final phase starts from this position with a rapid extension of the leg on the throwing arm side, that is the back leg, the rapid alignment of the shoulder axis with the pelvic axis and a violent outwards swing of the throwing arm, extended as much as possible, brought forwards by the straightening and advancement of the chest (photo 10, p. 169). The forward leg with the foot pointed functions as a support (photo 11, p. 169), while the arm finally whips forward to complete the kinetic chain initiated by extending the back leg, continued by the hips and the shoulders, and concluded by flexing the forearm on the upper arm and the hand on the forearm (photo 12, p. 169).

At the moment of release from the fingers the discus should have reached the maximum initial velocity for the optimal angle of elevation, with a strong rotary movement around the short axis imparted by the index finger of the throwing hand, clockwise for the right-handed thrower, anti-clockwise for the left-handed thrower. To slow the body's momentum, which could otherwise carry the thrower out of the circle and thus cause a foul, the athlete continues to rotate, placing the back foot in the place of the supporting foot and slowing down the speed of rotation. This point is the reverse, and can even involve another complete turn of the body to use up all the excess energy from the pivot.

Biomechanics. Bearing in mind that the throw has to conform with the regulations, the distance of the throw is determined by the speed and angle of release, and also by aerodynamic factors that influence the flight (Fig. 1, p. 167). The speed and angle of release are determined by the power and direction of the forces influencing the discus, and the time and distance over which these factors are applied. The height of delivery is determined by the position of the athlete's body at that moment and by his physical stature. The height of delivery is a very minor factor compared with the speed and angle of release, yet if these two factors remain constant, then a taller thrower who delivers the discus in an upright position, with his legs and trunk well stretched, will have an advantage over a shorter opponent.

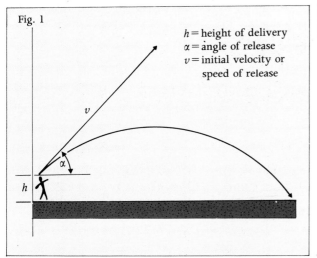

Fig. 1

h = height of delivery
α = angle of release
v = initial velocity or
      speed of release

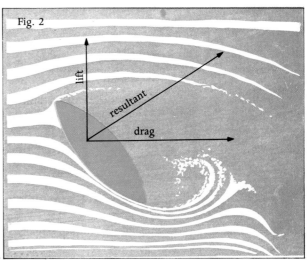

Fig. 2

lift

resultant

drag

Fig. 3

α = angle of release
β = angle of attitude
v = flight path of discus
c = centre of gravity of discus
γ = angle of attack

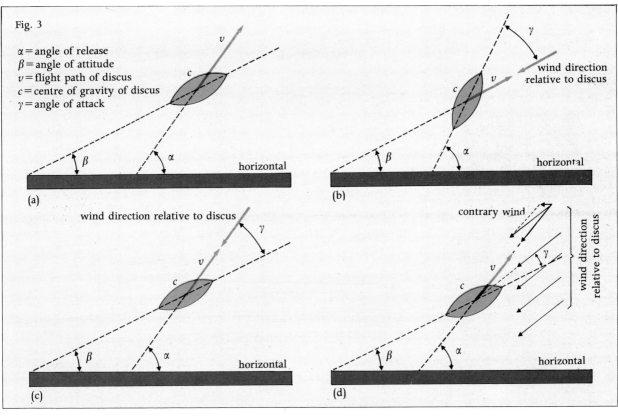

(a)

v

c

β

α

horizontal

(b)

γ

wind direction
relative to discus

c v

β α

horizontal

(c)

wind direction relative to discus

γ

v

c

β α

horizontal

(d)

contrary wind

v

γ

wind direction relative to discus

c

β α

horizontal

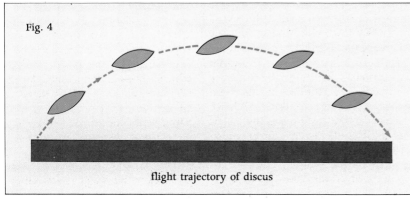

Fig. 4

flight trajectory of discus

The ballistics of the discus
The drawings on this page set out the aerodynamic factors that influence the flight of the discus and the length of throw.

The throw is affected by wind direction and by the inclination of the discus relative to the ground.

Aerodynamic factors. In the flight phase the discus is subjected both to gravity and to forces exerted on it by the air through which it passes.

When the discus is placed in a wind tunnel in which the speed of the air striking it can be varied, two effects are produced simultaneously:
(1) the direction of airflow round the discus is modified as shown in Fig. 2;
(2) the airspeed over the surface of the discus is reduced by coming into contact with the surface of the implement. These changes in speed and direction of the airflow occur because the discus exerts forces on the airflow

striking it. Consequently the air reacts by exerting equal and opposite forces on the discus.

The component of these forces acts in the same direction as the airflow before it strikes the discus, and is called drag (Fig. 2).

When a body moves in a fluid medium it is the drag, i.e. that component of the force exerted by the fluid on the body, that reduces the velocity of the body throughout its passage.

The component which acts at right angles to the line of resistance is called lift (Fig. 2).

When the air flows behind the discus (Fig. 2) the layer of air in contact with the discus itself is slowed down as a result of the forces exerted on it by the implement. This layer of air tends to slow down the next layer, and this slows down the next, and so on. The depth of air subject to this progressive slowing down further and further away from the surface of the discus becomes progressively greater in proportion to the size of the body struck by the air.

The amount of drag produced by a body moving in a fluid depends on a number of factors, including:

(1) the fluid's speed relative to the body;
(2) the surface of the body;
(3) the smoothness of the surface;
(4) the characteristics of the fluid.

The size of the forces exerted by the air and therefore the sum of their influence depends on:
(1) the speed of release;
(2) the angle of release, i.e. the angle between the horizontal and the direction in which the centre of gravity of the discus is moving immediately after delivery;
(3) the angle of inclination of the discus in relation to the horizontal,

otherwise called the angle of attitude, at the instant of delivery. Contrary to what might be expected, the angle at which the discus is delivered is not usually the same as that at which it is inclined relative to the horizontal: many good throwers aim slightly higher than the plane of the discus to achieve an angle of release greater than the angle of attitude (Fig. 3a);
(4) the wind speed;
(5) the angular velocity of the discus when delivered.

It is an extremely complex problem to determine the relative contribution of each of these factors.

How to throw the discus
The sequence shows Marco Bucci in each key position of the discus throw. Below can be seen the cross section of the discus.

Many attempts have been made to solve the problem, using a wind tunnel and measuring the forces exerted on the discus under widely varying conditions.

Particularly interesting are the experiments on the forces exerted on the discus by favourable and contrary air currents in relation to the length of throw.

The following conclusions have been reached: while contrary winds are useful for an increase of throw when they have a velocity of 11–13 km/h, with higher velocities the advantage diminishes until at a contrary wind velocity of 23 km/h it becomes a disadvantage. Favourable winds above 23 km/h are equally disadvantageous to the throw. Unfortunately the procedural details of these experiments have not been clearly explained, and there are also data from other investigations which contradict them. The following aerodynamic details have also been established:

(1) A thrower of average ability can benefit more from a contrary wind than a good thrower (because the percentage of influence relative to the wind is greater for the average thrower than for one who can achieve a higher release speed);

(2) it is impossible to determine an optimum wind velocity for the maximum distance;

(3) the discus is stable at angles of attack between 27° and 29°.

The angle of attack is the angle between the central plane of the discus and the flight path or relative airflow. If the discus is thrown in still air, the relative airflow in this case corresponds in speed and direction to the flight path of the implement. The angle of attack at the moment of delivery is therefore equal to the angle of attitude minus the angle of release (Fig. 3b). A positive angle of attack means that the underside of the discus is presented to the airflow, while a negative angle of attack (a common factor in good throws) means that the upper side is presented to the airflow (Fig. 3c).

If the discus is thrown with wind blowing, the wind speed must be taken into consideration to determine the force and direction of the wind relative to the angle of attack (Fig. 3d).

Some researchers have analysed the aerodynamic properties of a rotating discus, which had never been done before. They have discovered that at a wind speed of 33 m/sec. (118.8 km/h) the maximum value of the lift/drag ratio was achieved with an angle of attack of 9°, a result in complete accordance with various preceding data for velocities of around 30 m/sec. (108 km/h).

Other researchers set out to determine at what angles of attitude and release the discus should be thrown in order to travel the greatest possible distance for a particular initial velocity. From these investigations they were able to draw the following conclusions:

(1) the delivery speed is the most important factor in determining the length of throw;

(2) for any delivery speed the release angle is of major importance (for throwers of 50–60 m, release angles of around 35° are effective, whereas throwers who achieve shorter distances use a slightly greater release angle);

(3) the angle of attitude should be between 25° and 35°.

These conclusions which involve an angle of attack of between 0° and 15° seem at first sight to be in direct contrast to those previously mentioned which indicate that an angle of attack of 9°–10° is most likely to achieve the best lift/drag ratio.

The reason for this apparent contradiction lies in the fact that while the angle of attitude can remain almost constant during the flight, the relative wind direction and therefore the angle of attack changes constantly as the discus attains the highest point of its trajectory and then falls back to earth. The angle of attack imparted at delivery must, however, be such as to permit the best results over the whole trajectory rather than at just one point along it (Fig. 4). Data obtained from trying out various angles of release and attitude are scarce. All the same, what little has been learned indicates that experimental results are confirmed in practice.

REGULATIONS GOVERNING THROWING THE DISCUS

1. The order in which competitors make their attempts is to be drawn by lots.
2. When there are more than 8 competitors, each is to be allowed 3 attempts, and the 8 competitors with the best throws are each to be allowed 3 more attempts. When there are 8 or fewer competitors, each one is to be allowed 6 attempts. On the field each competitor is permitted to make 2 practice throws carried out under the supervision of the judges in the order of the draw, the competitors being called out by name. After the contest has started, the competitors are not allowed to use the circle or the throwing sector for warming up, either with or without implements.
3. Each contestant is to be placed according to the best of his throws.
4. The discus is thrown from a circle. The competitor must start his throw from a stationary position.
5. The competitor may touch the inside of the circle rim. The throw is foul and disallowed if the competitor, after entering the circle and starting his throw, touches with any part of his body the ground outside the circle or the upper part of the rim, or if he releases the discus incorrectly during execution.

Provided the above regulations are not infringed in the course of the attempt, a competitor may break off an attempt once started, may place his implement on the ground and/or may leave the circle before returning to a stationary position to restart his attempt.

6. The competitor may not leave the circle until the implement has landed. When he leaves the circle, his first contact with the upper edge of the rim or the ground outside the circle must take place completely behind the white line drawn outside the circle and passing invisibly through the centre of the circle itself.
7. In order for a throw to be valid, the implement must fall within the inside edges of the lines (5 cm wide) that mark a 40° throwing sector drawn so

that the lines of radius meet at the centre of the circle. The ends of the lines outlining the throwing sector are to be indicated with marker flags.

8. The maximum permissible slope of the ground within the throwing sector is 1/100.

9. The measurement of each throw must be taken immediately after the throw from the nearest mark left by the discus to the centre of the circle.

10. A distinctive stake or flag must be provided to indicate the best throw of each competitor, and placed along a line or tape outside the line of the sector. A marker must indicate the current world record and, where appropriate, the national record.

11. In the Olympic Games, the World Championships and continental or group Games or Championships, the only implements to be used are to be those supplied by the organizers and no modifications may be introduced during the contest. No competitor may bring any implement he wishes on to the field.

In regional contests, competitors may use their own implements provided they are checked and approved by the organizers before the contest and are placed at the disposal of all the competitors.

12. No expedient of any kind that in any way helps a competitor while executing his throw may be permitted. Only in the case of an open wound is the use of adhesive tape or sticking plaster allowed on the hands. The use of gloves is not permitted, but to obtain a better grip competitors may rub an appropriate substance on their hands and their hands alone. To protect the spine from damage a competitor may wear a belt of suitable material.

13. Competitors may not spray or spread any substance on the circle or the soles of their shoes.

14. The discus must be carried back to the circle, never thrown back.

15. CONSTRUCTION OF THE DISCUS. The body of the discus must be made of wood or other material inside a circular metal rim with a perfectly rounded border about 6 mm wide. There may be circular plates fixed centrally on either side. Alternatively the discus may be constructed without metal plates, provided the corresponding area is flat and the

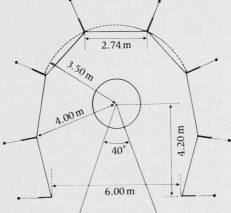

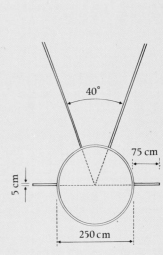

measurements and total weight of the implement meet the prescribed requirements.

The two sides of the discus must be identical and have no dents, protuberances or sharp edges. The sides must be tapered in a straight line from the beginning of the curve of the rim to a distance of 25–28.5 mm from the centre of the discus.

16. It must conform to the following measurements:

		Men	Women
Weight for the confirmation of a record	min.	2.000 kg	1.000 kg
Tolerance for the supply of competition implements	min.	2.005 kg	1.005 kg
	max.	2.025 kg	1.025 kg
Diameter of the metal plates or the flat central area	min.	50 mm	50 mm
	max.	57 mm	57 mm
Thickness at the centre	min.	44 mm	37 mm
	max.	46 mm	39 mm
Thickness of the rim 6 mm from the edge	min.	12 mm	12 mm

17. CONSTRUCTION OF THE DISCUS THROWING CIRCLE. The rim is made of sheet iron, steel or other material, the upper edge of which must be level with the surrounding ground.

The inside of the circle may be made of concrete, asphalt or other solid non-slip material. The surface of this inner part must be levelled and finished 2 cm (± 6 mm) below the edge of the rim.

18. DIMENSIONS. The internal diameter of the circle must measure 2.5 m (± 5 mm).

The circle must be at least 6 mm thick and be painted white.

19. A straight white line 5 cm wide must be traced outside the circle for a length of at least 75 cm either side of the circle. It may be painted or made of wood or other suitable material. The back edge of this white line is to coincide with the extension of an invisible line passing through the centre of the circle at right angles to the centre line of the throwing sector.

Safety cage for the discus.

1. All discus throws must be made from a cage that ensures the safety of the spectators, the competition officials and the contestants.

2. The cage must be designed, constructed and maintained so as to be able to block a discus of 2 kg moving at a speed of over 25 m/sec. The structure must be such as to prevent any danger of the discus, once blocked, rebounding outside the framework of the cage, back towards the athlete or over the top of the net.
3. The cage must be U-shaped, composed of at least 6 panels of netting each 3.17 m wide. The opening must be 6 m wide, situated 5 m in front of the centre of the throwing circle. The panels of netting must be at least 4 m high.

4. The netting for the cage should be of any suitable material such as cord of natural or synthetic fibre, or steel wire of roughly average elasticity. The maximum gauge of the mesh should be 5 cm for wire and 4 cm for cord.
5. The maximum danger splay for throwing the discus from this cage is approximately 98°, taking into consideration that there are both right- and left-handed throwers. The placing and angling of the cage on the in-field should therefore be determined by considerations of safety during use.

Training

Training methods for the individual throwing events are markedly similar, allowing them to be discussed all together. They fall into two groups: (a) training in technique; (b) strength training.

The first group includes all the exercises and procedures aimed at perfecting the way in which the movement is carried out, creating an exact rhythm for the throw and neat introduction of the various components in the kinetic chain. The aim is to master and weld together the various phases of the throw, working on each event's individual elements of technique (stance, preliminary swings, transition, run-up or turns, delivery and reverse). Particular care is taken over the most delicate of these moments, the passage from the phase of transition or run-up or turns, to the delivery or final phase. The phases are so bound together that the initial phase can consequently affect the whole execution of the throw. To this end exercises are required which reflect the entire technique of the throws themselves, complete or partial, from the stance onwards, or else auxiliary exercises imitating the basic action.

The second group includes exercises for improving the basic psycho-physical qualities most needed: the strength and speed of muscular contraction. Particularly important in

this discipline is the connection between strength and speed, in other words muscular power, which is usually developed and increased by exercises defined as indirect, using movements different from those specific to the discipline practised.

Since muscular power is the product of strength and speed of muscular contraction, we attempt first to increase the strength by exercises against moving resistances: weight-lifting (snatch, jerk, squat and clean), bench-press seated and inclined (bar-bell resting on the shoulders, driven vertically with the arms), pull-over (lying on bench, bar-bell is raised and lowered alternately above head and over body) etc. and muscle exercises against fixed resistances (isometrics), together with other exercises of muscular contraction with muscles in the extension phase such as hops and jumps. In the second stage we try to use the strength fostered by these indirect exercises in the specific event that is the object of the training, using movements or parts of movements similar to those required by the event's particular action.

To improve the speed of muscular contraction we use specific exercises under more difficult or easier conditions than those of an actual contest. For example, the shot can be made more difficult by throwing a heavier implement (e.g. 8 kg), or with the

body weight increased by a heavy jacket, etc. Conditions can be eased by using a lighter implement (a shot of 6 kg). Naturally this intense activity leads to muscle expansion and an increase in body weight. The weight of the throwing implements (excluding the javelin) in fact requires the thrower to have a considerable body mass that can impart to the implement a high initial velocity (e.g. in the order of 13.5 m/sec. for putting the shot about 20 m). It must also be remembered that the greater the athlete's height, the longer will be the throw for a given body weight, the trajectory in this case starting from a more forward point. Therefore the characteristics required for these events are high body weight and considerable stature.

In addition, the psychological qualities necessary to obtain results of international calibre are exceptional levels of determination, tenacity, will-power and, above all, self-confidence.

On the following pages are suggested typical training schedules for throwers of average national standard from 17 to 18 years old of both sexes. In the competitive period from mid-May to mid-June it is advisable to introduce 3 or 4 weeks of specific or supplementary work, as well as 3 weeks of similar work covering the August holiday.

Typical week in the general preparation period (November to January)

Session 1
• Lying on the back on the bench, butterfly exercise with 70% of max. load: 6 sets of 8 repetitions with 4–5 min. rest between the sets, imitating the throwing action with the arm.
• The same exercise lying on the stomach, 3 sets × 6 repetitions.
• Hanging from the bar, pull the chin up to touch it: 5 sets × 8 repetitions and appropriate rest intervals.
• Sitting astride the bench, twisting left and right, arms extended with 70% of max. load: 6 sets of 8 repetitions and appropriate rest intervals.
• On the horse or box, with bar-bell on the shoulders weighing 70% of max., half-squat (knee angle about 90°): 6 sets of 8 repetitions and appropriate rests.
• With bar-bell on the shoulders equal to 1.5 times the body weight, rise on tiptoe with the balls of the feet resting on a block at least 10 cm high: 4 sets of 10 repetitions plus rests.

• Lying on the back, raise hands and feet towards each other resting only on the buttocks: 4 sets of 5 repetitions (abdominal).
• Lying on the stomach, lift legs and chest, holding this position for several seconds before returning to rest: 4 sets of 15 repetitions plus rests (back).
• At the end of the session some suppling exercises for muscles and joints, especially the spine.

Session 2
• Jogging for 1.5–2 km to warm up.
• 15 min. free-standing gymnastics.
• 10 throws with a discus of 2.5 kg for men or 1.5 kg for women, from a standstill.
• 20 throws with regulation discus, from a standstill.
• 30 throws with regulation discus, watching the progression (speeding up).
• 10 sets of jumps over 10 hurdles

0.91 m and 0.76 m high and 2 m and 1.5 m apart respectively.
• 4 sets of 10 long jumps, taking off from alternate feet and landing in the sand. Go for the greatest possible length.
• 2–3 × 150 m at 70% of max. speed.
• 10 min. jogging and a few suppling exercises.

Session 3
• 25–30 min. jogging.
• 20 min. muscle extension and joint suppling exercises for all joints.
• Game of basketball, volleyball or handball.

Session 4
• Rest.

Session 5
• As Session 1.

Session 6
• As Session 2.

Typical week in the specific preparation period (February to March)

Session 1
• Butterflies lying face up on the bench, with a load 80% of max.: 4 sets × 6 repetitions plus 5 min. rest between sets, used in making throwing gestures.
• Butterflies face down: 1 set × 4 repetitions with 80% of max. load.
• Hanging from the bar, bring the chin up to touch it: 3 sets × 6 repetitions with extra weight of 5–10 kg hung round the waist, plus rests between sets.
• On the horse or box, bar-bell on the shoulders with 80% of max. weight, semi-squat with knee angle not less than 90%: 4 sets × 6 repetitions plus rests.
• With bar-bell on the shoulders equal to body weight, bending and stretching the legs, keeping back upright: 4 sets × 6 repetitions plus rests.
• Abdominals as in general preparation period.

• Dorsals as above.
• At the end of the session, a few suppling exercises for muscles and joints, especially the spine.

Session 2
• 1.5–2 km jogging to warm up.
• 15 min. free standing gymnastics.
• 20 throws with a discus of 2.5 kg for men or 1.5 kg for women, from the circle and from a standstill.
• 20 throws from a standstill with the regulation discus.
• 30 complete throws with the regulation discus, watching the increasing pace of the throw and the reverse.
• 10 sets of jumps with feet together over 10 hurdles 0.91 m and 0.76 m high and 2 m and 1.5 m apart respectively.
• 4 sets of 10 long-jumps, taking off from alternate feet and landing in the sand, always going for the longest distance.

• 10 × 5 hurdles of 0.91 and 0.76 m, with crouching start from blocks and a distance of 8 strides between the start and the first hurdle, and a distance of 3 strides between hurdles.
• 5 sprinting starts from blocks and 20 m sprint.
• 2–3 × 150 m at 80% max. speed.
• 10 min. jogging and a few muscle suppling exercises to finish.

Session 3
• 25–30 min. jogging.
• 20 min. exercises (see above).
• Ball game (as above).

Session 4
• Rest.

Session 5
• As Session 1.

Session 6
• As Session 2.

Typical week in the competitive period (April to September)

Session 1
- 25–30 min. jogging.
- 20 min. exercises for muscular extension and joint mobility for all joints.

Session 2
- Butterflies lying face up on the bench: 4 sets, the first of 5 repetitions with 75% of max. load, the second of 4 repetitions with 80%, the third of 3 repetitions with 85%, the fourth of 2 repetitions with 90%.
- Butterflies face down: 1 set × 6 repetitions with 70% of max. load.
- Hanging from the bar, bring the chin up to touch it: 4 sets, the first of 4 repetitions with a load of 80% of the maximum (tie bar-bell discs on a belt round the waist), the second of 3 repetitions with 85%, the third of 2 repetitions with 90%, the fourth 1 repetition with 95%.
- On the horse or box, with bar-bell on the shoulders with a load equal to 80% of the maximum, half-squat: 4 sets × 6 repetitions plus rests.
- With bar-bell across the shoulders equal to the body weight, bending and stretching the legs, keeping back upright: 4 sets × 6 repetitions.

- Abdominals and dorsals as in the specific preparation period.
- At the end of the session, a few suppling exercises for muscles and joints, especially the spine.

Session 3
- 1.5–2 km jogging.
- 15 min. free-standing gymnastics.
- 20 throws of the regulation discus from a standstill, watching the position of delivery.
- 30 complete throws of the regulation discus, watching the mounting pace of the throw and the reverse.
- 10 throws with a discus of 1.75 kg (men) or 0.75 kg (women) watching the progression and speed of execution.
- 5 sets of jumps with feet together over 10 hurdles 0.91 m and 0.76 m high and 2 m or 1.5 m apart respectively.
- 2 sets of 10 long-jumps with take-off from alternate feet and landing in the sand, trying for the greatest length.
- 5 × 5 hurdles as in the specific preparation period.
- 5 racing starts from blocks plus 20 m sprint.

- 2–3 × 150 m at 80% of maximum speed.
- 10 min. jogging, finishing with a few suppling exercises.

Session 4
- 1 km jogging to warm up.
- 15 min. free-standing gymnastics.
- 10 throws from a standstill with competition discus.
- 20 throws watching progression and reverse.
- 5 throws with discus of 1.75 kg (men) or 0.75 kg (women).
- 10 min. jogging, finishing with a few suppling exercises.

Session 5
- Rest.

Session 6
- Butterflies face up as in Session 2.
- Half-squats as in Session 2.
- Abdominals as in Session 2.
- Dorsals as in Session 2.
- At the end, a few suppling exercises for muscles and joints, especially the spine.

Session 7
- Competition.

Left. *The safety cage used for the discus to prevent it flying off into the crowd in the event of a throw getting out of control.*
Below. *One of the strength exercises practised by discus throwers.*

■ The stars ■

BUD HOUSER (USA)
In the 1920s the leading countries in this event were the USA and Finland. The star of this period was the American Clarence 'Bud' Houser, who trained under Dean Cromwell. Like most American undergraduates who took part in this event, Houser practised both the shot and the discus at top international level, two events considered a fair way apart today. In 1924 in Paris he won the Olympic gold medal in both events with 14.99 m and 46.15 m respectively. As a discus thrower he reached his peak in April 1926 at Palo Alto, when he gained his world record with a throw of 48.20 m. He used to do 1½ turns in the circle, moving with a rapid sequence of steps. At the shot he achieved 15.42 m, also in 1926. He returned to the Olympic arena in 1928 at Amsterdam and again won the discus, the first three athletes achieving distances within 22 cm.

ADOLFO CONSOLINI (ITALY)
Discovered during a promotional display in 1937, he took up athletics at the relatively advanced age of 20. In that same season he succeeded in throwing the discus 41.77 m, a distance that won him the national junior title at Florence. Over the following years he made continuous progress. By 1938 he had improved to European and world standard, throwing 48.02 m.

The first occasion on which Consolini exceeded 50 m was at Turin in 1940, and in 1941 he took the world record for the first time with 53.34 m. In the following years he lost and regained the world record, and took the world record twice more with 54.23 m in the spring of 1946 and 55.33 m in the autumn of 1948.

Consolini took part in four Olympics, although the two which were cancelled because of the Second World War would have found him on his best form. In London in 1948 he won the Olympic gold with 52.78 m, was then second (53.78 m) in Helsinki in 1952, sixth (52.21 m) at Melbourne in 1956 and seventeenth (52.44 m) in Rome in 1960.

Mac Wilkins

In the European field he was for many years practically unbeatable. Between September 1941 and June 1955 he was beaten by only one other European, his compatriot Giuseppe Tosi. He won the European title three times with 52.23 m in 1946 at Oslo, 53.75 m in 1950 at Brussels and 53.44 m in 1954 at Berne.

Six times European record holder, Consolini took the last of these records in December 1955 with 56.98 m, when he was nearly 39.

AL OERTER (USA)
His name is linked with one of the most prestigious records, that of the highest number of Olympic victories in one event. From 1956 to 1968 he won the Olympic discus title four times. More surprising is the fact that before each of these contests, Oerter was never the favourite, but just a contender for the medals. Three times out of the four he won by breaking his own record.

In 1956, when just 20, he went to the Melbourne Games and opened with a new Olympic and personal record of 56.36 m, which turned out to be the winning distance.

In 1960 at the Rome Games, Oerter won with a personal record of 59.18 m. His third victory in 1964 at Tokyo was also the most difficult. The world record holder at that point was the Czech Ludvik Daněk with 64.55 m. Oerter had injured his ribs and was advised not to compete by doctors. Wearing a harness and requiring ice packs at intervals on the affected area, he nevertheless demoralized the other competitors from the qualifying round onwards with a new Olympic record of 60.54 m. In the final Daněk was ahead until the fourth round (60.52 m) but in the next throw Oerter gave it all he had, winning with 61.00 m. Although not his best, the distance was enough to earn him his third gold medal.

The last of his four Olympic victories, in 1968 at Mexico City, was perhaps the least expected of all. Beforehand the favourite was Jay Silvester who not only held the world record with 68.40 m, but had beaten Oerter in that season's straight competitions on six out of seven occasions. However, Oerter claimed a point in his favour: lying fourth at the end of the second round, he threw a personal best of 64.78 m in the third, clinching it with two more throws of over 64 m. That was his fourth Olympic victory.

Oerter's name appears four times in the list of world records, the first with 61.10 m (1962) and the last with 62.94 m (1964). In 1969 Oerter decided to retire from athletics, but made a comeback in 1977 with results fairly close to those of his best days. Subsequently, he threw some sensational distances, reaching 69.46 m in spring 1980 when he was nearly 44. He also managed to come fourth in the Olympic trials the same year.

MAC WILKINS (USA)

The Americans, for many years at the top of this event, began to lose ground in the face of the European challenge in the 1980s. The last of them to be confirmed as number one in the world was Mac Wilkins, who was the first officially to break the 70 m barrier. This happened in 1976 at San José, California. A few days earlier Wilkins had taken the world record with 69.18 m. At San José he bettered that within a few minutes with 69.80 m, 70.24 m and 70.86 m.

In the summer of that year at Montreal, Wilkins won the Olympic title with 67.50 m, from the East German Wolfgang Schmidt. In the qualifying rounds the day before, the American had done better with 68.28 m, which still stands as the Olympic record. Incidentally, the discus is the only track and field event in which no world record has ever been set during the Olympic Games.

Wilkins is one of the most complete throwers ever. At various times in his career he has thrown the discus 70.98 m (1980), the shot 21.06 m (indoors in 1977), the hammer 63.66 m (1977) and the javelin 78.44 m (1970).

FAINA MYELNIK (USSR)

Between 1971 and 1975 this powerful Ukrainian woman set the world record eleven times, beginning with 64.22 m and reaching 70.50 m.

She made her international debut in Helsinki in 1971, where she won with her last throw of 64.22 m. The following year in Munich she won the Olympic title with 66.62 m.

She was supposed to be unbeatable but at the 1976 Olympics only made fourth place in the final.

Faina Myelnik first passed the 70 m mark on 20 Aug. 1975 in Zürich with 70.20 m and took the last of her world records (70.50 m) the following year at Sochi. However, after her defeat in Montreal she never seemed to be the athlete she had been. At the European Games, after the victory of 1971 and another in 1974, she dropped to fifth place in 1978.

EVELIN JAHL (GDR)

She has been the greatest woman competitor in the history of the discus. Between 1976 and 1981 she won all there was to win.

She first did well internationally at the 1976 Olympic Games in Montreal; barely 20 years old she threw 69.00 m, a new personal record which won her the title. In 1978, she won the European title in Prague. The following year she continued to dominate the field with victories in the European Cup and the World Cup. She won the Olympic title again in 1980 at Moscow, becoming the first woman to take two gold medals in this event. In 1981, following a defeat in the European Cup, she won in the World Cup.

She raised the world record on two occasions: 70.72 m in 1978 and 71.50 m in 1980.

WORLD RECORDS

Men

m

47.58 James Duncan (USA) 1912
47.61 Thomas Lieb (USA) 1924
47.89 Glenn Hartranft (USA) 1925
48.20 Clarence Houser (USA) 1926
49.90 Eric Krenz (USA) 1929
51.03 Eric Krenz (USA) 1930
51.73 Paul Jessup (USA) 1930
52.42 Harald Andersson (USA) 1934
53.10 Willi Schröder (Sweden) 1935
53.26 Archie Harris (Germany) 1941
53.34 Adolfo Consolini (Italy) 1941
54.23 Adolfo Consolini (Italy) 1946
54.93 Robert Fitch (USA) 1946
55.33 Adolfo Consolini (Italy) 1948
56.46 Fortune Gordien (USA) 1949
56.97 Fortune Gordien (USA) 1949
57.93 Sim Iness (USA) 1953
58.10 Fortune Gordien (USA) 1953
59.28 Fortune Gordien (USA) 1953
59.91 Edmund Piatkowski (Poland) 1959
59.91 Rink Babka (USA) 1960
60.56 Jay Silvester (USA) 1961
60.72 Jay Silvester (USA) 1961
61.10 Al Oerter (USA) 1962
61.64 Vladimir Trusenyov (USSR) 1962
62.45 Al Oerter (USA) 1962
62.62 Al Oerter (USA) 1963
62.94 Al Oerter (USA) 1964
64.55 Ludvik Danek (Czechoslovakia) 1964
65.22 Ludvik Danek (Czechoslovakia) 1965
66.54 Jay Silvester (USA) 1968
68.40 Jay Silvester (USA) 1968
68.40 Ricky Bruch (Sweden) 1972
68.48 John Van Reenen (S. Africa) 1975
69.08 John Powell (USA) 1975
69.18 Mac Wilkins (USA) 1976
69.80 Mac Wilkins (USA) 1976
70.24 Mac Wilkins (USA) 1976
70.86 Mac Wilkins (USA) 1976
71.16 Wolfgang Schmidt (GDR) 1978
71.86 Yuri Dumchev (USSR) 1983

Women

48.31 Gisela Mauermayer (Germany) 1936
53.25 Nina Dumbadze (USSR) 1948
53.37 Nina Dumbadze (USSR) 1951
53.61 Nina Romashkova (USSR) 1952
57.04 Nina Dumbadze (USSR) 1952
57.15 Tamara Press (USSR) 1960
57.43 Tamara Press (USSR) 1961
58.06 Tamara Press (USSR) 1961
58.98 Tamara Press (USSR) 1961
59.29 Tamara Press (USSR) 1963
59.70 Tamara Press (USSR) 1965
61.26 Liesel Westermann (W. Germany) 1967
61.64 Christine Spielberg (GDR) 1968
62.54 Liesel Westermann (W. Germany) 1968
62.70 Liesel Westermann (W. Germany) 1969
63.96 Liesel Westermann (W. Germany) 1969
64.22 Faina Myelnik (USSR) 1971
64.88 Faina Myelnik (USSR) 1971
65.42 Faina Myelnik (USSR) 1972
65.48 Faina Myelnik (USSR) 1972
66.76 Faina Myelnik (USSR) 1972
67.32 Argentina Menis (Romania) 1972
67.44 Faina Myelnik (USSR) 1973
67.58 Faina Myelnik (USSR) 1973
69.48 Faina Myelnik (USSR) 1973
69.90 Faina Myelnik (USSR) 1974
70.20 Faina Myelnik (USSR) 1975
70.50 Faina Myelnik (USSR) 1976
70.72 Evelin Jahl (GDR) 1978
73.26 Galina Savinkova (USSR) 1983

Al Oerter

Shot put
History

Putting the shot or throwing a stone ball was practised in Scotland and Ireland long before the last century; immigrants then took it to the USA, where it quickly caught on and produced its first champions.

Towards the mid-19th century, the weight of the shot, now made of iron, was standardized at 16 lbs (7.257 kg). It was thrown from a 7 ft square (2.135 m), and such a square was used in the first three Olympic Games.

In 1909 it was changed to a circle 7 ft in diameter, the front edge marked by a plank in the position of the present wooden stop-board.

The best practitioners of the early years adopted mainly individual techniques, usually employing their strength without it culminating in the present burst of explosive power. Their legs hardly helped at all to increase the final propulsion, which consisted of no more than a 45° turn, since they started in a position facing the direction of throw.

Only in the 1950s did shot putting start to make some headway in the athletics world, based on Parry O'Brien's style.

The technique of putting the shot
Marco Montelatici, one of Italy's best putters and the first to throw the shot beyond 20 m, demonstrates his technique in the photographs.

The shot has been included in the Olympic programme since 1896. At the St Louis Games of 1904 there was a contest with a 'heavy' shot weighing 65 lbs (25.4 kg). In the Olympics at Stockholm in 1912 and Paris in 1920, shot-putting contests were devised as a combined left and right hand event, putting first with one hand, then with the other.

Of all the throwing events, the shot is the only one held indoors.

TECHNIQUE

The shot must be thrown with one hand, from the shoulder. When the thrower has entered the circle to start his throw, the implement must be held near his chin and throughout all the movements the implement itself must never be moved behind his shoulder, otherwise the throw will be disallowed.

At present the most widely used techniques of putting the shot are the back-facing technique, named after O'Brien who invented it, and the rotational technique, named after Baryshnikov. Neither of these techniques contains any substantial difference between men and women.

The O'Brien technique can be described as follows (for a right-hander): the thrower takes up his starting position with his back facing the direction of the throw, standing at the rear of the circle, holding the implement resting on the base of the fingers of his right hand (photo 1, p. 177), his throwing arm bent at the elbow and the hand holding the implement resting on his shoulder, the fingers flexed and slightly apart. The body remains upright with the supporting leg (corresponding to the throwing arm) firmly placed with the toe at the very centre of the back of the circle (photo 2). In preparation for the glide, the thrower leans his body forward and at the same time bends his supporting leg, raising the other leg behind in order to balance the body on the supporting leg (photo 3). The free leg is now bent and brought close to the supporting leg (photo 4). Here begins the glide itself, with the left leg kicking rapidly backwards in the direction of throw, followed immediately by the straightening of the supporting leg and its successive snatching up underneath the body with the knee bent. In these movements the supporting leg slides on the flat of the foot, bringing the thrower firmly on to his right foot in the centre of the circle (photo 5), while his left foot immediately comes down against the stop-board, without changing the position of his upper body (6–7).

Having thus reached the throwing position, the legs straighten rapidly, the trunk lifts and slightly rotates (photo 8), and the shoulder, arm, and finally throwing hand drive forward in succession (photos 9–11), forming the kinetic chain that will give the implement the highest possible initial speed and the most favourable release angle, which will be smaller the greater the height of the thrower.

To prevent himself falling out of the front of the circle, which would render the throw foul, the athlete does a rapid scissor of the legs, changing his weight with a small jump from the left leg on to the right (photo 12).

The rotational technique, or Baryshnikov technique, basically uses the same general leg movements as those adopted by discus throwers (see the description of discus throwing), the upper body abiding by the international regulations that do not permit the implement to be placed behind the shoulder, nor moved away from it until the final phase. From the starting position, which is the same as that for the discus as far as the legs are concerned, the athlete pivots on the foot opposite the throwing arm and rotates anticlockwise if he is right-handed and clockwise if he is left-handed, and does a glide that brings him into a landing position very similar to that in the O'Brien technique, but with the advantage of having produced a rotational energy in his body that, when concentrated at the end of the kinetic chain building up to delivery, should give the implement a higher initial speed. The greatest difficulty in this technique comes in the reverse phase, because it is difficult to channel the energy developed by the rotation perfectly into the kinetic chain building up to delivery, which often means that the reverse becomes uncontrollable, causing the high probability of a no throw with the athlete falling outside the front of the circle or the shot landing outside the throwing sector.

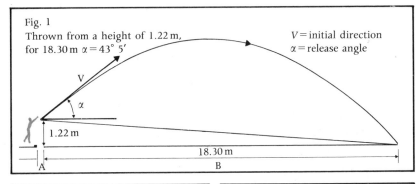

Fig. 1
Thrown from a height of 1.22 m, for 18.30 m α = 43° 5'

V = initial direction
α = release angle

1.22 m

18.30 m

A

B

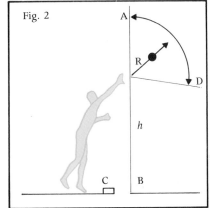

Fig. 2

A

R

D

h

C

B

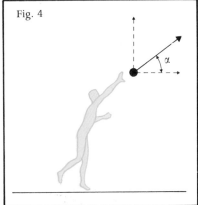

Fig. 4

α

BIOMECHANICS. The distance that is measured in a shot put is the sum of two distances:

(1) The horizontal distance A that the shot is carried beyond the vertical passing through the front limit of the circle, as far as the vertical passing through the point at which it is released from the thrower's hand (fig. 1);

(2) The horizontal distance B between the vertical passing through the point of release and the mark on the ground where the implement falls, i.e. while it is in flight (fig. 1). The first of these two distances is usually about 40 cm (fig. 3), dependent on the position of the body at the moment of release and by the athlete's physique, especially the length of his throwing arm.

The second is conditioned by the release speed, the release angle (fig. 4) and the height at which the shot is released, besides the air resistance encountered during flight.

The release speed (or initial velocity), without doubt the most important factor, is determined by the magnitude and direction of the forces applied to the shot, also by the distance and time over which these forces are applied (impulse). The release angle is determined by these two

Biomechanical data
Figs 1, 2 and 4 show the speeds and forces resulting from the shot being thrown.

factors: magnitude and direction of the forces applied. The optimum release angle is slightly under 45°, because there is a difference in level between the release point and the landing point (fig. 1). The extent of the release angle's divergence from 45° depends on the magnitude of the release speed and, to a lesser degree, the height of the release point. The lower the release speed and the higher the release point, the smaller will be the release angle (fig. 5).

The height of the release point is determined by the position of the body at that moment (fig. 3) and by the thrower's build. Other circumstances being equal, a tall athlete with long arms who achieves a final position with legs, hips, trunk and throwing arm well stretched at the moment of release, will succeed in throwing further than an athlete of different build or one who does not reach out so well. The effects of air resistance on putting the shot can be ignored.

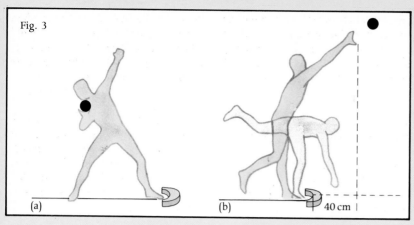

Fig. 3

(a)   (b)   40 cm

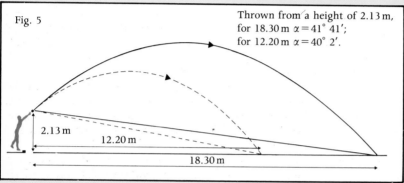

Fig. 5

Thrown from a height of 2.13 m,
for 18.30 m α = 41° 41';
for 12.20 m α = 40° 2'.

2.13 m
12.20 m
18.30 m

Biomechanical data

Fig. 5 illustrates the different lengths of trajectory in relation to two different release angles at the moment the shot is released.

40°

75 cm

122 cm

5 cm

213.5 cm

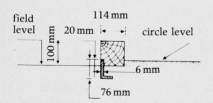

field level
circle level
114 mm
20 mm
100 mm
6 mm
76 mm

Implements and the circle

The photograph shows various types of implement, the regulation ones for both women and men, and other heavier and lighter ones used for training. The implements for adolescents must weigh 6 kg for boys and 3 kg for girls. The drawings show the throwing circle and the stopping-board with measurements.

REGULATIONS GOVERNING PUTTING THE SHOT

1. The order in which the competitors make their attempts is to be drawn by lots.

2. When there are more than eight competitors, each is to be allowed three attempts, and the eight competitors with the best throws are to be allowed three more attempts. In the case of a tie for eighth place, each competitor involved in the tie is to be allowed the three more attempts. When there are eight or fewer competitors, each one is to be allowed six attempts. On the field each competitor may, if possible, make two practice throws, but not more. These must be carried out under the supervision of the judges and in the order of the draw, and the contestants are to be called out by name. After the contest has started, the competitors are not permitted to use the circle or the throwing sector for warming up, with or without the shot.

3. Each competitor is to be placed according to the best of his throws.

4. The throw must be made from a circle. In the centre of the front half of the circle's circumference there must be a stop-board firmly fixed to the ground.

The throwing sector area may be surfaced with cinders or grass or any other suitable material on which the shot will leave a mark.

5. The competitor must start his throw from a motionless position within the circle.

The shot must be put from the shoulder using only one hand. At the moment when the competitor takes up his starting position in the circle, the shot must touch or be very close to his chin, and his hand must not be lowered from this position during the throwing action. The shot may on no account be carried behind the shoulder-line.

6. A competitor may touch the inside of the stop-board or the rim of the circle. The throw must be ruled a foul if the competitor, after entering the circle and starting his throw, touches with any part of his body the ground outside the circle or the upper edge of the rim or the stop-board, or if he releases the shot incorrectly during the execution of any attempt.

Provided the aforesaid regulations are not infringed in the course of the attempt, a competitor may break off an attempt once started, may place his shot on the ground and/or may leave the circle before returning to the motionless position to restart his attempt.

7. The competitor may not leave the circle until the shot has landed. When leaving the circle after it has done so, his first contact with the upper edge of the rim or the ground outside the circle must take place completely behind the white line drawn outside the circle and passing invisibly through the centre of the circle itself.

8. In order for a throw to be valid, the shot must fall in such a way that the mark nearest the circle left by its impact on the ground is between the inside edges of the lines (5 cm wide) that mark a 40° sector drawn so that the lines of radius meet at the centre of the circle.

The ends of the lines outlining the throwing sector are to be indicated with marker flags.

9. The maximum permissible slope of the ground within the throwing sector is 1/1000.

10. The measurement of each throw must be taken immediately after the throw, from the nearest mark left by the shot as it falls, to the inside of the rim of the circle, along the line from the mark made by the shot to the centre of the circle.

11. A marker flag or disc must be provided to indicate the current world record and, where appropriate, the national record.

12. In the Olympic Games, the World Cup and continental or group Games or Championships, the only implements to be used are those supplied by the organizers, and no modifications may be introduced during the contest. No competitor may bring whatever implement he wishes on to the field.

In regional meetings, competitors may use their own implements provided they are checked, approved and initialled by the display organizers before the contest and placed at the disposal of all the competitors.

13. No expedient of any kind (for example, binding two or more fingers together with adhesive tape) that in any way helps a competitor to execute his throw may be permitted. Only if it is necessary to cover an open wound is the use of adhesive tape or sticking plaster allowed on the hands. The use of gloves is not permitted.

To obtain a better grip contestants are authorized to rub an appropriate substance on their hands, and hands alone. To protect the spine from damage, a competitor may wear a belt of leather or other suitable material.

14. Competitors may not spray or sprinkle any substance on the circle or the soles of their shoes.

15. After the throw has been completed, the shot must be carried back to the circle, never thrown back.

16. CONSTRUCTION OF THE SHOT. The shot may be of solid iron or brass or any other metal no softer than brass, or else a shell of one such metal filled with lead or other material. It must be spherical in shape and its surface must be smooth.

17. It must conform to the following measurements:

18. CONSTRUCTION OF THE SHOT CIRCLE. The rim is made of a sheet of iron, steel or other suitable material, the upper edge of which must be level with the surrounding ground. The inside of the circle may be made of concrete, asphalt or other solid, non-slip material. The surface of this inner part must be levelled and finished 2 cm (± 6 mm) below the upper edge of the rim. A portable circle is acceptable if it conforms to the above specifications.

A white line 5 cm wide must be traced outside the circle for a length of at least 75 cm from either side of the circle. It may be painted or made of wood or other suitable material. The back edge of the white line is to coincide with the extension of an invisible line passing through the centre of the circle at right angles to the centre line of the throwing sector.

19. The internal diameter of the circle must measure 2.135 m (± 5 mm).

The circle must be at least 6 mm thick and be painted white.

20. The stop-board may be of wood or any other suitable material and must be bow-shaped so that its inside edge coincides with the inside edge of the rim, and also made in such a way that it can be firmly fixed to the ground.

21. The stop-board must measure 1.21/1.23 m inside length, 11.2/11.6 cm in width and 9.8/10.2 cm in height above the internal level of the circle.

22. The stop-board must be painted white.

			Men	Women
Weight for the confirmation of a record	min.		7.260 kg	4.000 kg
Tolerance for the supply of competition implements	min.		7.265 kg	4.005 kg
	max.		7.285 kg	4.025 kg
Diameter	min.		110 mm	95 mm
	max.		130 mm	110 mm

To the typical weekly training programme suggested for shot putters of 17–18 we would add a few ideas for younger putters.

It is of paramount importance that trainees under the age of 16 should form the clearest possible conception of the action fundamental to the event. They can be shown film sequences of throws by champions and also see them at work live by attending high level national and if possible international contests. They can compare film sequences of themselves with those of expert athletes. It is preferable to divide the annual cycle of work into three basic periods, excluding the indoor competitions (we are still talking about young people up to 16) even though shot-putting contests, alone of the throws, are possible indoors. Here are the periods suggested: general preparation from November to January; specific preparation from February to March; competitions from April to September. October can be a period of mild exertion.

All-important at a young age are rational eating habits in accordance with the high energy expenditure required by training, and also fairly strict rules of living, within the context of a school education and the need for recreation.

Session 1
• Lying face up on the bench, straighten and bend the arms carrying a bar-bell weighing 80% of the maximum that can be lifted: 4 sets of 6 repetitions with 5 min. rest between sets, used to perform throwing actions with the arm.
• On the horse or box, a bar-bell on the shoulder weighing 80% of max., half-squats with a knee-angle not less than 90°: 4 sets of 6 repetitions plus rests.
• In a sitting position astride the bench, holding a bar-bell on the shoulders weighing 80% of max., drive the bar-bell upwards until the arms are straight then relower it on to the shoulders: 2 sets × 4 repetitions plus rests.

WEEKLY TRAINING SCHEDULES

Typical week in the general preparation period (November to January)

Session 1
• Lying face up on the bench, straighten and bend the arms carrying a bar-bell weighing 70% of the maximum that can be lifted: 6 sets of 8 repetitions with 4 or 5 min. rest between sets, performing throwing actions with the arm.
• On the horse or box, a bar-bell on the shoulders weighing 70% of max., half-squats with a knee angle of about 90°: 6 sets × 8 repetitions plus appropriate rests between sets.
• With a bar-bell on the shoulders equal to 1.5 times body weight, rise on tiptoe with the balls of the feet resting on a block at least 10 cm high: 4 sets × 8 repetitions plus rests.
• In a sitting position astride the bench, holding a bar-bell on the shoulders weighing 70% of max., drive the bar-bell upwards until the arms are straight then relower it on to the shoulders: 4 sets × 6 repetitions plus rests.
• Lying face up, raise hands and feet to touch each other, resting only on the buttocks: 4 sets × 15 repetitions (abdominals).
• Lying face down, raise the chest and legs from the ground holding the position for several seconds before relowering them: 4 sets × 15 repetitions plus rests (back).
• At the end of the session, a few suppling exercises for muscles and joints, especially the spine.

Session 2
• 1.5 or 2 km jogging to warm up. 15 min. free-standing gymnastics.
• 10 puts with a shot of 8 kg (males) or 5 kg (females) from a standstill.
• 20 puts with regulation shot, from a standstill.
• 30 complete puts with regulation shot, watching the progression (speeding up).
• 10 sets of jumps over 10 hurdles 0.91 m high and 2.0 m apart (males) or 0.76 m high and 1.5 m apart (females).
• 4 sets of 10 long jumps, taking off from alternate feet and landing in the sand, aiming at the maximum distance possible.
• 2 or 3 × 150 m at 70% of maximum speed.
• 10 min. jogging and some muscle suppling exercises.

Session 3
• As Session 1.

Session 4
• As Session 2.

Session 5
• As Session 1.

Session 6
• As Session 2.

Session 7
• Rest.

Typical week in the specific preparation period (February to March)

- Abdominals and back muscles as in the general preparation period.
- At the end of the session, some suppling exercises for joints and muscles, with particular attention to the spinal column.

Session 2

- 1.5 or 2 km jogging to warm up.
- 15 min. free-standing gymnastics.
- 20 puts with a shot of 8 kg (males) or 5 kg (females) from a standstill.
- 20 puts from a standstill with the regulation shot.
- 30 complete puts with the regulation shot, watching the progression (speeding up).
- 10 sets of jumps with feet together over 10 hurdles 0.91 m high and 2.0 m apart (males) or 0.76 m high and 1.5 m apart (females).
- 4 sets of 10 long-jumps, taking off from alternate feet and landing in the sand, aiming for the maximum distance possible.
- 4 sets of 6 backward leaps.
- 10 × 5 hurdles of 0.91 m (males) and 0.76 m (females) with crouch start from blocks, a distance of 8 strides between the start and the first hurdle and 3 strides between hurdles.
- 5 racing starts from blocks plus 20 m sprint.
- 2 or 3 × 150 m at 80% of maximum speed.
- 10 min. jogging, finishing with some muscle and joint suppling exercises.

Session 3
- As Session 1.

Session 4
- As Session 2.

Session 5
- As Session 1.

Session 6
- As Session 2.

Session 7
- Rest.

Typical week in the competition period (April to September)

Session 1
- 25–30 min. jogging to warm up.
- 20 min. muscle stretching and joint suppling for all joints.

Session 2
- Lying face up on the bench, exercise as in the previous periods: 4 sets divided as follows: the first of 5 repetitions with 75% max. weight, the second of 4 repetitions with 80% of max. weight, the third of 3 repetitions with 85% of max. weight and the fourth of 2 repetitions with 90% of max. weight, with appropriate rests between sets.
- On the horse or box, a bar-bell on the shoulders weighing 80% of max., half-squats: 4 sets of 6 repetitions plus rests.
- Sitting astride the bench, holding a bar-bell on the shoulders weighing 80% of max., drive the bar-bell upwards and relower it on to the shoulders: 2 sets × 4 repetitions.
- Abdominals and back muscles as in the general preparation period.
- At the end of the session, some muscle and joint suppling exercises with particular attention to the spinal column.

Session 3
- 1.5 or 2 km jogging to warm up.
- 15 min. free-standing gymnastics.
- 10 puts from a standstill with the regulation shot.
- 30 complete puts with shot of regulation weight, watching the rhythm of the put.
- 10 puts with shot weighing 6.0 kg (males) or 3.5 kg (females).
- 6 sets of jumps over 10 hurdles 0.91 m high and 2.0 m apart (males) or 0.76 m high and 1.5 m apart (females).
- 4 sets of 10 long-jumps, taking off from alternate feet and landing in the sand.
- 4 sets of 6 backward leaps.
- 5 racing starts from blocks plus 20 m sprint.
- 10 min. jogging plus some muscle suppling exercises.

Session 4
- 1 km running to warm up.
- 15 min. free-standing gymnastics.
- 30 puts with regulation shot, the first 10 from a standstill, watching the reverse in both.
- 10 complete puts with a shot of 6.0 kg (males) and 3.5 kg (females).
- 10 min. jogging and some muscle suppling exercises.

Session 5
- Rest.

Session 6
- Exercise on the bench as in Session 2.
- Exercise on the box, half-squat as in Session 2.
- Abdominals and back muscles as in the general preparation period.
- At the end of the session, some suppling exercises for muscles and joints with particular attention to the spinal column.

Session 7
- Competition.

◼ The stars ◼

RALPH ROSE (USA)

The most versatile thrower at the beginning of the 20th century was the American Ralph Rose, a giant of 6 ft 6 in. (1.98 m) weighing in at 233 lbs (106 kg) who, although the shot was his main event, achieved outstanding results in the hammer and discus too. He was the prototype of the old style thrower, who was expected to be strong and nothing else. His movement on the putting circle was stripped down to a short bounce forwards after a 45° turn, delivering the shot from about the centre of the circle, his feet remaining quite close throughout.

In the shot he had two strong rivals in his compatriot Wesley Coe and the Irishman Dennis Horgan. The first of them to pass 15 m was Coe: 15.09 m in the 1905 American Championships. Two years later, Rose beat this with throws of 15.10 m and 15.12 m. His ascendancy culminated on 21 Aug. 1909 in San Francisco in a distance of 15.54 m, which remained unbeaten for 19 years.

In the Olympic Games he won six medals. He began in 1904 at St Louis (an almost exclusively American Olympics) with a gold in the shot, a silver in the discus and a bronze in the hammer. In 1908 in London, he won the shot again, and in 1912 in Stockholm he was second in the shot and won the two-arm shot. His personal best in the hammer was 50.10 m.

PARRY O'BRIEN (USA)

In the wake of Fonville and Fuchs, who could justifiably be called the first 'moderns', emerged the man who made greater history in the shot circle than any other, the Californian Parry O'Brien. At a time when the champion mentality was still low-key, O'Brien showed a professionalism that sometimes bordered on the fanatic. He studied the event in great detail and introduced a radical stylistic innovation. Starting with his back towards the throwing direction and the right foot behind, he used this as a fulcrum to execute a turn of 180°, then launched the shot from the opposite side of the circle to the stopboard. In this way he extended to the

Parry O'Brien

limit the channel through which the force of propulsion is applied to the shot. He paid a great deal of attention to speed; more than once, in the course of American tours abroad, he ran very useful laps in the 4 × 400 m relay.

O'Brien pushed up the world record by 1.30 m, taking it to 18.00 m on 9 May 1953 at Fresno, and to 19.30 on 1 Aug. 1959 at Albuquerque.

He took part in four Olympic Games, coming first in 1952 (17.41 m) and 1956 (18.57 m), third in 1960 (19.11 m) and fourth in 1964 (19.20 m).

O'Brien remained unbeaten for 116 contests between 1952 and 1956, the largest number of consecutive victories in any athletics event.

He reached the peak of his career at the age of 34 with 19.69 m (although in the meantime the world record had risen to 21.52 m). When he was 30 he threw the discus 60 m.

RANDY MATSON (USA)

He is the most recent world-class shot putter to be in that class in the discus too.

As an adolescent he was relatively lean, but he underwent a body-building programme, and at the height of his career he stood 6 ft 7 in. (1.99 m) and weighed 260 lbs (118 kg). He began to compete in senior class shot at the age of 18, and straight away put 18.44 m. The following year he qualified for the Tokyo Olympics, where he finished second with a new personal best of 20.20 m. Matson took the

world record in 1965, when he surpassed Long's record (20.68 m) with 20.70 m and then 21.05 m. A month later, he put 21.52 m, which was submitted to the IAAF and ratified. In 1968 at Mexico City he easily won the Olympic title with 20.54 m.

He gave the greatest demonstration of his double ability as shot-putter and discus thrower on 8 Apr. 1967, putting the shot 21.47 m and throwing the discus 65.16 m. The first was only a hair's breadth from his own world record of 21.52 m, and the second only 6 cm short of the 65.22 m record by the Czechoslovakian Ludvik Daněk.

After his victory in Mexico City, however, the Texan giant noticeably relaxed the pressure, but he went on competing, rather less strongly, for a number of years. From 1974 to 1975 he belonged to Mike O'Hara's professional troupe, and was still capable of throwing over 21 m.

BRIAN OLDFIELD (USA)

Oldfield never won Olympic medals and never set up an official world record, but he deserves a place of honour in the history of the shot for two reasons. First, for being the best exponent to date of the rotational style introduced by Aleksandr Baryshnikov, who in 1976 took the record to 22.0 m, and secondly, because he threw the three best lengths of all time, never confirmed by the IAAF, because he obtained them as a professional, while competing for Mike O'Hara's troupe.

A very large man with good speed, he had some success as an amateur too, before and after his professional interlude. In 1972 he threw 20.97 m

Udo Beyer

and qualified for the Munich Olympics, finishing sixth with 20.91 m, only 27 cm behind the winner Wladyslav Komar. His best time came after he had adopted the rotational style. He needed some time to perfect it, but then achieved throws of 22.86 m (10 May 1975), 22.45 m and 22.28 m. Doubts were raised about the authenticity of these results, obtained outside official athletics. Oldfield himself replied to his critics a few years later, when he was reinstated as an amateur in domestic athletics. In 1981 he raised the USA record to 22.02 m. He was 36, and it was six years since he had thrown 22.86 m. As further proof of his speed, he has thrown the discus 62.26 m.

UDO BEYER (GDR)

In an exemplary career he has won everything. He has twice raised the world record: to 22.15 m in 1978 at Göteborg, and to 22.22 m in 1983.

The big, powerful figure of the 18 year old Udo began to stand out clearly in the European Junior Championships of 1973 at Duisburg, when he won the shot with 19.65 m. The following year he went to the European Open in Rome and came eighth. His reign started in 1976 when he surprised many people by winning the Olympic gold at Montreal with 21.05 m, albeit in a very close finish with the Russians Yevgeni Mironov (21.03 m) and Aleksandr Baryshnikov (21.00 m). After that he was practically unbeatable until 1983. In this long period he rarely suffered defeats, and only one of these was important, the Moscow Olympics where he placed only third. In compensation he collected three World Cup victories (1977, 1979 and 1981) and two at the European Games (1978 and 1982).

In 1983 he began by beating the American Dave Laut, the present number one exponent of the rotational style, in the USA v. GDR match at Los Angeles, the actual occasion on which he took the world record to 22.22 m. Then he unfortunately damaged his ankle, which prevented him coming higher than sixth at the World Championships in Helsinki.

ILONA BRIESENIEK (GDR)

This East German girl dominated the women's shot scene from 1977 to 1982. By the end of that period she had obtained eight of the ten best results of all time.

Her credits include: one victory at the Olympic Games (1980), two European titles (1978 and 1982), three victories in the World Cup (1977, 1979 and 1981), and the world record of 22.45 m, which she has held since 1980. After failing a dope-test and being disqualified in 1977 she was reinstated by the IAAF in time to compete and win in the European Games at Prague in 1978. Brieseniek has had only one main rival, Helena Fibingerova, holder of the longest-ever throw, 22.50 m obtained indoors in 1977, but never confirmed as an official world record. Fibingerova finally turned the tables at the World Championships in Helsinki in 1983, winning with 21.05 m, while Brieseniek came third.

The German girl emerged at Duisberg in 1973, winning the European Junior title with 17.05 m. Three years later she took part in the Montreal Olympics, finishing sixth.

WORLD RECORDS

Men
m
15.54 Ralph Rose (USA) 1909
15.79 Emil Hirschfeld (Germany) 1928
15.87 John Kuck (USA) 1928
16.04 Emil Hirschfeld (Germany) 1928
16.04 Frantisek Douda (Czechoslovakia) 1931
16.05 Zygmunt Heljasz (Poland) 1932
16.16 Leo Sexton (USA) 1932
16.20 Frantisek Douda (Czechoslovakia) 1932
16.48 John Lyman (USA) 1934
16.80 Jack Torrance (USA) 1934
16.89 Jack Torrance (USA) 1934
17.40 Jack Torrance (USA) 1934
17.68 Charles Fonville (USA) 1948
17.79 Jim Fuchs (USA) 1949
17.82 Jim Fuchs (USA) 1950
17.90 Jim Fuchs (USA) 1950
17.95 Jim Fuchs (USA) 1950
18.00 Parry O'Brien (USA) 1953
18.04 Parry O'Brien (USA) 1953
18.42 Parry O'Brien (USA) 1954
18.43 Parry O'Brien (USA) 1954
18.54 Parry O'Brien (USA) 1954
18.62 Parry O'Brien (USA) 1956
18.69 Parry O'Brien (USA) 1956
19.06 Parry O'Brien (USA) 1956
19.25 Parry O'Brien (USA) 1956
19.25 Dallas Long (USA) 1959
19.30 Parry O'Brien (USA) 1959
19.38 Dallas Long (USA) 1960
19.45 Bill Nieder (USA) 1960
19.67 Dallas Long (USA) 1960
19.99 Bill Nieder (USA) 1960
20.06 Bill Nieder (USA) 1960
20.08 Dallas Long (USA) 1962
20.10 Dallas Long (USA) 1964
20.20 Dallas Long (USA) 1964
20.68 Dallas Long (USA) 1964
21.52 Randy Matson (USA) 1965
21.78 Randy Matson (USA) 1967
21.82 Allan Feuerbach (USA) 1973
21.85 Terry Albritton (USA) 1976
22.00 Aleksandr Baryshnikov (USSR) 1976
22.15 Udo Beyer (GDR) 1978
22.22 Udo Beyer (GDR) 1983

Women
9.57* Hilde Köppl (Austria) 1926
14.38 Gisela Mauermayer (Germany) 1934
14.59 Tatyana Sevryukova (USSR) 1948
14.86 Klaudia Tochonova (USSR) 1949
15.02 Anna Andreyeva (USSR) 1950
15.28 Galina Zybina (USSR) 1952
15.37 Galina Zybina (USSR) 1952
15.42 Galina Zybina (USSR) 1952
16.20 Galina Zybina (USSR) 1953
16.28 Galina Zybina (USSR) 1954
16.29 Galina Zybina (USSR) 1955
16.67 Galina Zybina (USSR) 1955
16.76 Galina Zybina (USSR) 1956
17.25 Tamara Press (USSR) 1959
17.42 Tamara Press (USSR) 1960
17.78 Tamara Press (USSR) 1960
18.55 Tamara Press (USSR) 1962
18.55 Tamara Press (USSR) 1962
18.59 Tamara Press (USSR) 1965
18.67 Nadyezhda Chizhova (USSR) 1968
18.87 Margitta Gummel (GDR) 1968
19.07 Margitta Gummel (GDR) 1968
19.61 Margitta Gummel (GDR) 1968
19.72 Nadyezhda Chizhova (USSR) 1969
20.09 Nadyezhda Chizhova (USSR) 1969
20.10 Margitta Gummel (GDR) 1969
20.10 Nadyezhda Chizhova (USSR) 1969
20.43 Nadyezhda Chizhova (USSR) 1969
20.43 Nadyezhda Chizhova (USSR) 1971
20.63 Nadyezhda Chizhova (USSR) 1972
21.03 Nadyezhda Chizhova (USSR) 1972
21.20 Nadyezhda Chizhova (USSR) 1973
21.57 Helena Fibingerova (Czechoslovakia) 1974
21.60 Marianne Adam (GDR) 1975
21.67 Marianne Adam (GDR) 1976
21.87 Ivanka Khristova (Bulgaria) 1976
21.89 Ivanka Khristova (Bulgaria) 1976
21.99 Helena Fibingerova (Czechoslovakia) 1976
22.32 Helena Fibingerova (Czechoslovakia) 1977
22.36 Ilona Brieseniek (GDR) 1980
22.45 Ilona Brieseniek (GDR) 1980
22.53 Natalya Lisovskaya (USSR) 1984

* 5 kg shot

Hammer

The hammer throw has distant origins in the Celts of Scotland and Ireland, who used to throw a blacksmith's hammer, and later an implement consisting of an iron ball similar to the present one but with a rigid wooden handle; this then became a steel chain and finally a steel wire with a triangular grip. The weight of today's hammer, 7.260 kg, was fixed at the end of the 19th century. The diameter of the circle adopted when this event was first contested at the Paris Olympics in 1900 was 9 ft (2.74 m), and this was subsequently reduced to the 7 ft (2.135 m) in use today.

Like the discus and the javelin, the hammer is not normally thrown indoors. There is, however, an American-brand winter version that has also been introduced indoors in the Soviet Union. This involves throwing a hammer with a handle and is used only in indoor USA–USSR contests. The implement is an iron ball weighing 35 lb (15.855 kg), the handle being fixed to it by a very short chain, which reduces the turning radius. The lower speed of the turns, dictated by the increased weight of the implement, obviously reduces the length of the throws.

THE TECHNIQUE OF THE HAMMER THROW

The hammer, like the discus, is thrown from a circle 2.135 m in diameter and must fall within a 40° sector. The throwing techniques most widely adopted today may be described as follows: the athlete takes hold of the implement by the handle, as shown in photo 1, with his gloved hand (left if he rotates anticlockwise, right if clockwise), with the upper edge of the handle resting across the joints of his middle or end phalanxes, and the other hand overlapping the first, and takes his stance with his back facing

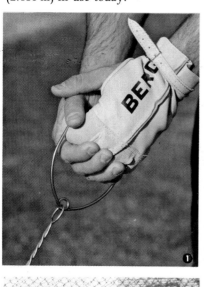

the direction of throw, his legs slightly apart, his knees bent, and his feet touching the rim at the back of the circle. The hammer head may be resting inside or outside the circle, or suspended. The athlete then performs a few pendulum swings which lead into the preliminary swings, rotationary movements using only the arms and upper body, which give the implement the necessary speed before starting the turns, and allow the athlete to adjust his balance.

Most athletes at present use two preliminary swings and three turns, but there has been a recent tendency to use two or three swings and four turns. This causes considerable problems, given the limited space within the circle. The plane of the preliminary rotations is not horizontal but slightly inclined, so that the implement is swinging up and down.

These rising and falling phases of the orbit described by the hammer head are identified as the low point and the high point of the orbit in relation to the plane of the circle. After the preliminary swings (photos 2−5) the athlete goes into the transition at the moment when the hammer head passes through the low point, which occurs in front of him and slightly towards the direction of the knee of the pushing leg. As soon as the hammer head begins to turn in the orbit, the athlete raises the ball of his supporting foot and pivots on the heel, while the other foot turns on the flat, pushing towards the circle, then lifts and follows the hammer round (photo 6).

When the hammer head reaches the high point of the orbit the athlete tilts on to the outside edge of his supporting foot (at this point he is nearly airborne) and comes down on to the flat of the same foot. The hammer head goes into the downward phase of its orbit and the pushing foot quickly makes contact with the back of the circle; this contact must occur before the hammer head overtakes the axis between the two feet (photo 7). There is a displacement angle between the axis of the hips, which are ahead, and that of the shoulders; the arms are both straight, forming an isosceles triangle, the invisible prolungation of the wire as far as the athlete's chest being its height (photos 8−9). When the hammer head passes the low point again, the first turn is complete and the second begins, which is performed in the same way but at a higher speed and with a more marked inclination of the plane of orbit (photos 10−11). This continues for

In photo 1, the correct grip for the hammer is shown; photos 2−12 show each part of the action for throwing the hammer. The athlete is Sergei Litvinov, in the European Championships of Athens in 1982 (Photographs by Helmar Hommel).

three or four turns according to the technique adopted.

Those athletes who complete four turns usually prefer to perform the first entirely on the flat of the pivot foot (as in the discus). This reduces by one step the distance the athlete advances across the circle, which in the case of the four-turn technique often results in a no-throw, since 2.135 m is a very limited space. At the end of the last turn, when the hammer head is still behind the hip axis and the pushing foot is coming to the ground, the final or delivery phase begins; this is performed by turning and straightening the legs and strongly stretching the spine. The arms, well extended from the shoulders, sweep violently upwards, and when they can exert no more force on the implement the fingers release their grip. The pivot leg now becomes the supporting leg (photo 12).

In the hammer, the reverse action is not as frequently used as in the other throwing events, because a good performance should enable the athlete to remain perfectly balanced within the circle at the moment he releases the hammer. Nevertheless, since technical perfection is rare, one often sees a recovery action to stop the throw being fouled by the athlete being unable to stop himself coming out of the circle, even with only part of his body, before the implement has landed. The athlete changes his legs over to get out of the twisted position in which he has delivered the hammer, assuming a reverse position similar to that of discus throwers.

Biomechanics

The distance of a hammer throw executed in accordance with the regulations depends on:
• the initial velocity;
• the release angle;
• the height of release;
• air resistance during flight.

The initial velocity. Since the hammer is initially stationary, the velocity it later acquires will depend on the nature of the forces exerted upon it to produce its movement according to Newton's second law.

The forces that the thrower exercises upon the hammer are applied to the handle and transmitted through

the wire to the head. Since the wire is light and fine, only those forces exercised along the length of the wire are active in influencing the movement of the implement's head. If the wire is aligned so that an invisible extension of it passes through the axis around which the hammer is rotating, all the

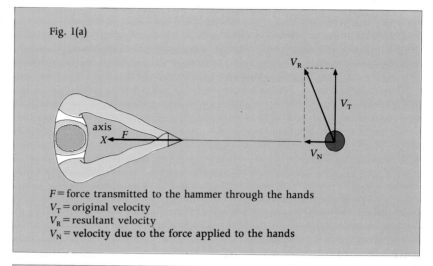

Fig. 1(a)

F = force transmitted to the hammer through the hands
V_T = original velocity
V_R = resultant velocity
V_N = velocity due to the force applied to the hands

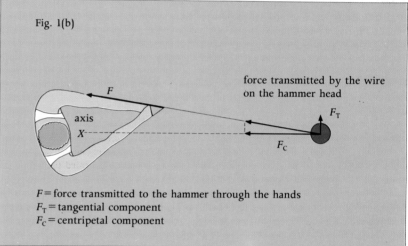

Fig. 1(b)

force transmitted by the wire on the hammer head

F = force transmitted to the hammer through the hands
F_T = tangential component
F_C = centripetal component

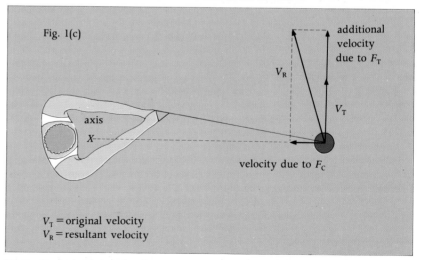

Fig. 1(c)

additional velocity due to F_T

velocity due to F_C

V_T = original velocity
V_R = resultant velocity

Biomechanics of hammer throwing
The three drawings above illustrate the transmission of force from the thrower to the implement through his two-handed grip on the handle, and trace the directions of the velocity resulting from the various forces acting on the hammer.

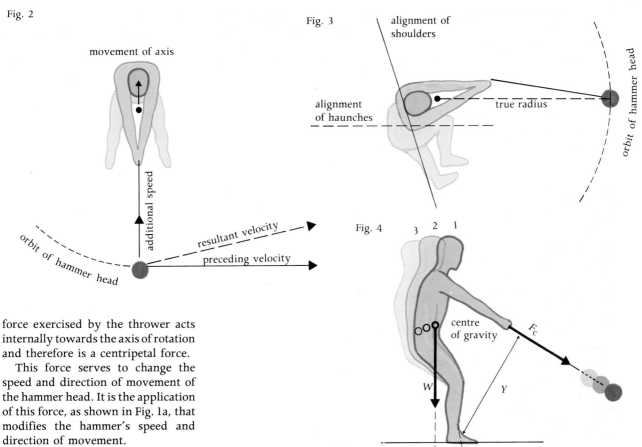

Fig. 2

movement of axis

additional speed

resultant velocity

preceding velocity

orbit of hammer head

Fig. 3

alignment of shoulders

alignment of haunches

true radius

orbit of hammer head

Fig. 4

3 2 1

centre of gravity

F_c

W

Y

X

axis

R

1 = entry position on first turn
2 = entry position on second turn
3 = entry position on third turn

force exercised by the thrower acts internally towards the axis of rotation and therefore is a centripetal force.

This force serves to change the speed and direction of movement of the hammer head. It is the application of this force, as shown in Fig. 1a, that modifies the hammer's speed and direction of movement.

But if the wire and its extension form an angle with the axis of rotation, the forces exercised along its length have the effect of producing not only centripetal components but also tangential ones (Fig. 1b). This brings about an increased velocity of the hammer head in both directions (Fig. 1c).

These facts raise the question as to which of these two factors is the more important. A numerical example will provide the most appropriate answer. Suppose that an athlete exercises a given force for a determinate period of time, and as a result the speed of the hammer head is changed by 3 m/sec. If we suppose the previous speed of the hammer head to have been 21 m/sec. (75.6 km/h) and the force is exercised *in the direction of movement* of the hammer, the resultant velocity, after the application of the force will be 21 + 3 = 24 m/sec. (86.4 km/h). However, if the athlete applies the same force *at a right angle to the direction of movement* of the hammer head (Fig. 2), the resultant velocity will be rather lower, namely:

$$\sqrt{21^2 + 3^2} = 21.2 \text{ m/sec.}$$

(76.32 km/h).

Finally, if the force is applied at an angle between 0° and 90°, the resultant velocity will have a corresponding intermediate value:

Angle (degrees)	Resultant velocity	
	m/sec.	km/h
0	24	86.04
15	23.9	86.04
30	23.6	84.96
45	23.2	83.52
60	22.6	81.36
75	21.9	78.84
90	21.2	76.32

Although the total value of the angle that the thrower can achieve between the direction of the wire and the invisible radius that connects the hammer head to the rotational axis is only a few degrees (Fig. 3), the advantage it confers is important as far as increasing the velocity of the hammer is concerned. The factors that influence the release velocity are included in the equation: V = *wr* which expresses the value of the tangential velocity as a function of the angular velocity and the radius.

From this equation the following conclusions may be drawn:
(1) where the angular velocity is constant, the greater the radius, the greater will be the hammer's tangential velocity;
(2) where the radius is constant, the greater the angular velocity at which the hammer is rotated, the greater will be the tangential velocity;
(3) in any case the greatest tangential velocity will be obtained when both these factors, the angular velocity and the radius, are at their maximum.

If the tangential velocity increases, so the value of the centripetal force increases that the athlete must exercise to maintain the hammer in an orbit around his rotational axis.

This increase in centripetal force is accompanied by an identical increase in the centrifugal force that the hammer exerts in reaction on the athlete.

This centrifugal force requires the athlete to modify continuously the position of his own body in order to maintain his equilibrium.

The athlete is subject to three forces:

(1) gravitational force, that is his own weight acting through his own centre of gravity;

(2) centrifugal force, applied through his hands to the hammer;

(3) the reaction of the ground, applied to his feet.

Now, if the athlete is to avoid turning forwards or backwards around a transverse axis passing through his feet, the momentum of his weight relative to this axis must exactly balance the opposite momentum represented by the centrifugal force, (assuming that the force of reaction of the ground acts through the axis and therefore generates no momentum). To establish equilibrium between the two moments while the centrifugal force is increasing, the athlete is obliged to modify his body position progressively, 'sitting' to counterpoise the hammer (Fig. 4).

This action involves moving the centre of gravity downwards and backwards by flexing the hips and knees, and so diminishes the vector of centrifugal force while increasing the vector of body weight, thus ensuring equilibrium between the two moments.

The height of release. This depends principally on the athlete's body position at the moment he releases the implement and on his physical characteristics. However, the differences between various throwers are so small as to have little consequence.

Release angle. Since the hammer is released in the delivery at about shoulder height, that is about 1.50 m above the level of the ground where it will fall at the end of its trajectory, the optimum release angle is slightly less than 45°, approximately 43° or 44° for throwers of distances over 50 m.

Air resistance. The effect of air resistance on the distance of hammer throws is generally held to be very little. Figures of the order of a 1% reduction in distance at sea level have been suggested.

REGULATIONS GOVERNING THE HAMMER THROW

1. The order in which the competitors make their attempts is to be drawn by lots.

2. When there are more than eight competitors, each is to be allowed three attempts, and the eight competitors with the best throws are to be allowed three more attempts. In the case of a tie for eighth place, each tied competitor is allowed three more attempts. When there are eight or fewer competitors, each one is allowed six attempts. On the field each competitor may make two practice throws, but no more. These must be carried out under the supervision of the judges and in the order of the draw, and the contestants are to be called out by name. After the contest has started, the competitors are not permitted to use the circle or the throwing sector for warming up, with or without a hammer.

3. Each competitor is to be placed according to the best of his throws.

4. The use of gloves is allowed in order to protect the hands. The gloves must be soft, back and front, and the fingertips must remain uncovered, i.e. the glove fingers must not have closed ends.

No expedient of any kind (for example, binding two or more fingers together with adhesive tape) that in any way helps a competitor to execute his throw may be permitted.

Only if it is necessary to cover an open wound is the use of adhesive tape or sticking plaster allowed on the hands. To protect the spine from damage, a competitor may wear a belt of leather or other suitable material.

To obtain a better grip, contestants are authorized to rub an appropriate substance on their hands and their hands alone. Competitors may not spray or sprinkle any substance on the circle or the soles of their shoes.

5. The hammer must be thrown from a circle. The competitor must start his throw from a motionless position. In the starting position before the preliminary swings and turns, the competitor may if he wishes rest the head of the hammer on the ground outside the circle.

The competitor may touch the inside of the rim of the circle.

6. A throw should not be deemed foul if the hammer head touches the ground in the course of the competitor's preliminary swings and turns; but if, after having touched the ground, he breaks off the throw in order to begin afresh, this counts as a valid attempt.

7. The throw is foul and must be disallowed if the competitor, after entering the circle and starting his throw, touches with any part of his body the ground outside the circle or the upper edge of the rim, or if he releases the hammer incorrectly during the execution of any attempt.

8. Provided the aforesaid regulations are not infringed in the course of the attempt, a competitor may break off an attempt once started, may place his implement on the ground, and may leave the circle before returning to the stationary position to restart his attempt.

9. Should the hammer break during the throw or while in the air, this shall not count as an attempt, provided the throw has been carried out according to the rules. Should the competitor by reason of the above lose his balance and commit a foul, this shall not be counted against him.

10. The competitor must not leave the circle until the implement has landed. When leaving the circle, his first contact with the upper edge of the rim or the ground outside the circle must take place completely behind the white line drawn outside the circle and passing invisibly through the centre of the circle itself.

11. The hammer must be carried back to the circle, never thrown back.

12. In order for a throw to be valid, the implement must fall in such a way that the mark nearest to the circle left by its impact on the ground is between the inside edges of the lines (5 cm wide) that outline a 40° sector drawn so that the lines of radius meet at the centre of the circle. The ends of the sector marking lines must be indicated with marker flags. To determine indisputably whether the throw is valid according to the above standards, the judge must decide whether 'the mark nearest to the circle', i.e. the spot where the stake is to be planted from which to measure the throw, lies within the sector, even when part of the mark left by the implement lies

outside the sector. Therefore a throw is not established as valid until after the stake has been planted. If the stake cannot be planted because it would be on the line or outside it, the throw is ruled out.

13. The measurement of each throw must be taken immediately after the throw, from the nearest mark left by the head of the hammer as it falls, to the inside of the rim of the circle, along the line from the mark made by the implement to the centre of the circle.

14. A distinctive stake or flag must be provided to indicate the best throw of each competitor and must be placed along a line or tape outside the throwing sector lines. A marker flag or disc must be provided to indicate the current world record and, where appropriate, the national record.

15. CONSTRUCTION OF THE HAMMER CIRCLE. The rim is made of sheet iron, steel or other suitable material, the upper edge of which must be level with the surrounding ground.

The inside of the circle may be made of concrete, asphalt or other solid, non-slip material. The surface of this inner part must be levelled and finished 2 cm (± 6 mm) below the upper edge of the rim.

DIMENSIONS. The internal diameter of the circle is to measure 2.135 m (± 5 mm).

The circle is to be at least 6 mm thick and be painted white. A white line 5 cm wide must be traced outside the circle for a length of at least 75 cm from either side of the circle. It may be painted, or made of wood or other suitable material. The back edge of this white line is to coincide with the extension of an invisible line passing through the centre of the circle at right angles to the centre line of the throwing sector.

The hammer may be thrown from a discus circle, provided that the diameter of this circle has been reduced from 2.50 m to 2.135 m by the insertion of an inner ring that must not be dangerous for competitors.

16. The maximum permissible slope of the ground within the throwing sector is 1:1000.

17. In the Olympic Games, the World Cup and continental or group games or championships, the only imple-

ments to be used are those supplied by the organizers, and no modifications may be introduced during the contest. No competitor may bring whatever implement he wishes on to the field.

In regional meetings competitors may use their own implements provided they are checked, approved and initialled by the organizers before the contest, and placed at the disposal of all the competitors.

18. CONSTRUCTION OF THE HAMMER. The hammer has three parts: a metal head, a wire and a grip.

19. HEAD. The head may be of solid iron or other material not softer than brass, or a shell of such metal filled with lead or other solid material. It must be completely spherical with a minimum diameter of 110 mm.

If a filler is used, it must be inserted in such a way that it does not move about and the centre of gravity is no more than 6 mm from the centre of the sphere.

20. WIRE. The wire is a single, not spliced steel wire no less than 3 mm in diameter, which must not be liable to stretch noticeably during the throw and may be twisted at one or both ends as a means of attachment.

21. GRIP. The grip may consist of a single or double loop but it must be rigid with no movable joints of any kind, and be such that it cannot lengthen appreciably during the throw.

It must be attached to the wire in such a way that it cannot turn into the twists of the wire, thus increasing the overall length of the hammer.

22. ATTACHMENT OF THE WIRE: The wire is attached to the head by means of a pivot, which may be simple or on ballbearings. The grip must be attached to the wire by a twist, but a pivot may not be used.

23. The hammer must conform to the following measurements:

Centre of gravity of the head: not more than 6 mm from the centre of the sphere.

It should, for example, be possible to balance the head, without wire and grip, on a level, sharp-edged, circular hole 12 mm in diameter.

24. CAGE FOR THROWING THE HAMMER: The hammer must be thrown from inside a cage that ensures the safety of spectators, officials, competitors and athletes involved in other contests. As said before, the hammer may also be thrown from a discus circle provided a ring is inserted to reduce the diameter from 2.50 m to 2.135 m, and provided the cage is capable of stopping a hammer of 7.260 kg, being composed of a minimum of seven panels of netting 2.74 m wide and 5 m high, the width of the opening being 6 m.

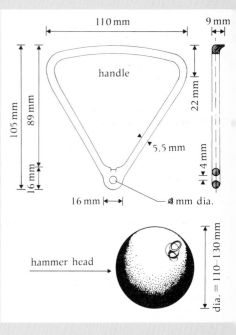

The above diagrams show the relevant dimensions for the handle and the hammer head.

Overall weight of the hammer when ready for throwing		
Weight for the confirmation of a record	min.	7.260 kg
Tolerance for the supply of competition implements	min.	7.265 kg
	max.	7.285 kg
Overall length of the hammer when ready for throwing, measured from inside the grip	min.	117.5 cm
	max.	121.5 cm
Diameter of the head	min.	110 mm
	max.	130 mm

Training

For young throwers under 16 who have decided to take up the hammer, the primary objective must be technical perfection, to be achieved gradually through a clear and thorough knowledge of the event. Film sequences of throws by champions and seeing them live at top-class meetings are invaluable for teaching this sort of thing. During power training, the young hammer thrower must always bear in mind the nature of the throw, the weak points in his own technique and the need to correct them, naturally with the help of his coach. Comparison of films of his own performance with those of expert athletes is extremely useful.

The typical training weeks that follow are suggested for 17–18 year olds with some experience of hammer throwing. As with discus throwing, during the competition period (April to September) it is a good idea to insert two intervals of specific work between May and June and in mid-August. Mild work is advisable in October, also defined as active rest.

WEEKLY TRAINING SCHEDULE

Session 1
• Pull the bar-bell up to the chin with a weight 70% of max.: 6 sets × 8 repetitions with 3–4 min. rest between sets.
• In a sitting position astride the bench, drive the bar-bell upwards from the shoulders with 70% of max.: 6 sets × 8 repetitions plus appropriate rests between sets.
• Heavy athletics snatch exercise with 70% of max.: 6 sets × 8 repetitions.
• On horse or box, half-squats with 70% of max. weight: 6 sets × 8 repetitions plus rests.
• From the half-squat position, with springs fixed from a side wall to the knees: 4 sets of 8 repetitions with an effort equal to 80% of max.
• Abdominals: 4 sets × 15 repetitions.
• Back: 4 sets × 15 repetitions.
• At the end of the session, some muscle and joint suppling exercises, especially for the spinal column.

Session 2
• 1.5–2 km jogging.
• 15 min. free-standing gymnastics.
• 10 throws with a hammer of regulation length weighing 8 kg.

Typical week in the general preparation period (November to January)

• 30 complete throws, watching throwing rhythm and progression.
• 10 sets of jumps over 10 hurdles 0.91 m high and 2 m apart.
• 4 sets of 10 standing long jumps with feet together and landing in the sand, trying for the greatest possible distance.
• 2–3 × 150 m at 70% of maximum speed.
• 10 min. jogging and some muscle suppling exercises.

Session 3
• 25 or 30 min. jogging.
• 20 min. muscle extension and joint mobility exercises for all the joints.
• Game of basketball, volleyball or handball.

Session 4
• Rest.

Session 5
• As Session 1.

Session 6
• As Session 2.

Session 7
• Rest.

Session 1
• Pull the bar-bell up to the chin with a weight 80% of max.: 4 sets × 6 repetitions plus rests.
• From a sitting position astride the bench, drive the bar-bell upwards from the shoulders with 80% of max. weight: 4 sets × 6 repetitions plus rests.
• Heavy athletics snatch exercise with 80% of max. weight: 4 sets × 6 repetitions.
• On horse or box, half-squats with 80% of max. weight: 4 sets × 6 repetitions plus rests between sets.
• From the half-squat position with springs fixed from a side wall to the knees: 4 sets × 8 repetitions with an effort equal to 80% of max.

Session 1
• 25 or 30 min. jogging.
• 20 min. muscle extension and joint mobility exercises for all the joints.

Session 2
• Pull the bar-bell up to the chin: 4 sets, the first of 5 repetitions with 75% of max. weight, the second 4 repetitions with 80% of max. weight, the third of 3 repetitions with 85% of max. weight and the fourth of 2 repetitions with 90% of max. weight.
• From a sitting position astride the bench, drive the bar-bell upwards from the shoulders with 85% of max. weight: 2 sets × 8 repetitions.
• Heavy athletics snatch exercise: 4 sets, the first of 5 repetitions with 75% of max. weight, the second of 4 repetitions with 80% of max. weight, the third of 3 repetitions with 85% of max. weight and the fourth of 2 repetitions with 90% of max. weight.
• On the horse or box, half-squats with 80% of max. weight: 4 sets × 6

Typical week in the specific preparation period (February to March)

- Abdominals: 4 sets × 15 repetitions.
- Back: 4 sets × 15 repetitions.
- At the end of the session, some muscle and joint suppling exercises, especially for the spinal column.

Session 2
- 1.5 or 2 km jogging.
- 15 min. free-standing gymnastics.
- 10 throws with a hammer of regulation length weighing 8 kg.
- 30 complete throws, watching throwing rhythm and progression.
- 10 sets of jumps over 10 hurdles 0.91 m high and 2 m apart.
- 4 sets of 10 standing long jumps with feet together and landing in the sand, trying for the greatest possible distance.

- With a shot of 7.257 kg or a 10 kg bar-bell disc, perform about 20 two-handed throws backwards over the head.
- 2−3 × 150 m at 80% of max. speed.
- 10 min. jogging and some muscle suppling exercises.

Session 3
- 25 or 30 min. jogging.
- 20 min. muscle extension and joint mobility exercises for all the joints.
- Game of basketball, volleyball or handball.

Session 4
- Rest.

Session 5
- As Session 1.

Session 6
- As Session 2.

Session 7
- Rest.

Typical week in the competition period (April to September)

repetitions plus rests between sets.
- From the half-squat position, with springs fixed from the knees to a side wall: 4 sets × 6 repetitions with an effort equal to 85% of max.
- Abdominals: 4 sets × 15 repetitions.
- Back: 4 sets × 15 repetitions.
- At the end of the session, some muscle and joint suppling exercises, especially for the spinal column.

Session 3
- 1.5 or 2 km jogging.
- 15 min. free-standing gymnastics.
- 10 complete throws with a regulation hammer, watching the reverse.
- 30 complete throws with regulation hammer, watching the throwing rhythm and the progression.
- 10 throws with a hammer of regulation length weighing 6 kg, watching the speed of execution and the progression.
- 4 sets of jumps over 10 hurdles 0.91 m high and 2 m apart.

- 4 sets of 10 long jumps with feet together and landing in the sand, trying for the greatest possible distance.
- With a shot of 7.275 kg or a 10 kg bar-bell disc, perform about 20 two-handed throws backwards over the head.
- 2−3 × 150 m at 80% of max. speed.
- 5 or 6 racing starts from blocks with about 20 m sprint.
- 10 min. jogging and some muscle suppling exercises.

Session 4
- 1 km jogging to warm up.
- 15 min. free-standing gymnastics.
- 30 throws with regulation hammer watching the throwing rhythm and the progression.
- 10 throws with a hammer of regulation length weighing 6 kg, watching the speed and the progression.
- 10 min. jogging and some muscle suppling exercises.

Session 5
- Rest.

Session 6
- Chin pulls as in Session 2.
- Half-squat exercises on the box as in Session 2.
- Heavy athletics snatch as in Session 2.
- Abdominals and back as in Session 2.
- At the end of the session, some muscle and joint suppling exercises with particular attention to the spinal column.

Session 7
- Rest.

■ The stars ■

PAT O'CALLAGHAN (IRELAND)

Towards the end of the 19th century, the Irish played an important part as pioneers of the throwing events, particularly in the shot and hammer. Most of the champions from Ireland emigrated to the USA to get away from the economic conditions of their home country, and several of them rose to world fame there.

However, one great athlete who did not leave his country and who won two Olympic titles was Pat O'Callaghan, a likeable extrovert who in the 1920s and early 1930s reigned supreme in the hammer. He started by practising all sorts of events but concentrated on the hammer from 1927 onwards. At the first official trials he threw 41.49 m, and by the end of the season he had reached 46.17 m, which placed him among that year's top 20 specialists.

In 1928 he travelled to Amsterdam for the Olympic Games, where he astonished both the Scandinavians and Americans by out-throwing them all on his fifth attempt with 51.39 m. Four years later at Los Angeles it was the same story; this time O'Callaghan won with his very last throw of 53.92 m.

He never gained an official world record, but on 22 Aug. 1937 he threw the hammer 59.55 m, nearly two metres further than the previous world record of Pat Ryan. The result could not be ratified by the IAAF because the federation Callaghan belonged to at the time, NACA, was not recognized by the international organization. For the same reason O'Callaghan had not been able to enter the 1936 Olympics.

He was very versatile for his time, clearing 1.88 m in the high jump and putting the shot 14.75 m.

HAROLD CONNOLLY (USA)

Having got in touch with the German school, Connolly reached world class in 1956, the year in which the Russians began to make their mark. Connolly soon found a great rival in the Russian thrower, Mikhail Krivonosov. Connolly chalked up his first win over the Russian with a

Hal Connolly

throw of 66.71 m in Boston (a result never submitted for IAAF ratification). A few days later Krivonosov replied in Tashkent with 67.32 m. Connolly had the last word in the pre-Olympic phase, when he threw 68.54 m at Los Angeles. These results created great expectancy for the hammer competition in November at the 1956 Olympics. Here Krivonosov, capable of throwing the discus over 51 m, quickly took the lead with 63.03 m, but finally the powerful Connolly took the gold with 63.19 m.

In 1958 the American increased his distance to 68.68 m, and on 12 Aug. 1960 he was the first to exceed 70 m, with a distance of 70.33 m. Things went badly for him at the Rome Games, however, where 63.59 m placed him eighth in a competition won by the Russian Vasily Rudenkov. Connolly bettered the record on other occasions, finally pushing it to 71.26 m in 1965. The year before at the Tokyo Games he had again been pushed out of the medals by the Russians, finishing no better than sixth.

ANATOLI BONDARCHUK (USSR)

In recent years the hammer has become the exhibition event of Russian athletics, to the point where in the 1982 season the world ratings showed 30 Russian names among the top 50. One man who did a great deal to promote this domination is Anatoli

Bondarchuk, a Ukrainian who was a great athlete himself before becoming a coach. He reached his peak in 1969, twice pushing up the world record: 74.68 m when he won the European title at Athens, and 75.48 m shortly afterwards at Rovno.

At the Munich Olympics in 1972 he won the gold medal with 75.50 m. Four years later, at the age of 36, he succeeded in qualifying for the Olympic team, and at the Montreal Games he supported his young compatriots Sedykh (his pupil) and Spiridonov, taking the bronze medal.

YURI SEDYKH (USSR)

A pupil of Bondarchuk, he emerged at the 1973 European Junior Championships in Duisburg when he was 18, and won with 67.32 m. He competed at senior level at the 1976 Montreal Olympics, where he won with 77.52 m. Four years later, when the Soviet Union already had several 80 m specialists, he had to fight hard to get into the team for the Moscow Games but he made it, raising the world record to 80.64 m in his qualifying throw. But a few weeks later he was eclipsed by Sergei Litvinov, who reached 81.66 m. Sedykh grabbed back his record in the Olympic final, achieving 81.80 m on his first throw. Sedykh has two European titles (1978

Anatoli Bondarchuk

Yuri Sedykh, current world record holder in the hammer.

and 1982) to his credit, and only in 1983 did he yield to Litvinov, who won at the World Championships with 82.68 m, while Sedykh was second with 80.94 m. Again in 1984, Sedykh won back his record with a superb throw of 86.34 m.

SERGEI LITVINOV (USSR)

The idea of completing four instead of three turns in the circle was introduced in the 1950s by the Russian Stanislav Nyenashev, and this method has been revived and perfected by Sergei Litvinov. At first Litvinov often incurred 'no-throws' because he found it difficult to stay in the circle but, in the end, he managed to correct the problem without sacrificing his speed. Litvinov exceeded 60 m for the first time at the age of 16, and 70 m at 18. In 1980 he took the world record with 81.66 m, but at the Moscow Olympics Yuri Sedykh beat this with a new world record of 81.80 m, and Litvinov had to be content with 80.64 m and the silver medal. Even in 1982 Litvinov suffered in the big contests because of his frequent no-throws. He regained the world record with 83.98 m, but in the European Games at Athens he had a bad day and finished third behind Sedykh and Igor Nikulin.

In the absence of Sedykh, Litvinov had gained his first important success in the 1979 World Cup at Montreal. Everything went well for him in 1983: after a world record of 84.14 m in the spring, he asserted himself with 82.68 m at the World Championships in Helsinki. On that occasion he did not make a single no-throw, and in three of his six throws he outdid Sedykh's best distance, the 80.94 m which put him in second place.

WORLD RECORDS

m
57.77 Patrick Ryan (USA) 1913
59.00 Erwin Blask (Germany) 1938
59.02 Imre Németh (Hungary) 1948
59.57 Imre Németh (Hungary) 1949
59.88 Imre Németh (Hungary) 1950
60.34 Jozsef Csermák (Hungary) 1952
61.25 Sverre Strandii (Norway) 1952
62.36 Sverre Strandii (Norway) 1953
63.34 Mikhail Krivonosov (USSR) 1954
64.05 Stanislav Nyenashev (USSR) 1954
64.33 Mikhail Krivonosov (USSR) 1955
64.52 Mikhail Krivonosov (USSR) 1955
65.85 Mikhail Krivonosov (USSR) 1956
66.38 Mikhail Krivonosov (USSR) 1956
67.32 Mikhail Krivonosov (USSR) 1956
68.54 Harold Connolly (USA) 1956
68.68 Harold Connolly (USA) 1958
70.33 Harold Connolly (USA) 1960
70.67 Harold Connolly (USA) 1962
71.06 Harold Connolly (USA) 1965
71.26 Harold Connolly (USA) 1965
73.74 Gyula Zsivótzky (Hungary) 1965
73.76 Gyula Zsivótzky (Hungary) 1968
74.52 Romuald Klim (USSR) 1969
74.68 Anatoli Bondarchuk (USSR) 1969
75.48 Anatoli Bondarchuk (USSR) 1969
76.40 Walter Schmidt (FGR) 1971
76.60 Reinhard Theimer (FGR) 1974
76.66 Aleksey Spiridonov (USSR) 1974
76.70 Karl-Hans Riehm (FGR) 1975
77.56 Karl-Hans Riehm (FGR) 1975
78.50 Karl-Hans Riehm (FGR) 1975
79.30 Walter Schmidt (FGR) 1975
80.14 Boris Zaichuk (USSR) 1978
80.34 Karl-Hans Riehm (FGR) 1978
80.38 Yuri Sedykh (USSR) 1980
80.46 Jüri Tamm (USSR) 1980
80.64 Yuri Sedykh (USSR) 1980
81.66 Sergei Litvinov (USSR) 1980
81.80 Yuri Sedykh (USSR) 1980
83.98 Sergei Litvinov (USSR) 1982
84.14 Sergei Litvinov (USSR) 1983
86.34 Yuri Sedykh (USSR) 1984

Sergei Litvinov

Javelin

History

The javelin featured in the Olympic programme in Ancient Greece as part of the pentathlon, so it is surprising that it was not brought back straight away with the modern Olympics in 1896.

The ancient javelin had a grip in the form of a small loop through which the athlete slid his index and middle fingers, enabling him to exert more force on the implement.

In the 19th century javelin contests were not merely a trial of distance; precision mattered too, the implement being aimed at fixed targets. The javelin was not reintroduced into the modern Olympics until the fourth competition in London in 1908.

In the 1912 games the combined left- and right-handed version of the event was used, now discontinued. There were two styles of throwing up to the turn of this century: holding the implement in the middle, at its centre of gravity, or with a free-style grip, towards the tail.

With the free-style grip being outlawed, javelin throwers have striven to make the device remain airborne for as long as possible, by trying to improve its aerodynamics while still conforming to the International Regulations. One attempt, by Franklin Held in the 1950s, involved making the rear part of the grip thicker, but there was a snag: the javelin fell flat, which was ruled invalid, so most attempts with it were no-throws.

At the same time, Spanish researchers re-examined the possibility of rotating the implement before launching it, therefore being thrown

1   2   3   4

in the same way as the discus and the hammer, but this attempt to revive a method previously quashed by the IAAF made no headway.

The most recent innovation has been a javelin modified by the Held family to have improved aerodynamics; Tom Petranoff used this model to set a new world record for the javelin in 1983 of 99.72 m.

The technique of the javelin

The javelin is the only one of the throwing events not to be made from a circle, a straight run-up being used instead. The implement must fall point first within a 29° sector centering on the runway 8 m behind the scratch-line. The throwing techniques used at present vary in the method of carrying the implement and in the number of special strides. Schematically these variations can be

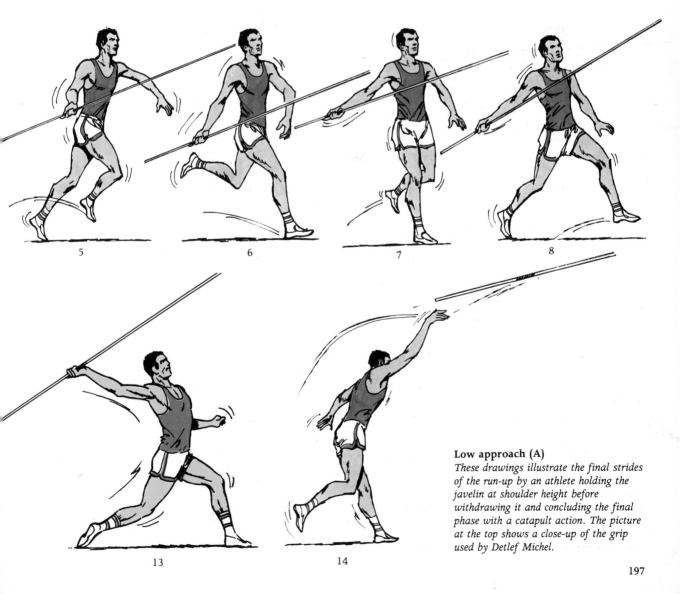

5   6   7   8

13   14

Low approach (A)
These drawings illustrate the final strides of the run-up by an athlete holding the javelin at shoulder height before withdrawing it and concluding the final phase with a catapult action. The picture at the top shows a close-up of the grip used by Detlef Michel.

1   2   3

8   9   10

summed up as follows (see drawings A and B): in the starting position, the athlete holds the javelin as shown in the first drawing, with the throwing arm flexed at the elbow, the hand holding the implement head-high, the point aimed slightly downwards. Keeping the javelin in this position, the athlete carries out a standard run-up, raising his knees well, until he reaches his check mark placed next to the runway where he will begin to move the implement backwards, either with a movement down in front and then back (A 1–7) or straight back (B 1–4). This is the point at which the three different techniques begin. There can be 3, 5 or 7 special strides (the most popular method at present uses 5) and the purpose is to bring the athlete to the cross-over stride or lay-back phase which is the most controversial and crucial phase before the actual throw (A 10–11, B 6–7).

In this phase, with a push from the foot opposite to the throwing arm, the pelvic axis turns outwards through 20° and aligns with the shoulder axis, while the foot on the same side as the throwing arm turns to point 30° away from the direction of run-up.

The lay-back phase begins by landing on the foot on the side of the throwing arm with that knee bent (A 11–12, B 8–9), and then taking an extended stride on the other, followed by a straightening of the first leg, while the shoulder and throwing arm are kept in the drawn-back position so as to create the throwing arc, consisting of the kinetic chain of foot–knee–hips–shoulder–elbow–wrist (A 13, B 10).

The final delivery phase, firmly supported on the front leg, requires the throwing shoulder to whip forward with all the joints concerned (hips–shoulder–elbow–wrist) being braced in turn, allowing energy to pass through the successive segments of the kinetic chain, transferring the maximum possible velocity to the implement for the optimum release angle (A 14, B 11).

Now, to stop himself fouling the scratch-line, the athlete performs a reverse action bringing the back leg forward, lifting the supporting leg up and back, thus recovering his balance and keeping himself behind the line so that the throw will be valid (B 12–14). The implement must land within the throwing sector and is also required to land point first and break the turf.

Biomechanics. The basic factors that determine the distance measured in the javelin throw, according to the international rules, are the same as for the discus, namely:
release speed;
height of release;
release angle;

4　　　　　　5　　　　　　6　　　　　　7

11　　　　　　12　　　　　　13　　　　　　14

aerodynamic factors at work during the flight.

The aerodynamic factors assume even greater importance in the javelin than for the discus.

Studies in this area have been very limited, and the question of the javelin's flight phase is still a long way from being fully investigated. In particular, there are no sufficiently precise and widely accepted ideas as to the optimum release angle, the angle of attack, or the degree of rotation about the implement's major axis to be imparted at the moment of release.

The difficulty of arriving at conclusions about these factors has been offset by the development of new models of javelin, the so-called aerodynamic javelins.

By improving the surface, carefully placing the centre of gravity and other such details, javelin designers are capable of perfecting the implement's aerodynamic properties to such a point that the type of javelin used is a decisive factor in the result.

It is estimated that the type of javelin used may bring about variations in the length of throw of the order of 3–6 m, compared with an 'old-style' javelin.

However, although evidence about the aerodynamic behaviour of the javelin in flight is as yet inconclusive, a few points are generally held to be certain:
the release (or initial) speed is by far the most important factor in determining the distance of the throw;
the optimum release angle depends on the type of javelin used. (The optimum angle of release for non-aerodynamic javelins was probably around 35° or 40° for experienced throwers. For the aerodynamic javelin, however, the optimum release angle is so varied that it is impossible to give any common figure. It has only been confirmed that it is markedly smaller

High approach (B)

These drawings, by contrast, illustrate an athlete holding the javelin at head height and withdrawing it with a twist of his body before exploding into the final catapult and recovering with a cross-over action of the legs.

than that used with non-aerodynamic javelins.);

although there is little information on the optimum angle of attack at the moment of release, most throwers favour an angle of attack coinciding with the angle of release; the rotation around the implement's major axis imparted at the moment of release is considered a beneficial stabilizing factor.

REGULATIONS GOVERNING THE JAVELIN THROW

1. The order in which the competitors make their attempts is to be drawn by lots.

2. When there are more than eight competitors, each is to be allowed three attempts, and the eight competitors with the best throws are to be allowed three more attempts. In the case of a tie for eighth place, each tied competitor is to be allowed three more attempts. When there are eight or fewer competitors, each one is to be allowed six attempts. On the field, each competitor may make two practice throws. These must be carried out under the supervision of the judges and in the order of the draw, and the competitors must be called out by name. After the contest has started, the competitors are not permitted to use the runway or the throwing sector for warming up, with or without a javelin.

3. Each competitor is to be placed according to the best of his throws.

4. No expedient of any kind (for example, binding two or more fingers together with adhesive tape) that in any way helps a competitor to execute his throw may be permitted. Only if it is necessary to cover an open wound is the use of sticking plaster or adhesive tape allowed on the hands. To protect the spinal column from damage, a competitor may wear a belt of suitable material. To obtain a better grip, competitors may spread a suitable substance on their hands, and their hands alone. The use of gloves is not permitted.

5. The javelin must be held by the grip. It must be thrown from above the shoulder or the upper throwing arm, and must not be thrown by catapult, nor rotation. Unorthodox styles are not permitted.

No throw is valid unless the metal point touches the ground before any other part of the javelin.

The throw is foul if the competitor touches with any part of his body the scratch-line or the lines traced from its ends at right angles to the parallel lines, or the ground beyond the scratch-line or the other said lines.

At no time after preparing to throw and until the javelin has been released into the air, may the competitor turn round so that his back is towards the direction of the throw.

A competitor may not leave the runway before the javelin has touched the ground. He must then leave the runway in an upright position, from behind the scratch-line and the lines drawn from the ends of it.

Should the javelin break during a throw, this is not to be deemed an attempt, provided the action itself has been carried out according to the rules.

6. A no-throw or an incorrect release of the implement shall be registered as an invalid attempt.

7. The javelin must be carried back to the runway, never thrown back.

8. RUNWAY AND THROWING SECTOR. The length of the runway must be no more than 36.50 m and no less than 30 m and must be indicated by two parallel lines 5 cm wide and 4 m apart. The throw is to be made from behind a curved scratch-line which shall be an arc on a radius of 8 m; this arc may be painted or made of wood or metal, 7 cm wide, white in colour and level with the ground. Two lines must be traced from the ends of the arc at right angles to the parallel lines that indicate the sides of the runway. These lines must be 1.50 m long and 7 cm wide. The maximum permissible slope of the ground within the runway is 1:100 sideways and 1:1000 in the direction of running. The maximum permissible slope within the throwing sector is 1:1000.

9. No check-mark may be placed on the runway, but competitors may place check-marks (provided by the organizers) next to the runway.

10. All valid throws must fall within the inside edges of the 5 cm wide lines that indicate the 29° throwing sector, marked on the ground by the extension of the lines from the centre of the invisible circle of which the scratch-line forms an arc, through the point where this arc joins the lines that indicate the sides of the runway. The ends of the radial lines must be indicated with marker flags.

11. The measurement of each throw must be taken immediately after the throw, from the nearest mark left by the javelin head to the inside edge of the scratch-line, along a line between the mark and the centre of the circle of which the scratch-line is an arc.

12. A marker stake or flag must be provided to indicate the best throw of each competitor, and must be placed along a line or tape outside the sector lines. A marker flag or disc must be provided to indicate the current world record and, where appropriate, the national record.

13. In the Olympic Games, the World

Prescribed measurements for the javelin

		Men	Women
Weight (including the binding of the grip) for the confirmation of a record	min.	800 g	600 g
Tolerance for the supply of competition implements	min.	805 g	605 g
	max.	825 g	625 g
Overall length	min.	260 cm	220 cm
	max.	270 cm	230 cm
Length of metal head	min.	25 cm	25 cm
	max.	33 cm	33 cm
Distance from the point of the metal head to the centre of gravity	min.	90 cm	80 cm
	max.	110 cm	95 cm
Diameter of the thickest section of the shaft	min.	25 cm	20 cm
	max.	30 cm	25 cm
Length of the bound grip	min.	15 cm	14 cm
	max.	16 cm	15 cm

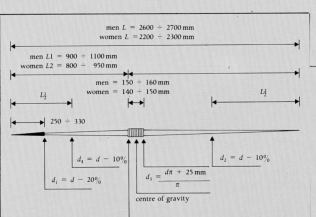

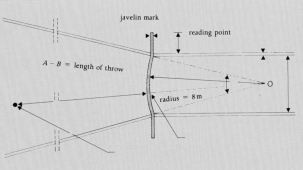

Javelins and the runway
Left: *Regulation measurements for the javelin, for both men and women.*
Right: *Details of the end of the runway and the throwing sector.*

Cup and Continental or Group Games or Championships, only javelins supplied by the organizers are to be used, and no modifications may be introduced during the contest.

No competitor may bring any implement on to the field. In regional meetings competitors may use their own javelins, provided they are checked, approved and initialled by the organizers before the start of the contest and are placed at the disposal of all the competitors.

14. CONSTRUCTION. The javelin comprises a metal head, a shaft and a grip bound with cord. The shaft may be of wood or metal to which is fixed a metal head ending in a sharp point.
15. The binding must be at about the centre of gravity, with no straps, notches or corrugations of any sort on the shaft. The binding must be of uniform thickness, not more than 25 mm.
16. The cross-section must be perfectly circular from one end of the implement to the other, and its maximum diameter must be under the grip. From the grip, the javelin must gradually taper towards the metal head and the tail. The line from the end of the grip to the metal head may be straight or slightly curved, but the curve must be gradual, and there must be no sudden alterations in the diameter of the section throughout the length of the javelin. NB – Although the cross-section should be circular, a maximum difference of 5% is allowed between the larger and smaller diameters, which would make it oval. The average of the two diameters must correspond to the specifications given.
17. The javelin must have no moving parts or other device that during the throw could alter the centre of gravity or the characteristics of the throw.
18. The tapering of the shaft from its maximum diameter to the point of the metal head or the tail must be such that the diameter halfway between the end of the binding and either end does not exceed 90% of the maximum diameter of the shaft, and at a point 15 cm from either end, 80% of the maximum diameter.

Training

For the javelin as for sprinting, natural gifts are the fundamental requirements that make a champion. So youngsters not naturally predisposed towards this sort of throw are ruled out, and only those who display the necessary characteristics to an outstanding degree are successful. Technical training and strength development will make the most of these gifts.

For the young javelin thrower under 16 we would suggest trying to pinpoint technical defects by comparing their own performances with those of experienced athletes, particularly champions. Technique can also be learned by studying athletes in action at big meetings. Obviously it is hard to learn technique correctly and develop mental and physical powers to the full unless sensible eating habits and a reasonable lifestyle are followed.

We suggest the following typical weeks for 17–18 year-old javelin throwers. Here too, during the competitive period two phases of specific work should be inserted between May and June (3–4 weeks) and in August (3 weeks). In October a period of active rest is advisable to allow the athlete to recuperate.

WEEKLY TRAINING SCHEDULES

Typical week in the general preparation period (November to January)

Session 1

• Lying face up on the bench, butterfly exercise with a weight of 70% of the max.: 6 sets of 8 repetitions with appropriate rests.

• From the same position, the exercise illustrated in Fig.1: 6 sets of 8 repetitions with 70% of max. weight and appropriate rests between.

• The exercise illustrated in Fig.2: 6 sets of 8 repetitions with a 10 kg disc on the bar-bell.

• On the horse or box, a bar-bell on the shoulders with weight corresponding to 70% of max., half-squats: 6 sets × 8 repetitions plus rests between sets.

• With a bar-bell on the shoulders equal to 1.5 times bodyweight, rise on tiptoe with the balls of the feet resting on a block at least 10 cm high: 4 sets × 10 repetitions plus rests.

• Lying face up, raise hands and feet to touch each other, resting only on the buttocks (abdominals): 4 sets × 15 repetitions.

• Lying face down, raise the chest and legs from the ground, holding the position for several seconds before relowering them (back): 4 sets × 15 repetitions.

• At the end of the session, a few muscle and joint suppling exercises for all joints, especially the spine.

Session 2

• 1.5–2 km jogging to warm up.

• 15 min. free-standing gymnastics.

• 10 javelin-style throws from a standstill with a weight of 3 kg for boys and 2 kg for girls.

• 20 throws from a standstill with a regulation javelin.

• 20 complete throws with a regulation javelin, watching the rhythmic progression of the special strides.

• 10 two-handed throws backwards over the head with a weight of 4 kg for boys and 3 kg for girls.

Session 3

• 25–30 min. jogging.
• 20 min. muscle extension and joint mobility exercises for all joints.

• Game of basketball, volleyball or handball.

• 10 sets of jumps over 10 hurdles 0.91 m high and 2 m apart (boys) and 0.76 m high and 1.5 m apart (girls).

• 4 sets of 10 long-jumps, taking off from alternate feet and landing in the sand, always trying for the longest distance possible.

• 2–3 × 150 m at 70% max.

• 10 min. jogging and a few muscle suppling exercises.

Session 4
• Rest.

Session 5
• As Session 1.

Session 6
• As Session 2.

Session 7
• Rest.

Fig. 1

Fig. 2

Session 1

• Lying face up on the bench, butterfly exercises with 80% of max. weight: 4 sets of 6 repetitions with rests between sets.

• From the same position, the exercise shown in Fig.1: 4 sets of 6 repetitions with 80% of max. weight, plus rests.

• The exercise shown in Fig. 2: 6 sets × 8 repetitions plus rests.

• On the horse or box, with a bar-bell on the shoulders weighing 80% of max, half-squats: 4 sets × 6 repetitions plus rests.

• With a bar-bell on the shoulders equal to body-weight, bend and straighten the legs, keeping the body upright: 4 sets × 6 repetitions plus rests.

Session 1
• 25–30 min. jogging.

• 20 min. muscle extension and joint mobility exercises for all joints.

Session 2

• Lying face up on the bench, butterfly exercise: 4 sets, the first of 5 repetitions with 75% of max. weight, the second 4 repetitions with 80%, the third 3 repetitions with 85%, and the fourth 2 repetitions with 90%, plus rests between sets.

• From the same position on the bench, the exercise shown in Fig.1: 4 sets, the first of 5 repetitions with 75% of max. weight, the second 4 repetitions with 80%, the third 3 repetitions with 85% and the fourth 2 repetitions with 90%, plus rests between sets.

• The exercise shown in Fig. 2: 6 sets × 8 repetitions plus rests.

• On the horse or box, with a bar-bell on the shoulders weighing 80% of

Typical week in the specific preparation period (February to March)

- Abdominals and dorsals as in the general preparation period.

- At the end of the session, some muscle and joint suppling exercises, particularly for the spinal column and shoulders.

Session 2
- 1.5–2 km jogging.

- 15 min. free-standing gymnastics.

- 15 throws from a standstill with a 2 kg weight for boys and a 1.5 kg weight for girls.

- 20 throws from a standstill with the regulation javelin.

- 20 complete throws with the regulation javelin, watching the rhythmic progression of the special strides.

- 15 two-handed throws backwards over the head with a 3 kg weight for boys and a 2 kg weight for girls.

- 10 sets of jumps over 10 hurdles, 0.91 m high and 2 m apart for boys, and 0.76 m high and 1.5 m apart for girls.

- 4 sets of 10 long-jumps, taking off on alternate legs and landing in the sand, always trying for the longest distance possible.

- 10 × 5 hurdles of 0.91 m for boys and 0.76 m for girls, with crouch start from blocks and a distance of 8 strides between the start and the first hurdle and 3 strides between hurdles.

- 5 crouch starts from blocks plus 40 m sprint.

- 10 min. jogging, finishing with some muscle suppling exercises.

Session 3
- 25–30 min. jogging.

- 20 min. muscle extension and joint mobility exercises for all joints.

- Game of basketball, volleyball or handball.

Session 4
- Rest.

Session 5
- As Session 1.

Session 6
- As Session 2.

Session 7
- Rest.

Typical week in the competition period (April to September)

max., half-squats: 4 sets × 6 repetitions plus rests.

- With bar-bell on the shoulders equal to body weight, bend and straighten the legs, keeping the body upright: 4 sets × 6 repetitions plus rests.

- Abdominal and back exercises as in the general preparation period.

- Finally some muscle and joint suppling exercises, especially for the spinal column and the shoulder.

Session 3
- 1.5–2 km jogging.

- 15 min. free-standing gymnastics.

- 10 throws from a standstill with regulation javelin.

- 20 complete throws with the regulation javelin, watching the rhythm of the special strides and the delivery.

- 10 throws from a standstill with a javelin of 600 g (boys) and 450 g (girls).

- 10 sets of jumps over 10 hurdles 0.91 m high and 2 m apart (boys) and 0.76 m high and 1.5 m apart (girls).

- 4 sets qf 10 long-jumps, taking off from alternate feet and landing in the sand, trying for the maximum possible distance.

- 10 × 5 hurdles of 0.91 m for boys and 0.76 m for girls with crouch start from blocks and a distance of 8 strides between blocks and the first hurdle and 3 strides between hurdles.

- 5 crouch starts from blocks plus 40 m sprint.

- 2–3 × 150 m at 80% of max. speed.

- 10 min. jogging and some muscle suppling exercises to finish.

Session 4
- 1 km jogging to warm up.

- 15 min. free-standing gymnastics.

- 20 complete throws with the regulation javelin, watching the rhythm of the special strides and the delivery.

- 10 throws from a standstill with a javelin of 600 g (boys) and 450 g (girls).

- 10 min. jogging and some muscle and joint suppling exercises.

Session 5
- Rest.

Session 6
- Lying face up on the bench, exercise as in Session 2.

- From the same position, exercise as in Session 2.

- Half-squat exercise on the horse or box as in Session 2.

- Abdominal and back exercises as in the general preparation period.

- Finally, a few muscle and joint suppling exercises, especially for the spinal column.

Session 7
- Competition.

The stars

JONNI MYYRÄ (FINLAND)

This farmer from Savitaipale began the tradition of javelin throwing in his country. At the age of 20 he entered the Stockholm Olympics and came eighth. He first achieved a world record distance in 1914 with a throw of 63.29 m, but this result, together with two successive ones (64.81 m in 1915 and 65.55 m in 1919), was never ratified by the IAAF. The only one of his record throws to appear in the record books was the 66.10 m that he achieved in August 1919.

With these results behind him, Myyrä entered the Antwerp Olympics as hot favourite, and won easily with 65.78 m, three of his compatriots gaining the next three places, there being no limit on the number of competitors from the same nation in one event in those days. Four years later in Paris he again won the Olympic gold, and he was 32 by this time. He subsequently emigrated to the USA, where he achieved two superb results unofficially: 68.55 m in the javelin at Richmond, California in 1926, and 48.80 m in the discus in New York in 1925.

MATTI JÄRVINEN (FINLAND)

This most famous of Finland's great javelin throwers was unchallenged in the event for nearly a decade, pushing up the world record from 71.57 m in 1930 to 77.23 m in 1936.

He came from a family of athletes, and was the youngest and most famous of the four.

In 1926, Matti was capable of throwing the javelin 54.26 m, an extraordinary feat for a 17 year-old in those days. Soon afterwards, he injured his elbow, had to undergo an operation and was out of action until 1929. However, he made a superb comeback, becoming national champion with 66.18 m, and at the end of the year he was top of the season's world list with 66.75 m. After his first official world record of 72.38 m in 1930, he followed up with no fewer than 10 more up to the 77.23 m in June 1936. In the Los Angeles Olympics (1932) he won with 72.71 m. In 1936 Matti sustained a back injury

and arrived somewhat under-prepared for the finals in Berlin. He could manage only fifth place, while his compatriots Nikkanen and Toivonen took silver and bronze behind the German Gerhard Stöck.

JANIS LUSIS (USSR)

Lusis is the only athlete to have won the title four times in the same event at the European Championships: in 1962 at Belgrade (82.04 m), in 1966 at Budapest (84.48 m), in 1969 at Athens (91.52 m) and in 1971 at Helsinki (90.68 m). At the Olympic Games he has won all three medals, bronze in 1964 in Tokyo (80.57 m), gold in 1968 at Mexico City (90.10 m) and silver in 1972 at Munich (90.46 m). On this last occasion he lost to the West German Klaus Wolfermann by only 2 cm.

Lusis was the second javelin thrower to exceed the 90 m mark, after the Norwegian Terje Pedersen's 91.72 m in 1964. He claimed the world record for the first time in 1968 at Saarijärvi, Finland, with 91.98 m, and in 1972 at Stockholm with 93.80 m. In the course of his career he threw over 90 m nine times. He has also demonstrated his versatility as a decathlete.

MIKLÓS NÉMETH (HUNGARY)

The son of a former Olympic champion and world record holder in the

Above, the East German Detlef Michel who won the javelin at the World Championships in 1983.

hammer, Miklos Németh had to persevere for many years before he achieved success in the javelin. This was at the age of 30 when in the 1976 Olympic Games in Montreal he won the javelin with 94.58 m, a new world record.

By 1967 Németh was already a world class thrower with 87.20 m, but then for quite a time his results in big competitions came short of expectations. In the 1968 Olympic Games, because of a slight injury, he did not

Miklós Németh

manage to qualify for the final. In the European Games he finished ninth in 1971 and seventh in 1974. In the 1972 Olympic Games, he again placed seventh.

In 1975 he joined the élite band of 90 m throwers by throwing 91.38 m, followed by his Olympic success. After this he continued to distinguish himself in the international field, and placed eighth in the 1980 Moscow Olympics.

DETLEF MICHEL (GDR)

Michel is the reigning world champion thanks to his victory at the 1983 World Championships at Helsinki.

At 17 he could already throw 75.80 m, but an accident slowed down his progress for a while. He went over 80 m at the age of 20, and made his first good competitive throw in 1978, taking fourth place in the Prague European Games. In 1980 he reached 90 m, but suffered bitter disappointment at the Moscow Games when he was eliminated in the qualifying rounds.

Since 1981 he has shown growing steadiness, being at home in big contests: first in the European Cup, second in the 1981 World Cup and third in the 1982 European Games.

In 1983 he equalled the European record with 96.72 m, and contested the American Tom Petranoff's supremacy. Petranoff won the first of two straight contests in June at Los Angeles, with 94.62 m to Michel's 92.08 m, but the East German had the last word at the Helsinki World Championships, throwing 89.48 m compared with Petranoff's 85.60 m.

On 8 June 1983, the day Michel threw his European record distance in Berlin, he performed five throws between 90.30 m and 96.72 m, which gives an idea of his consistency.

TOM PETRANOFF (USA)

American javelin throwers have in the past often been the target of jibes. The well-known American coach Dean Cromwell made the remark to a group of foreign experts: 'All I can tell you about the style of American javelin throwers is that it's not worth copying.' However, another javelin expert, Matti Järvinen, the great Finnish champion of the 1930s, made this prophecy: 'When the Americans,

with their great athletic resources, learn to throw properly, we shall get a three-figure world record.

Tom Petranoff came amazingly close to the 100 m mark on 15 May 1983 when he threw 99.72 m, exactly 3 m more than the then world record of the Hungarian Ferenc Paragi.

Petranoff had been known to have enormous potential since 1977. He was 19, and was pitcher for a San Diego baseball team. He knew he had a powerful arm and one day, while crossing a sports field, he was surprised to see someone of much slighter build than himself throw a javelin beyond 70 m. This spurred him on to try the javelin himself. His first official attempt was over 60 m, a few months later he became US junior champion, and in the meeting in that class with the Soviet Union he reached 77.48 m. After this superb start things went ahead rather more gradually, but still he reached 85.44 m in 1980 and 88.40 m in 1982.

In 1983 he enjoyed an exceptional season, exceeding 90 m in 13 meetings. On many occasions he used a new type of javelin, the Custom 3, not accepted by the IAAF for the 1983 World Championships simply because it had been on the market for less than a year. However, with a traditional implement, the Custom 2, he still managed to throw 94.88 m at Tampere, Finland. Using the same implement, but on a bad day

Tom Petranoff

Ruth Fuchs

weatherwise, he could manage only 85.60 m in the World Championships, having to resign himself to second place behind the East German Michel.

ELVIRA OZOLINA (USSR)

For many years this student from Leningrad remained at the top in the women's javelin. She won international records and successes under her maiden name of Ozolina, but achieved her personal best distance after marrying Janis Lusis.

As an athlete Ozolina had great agility (11.4 sec. in the 80 m hurdles) and her name figures three times in the record books: 57.92 m and 59.55 m in 1960, and 59.78 m in 1963. On 27 Aug. 1964, at Kiev, she was the first woman in the world to pass the 60 m mark, reaching 61.38 m on her last throw. For some unknown reason, this result was never confirmed, so the first official 60 m thrower in the women's javelin was the Russian Yelena Gorchakova, with 62.40 m at the Tokyo Olympics.

Having won at the Rome Olympics and the 1962 European Games in Belgrade, Ozolina finished only fifth in Tokyo, and after this recurrent injuries prevented her making progress in the event for a while. She did not lose interest, however, and as late as 1973, when 34, she threw a personal best of 63.96 m, putting her second on the all-time list, after the East German Ruth Fuchs.

RUTH FUCHS (GDR)

On 11 June 1972, the Russian Gorkachova's 1964 record of 62.40 m was bettered first by the Pole Ewa Gryziecka in Bucharest with 62.70 m, then by the East German Ruth Fuchs at Potsdam with 65.06 m.

At the Munich Olympic Games shortly afterwards it became obvious that Fuchs was going to dominate the event for some time, when she won with 63.88 m. With her sound physique and unyielding nerves, she dominated the world javelin scene from 1972 to 1980. She improved the world record a further five times, skimming the 70 m mark with 69.96 m in April 1980. In Montreal 1976 she had retained the Olympic title, becoming the only woman to do so in this event. She twice won the European title (1974 and 1978) and twice repeated her success in the World Cup (1977 and 1979). Her run of success ended at the 1980 Moscow Olympics when, to everyone's surprise, she managed only ninth place.

TIINA LILLAK (FINLAND)

Finland's highly successful male athletes have as yet been joined by very few women. The first Olympic medal to be won by a Finnish woman went to Kaisa Parviainen, who took the silver for the javelin in 1948.

This was followed in 1983 by the victory of Tiina Lillak at the Helsinki World Championships. She came to public notice in 1982 when she took the world javelin record with 72.40 m, although she lost it again only a few months later to a Greek, Sofia Sakorafa, who threw 74.20 m at a meeting in Crete. That summer, in the European Games at Athens, Lillak placed only fourth in the women's javelin.

In 1983 she regained the world record with a throw of 74.76 m, and won with a throw of 70.82 m at the Helsinki World Championships. On this occasion, however, she left her winning throw until late in the competition overtaking on her last attempt the British girl Fatima Whitbread, who had dominated the contest since her first-round throw of 69.14 m. In the 1984 Olympics she won a silver medal behind the British girl Tessa Sanderson.

Tiina Lillak

WORLD RECORDS

Men	Women
m	m
62.32 Erok Lemming (Sweden) 1912	46.74 Nan Gindele (USA) 1932
66.10 Jonni Myyrä (Finland) 1919	47.24 Anneliese Steinhauer (Germany) 1942
66.62 Gunnar Lindström (Sweden) 1924	48.21 Herma Bauma (Austria) 1947
69.88 Eino Penttilä (Finland) 1927	48.63 Herma Bauma (Austria) 1948
71.01 Erik Lundqvist (Sweden) 1928	49.59 Natalya Smirnitskaya (USSR) 1949
71.57 Matti Järvinen (Finland) 1930	53.41 Natalya Smirnitskaya (USSR) 1949
71.70 Matti Järvinen (Finland) 1930	53.56 Nadyezhda Konyayeva (USSR) 1954
71.88 Matti Järvinen (Finland) 1930	55.11 Nadyezhda Konyayeva (USSR) 1954
72.93 Matti Järvinen (Finland) 1930	55.48 Nadyezhda Konyayeva (USSR) 1954
74.02 Matti Järvinen (Finland) 1932	
74.28 Matti Järvinen (Finland) 1933	55.73 Dana Zátopkova (Czechoslovakia) 1958
74.61 Matti Järvinen (Finland) 1933	57.40 Anna Pazera (Australia) 1958
76.10 Matti Järvinen (Finland) 1933	57.49 Birute Zalogaitite (USSR) 1958
76.66 Matti Järvinen (Finland) 1934	57.92 Elvira Ozolina (USSR) 1960
77.23 Matti Järvinen (Finland) 1936	59.55 Elvira Ozolina (USSR) 1960
77.87 Yrjö Nikkanen (Finland) 1938	59.78 Elvira Ozolina (USSR) 1963
78.70 Yrjö Nikkanen (Finland) 1938	62.40 Yelena Gorchakova (USSR) 1964
80.41 Bud Held (USA) 1953	62.70 Eva Gryziecka (Poland) 1972
81.75 Bud Held (USA) 1955	65.06 Ruth Fuchs (USSR) 1972
83.56 Soini Nikkinen (Finland) 1956	66.10 Ruth Fuchs (USSR) 1973
83.66 Janusz Sidlo (Poland) 1956	67.22 Ruth Fuchs (USSR) 1974
85.71 Egil Danielsen (Norway) 1956	69.12 Ruth Fuchs (USSR) 1976
86.04 Al Cantello (USA) 1959	69.32 Kathy Schmidt (USA) 1977
86.74 Carlo Lievore (Italy) 1961	69.52 Ruth Fuchs (USSR) 1979
87.12 Terje Pedersen (Norway) 1964	69.96 Ruth Fuchs (USSR) 1980
91.72 Terje Pedersen (Norway) 1964	70.08 Tatyana Biryulina (USSR0 1980
91.98 Janis Lusis (USSR) 1968	71.88 Antoaneta Todorova (Bulgaria) 1981
92.70 Jorma Kinnunen (Finland) 1969	
93.80 Janis Lusis (USSR) 1972	72.40 Tiina Lillak (Finland) 1982
94.08 Klaus Wolfermann (GDR) 1973	74.20 Sofia Sakorafa (Greece) 1982
94.58 Miklós Németh (Hungary) 1976	74.76 Tiina Lillak (Finland) 1983
96.72 Ferenc Paragi (Hungary) 1980	
99.72 Tom Petranoff (USA) 1983	
104.80 Uwe Hohn (GDR) 1984	

Index